Heathen Soul Lore Foundations

Ancient and Modern Germanic Pagan Concepts of the Souls

Winifred Hodge Rose

With original artwork by Dale Wood

Heathen Soul Lore Series Book I

Wordfruma Press

2021

©2021 Winifred Hodge Rose. Dale Wood artwork ©2021 Dale Wood. All rights reserved for all original material in this book. Brief quotations are allowed, for the purposes of news reporting, criticism, comment, scholarship, research, or teaching.

Wordfruma Press
Urbana Illinois USA

WordfrumaPress.com

ISBN:
978-1-7379327-5-8 (Hardcover, color illustrations)
978-1-7379327-0-3 (Hardcover, grayscale illustrations)
978-1-7379327-2-7 (Paperback, grayscale illustrations)
978-1-7379327-3-4 (EPUB, color illustrations)
978-1-7379327-6-5 (EPUB, grayscale illustrations)
978-1-7379327-4-1 (PDF, color illustrations)
978-1-7379327-7-2 (Kindle E-book, color illustrations)
978-1-7379327-8-9 (Kindle E-book, grayscale illustrations)

Library of Congress Control Number: 2021920023

Cover art: Dale Wood
Cover Design: Winifred Hodge Rose

Dedication

To the Feorhcynn: the Kindred of the Ferah-Soul, all beings who share in the life-force of Midgard. May we all flourish, in balance with one another.

To the Aldr-beornum, the Eldi-barn: human beings. We are the Children of Time, who share the gifts of the Aldr-Soul: our mortal realm, our lives in Time, the beauty of the ephemeral which creates, layer by layer, the intricate structure of all-that-is. May we be mindful of this subtle power to shape our lives and our world, and use it wisely.

Cover Painting: "Embracing the Souls" by Dale Wood

The soulful watercolor landscape on the book cover was painted by Dale Wood, a few nights after his grandmother passed away, as he sat beside what had been her bed while he cared for her during the end of her life. She had always been a great supporter of his artistic work. This image and his grandmother came into his mind as he proofread the manuscript of this book, and he shared it with me, which led to our collaboration. I see a shape in this lovely painting: the image looks to me like a woman holding a landscape in her embrace. The rise on the right side of the painting is like her head, the wooded ridges running along the top and bottom of the painting look like arms stretched out. In the center is a soft, billowy landscape, like a grandmother's soft embrace. The trees, appearing and disappearing into the mist, are like the souls which sometimes are perceptible to our awareness, other times not. This could be a grandmother, or the Earth Mother. The whole scene is evocative of the mysteries of the souls and the Deities, and of the love that reaches, soul to soul, across the boundaries of the Worlds.

This vista of a rolling landscape draws us onward to explore the unknown. By Dale Wood.

Table of Contents

Introduction to Heathen Soul Lore 1
   Studying Ancient Heathen Concepts 2
   Presenting Modern Heathen Concepts 7
1. Definition and Overview of Heathen Souls 9
   One Soul per Person, or More? 11
   Defining a Soul 14
   A Brief Summary of Each Soul 16
      Ferah 17
      Ahma 18
      Ghost 19
      Hama 20
      Aldr 21
      Saiwalo 22
      Hugr 24
      Mod 25
      Sefa 26
      Associated Spirits 28
2. The Awakening of the Souls 29
3. Born of Trees and Thunder: The Ferah Soul 41
   Connections between Trees and Life-Soul 42
      Table 1: Trees and Life-Soul Words 42
      Table 2: Words Derived from *perku 43
   Ferah and the Gods 44
      Table 3: Gods, Earth, Sky Powers 45
   The Evolutionary Perspective 49
   The Nature of the Ferah 51
   Ferah, Law, and Priesthood 56
   Ferah and Sacrifice 60

The Ferah at Death 61
Development and Psychology of Ferah 65
Ferah and Magic 67
Summary 68
In Closing 68

4. Ǫnd, Ahma, Ghost and Breath: Their Basic Nature 71
The Breath 72
Table 4: "Breath" Words 73
Enter the Ghost 75
The Meanings of Spirit 77
Table 5: Distribution of Germanic 'Spirit' Meanings ... 78
Ghost and Mind 80
Table 6: Spirit and Mind Meanings 85
Table 7: Illness or Health of Ghost 86
The Impoverishment of the Ghost 87
Summary of Meanings, and Modern Heathen Usage 87
In Closing 89

5. Ghost Rider: Athom, Ghost, and Wode in Action 91
Origin and Afterlife of Ghost and Ahma 93
Athom and Ghost 96
Wode 103
The Otherworldly Nature of the Ghost 115
Summary 123
In Closing 124

6. The Shape of Being Human: The Hama Soul 127
The Gifts of Loðurr 132
1. The Gift of Lá 132
2. The Gift of Læti 134
3. The Gift of Litr 136

The Gift-Giver	139
The Lich-Hama	142
Anglo-Saxon Hiw	144
The Hama in the Womb	147
The Hama as Healer	152
The Hama After Death	153
Examples of Hama Words	155
Summary	156
7. Aldr and Orlay: Weaving a World	**159**
Nourisher and Life-Span	162
A Greek Soul-Cognate: the Aion	165
The Footholds of the Aldr / Aion	167
Aldr-Wita: Holistic Health Practice	168
Aldr and Orlay	172
Werold: Our World as Aldr's Soul-Skin	176
Godly Patrons of Aldr	179
The Afterlife of Aldr	182
Summary	188
In Closing	188
8. Dances with Daemons: The Mod Soul	**193**
Basic Meanings	195
Mod as Daemon	201
Mod as Daemon of Sickness	206
The Implications of Human-Mod Co-evolution	213
The Afterlife of Mod-Soul	217
Mod's Potency and the Holy Ones	220
In Closing	223
9. Hunting the Wild Hugr	**227**
Root-complex #1: 'Shining'	230

Root-complex #2: 'Mounds and Wights' 231
    The Kaunaz Rune 233
    Root-complex #3: 'The Unborn, Swelling' 235
    'Swollen with Power and Wind' 236
    Root-complex #4: 'An Eldritch Cry' 239
    Root-complex #5: 'Excitation, Stirring up the Soul' 241
    Root-complex #6: 'The Watcher; Magical Force' 243
    Afterlife and the Ancestral Connection 245
    Origins and Evolution of Hugr 247
    The Tale of the Hugr 250

10. Who is Hugr? 253
    Basic Meanings 254
    Three Domains of Hugr 258
    Hugr and the Heart 260
    Hugi 'Wallows' Within the Breast 266
    The Roots of Hugr 267
    Clarifying the Hugr 270
    Summary 274
    A Meditation on the Hugr's Power 274

11. The Occult Activities of the Hugr 277
    Part 1: The Actions of the Hugr in Nordic Folk Beliefs 277
        Desire, Longing, Envy, Hatred 280
        Hugr as Fore-runner, Hugboð, and Warder 286
        The Wind of the Troll-wife 289
        Hugham: The Hugr Takes Shape 290
    Part 2: Hugr's Involvement in Magical and Esoteric Practices 293
        Rede-Giver 294
        Ancestor-Work 296
        Spellcraft and Runecraft affecting the Hugr 298

- The Double and Animal-Double 302
- Seiðcraft 305
- A Glimmer of Anglo-Saxon Magic 307
- Swelling of the Hugr 311
- Summary and Closing 313

12. Sefa: The Soul of Relationship 317
- Shaping our Understanding of Sefa 317
  - Related words: 317
  - Possible Roots: 318
  - Some Examples of Sefa in Old Texts 320
- Sjöfn, Sif, and their Companions 322
- Vulnerability of Sefa 325
- Modsefa / Modsebo 328
- The Wunjo Rune 334
- Summary 335

13: Hel-Dweller 337
- Hel as the Hidden Land 341
- Faring to the Edge of Hel 343
  - Hervör's Tale 343
- Common Motifs Relating to Hel and the Dead 348
  - Brynhild's Ride to Hel 348
  - Baldr's Dreams 350
  - Hermoðr's Journey 351
  - Thorstein Cod-Biter 352
- Hel-Motifs in Tales of Hidden Lands 353
  - Skirnir's Journey 353
  - Svipdag's Quest 356
  - Fairy Tales 359
  - Frau Holle and Walburga 360

Some Overarching Themes	363
14. The Soul and the Sea	367
Where does 'Saiwalo' come from?	368
Weisweiler's Exploration of *Saiwalo	369
Other Folklore about Souls and Water	377
A Dash of Salt	379
Salt / Sweet, Grasping / Giving	383
Summary	386
Hail the Holy Ones	387
15. What Happened to Heathen Saiwalo?	389
The Sawol in *Beowulf*	393
The Ferah-Saiwalo Dynamic	398
Ghost versus Soul	405
What's the Big Deal?	409
Impacts of Changing Ideas about the Soul	413
Summary	415
Interlude: A Short Essay on the Eormen-Soul	421
16. The Alchemy of Hel	425
Part 1. Alchemy, Ginnungagap, & the Coalescence of Hel	427
Alchemy in this Context	427
Why Alchemy?	429
The Mighty Gap of Potential	430
The Coalescence of Hel	434
Summary of Part 1	440
Part 2. Generation, Coagulation, Dwimor and Dwimoring	440
Spontaneous Generation	440
Coalescence and Coagulation	443
The Roots of Dwimor	445
The Dwimor in Midgard	447

 Dwimoring 450
Part 3: Images; Polarity of Saiwalo and Ahma; Precipitation 453
 Dwimor-images 453
 The Poles of Saiwalo and Ahma 455
 The Alchemy of Images 457
 Precipitation 460
Part 4. Hel: An Ecological Perspective 461
 The Impact of Christianity on Hel 464
 Our Responsibility during Midgard Life 468
Part 5. Stages of Alchemical Transformation 471
 The Chthonic Forces 474
 Differences between Hugrs and Saiwalo-Dwimors 476
 The Alchemical Processes 478
 Necromancy and Arcane Knowledge 486
Part 6. The Permeability of Hel 488
 Where do Hugrs come from? 488
 Back-Door Connections 491
17. The Arising of the Self 497
 The Emergent Self 499
 The Midgard Self 501
 The Holographic Self 503
 Summary 506
18. Closing Thoughts and Topical Summaries 507
 Another Look at Multiple Souls 508
 Origins, Nature, and Destinations of the Souls 509
 Soul-Footholds 514
 Different Religions, Different Perspectives 516
 The Meaningfulness of Soul Lore Study 518
Acknowledgements 521

Word-Hoard / Glossary 525
Photograph and Artist Credits 541
Book-Hoard / Bibliography 549
About the Author and Artist 559
A Word about Wordfruma Press. 563

Introduction

Introduction to Heathen Soul Lore

What is a soul? What does it mean to have one? Or more than one? Can a soul be gained or lost? Where does it come from? Where does it go to? Questions such as these have likely occupied peoples of all times and places throughout human history. There is nothing surprising about this interest, since inquiries and understandings of the soul explore the roots of living and being, of self and other, and the mysteries of subjective time and of the unseen world which offers only hints of its presence in our ordinary lives. Exploration of these questions is a primary purpose of all religions and forms of spirituality. My own undertaking is to explore these questions from a Heathen perspective.

The term 'Heathens', or 'people of the heath,' is used to describe the ancient paganisms of the tribes who spoke the old Germanic languages of Europe, including Anglo-Saxon, Old Saxon, Old Norse, Old High German, Gothic, Frisian, Frankish, and other related languages. They left clues to their philosophies and world-views, their understandings of religion, the world, and life in general, in their poetry and art, their languages and laws, their folklore and customs.

Aspects of these ancient paganisms are brought forward into present-day Heathen beliefs and practices. There are many styles of modern Heathen practice, and many modern Heathen scholars who research ancient practices and beliefs to enrich the modern foundations of our troth. (For a thorough review of ancient and modern

Heathen history, see Waggoner, *Our Troth, Vol. 1: Heathen History*.) This book expresses my own perspectives, with grateful acknowledgement toward the many sources, past and present, Heathen and non-Heathen, that have influenced my thoughts.

Studying Ancient Heathen Concepts

How does one study ancient concepts and beliefs about something as abstract as "the soul"? Archaeological artifacts and pictorial art can offer only a few hints. Written information about ancient Germanic Heathen concepts comes almost entirely from accounts by Christians whose lifelong efforts were devoted to eradicating pre-Christian beliefs, and who generally made little effort to understand the subject. We have somewhat better luck when we turn to the oldest written poetry. But even here there is the problem of trying to understand and translate unfamiliar concepts couched in ancient languages, and the subject matter of these poems is seldom focused on the nature of the soul, at least not by our modern concepts about what a 'soul' is.

My primary approach has been to focus on words themselves, words from all of the ancient Germanic languages that give us clues to concepts of the soul. I view words as 'artifacts' of concepts, similar to the way archaeological objects are artifacts of culture. Ancient objects can teach us much about a culture, though there are limitations to this knowledge, and ancient words can teach us much about the conceptual world of the speakers, though again there are limitations.

But words, standing alone, are not sufficient. An arrowhead or a potsherd that shows up in somebody's junk collection in the attic tells us far less than the same item

Introduction

could tell if it had been found in place by an archaeological team, in context with other items that collectively record a culture in a specific time and place. In the same way, simply getting a modern translation of an ancient word out of a dictionary can be fairly uninformative, and often actively misleading, in comparison to reading and understanding that word in place in its original text. And even this does not go far enough. Not only must an object or a word be understood in its own context. The larger entities – cultures and concepts – must in turn be taken in context: their histories and their interactions with other surrounding cultures and concepts. In my efforts here, I have also looked at early Christian concepts as they were at the times when they first began to influence the religious thought of the various Germanic peoples.

The core of my approach is this: I have taken words relating to the soul from dictionaries of Anglo-Saxon, Old Norse, Old Saxon, Old High German, and Gothic languages, and then read through many textual passages in these languages where those words appear, to get a sense of them in context. Some of these texts were non-Christian writings, such as poems, sagas, and miscellaneous records. But many of the writings were specifically Christian in nature: retellings of New Testament events in the Germanic languages, translations or discussions of Christian scripture and theology, and also applications of classical Greek, Roman and Hellenistic philosophy to Christian thought. These were important because of their subject matter, focusing on soul, spirit and related topics directly relevant to my purpose.

Among the most enlightening questions for me to pursue have been: which Germanic words were used to translate which Latin or Greek words, and why? How well do Christian terms, as expressed mostly in the Latin language, translate into Germanic terms? What happened to the concepts when they were translated into a different language family? Were they altered by being translated into words that evolved within in a very different, Heathen, world-view? To find answers to these questions I also referred to Latin and Greek texts, mostly from the Old and New Testaments, looked at how these were translated into Germanic languages, and studied modern scholars who pursued these topics.

One of the most useful texts for this effort has been the Old Saxon *Heliand*. This epic poem, dating from the first half of the 9th century, is not a word for word translation but a retelling of the Christian gospel using very traditional Germanic imagery and language. It presents Jesus as the leader of a Germanic-style band of oathed companions (his disciples), where Peter is his personal sword-thane, and all are referred to as 'heroes.' They go fishing not in the calmness of an inland lake, but in their oceangoing longboats, battling horrendous tides and winds, just as the Vikings do. The angels announcing Jesus' birth come not to shepherds but to the guards of the King's prize horse herds.

Mary is presented not as a simple village girl but as a woman of the nobility, descendant of kings, possessed of all a noblewoman's qualities as would be appropriate for a Germanic heroine. The scene of Jesus' trial before Pontius Pilate, more detailed than the original, illustrates the Germanic love of dramatic judicial ordeals and details of law. At Jesus' baptism, the dove with a message from his God alights on Jesus' shoulder and speaks in his ear, just as Odin's ravens Huginn and Muninn swoop to his shoulder

Introduction

with their messages. Nazareth, Jerusalem, and other towns are described as 'high-timbered' fortified burgs on hilltops.

Every detail of the poem is described in traditional poetic form, words and imagery that would resonate with Germanic Heathens. This was the intention of the author, likely a Saxon monk, who may well have been a convert from Heathenism himself, and was certainly writing for a Heathen population very unwilling to convert to the religion of their hated Frankish conquerors. (A good reference for the historical context of this poem is Murphy's *The Saxon Savior*.)

Thus, although the subject matter of the poem is Christian, the vocabulary and concepts are rooted in traditional Heathen thought. A modern scholar describes the *Heliand*-poet as having "an astonishingly rich vocabulary for describing soul-related characteristics and feelings" (Eggers p. 11). There is not a single, simple translation of soul-words here. For example, the Christian Latin term *anima*, modern English 'soul', is translated into a large variety of different Saxon words, depending on the context, showing that there is not a one-to-one correspondence of terminology, and the same occurs for *spiritus* (spirit), *mens* (mind), *vita* (life), *cor* (heart) and many other words relating to 'the soul'. The lack of a one-to-one correspondence is not surprising when one comes to believe, as I have, that Germanic Heathenry recognizes multiple souls as opposed to only one or two, soul and spirit, as posited in Christian thought. By comparing words and concepts from the Latin texts and looking at how they were transformed by the Saxon retelling, we can learn far more about ancient Heathen beliefs than might be expected from reading a Christian work.

I also found some very interesting parallels between ancient Germanic and Homeric (archaic) Greek concepts of the soul, and compared words and concepts in other Indo-European languages as well. I have supplemented this effort with folklore and folk beliefs from different cultures, comparative religion and anthropology, modern theories about the soul, and my own explorations and insights as a modern Heathen spiritual practitioner. Hopefully, I have made it clear throughout the book as to which conclusions come from academic and textual references, and which ones are my own, so that the reader can evaluate them accordingly.

Is the end result of all this effort a perfect, incontrovertible Heathen doctrine of the soul(s)? No, it is not! Almost certainly, such a thing never existed and probably never will. For any theory of Heathen beliefs about the soul, including my own, I could point to historical and linguistic evidence that fails to support or even actively contradicts it. We are talking about related groups of people, languages and cultures that were widely spread in time and space, that were influenced by and exerted influence on their surrounding neighbors, that did not communicate and store information via writing, and that did not think in terms of doctrine, dogma, or other forms of enforced consistency.

For these ancient peoples, religion was not a matter of the individual soul's salvation or damnation based on specific beliefs. It was a matter of maintaining beneficial relationships among people, between people and their Deities, and with the natural world. The important thing was not dogmatic details of belief, but right action that maintained the vital balances in the world. This does not mean that their own souls were not a significant matter for them. It only means that there was a lot of room for personal and local interpretations and variations, which took place within a common overall world-view but was not rigidly constrained by it.

Presenting Modern Heathen Concepts

What I present here is a set of concepts I call Heathen soul lore, drawn from different Germanic Heathen places and times, which I believe to be a supportable interpretation of available evidence from many different venues. I have worked to draw this material together into a coherent whole, a modern but lore-based perspective on Heathen spiritual belief. It is my hope that this work will contribute to the present-day practice of Germanic Heathenry and to the general study of religion and spirituality, including various other branches of modern Paganism.

In all of my soul lore study, I have paired two approaches and orientations: a scholarly, analytical, and reasoned approach, and a personal, spiritual, experiential approach. My work as a whole is not a scholarly enterprise *per se*; rather, I use the scholarly approach to discover a place to begin, and directions for further explorations. Scholarly work lays the foundations, but my true, ongoing work is spiritual and experiential.

This volume, Book I of my Heathen Soul Lore series, lays out the knowledge-foundations for my approach to soul lore. Book II of this series, *Heathen Soul Lore: A Personal Approach*, provides further in-depth discussion of the souls from a more personal, applied perspective, and offers exercises and guidelines for those who wish to pursue Heathen soul practice in daily life.

I believe that our imagination is a crucial cognitive faculty for exploring and understanding our souls and the worlds they inhabit. From time to time throughout this book, I present my ideas in story form, or make use of more poetic imagery and analogies to explain the ideas, in order to encourage imaginative engagement in the reader. Chapters 2 and 16 are examples of this.

The illustrations, also, are chosen to stimulate engagement of the reader's imagination, and to encourage meditation on the ideas presented here. Please note that artist names are generally presented with their paintings, while longer credits, as required, are listed by page number in the section "Photograph and Artist Credits" toward the end of the book.

I want to point out that there is a good deal of other modern Heathen writing on these subjects, worthy of pursuit whether my ideas are in agreement with them or not! Heathen soul lore and other knowledge is an organic growth, sending forth many fertile sprouts of different kinds, full of life and vigor. Long may it be so! We seek what nourishes our own souls: that is the ultimate criterion for choosing any lore, any path, any way of life. My hope is that our soul lore explorations here will prove nourishing to you, and stimulate you to further pursue the learnings of the souls in whatever directions draw you.

Chapter 1

Asgard and Bifröst, by Otto Schenk

The Overview.

1. Definition and Overview of Heathen Souls

The first step in pursuing a study of Heathen souls is to define what I mean by a 'soul.' There are two main approaches to this definition that I'm aware of. One of them I'm calling the 'psychological theory of the soul': the study of the faculties, capabilities and qualities within a person, their 'soul parts', which interface systematically within an overall holism. Examples are the faculties of Thought, Emotion, Will / Volition, as well as life-supporting functions, and in more religious or esoteric contexts an afterlife entity and perhaps a soul-guide. In this view, these parts are subsidiary to the whole: "A person has a soul," rather than "Souls take on personhood."

This psychological approach started in a systematic way in the West, as far as I'm aware, with the ancient Greek philosophers Plato and Aristotle, and has influenced ideas about the soul or the inner self in many philosophical, religious, and scientific streams of thought up to the present day. The modern word 'psychology' meaning 'science of the soul', describes a field of study based on these premises, though their focus is more on secular ideas about the 'Self' in place of religious ideas about the 'Soul.' Modern Heathen thinkers have developed this approach further in very useful ways, which can support various methods of spiritual and esoteric practice within a Heathen context.

My study of Heathen soul lore over the past two decades and more has led me to take a different perspective on defining what a soul is, one which is perhaps more 'primitive' from a modern perspective, especially a materialist one. Part of the reason I have taken a different approach is because I began this whole enterprise by searching for linguistic and other evidence of shamanistic beliefs and practices in Heathen Anglo-Saxon England. I found some interesting words, charms, and references, and published some of my results in my article "An Anglo-Saxon Charm Against a Dwarf: Shapeshifting, Soul Theft, and Shamanic Healing". But it made me realize that I couldn't pursue this path any further until I understood more of their beliefs about souls and spirits.

The entire focus and belief-system of any kind of shamanism depends on a deep, culture-based understanding of souls and spirits, because these are the 'basic units', if you will, of what a shaman works with. Shamans make use of spirits, and / or are used by them, for healing, exorcising, cursing and bewitching. They work upon the souls of others, while strengthening their own soul-capabilities and protecting their own souls against the stresses and strains of such work. Souls and spirits are the basic material of shamanistic activity.

Without an understanding of a given culture's beliefs about souls and spirits, one cannot understand that culture's involvement with any kind of spirit work: shamanism, spiritual healing, religious practices, priestly work, afterlife beliefs, oracular work, necromancy, etc.

So, I put my exploration of traces of Anglo-Saxon shamanism on pause, while I explored for traces of Heathen beliefs about the soul. I figured I'd spend a few months on that, then get back to the shamanism. Fifteen years after publishing the first article in my "Heathen soul lore" series, I'm still working hard on these beliefs about the souls, and have a great deal more in the pipeline! After taking the first steps in this direction, an amazing and inspiring spiritual vista began to open up before me, which I try to share through my writing, and expect to explore with wonder for the rest of my life.

One Soul per Person, or More?

Coming toward the question of 'what is a soul' from the direction of shamanism rather than from the direction of formal philosophy, monotheistic religion, or modern psychology, leads to a different kind of understanding, in my experience. In this view, souls are actual beings in their own right.

In contrast to what I am calling the 'psychological theory of souls,' where we have one soul comprised of several dependent parts, I take an approach that I call the 'existential theory of souls', meaning that humans are comprised of several distinct souls that exist in their own right, interacting with each other and the body to form a living person. Hence, "souls take on personhood," rather than "a person has a soul."

While they interact to form a living person, linked with a physical body in Midgard, distinct souls each have their own nature, their own abilities, behavior, functions, cosmological source, and afterlife fate. Some of them are capable of independent action, such as giving us advice, knowledge, premonitions of things our everyday mind does not know. These more independent souls can sometimes exit from the living body and act independently, or can be extracted from the living body by malicious magic, as is told in folklore of Germanic (and most other) lands, and as I explore in my writing. Some of the souls have active, independent afterlives and before-lives, as well.

I, and most other modern Heathens, are often critical of depending too heavily on 'functional' definitions of our Deities, and of other pantheons as well: the 'department store' idea of having 'a God of this' and 'a Goddess of that', where the main trick of religious practice is to figure out the 'right' Deity for one's petitions. We consider our Deities to be complex, multifaceted beings, highly developed individuals, not neatly-packaged 'functions', and we pursue our relations with them based on this understanding.

I take the same attitude towards our full-souls, versus soul-parts. The idea that we have 'a (single) soul-part for thinking', 'a part for emoting', 'a part for remembering', and so forth, doesn't sit with my understanding of our souls. Like the Deities, I think our souls are individual beings who have their own capacities or 'parts', with a lot of overlap and interconnection with each other. For both Deities and souls (and people, too), the important thing is to work on our understanding of, and relationships with, each of them as

Definition and Overview

individuals, rather than focusing on some tightly-structured system of categorization.

Based on many years of reading anthropological and comparative religious studies, I would say that belief systems positing that humans have more than one soul are far more common than belief-systems positing only one soul. Hinduism, Buddhism, Daoism, ancient Judaism, archaic Greek religion, and many past and present traditional, animistic, and tribal religions (including, in my understanding, historical Heathen beliefs) are examples, ranging from simple binary or ternary soul-concepts to very complex understandings of multiple layered and interwoven souls.

Even in Christianity, there is linguistic usage that differentiates 'soul' versus 'spirit', although confusingly people are considered to have only a single soul. This goes back to the founding texts from which the Christian version of the Bible was derived, written in Hebrew and Greek and then translated into Latin. Each of these languages had several distinct words for souls: *ruach, nefesh,* and *neshama* in Hebrew, *pneuma* versus *psyche* in Greek, *spiritus* versus *anima* in Latin. The very language-roots that supported the languages through which Christian thought developed and was expressed, recognize more than one soul.

Though the idea that we have more than one soul may seem strange to the modern Westerner (if indeed one believes in any soul at all), to a great many people around the world, past and present, this is the normal understanding. I argue that this is true about the ancient beliefs of Germanic-speaking Heathen tribes, as well.

Defining a Soul

Here are the criteria I use to define what a soul is.

1) It confers life by its presence with the body, and its departure is synonymous with physical death. The souls which fit this definition I call the Life-Souls.

Or, conversely,

2) It is capable of leaving and returning to the living body as an active metaphysical entity, either intentionally or inadvertently (for example during sleep and dreaming, or as the result of shock or trauma). It may also be removed from the body, or prevented from returning to it, by hostile supernatural or magical acts, which have deleterious but not immediately fatal results for the body. I call these the Daemon souls or Wander-Souls.

In addition:

3) Some souls are considered to have an independent afterlife and perhaps a before-life existence, and may reincarnate. Having an independent afterlife indicates that this is an existential soul-being, not simply a psychological part of a person. Some, but not all, of the Heathen souls I've identified have this characteristic.

There is a partial exception: the *Sefa*, which has many soul-like characteristics but does not fit into any of these criteria. I think that Sefa comes into being through the interaction

Definition and Overview

and synergy of all our other souls together, as I discuss in more detail in Chapter 17.

In order to identify specifically Heathen souls according to these criteria, I require that the word for that soul is present in all of the old Germanic languages that I've examined throughout this study, namely Old Saxon, Anglo-Saxon, Old Norse, Gothic, and Old High German. The selection of these languages is based on the availability of useful textual materials, and fortunately they represent the major branches of the old Germanic languages: Northern (Norse), Western (Saxon branches), Southern (Old High German), and Eastern (Gothic).

The meanings of the soul-words may not be identical among these languages, but they need to be very close in meaning in order to qualify for my selection. I've established this not simply through looking up the words in modern dictionaries, but by reading old texts in all these languages in order to understand the soul-words in their original contexts.

The one exception to this requirement that the soul-words must exist in all the languages is the actual word 'soul' itself, or rather, its ancestors: *Saiwalo, Saiwala, Seola, Siole, Sele, Sawol, Sawl,* etc. This word is present, with the same meaning of an afterlife being, a 'shade', in all the ancient and modern Germanic languages except for Old Norse, which borrowed the word *Sál* from Anglo-Saxon during the conversion to Christianity. In Chapters 14 and 15 I discuss this matter further.

In addition to these 'full-souls' there are faculties and capabilities, or 'soul-parts', within humans which were certainly recognized and valued by ancient Heathens, and were considered so powerful that they were sometimes poetically personified. Among these are the Will, Heart, Thought, Wish, and many others. These are psychological faculties of a person, the subjects that are considered when using the psychological theory of the soul.

Often in the old literature, these faculties were used as poetic synonyms for the souls, to enrich the vocabulary and imagery of the poem. For example, the Heart and the *Hugr* soul are very closely connected, as I show in Chapter 10, so that Heart and Breast are often used as poetic variants for the Hugr soul. The faculty of Thought is often treated as being synonymous with the Hugr, as well, though Hugr has meanings that extend well beyond 'Thought' and show Hugr's true personhood rather than Hugr being a single faculty such as 'Thought.'

In my understanding of soul lore, these faculties, capabilities and qualities all belong to various of the full-souls themselves. For example, most of the souls have a Will of their own, with the Mod and Hugr souls being particularly powerful in this respect. Most of the souls are capable of deep Thought and other mental and emotional activities, and have their own residence or foothold within our body or certain body parts or actions, which can be used synonymously for the soul, as I mentioned with Heart and Hugr. An example of this is the very close connection between our Breath and the Ahma soul, such that the breath and the soul-word *(Ahma, Ǫnd, And, Athom, Æðm, Atem, etc.)* can be used synonymously. All of these matters are discussed in more detail in chapters about each of the souls.

A Brief Summary of Each Soul

In developing my approach to soul lore, I've chosen to use specific names of the souls from different Germanic languages based on these considerations: (1) ease of pronunciation for modern English-speakers; (2) avoiding confusion with other similar but unrelated English words (for example, the Anglo-Saxon soul-word *feorh* is easily confused with English 'fear'); (3) avoiding words which may be interpreted in different ways by modern Heathens, such as *Ǫnd*; and (4) based on which language encompasses the broadest understanding of each soul.

I must emphasize that these summaries reflect my own understanding, which is based on ancient sources and modern scholarship, but goes beyond these into my own interpretations. All of my writing is intended to enrich and inspire modern Heathen spiritual practice, rooted in ancient beliefs but living and growing in today's world.

I. The Life-Souls

Ferah

(Feorh, Ferhth, Fjör, Fairhw, Ferh, Ferch, Verch. 'Ferah' is the Old Saxon word. Pronounced 'FAIR-ah.')

This is a very ancient word, going back to the Proto-Indo-European (PIE) word **perku*, meaning 'life-soul' or animating principle. It is connected with PIE words for 'chest / breast', for oak, pine, fir, and other trees, for earth and mountains, and is related to the name of the PIE Thunder-God **Perkwunos* and with the verb 'to strike'. The Norse Deity-names Fjǫrgyn and Fjǫrgynn, and a plural Norse word for 'Gods', *fjarg*, are all descendants of these words.

Ferah is a vitalizing Life-soul not only in humans, but in animals, trees, and other living entities as well. A lovely

Anglo-Saxon word is *feorh-cynn*, 'the kindred of the living, of those who share the Ferah soul'. As I understand it, Ferah was the soul enclosed within the Trees that were transformed into the mythical first humans, Ask and Embla. The Tree-Ferahs were first released from the trees by Thor's mighty Hammer-strike, then given the gifts of breath, spirit, wode, the human body-shape and its abilities, by Odin and his brothers as they shaped the mythical first humans.

Ferah is a vitalizing, life-giving substance that fills us during life, and mysteriously leaves at death. Ferah has personal characteristics such as wisdom, piety, emotions and thoughts, and connects us with the great Powers of Nature, Earth and Sky. It is perceptive, aware and responsive to everything in our environment, and is the locus of our bodily sensations and reactions to events around us.

In my understanding, our individual Ferah comes into being during conception as egg and sperm unite in a lightning-flash of power and set the forces of life into action, followed in due time by the thunder of the heartbeat and the lightning-energy of all our body's bioelectrical functions.

Ahma

(Ǫnd, And, Æðm, Athom, Ethma, Atum, Atem, Adem. 'Ahma' is the Gothic word. Pronounced 'AH-ma.')

All of these words go back to Proto-Indo-European words for both 'breath' and 'spirit,' and are linguistically related to the Hindu Atman, the highest, most refined soul in Hindu belief. In the Germanic languages, these words applied to the indwelling human spirit. In Old Norse and Gothic they also applied to otherworldly beings like ghosts, devils, dwarves, and other wights. The Christian Holy Spirit

Definition and Overview

was called by variations of this word in the different languages, such as *Ahmeins Weihis* in Gothic and *Hellige Ånd* in modern Norwegian.

Ahma is our 'spirit' and is the channel for divine gifts of inspiration and the highest mental abilities such as abstract thought and inspired creativity. This soul, in human form, is more connected with the divine realms and cosmic powers, and less concerned with earthly, mundane matters than many of our other souls.

Ghost

(*Gast, Gest, Geist, Keist, Geest.* 'Ghost' is the modern English form of the old Germanic word.)

Some of the old Germanic languages (Anglo-Saxon, Frisian, Old Saxon, Old High German) split the concept of Ahma into two, with their Ahma-related words applying primarily to 'breath' (including the Divine Breath), and another word *Gast, Geist, etc.* applying more to spirits and wights, though there was some parallel usage. Ghost-words applied to the inner spirit of a person, to spirit-beings such as ghosts, and to physical but otherworldly, supernatural beings such as dragons, wights, and monsters (e.g. Grendel, called an *ellor-gast*, an alien spirit, in Anglo-Saxon, even though he was a physical being). In these languages, the Christian Holy Spirit was called *Holy Ghost, Halig Gast, Heilige Geist, etc.*

In my conceptualization of Heathen soul lore, our Ghost and Ahma souls are intimately related in this way: Ahma is the sacred breath, the unchanging and formless material of spirit, while Ghost is Ahma's hama or soul-skin, a pod that shapes and encloses our formless Ahma into a personal being with its own character: our Ghost. While, as

I see it, Ahma is united with the impersonal, undifferentiated sacred power out of which everything flows, Ghost interacts with personal Deities and with the mundane world of Midgard on a person-to-person level, while still accessing the powers of our Ahma spirit.

Though the Ghost is a Life-soul, conferring life through the breath, it can also act as a Wander-Soul through temporary flight from the body during trance, dreams, coma, and near-death experiences, while remaining linked to the body through slow, deep breathing.

As we inhale our first breath when we are born, our Ahma enclosed within our Ghost rides in upon our breath and takes root within us. After death, when we 'give up the Ghost', our Ghost may join our closest Deities in their God-Homes. If it cannot fully let go of earthly life, it may wander as a haunt on the edges of Midgard. If our Ghost during life does not feel attached to any Deities nor drawn to haunt Midgard, then according to my understanding, it will likely dissolve its shape and revert to the undifferentiated Ahma state after death.

Hama

(*Hama, hamr, hamo. Hama* is the Anglo-Saxon term. Rhymes with 'Mama'.)

This word means 'a covering'. Hama is our human shape, a gift of the Gods: a shaped soul-energy which arises within the womb and placenta where a newly-conceived child lies. It holds the pattern of our physical body, and guides its formation during our growth in the womb. Hama also provides the pattern which guides the energies that heal and restore our body after injury or illness. The *hamingja* (ha-ming-ya) is a spirit of luck which is attached to the

Definition and Overview

structures of the womb (placenta, caul, afterbirth), is born with us, accompanies us during life, and governs the nature of our luck.

In my understanding, Hama consists of three parts, given to Ask and Embla when humans were first formed from trees. *La* or *Lö* is the spiritual energy of the blood which invigorates our body. *Læti* refers to our ability to take physical action, to speak, and to engage in social behavior. *Litr* is our unique physical appearance, including the light of our souls shining through our body and our face, our countenance. Our *Lichama* or Lich-Hama is our living body, the combination of our Lich, our physical body, plus our Hama soul which governs the body and its many abilities.

After death the Hama decomposes along with the Lich, as it releases into the ambient energy of life, unless, as is told in chilling folk-tales, it re-animates its body to become a Draugr, an animated corpse.

Aldr

(*Ealdor, Eldi, Alds*. Aldr is the Old Norse term. Pronounced 'AHL-dr.)

Aldr stems from the root **al* and *alan*, meaning 'to nourish.' It is a life-soul which channels spiritual energy to nourish and heal our Hama and our living body, our Lichama, nurturing it over many years so that it lives long and reaches old age. The word 'old' is derived from this root, as are words for life-span and for an age of time. A word for 'killer' in Anglo-Saxon was *ealdor-bana* or Aldr-bane; likewise there is the Old Norse phrase for killers, *aldrs synjuðu*, meaning 'Aldr-snatchers', showing that Aldr is necessary to maintain life.

As the Hama shapes and empowers our physical body and life in space, Aldr governs our 'body and life in time'. It is shaped and given to us by the Norns when we are born, drawn from the Well of Wyrd, and is linked with our ørlög and wyrd, the patterns that shape and are shaped by our life-events. Aldr triggers time-dependent physical changes such as puberty and menopause, and governs the timing of events related to our ørlög throughout our lifetime.

During life Aldr weaves its own hama or soul-skin, like a cloak or a cocoon, made up of all the deeds and events of our lives. This soul-skin is called our Werold ('man-age'): it is our own personal world, made up of our cumulative experiences and deeds over our whole lifetime. It is because of Aldr that we humans have the ability to view our life as a meaningful whole, our life-span as an entity woven within the dimensions of Time and Wyrd.

Saiwalo

(*Saiwala, Seola, Siola, Sawol, Seula, Sele, Sela, Sal.* Saiwalo is the Proto-Germanic word. Pronounced 'SIGH-wa-low'.)

This is the word that descended to become modern English 'soul', with similar words in all the other modern Germanic languages. In Heathen times Saiwalo was understood to be the soul which goes to Hel after death, where it continues existing as the 'shade'. Unlike most of the other souls, during life Saiwalo has little involvement in everyday Midgard activities and our personality, except for its role as a life-soul which keeps the body alive by its presence. When Saiwalo departs, the body is *sawol-leas*, soulless and dead.

Definition and Overview

When Christian missionaries began their work of translating Christian teachings into the Germanic languages, preaching that 'the soul' must be saved by Christ or else end up in a place of eternal torment and damnation, it was clear to them that Saiwalo and Hel were the closest match among the Heathen soul-word candidates for these roles, based on what was already believed about Saiwalo as an afterlife soul going to a place called 'Hel'.

The word-root of 'Hel' means 'hidden, concealed'; Heathen Hel was not seen as a place specifically for punishment. Heathen Hel is the Hidden Land, told of in endless myths, folktales, fairy tales, fantasies, experienced in dreams and trance-work. It contains sources of benevolence, reunion, rootedness, distress, emptiness, neediness, riches, power, beauty, mystery, arcane knowledge. Its denizens are the Saiwalo souls who shape their surroundings through their powers of imaging and their experiences during life.

The Christian missionaries chose one soul, out of the multiplicity of Germanic Heathen choices, to dub 'the one and only soul', destined for heaven or hell according to Christian rules. Ironically, this meant that the words for all the other souls recognized by Heathen belief either dropped out of the various Germanic languages entirely, or remained but changed their meanings, or else were eventually subsumed as 'parts' of what was once the Saiwalo soul and then became "The (only) Soul". As I show in Chapter 15, the other souls were definitely not seen as 'parts' of Saiwalo during Heathen times.

II. The Daemon Souls or Wander-Souls

Hugr

(Hugi, Hyge, Hugs, Hei, Hu. Hugr is the Old Norse word. Pronounced 'WHO-gr.').

Hugr is very closely related to the abilities and capacities of both the intellect and the heart. It resides around the heart where, under the influence of strong emotion or the raising of occult power, it wells up and swells within the breast until it bursts out as emotional expression or as magical power. Hugr is the soul which can most easily leave our physical body on its own errands, as is told in Norse folklore up until recent times, and can, rarely, appear as our Doppelgänger or in animal form at a distance from the body.

Hugr is associated particularly with domains of Thought that help us deal with everyday challenges of social and practical life, as opposed to the more abstract kinds of Thought associated with Ahma and Ghost. Hugr is a soul within us who loves, who has desires and longings, envy and cravings, intentions, strong emotions and subtle thoughts. It is fully embedded in and focused on our life in Midgard, and serves as our 'inner warder,' subtly helping us resist social pressures, deception and manipulation by other people. It is, among other things, a guardian of our personal boundaries. However, it may engage in manipulation of other people itself, in pursuit of its own desires, if it fails to develop self-restraint.

After death, Hugr sooner or later is likely to reincarnate, but a mature and seasoned afterlife Hugr may also spend time as an ancestral spirit, a *Dis* (female) or *Alf*

Definition and Overview

(male) of our physical or spiritual line who offers guidance, rede and wisdom from the spirit-world to the living. An angry, envious, hateful or vengeful Hugr after death may become an afflicting spirit, given many names in folklore such as Hag, Murk-Elf, Night-mare, etc. It will seek to cause illness, nightmares, ill luck, accidents, elf-shot, and other such misfortunes for the living.

Mod

(Moðr, Moths, Mot, Muat, Muot, Moet, Mut, Mood, Mo. Mod is the word in Anglo-Saxon and Old Saxon. Pronounced 'mode'.)

Mod and Hugr souls have a great deal in common. Both of them are sources of strong emotion, courage, determination, strategic and practical thinking. Both of them can serve as inner rede-givers, offering insights and knowledge not available to our conscious minds. Both are involved with our intentions that lead to actions. Both can flood us with negative emotions such as rage, envy, or cruelty, or throw us into moods and tempers, good or bad. The two of them provide a great deal of what we experience as 'character' and 'personality' within ourselves and others.

Mod is especially associated with strength of body, mind and will-power, and is a characteristic of Thor, his sons Magni (Might) and Móði (Mod-y), and his daughter Thruðr (Strength). Mod was also the word used to translate Latin *virtus* or 'virtue', in the sense of possessing some out-of-the-ordinary power, like the healing 'virtue' of herbs, or the power in a magical item. Even a good beer was considered to have Mod-power, its own virtue or special quality of flavor and potency. Thunder-clouds, mighty ocean waves, uncastrated male animals like stallions, bulls and rams, and the mighty aurochs mentioned in the Anglo-Saxon rune-poem for Ur: all of these were also called 'mod'.

Mod does not willingly leave the body as Hugr can do, but it can be weakened or removed from the body of humans and animals through the agency of illness, or by magical or supernatural means. Many medieval spells sought to restore mod-energy to an ill, lethargic, weak or depressed person or domestic animal by ousting the wight, witch or sorcerer that was afflicting their Mod-power.

There's reason to believe that Mod originated as a daemon, an elemental spirit of nature, an expression of natural power, and that some of these elemental spirits, ages ago, began to associate more and more closely with humans, animals, Deities, and wights. Gradually they became more integrated with their hosts, just as, on the physical level, micro-organisms like viruses and bacteria gradually integrated with our microbiome and even our genome, and during evolution changed our nature to a degree. In humans, through the influence of our other souls, over evolutionary time our inner Mod became more human-like, more integral to our 'soular-system', while still bearing within itself the power and wildness of its elemental roots.

Sefa

(Sefa, seofa, sebo, sefi. Sefa is the Old Norse and Anglo-Saxon word. Pronounced 'SAY-fah'.)

This word descends from or is closely related to several words with these meanings: the 'self', the ability of the self to sense and perceive what is around it, and kinship and relationship. It is related to the name of the Norse Goddess Sjöfn, who promotes and protects love, affection, and relationships, and to the Goddess-name Sif, wife of

Definition and Overview

Thor, whose name is related to 'sib' (sibling) and words for 'relative, relationship' in all the Germanic languages. In Old English, *sibb* meant 'kinship, relationship, love, friendship, peace, happiness'. Proto-Germanic **sibja* meant literally 'one's own', a blood relation. Sib-related words indicating 'relationship' occur in all the old and modern Germanic languages.

The basic meaning I derive for Sefa is "our self, with its abilities to sense, notice, perceive and understand, and that which is connected to our self through relationship, love and affection." Further meanings of this word are related to awareness, noticing, paying attention to, as well as soothing and quieting. These are all faculties of our Self that are needed to promote strong relationships between people who understand one another well, pay attention to and care for one another.

I associate the word 'caring' in all its meanings with Sefa, along with the perceptive insights that are gained from sincerely caring about others. A nutshell-meaning of Sefa, to me, is 'the one who cares' within ourselves, whether that caring is related to people or other beings or things, or to any kind of situation or idea that one may care about. This includes the meaning of 'cares' as 'worries, sorrows, concerns,' as well as the meaning of caring *for* someone or something, and caring *about* anything. Sefa-soul includes the energy and the link between our self and whatever we care about, whether concrete (like another person, or the environment) or abstract (like the ideas of justice, beauty, kindness, honor).

Sefa is not a daemon-soul, but as it is closely linked with Hugr and Mod, I include it with these other two souls as a group.

Associated Spirits

There are many fascinating accounts throughout the lore of Germanic lands and peoples, relating to spirits or wights which accompany some or all humans, and who are associated with peoples' kinship lines, household, land, crops, crafts, paranormal powers, activities of many kinds. They are a major source of the luck or ill-luck that affects human lives. Much has been written about them elsewhere, both by academic scholars and by practicing Heathens. Though I mention these spirits from time to time in my soul lore studies, they are not a primary focus of my work, simply because there is already so much for me to explore regarding our own inherent souls.

Opening our awareness to our souls, and to the souls of others, enables us to view the complex topographies of physical, social, psychological, and metaphysical life with clearer, more discerning eyes.

Chapter 2

2. The Awakening of the Souls

Here I'm presenting a story about my understanding of the souls and the Worlds they are connected to, based on ancient lore, but expanded further. There are different ways that souls can be understood, including the degree to which they are dependent upon any Deities. I'm offering a particular perspective, but others can be taken. This is an exploration of how we are formed, how each of us comes into being, the coalescence of all our souls with our body as we live our life in Midgard. I present this in the form of a story or a meditation, and invite you to picture it and follow it in your imagination, as well as your intellect. This story is intended to provide an overall context within which to place the discussions of the individual souls in the following chapters.

Ginnungagap

There is Fire and there is Ice. They form the poles of *Ginnungagap*, the Gap of Magical Potential, the great void that holds all potential Being within itself. The polarities of heat and cold meet in the middle and form a vast space of roiling mist and steam: this is Mist-World or *Niflheim*. Here, all-that-might-be exists as wisps and shifting forms and energies, ever flowing and reshaping. Here is where *Ahma* arises, also called *Önd* and *Athom:* the sacred breath of Spirit that flows through all existence.

Through this space of Ginnungagap currents of enormous power flow, generated by the primal polarities of Fire and Ice, and in the center they meet and swirl into a gigantic, churning fountain of energy called *Hvergelmir*, the Roaring Cauldron. Up and out it bursts, perpetually re-creating space-time by its existence and motion. This is the source of all the forces operating in the Worlds, flowing forth in the shape of the *Elivagar*, the mighty rivers of energy that feed the Worlds and form the turbulent boundaries between them.

The Elivagar billowing out from Hvergelmir.

As Hvergelmir's energy-fountain billows up, it begins its first stage of condensation, forming the World of *Hel*, the

The Awakening of the Souls

Womb of Souls. Hel is not the dumping ground of the dead. Rather, it is here that the potentialities of Mist-World, all the swirling Might-Be's, take the first steps toward becoming beings in their own right.

These beings, the Saiwalo souls, arise in Hel. They are formed, as everything is, from the Ahma-Mist, the Ǫnd-Spirit-Breath, arising from Mist-Home. The currents of Hvergelmir and the mighty Elivagar, the cosmic fountain and rivers of power, stir these mists. The roots of the World-Tree stabilize them, Mimir's Well feeds them, the primal Powers of the Worlds flow through them. And thus, our *Saiwalo* souls are stirred into being.

The Saiwalo forms a Dwimor, an image of the person-to-be. (John Bauer, artist.)

The Saiwalos are the first souls to begin the coalescence into individual beingness. To further this process, each Saiwalo forms and feeds a phantom, a spiritual shape called a *Dwimor*, which the Saiwalo projects from Hel into our world of Midgard. Dwimor is the soul-image of the person-to-be, flowing out from the Saiwalo soul into Midgard.

In Midgard, the Dwimor-image remains connected to Saiwalo, channeling flows of energy between Hel and Midgard. Dwimor serves as a spindle or a magnet, collecting all our other souls around it. Our Saiwalo with its Dwimor is the center of gravity that holds all our souls together during our life in Midgard. At the end of our physical life, our Dwimor departs Midgard as a phantom, and returns to the Saiwalo soul who generated it.

What is it that calls this Dwimor-image into being from Saiwalo? What urge does Saiwalo feel, that moves it to form a Dwimor and send it forth into Midgard? A sacred spark is lit, a spiritual fire ignites, and its beauty and power draw the Dwimor forth from its Saiwalo-soul in Hel, pulling it up into Midgard. This sacred spark is our *Ferah* soul, ignited when egg and sperm meet in the act of conceiving a physical body, a Lich.

Ferah is the power of lightning and thunder, the power of earth and mountains, of sky and storm. It flows through Thor and his Mother Earth, and into humans, animals, trees, all the beings of Nature. As the lightning-strike of Ferah-life begins in the womb, the complex flows of energy acting through the Dwimor cause each Ferah to become a unique individual, imprinted by the Dwimor-image and formed from the life-power of Earth and Sky. Thus Ferah-soul and Saiwalo-soul meet together, bridging the sacred energies between Midgard, the Home of Life, and Hel, the Womb of Souls.

The imprint of our soul-image that our Dwimor shares with Ferah-soul now flashes out like lightning, giving forth an echo that coalesces into our *Hama* soul, which links to the genetic imprint of the newly-conceived being. This is the soul which shapes our physical body, our Lich, with its ability to take action, to speak and behave as humans do, and take on human appearance. Odin's brother gave the template for the human Hama soul to Ask and Embla. That template is passed down to the present day by the power of the Hama. As our Hama-soul shapes our physical body, our Lich, the two of them blend together and become our *Lich-Hama:* our living, ensouled physical body. Hama gives us all the essential tools to function as humans in Midgard, including speech and the ability to interact in social groups.

The Dwimor imprints the Hama with its image, then the Hama shapes the physical body, the Lich. (John Bauer, artist.)

As we grow within our mother's womb, there are now three Life-souls at work to shape this growth. Our Dwimor, sent forth from Saiwalo, offers an image of what we can become: an image which will grow and change with us during our full lifetime, influenced by all our souls and our surroundings. Our Hama shapes our physical body and the many abilities our body gives us, including speech and brain-power. Ferah provides the energy for growth and change: the thunder that starts our infant heart beating, the lightning of bioelectric activity that runs through our nerves and all our cellular interactions, triggering growth and change. All the sensations and perceptions of our Lich, our body, are felt and perceived through our Ferah, which permeates and fills our Lich as a subtle energy-form.

Now our living body, our Lich-Hama, is finishing its formation in the womb, and we approach the time of our birth. The Norns draw forth from their Well our *Aldr* soul, and shape this soul to guide our life through the mysterious dimensions of Time and Wyrd. To this soul is attached our *ørlög*, the threads from the past with all their potentials and pitfalls. Aldr guides the timing of physical changes in our body, and the timing of wyrd-filled events in our lives, through its connection with the Norns. Aldr is also the Nourisher and Healer: a close-to-physical soul-being who funnels subtle energy into our Lichama, giving us vigor and health, and governing the span of our life.

Now the wyrded moment comes, guided by the Holy Ones and the stars, when we leave our mother's womb and enter Midgard as a being in our own right. At this momentous instant, we draw in our first breath, and with this breath our *Ghost* rides in and roots itself within us. Ghost is shaped out of the Ǫnd or Ahma, the Spirit-Mist that hovers timelessly over Ginnungagap. The Holy Ones attending our birth grasp a portion of Ahma / Ǫnd, and wrap it in a soul-skin to give it shape, cohesion, personhood, and the spirit-likeness of our Lich.

This Ǫnd wrapped in soul-skin is our Ghost: our own personal Spirit or Ahma, enlivened by the power-filled spirit-mist arising from Ginnungagap. Ghost is like a pod wrapped in a membrane, floating in the timeless fields of Ahma over Ginnungagap. Ghost pulsates within this field of Ǫnd, drawing Ǫnd into and out of its soul-skin, and causes our Lichama, our body, to do the same in Midgard. This is the process of breathing: our Ghost breathes Ǫnd, our Lich-

The Awakening of the Souls

Hama breathes air. They synchronize together, filling us with Life and Spirit.

As our Ghost settles into our soul-household, it attunes to the shape of our Dwimor-phantom. Thus, we have two phantom-souls who, in the afterlife or during disembodied visions, will bear the appearance of our Midgard-self: our Ghost and our Dwimor.

So here we have the tally of our six Life-Souls:
~ Hel-Dwelling Saiwalo with its Dwimor,
~ Ferah the Fire of Life,
~ Hama the Shaper,
~ Aldr the Nourisher, Time-Keeper, and Bearer of ørlög,
~ The sacred breath of Ahma or Ǫnd,
~ and our Ghost, our personal Spirit, which wraps our Ahma within it.

There are two other souls, Daemon souls rooted in Midgard, who have been hovering over, and influencing, our conception, gestation and birth. *Hugr's* nature is rooted in Desire, Wish, Longing. It is open to love, and springs from deep wells of the human past. Hugr is an ancestral soul who reincarnates in the body to experience Midgard life, again and again. This is how Hugr grows mightily in knowledge, wisdom, power, subtlety.

The Hugr-souls of our ancestors, and the Hugr-soul wishing to incarnate into our new body, spark desire and love in our parents at the time of our conception. The powerful desire of the hovering Hugr to reincarnate draws egg and sperm into full union.

As the spark of life begins, a *Mod* soul, a nature-spirit or elemental who has evolved along with humans, brings its own power to bear. Mod's powers are Strength, Will, and Determination, carried to a very high level. This hovering Mod-soul, seeking a physical body in Midgard, fills the new spark of life with strength and will to live and thrive, to grow to fulfill its full potential.

Mod and Hugr, these powerful Midgard souls, help us, the new person, to set deep roots into Midgard, rooting solidly into human life with all its complexity and richness. At first these Daemon souls are only loosely associated with our infant Lich-Hama. Some of their traits are strong in small children. Tempers and moods, willfulness and determination, basic traits of character: Mod and Hugr begin by attaching themselves to us in these ways. *Sefa* also begins to grow within us at this time: our sense of self, the perceptiveness this gives us regarding how our self relates to others, and our desire and need for relationship throughout our life.

As time goes on and we grow and mature, Hugr and Mod gradually knit themselves more tightly with our Life-souls as a well-functioning group, our 'soular system' or our *Hiwscipe* or *Hiwship*, as I like to call it in Anglo-Saxon: our soul-household. Sefa, our sense of self and how we relate to others, grows along with this.

Hugr and Mod bring intelligence and social skills, courage and strength of character, wisdom and guidance. These souls grow stronger and deeper through our experience of life. Thus they are able to express their characters, their desires, their will, their moods and tempers, their thoughts and actions, through this new person and into the rich and challenging world of Midgard. Sefa-soul helps to moderate the sometimes selfish or thoughtless powers of Mod through a soul-part blended between them: our

The Awakening of the Souls

Modsefa. Hugr's warding powers protect the tender Sefa, the relationship-soul, from being abused or drained.

As we grow into childhood, Ferah is an influential soul, igniting in us the love of nature that most children have, when given the opportunity. Playing with animals, watching the clouds, climbing trees, splashing in water and mud, learning to swim, hunting for rocks and bugs: through these activities Ferah awakens our awareness of its deep roots in natural life. We become aware that we are members of the *Feorh-cynn*, the kindred of all living beings.

Firi-barn, child of Ferah. Deep in their hearts, children know their kinship with all who bear the Ferah life-soul, the living-beings of the Feorh-cynn.

Ferah brings with it a natural sense of piety, of connection with Holy Ones both great and small, and when well-nurtured it gives us, as children, the innocent and lovely sense of connection with Holiness. Ferah has a strong sense of the natural laws that govern fruitful interactions between humans and Deities, humans and Nature. Thus, the Old Saxons referred to a wise and devout person as *feraht*. "The folk" were called *firihi*, after Ferah, and *firi-barn*: the children of Ferah.

Aldr nourishes our souls and our life, and triggers the many stages of growth and change as we navigate childhood, adolescence, adulthood, and old age. It gives us our sense of time passing, of wyrd and ørlög and the meaning these hold for our life. And it gives us the ability to see and understand our life as a whole: our life as a soul-garment that we weave, day by day, throughout our lives. Aldr is so important to human life that, again and again in the old writings, human beings are called *aldr-beornum* and *eldi-barn:* the Children of Aldr, Time-Children, mortal beings.

As small children, we often sense the presence of our Ahma and Ghost, with their connection to the timeless source of divine inspiration and power, though we have no way to express this understanding in words. As we mature, Ahma-power is best expressed through moments of inspiration, creativity of all kinds, and in brilliance of intellect.

As we grow and our 'soular-system' or Hiwship consolidates and integrates, we become more and more able to access and express all our souls. We ourselves link all the Worlds together through our souls and body, our thoughts and deeds, our care for ourselves, for each other, and for this beautiful world of Midgard.

The Ferah Soul

Ferah soul is sparked into being by lightning...

Heathen Soul Lore

...and born from trees.

Chapter 3

3. Born of Trees and Thunder: The Ferah Soul

As Bor's sons were going along the sea strand they found two trees, and took up the trees and shaped men therefrom. ...They gave them clothing and names, calling the karl-man Askr and the woman Embla. (From *Gylfaginning* in the Prose Edda.)

Odin said:
My clothes I gave, along the way,
To two tree-people.
They thought themselves heroes when they had clothing;
The naked person is ashamed.
(*Havamal* verse 49, in the Poetic Edda, my translation.)

Until three came, crossing over from elsewhere,
Potent and loving Æsir from their homes.
And found on the land Ask (Ash) and Embla (?Elm),
With little megin, lacking ørlög.
(without human power and destiny)
(*Völuspá* verse 17, in the Poetic Edda, my translation.)

In these beautiful passages from the Old Norse lore, we see that in the misty depths of time, the Gods shaped human beings out of trees. This belief is common to other Indo-European peoples, and other peoples of the world as well.

But why trees? The Abrahamic religions and some other religious traditions maintain that humans were shaped from earth, and other traditions tell of yet different origins, but our own faith links us with the trees. What is it about trees that makes them suitable for this transformation? Let us first explore what scholars can show us about the Indo-European linguistic connections between trees and vital essence or life-soul, as shown in Table 1. (Note that in the process of language evolution, the sounds 'p' and 'k' often transmute to the sounds 'f' and 'h', respectively.)

Connections between Trees and Life-Soul

Table 1: Trees and Life-Soul Words

Language	Trees	Life-Soul
Proto-Indo-European	*perkwu = oak	*perku
Proto-Germanic Gothic	*ferhwa = oak *furhwon = fir furh-jon = fir	*ferhwa
Old High German/ Old Saxon/ Old Frisian Lombardian	fereh-eih = oak foraha = pine fereha = oak	ferah, ferh, ferch, verch
Old Norse	fjörr = tree fura = pine fyri = fir	fjör = life-soul, pith fjörr = living being
Anglo-Saxon	furh = pine	feorh, ferhð
Modern English Modern German	fir tree Föhre = pine	--

The Ferah Soul

(* The asterisk is used before Proto-Indo-European (PIE) and Proto-Germanic words to indicate that these words are reconstructed using linguistic science. There are no written records of their language going back to the time before the Indo-European peoples split off from one another.)

Votive offerings to a group of Germanic Matron-Goddesses, dating to the time of the Roman Empire, link these two groups of meanings very neatly. The Goddesses are called *Alaferhwiae*, 'The All-Ferhw-Ones', and their votive stones show images of trees. The name has been variously interpreted as 'the great life-giving ones' and 'the goddesses belonging to all trees' (Simek p. 5). In my view the connection between trees and life-soul removes any contradiction between these interpretations.

There are many more words derived from those listed above, that flesh out our understanding of the Germanic life-soul concept. Table 2 shows just a few of them.

Table 2: Words Derived from *perku

Language	Term	Translation
Proto-Indo-European	*perku	chest, rib (the place where the soul lives)
Gothic	Fairhwus	the world, "house of the fairhw"
Anglo-Saxon	feorhus (feorh-hus) feorhbana feorhbera feorhcynn ferhth	- body, chest, "house of the feorh" - feorh-bane, murderer - feorh-bearer, living being - feorh-kin, kindred of the living - mind, intellect, spirit
Old Saxon	firibarn firihi feraht	- child of humankind - the folk - devoutly wise

All of these terms link together: (a) trees, (b) the vital principle or life-soul, (c) the human body as the dwelling place for this soul, (d) wisdom as the expression of this soul, (e) the idea of humans as 'children of this soul', and (f) the kinship among all humans, which is conferred by their common possession of this soul. Terms like *Feorhcynn* and *Fjǫrr* can also apply to all living beings, not only humans.

Ferah and the Gods

Though in biological, evolutionary terms, humans are more closely connected with animals than with trees, there is a unique characteristic that trees and humans share: we are both upright, vertical, and by our upright nature we serve as conduits between earth-power and sky-power.

Table 3 shows the close linguistic connections between the life-soul words I listed above and Gods, Earth and Sky powers.

Table 3: Gods, Earth, Sky Powers

Language	Life-Soul	Earth / Deity	Thunder / Deity
Proto-Indo-European	*perku	--	*Perkwunos Thunder God
Proto-Germanic	*ferhwa	*fergunja=mountain	
Old Norse	fjör	-Fjörgyn (Earth Goddess) - Fjörgynn (father of Frigg) - fjarg ("Gods," plural form) -fjarghus (Gods' house, temple)	Thor Thunder-God, son of Fjörgyn Earth-Goddess
Old Prussian	-	--	- percunis = thunder
Lithuanian, Latvian			- Perkunas Thunder-God
Old Russian			- Perunu Thunder- God
Anglo-Saxon	feorh	fyrgen = forested mountain	–
Middle High German	verch	virgunt = ditto	
Gothic	fair, fairhw	fairgunni = forested mountain region	–

Heathen Soul Lore

There seems to be what semanticists call a 'bundle' of meanings rooted in Proto-Indo-European that includes closely-related words for: oak / tree, Thunder-God, strike (**per*), and stone. There are various views as to which words are more closely derived from each other, but there is also a general sense that all of these words are interrelated. The Thunder-God strikes trees with a thunderbolt in the form of a stone hammer, causing lightning and fire to spring out. The 'stone' connection extends into the word-domain of rocks, mountains and other earth features. Thus, **Perkwus*, the Oak, is the bridge that links **perku / fairhw / ferah*, the life-soul, with **Perkwunos* Thunder-God, his stone hammer and his strike, his **per*. Oak is the bridge between soul and God-power.

A shadowy Storm-God strikes the trees with lightning.

There is a widely-held belief that when the thunderbolt strikes the oak, it does not 'cause' fire in the tree, but rather 'releases' the fire that is already within it. This reminds me of the Old English rune poem for Yew *(Eihwaz)*, which calls Yew the "keeper of the fire." This is also the reason why the Need-Fire, made with a fire-drill, is the most sacred form of 'domesticated' fire: fire is not brought to the wood, rather fire is released from it by the drill.

The idea of a God releasing fire from a tree is very close to the idea of Gods shaping, or even 'releasing' humans from trees, fire being a frequent analogy for 'life.' I speculate that Thor, as well as (obviously) his Mother Fjǫrgyn / Earth, is deeply involved in bringing into being and nurturing the Ferah souls of trees and other living beings. Though science doesn't yet completely understand how life began on Earth, among the ideas considered for this are the roles of meteorites and lightning: Thor and his Hammer stand behind these images too! We see Thor as a life-giver when he swings his Hammer over the bones of his slaughtered goats, bringing them back to life. His Hammer brings fertility to the lap of the bride and ripeness to the fields of gleaming grain.

With all of this, I wonder whether Thor was the one, in much earlier times than we have records for, who was credited with bringing human life from trees. Based on linguistic clues this would make sense; he would not necessarily have been the one giving specific gifts such as Ǫnd or Wode, but he and his Hammer might have been the actual 'releaser' of the human life-soul from the wood, just as he releases fire from within it. As I shall show farther on, the word 'release' is also used to describe what happens to the Ferah at the moment of death, the other end of the process.

So, here is a story of beginnings, expanded from the Old Norse tales:

Trees, rooted in Mother Earth, attract lightning bolts, Sky-God power. And so, one mythic day, Thor rode the clouds above a forest in his beloved Midgard, while from Asgard three mighty brothers set forth in that direction, all coming at last to a strand between the forest and the sea. This slender strip of no-man's-land stood between Land and Sea, Here and Otherworlds, Matter and Spirit. Together the Gods came across two trees there, trees with great Ferah-spirits of their own that drew the Gods' awareness like magnets. Raising his Hammer, the Hallower of Midgard gave the life-releasing blow, striking one tree on the fore-swing and the other on the back-swing. The trees-becoming-humans stood there between Mother Earth and Father Sky, between negative and positive poles of power, and felt the God-mains flowing through them in brilliant surges of actinic light.

From Asgard to Midgard.

And so the Ferah-souls within these trees burst forth as flames and were transformed into Ferahs of new beings, human beings, different but akin to the ancient spirits of the woods. The Sons of Bor gave their great gifts: breath and spirit, wode and speech. They clothed these transformed Ferah-spirits with the human shape, the Hama, so they would not be naked spirits in a world of tree-clothed wights. Human Hamas are so skillful and powerful that Ask and Embla, as Odin remarked, felt like heroes when they had been so clothed!

At Ragnarök, human souls will take shelter within the beleaguered Tree. Then, at the beginning of the new cycle of time, Lif and Lifthrasir will come forth as flames of life from the sheltering wood, just as their forebears Ask and Embla did, so many generations before.

The Evolutionary Perspective

In our myths about the creation of humans from trees, we can view our primal human substance literally as trees, or we can view it as the Ferah soul-substance itself: Ferah which gives life to all physical beings and which shares its name with trees, storm powers and earth powers. I follow both beliefs in different layers of my consciousness. At the mythic level of consciousness I find the idea of descent from trees to be deeply meaningful; all that I wrote, above, is true to me in a way that has no need for scientific logic.

At the more modern, scientific level my understanding is that our Ferah life-soul goes way back to pre-human stages of evolution. At some point during the physical process of evolution, the Gods gave pre-human beings a human spirit, human qualities and powers, and the Norns gave us the collective ørlög, the fate, of human-ness.

Thus we made the shift from pre-human to human beings, bringing our Ferah with us, and along with it our kinship with the Feorhcynn, the kindred of all living beings.

The family tree. (Relief from Mother Hulda / Frau Holle Fountain, Eschwege.)

Ferah can be understood as the soul which places us in an evolutionary context and connection with the other forms of life in Midgard. As humans emerged from pre-human beings, Thor and the other *Fjarg*, the Gods and Goddesses, played a great role in this process. From Thor's lightning, humans first obtained their fire, and his stone hammer was the prototype for tools that brought food and other needs to our forebears: throwing axes, hoes, and other tools and weapons. Midgard's Defender, a patron and inspirer of everyday, life-sustaining work, was with us back then, too!

As I mentioned above, the PIE words **perku* (life-soul), **perkus* (chest, breast), and **per* (to strike) are all closely related to words for the Thunder-God and his actions. The

Latin root of our word 'percussion' comes from the same source. These words are all part of a logic-circle that looks like this: *life-soul / chest / heartbeat / drumbeat / thunder / Thunder-God / God-power / life-soul.* In addition to the thunder / heartbeat aspect, there is the element of lightning / electricity and its functions in our body. Our brain and nervous system functions, inter-cellular reactions, and the regulation of our heartbeat, are just a few examples of the essential bio-electric life-functions set into motion within us by the God of Lightning.

There are three ancient words that well capture the interconnection of humans, the world, and the Gods: each is the same word in a different language; each expresses one aspect of the whole. Anglo-Saxon *feorhus* means 'house of the Feorh', and it refers to the body, sometimes just the chest, as the home of the Ferah-soul. Gothic *fairhwus* means 'house of the Fairh,' and refers to the world as a whole, the place where all Ferah-souls live their lives. And Old Norse *fjarghus,* "house of the Fjarg," is the temple or Gods-house, the place where the Gods who give life and soul are honored in Midgard.

The Nature of the Ferah

Without Ferah, there is no life. Grimm mentions that one of the many German folk-names for the personified figure of Death is the *ferch-grimme,* a monstrous figure who "has designs upon the life or soul (ferch)" (p. 849). Ferah is so much associated with life that often modern scholars simply translate the Germanic Ferah-words as 'life', which works alright in most contexts as long as we understand what is meant by 'life.' We are not speaking of life-span, lifetime, the duration of life: this is the domain of our Aldr soul. We are also not speaking of anything like life-style, way of life, making a living. Nor is Ferah some kind of philosophical abstraction or amorphous biological principle. Although modern linguists translate the PIE *perku* as 'life force, vital principle,' I doubt that our Indo-European forebears thousands of years ago thought in terms of "principles" and "forces;" they probably thought in much more concrete, substantive terms.

The Germanic Ferah-as-life was conceived of as an actual substance which conferred life by its presence, and caused death by its absence. It was pictured as a fluid substance which fills the body: the term *ferahes gifullid*, filled with Ferah, is used a number of times in the Old Saxon *Heliand*, particularly with reference to Jesus as one who was filled with an especially sacred and powerful Ferah soul. (The *Heliand* is an Old Saxon poem that retells the Christian gospel story in very Germanic imagery and language, a useful resource for understanding how native Saxon words relating to the souls were used.)

In the description of Jesus' resurrection, the *Heliand* author says that after his death the Ferah was no longer within the flesh, but then the flesh was again 'filled' with Ferah at the time of resurrection (l. 5852). The quasi-material nature of Ferah also comes across in a phrase from *Beowulf*. When Beowulf is facing the dragon, he knows that his Feorh will not be "wrapped in flesh" for very much longer; he knows that death and Wyrd are very near (ll. 2419 ff.).

We get an impression here of something like an etheric substance which is congruent with the physical body during life. It is both similar and dissimilar to the etheric body as it is understood today. The etheric-substance nature of the Ferah is quite clear from the ancient descriptions, and

The Ferah Soul

as I shall discuss below, many of our body-related sensations and instincts seem to be rooted as much in our Ferah as they are in our Lich, our physical body. In this much, the Ferah is similar to the modern etheric body concept. But it is different in that the Ferah is not a template which shapes our physical body; in Germanic thought, this role is played by the Hama. Nor can the Ferah leave the body and roam outside it during life, as the etheric body is understood to be capable of: that is a power of other souls.

The Ferah registers all the sensations, perceptions and emotions that occur within the Lich. For example, the Anglo-Saxon *Sið Gealdor* or journey-charm contains the line "may my Feorh never be frightened" by the perils of travel (Storms p. 216-223). The Feorh can suffer *feorhcwala*, torment and torture of the Feorh, when the body is wounded, tortured, or mortally ill. The mortally-wounded Grendel in *Beowulf* is called *feorhseoc* (feorh-sick). In the *Heliand*, the author says that when one is captured, one's enemies have power over the Ferah, but not over the Seola (Saiwalo soul) (ll. 1904-6). The Old High German poet Otfrid used the phrase *ferahe stechan*, to 'stab the Ferah' (Becker p. 34): when the body is stabbed, the Ferah is, too. These are examples of the close connection between the Lich and the Ferah: the Ferah is the one that actually perceives and feels cues in the environment (frightening situations, threat of injury), which set in motion instinctive and physiological responses within the Ferah-Lich complex, such as fear, pain, fever, etc.

There's an intriguing mention of the Ferah / Fjǫr in *Hervör's Saga* (Tunstall, Ch. 4). The Viking-leader Hervör has gone to the burial mounds of her father and his eleven brothers, all berserks who died in battle, to take her father's sword Tyrfing from his howe. Much argument ensues between Hervör and the shade or Dwimor of her father Angantyr Arngrimsson, who doesn't want to give her the sword because it will bring ill luck to her and her line.

Finally Hervör gets the sword, and as Angantyr bids her farewell, he makes a statement that sounds like a father's blessing, but hampered because he is dead and she is living. He tells her: "Freely I'd bestow on you the Fjǫr of twelve men, if you trust in the might, power and courage, and all the good that Arngrim's sons left behind themselves." (My translation; the original: *"Flótt gæfak ðér tólf manna fjǫr, ef ðú trúa mættir, afl ok eljun, allt it góða ðat er synir Arngríms at sik leifðu."*)

This seems to be simply his good wishes toward her, since presumably the Fjǫrvi of the dead are no longer available. But the description "might, power and courage, and all the good" gives us some idea of what the gift of Fjǫr would involve, if it were possible to give it. It's also intriguing to meditate on the idea of 'giving Fjǫr / Ferah', and what that might mean in a metaphysical sense. I believe this relates to the connection between Ferah and sacrifice (see below).

The Ferah is intimately involved with all the vital functions of our body: our physiology and metabolism, our neurotransmitter and endocrine functions, our responses to environmental cues, and our growth and deterioration in youth and age, health and disease. I believe that the channels and reservoirs of the life-energy, sometimes called Qi or Prana, are located within the Ferah, another point of commonality between Ferah and the modern etheric body concept. All of these life functions are logical outgrowths of Ferah's intimate connection with nature and all the powers and energies of nature, both mundane and divine.

The Ferah Soul

Beyond physical and environmental responsiveness, our Ferah soul can feel 'higher' emotions, and can be characterized by different qualities such as wisdom, holiness, or cruelty. The Gothic word *wai-fairhwjan* means 'wail-fairhw-ing', vocally expressing heartfelt grief that is felt in the Ferah. The Ferah is present in the accord or discord existing between people: in *Skirnismal* of the Poetic Edda, Gerðr says angrily to Skirnir that she will never live with Freyr with their Fjǫrs in good accord together (vs. 20). In the Old Saxon *Heliand*, the disciples of John the Baptist are described as *helagferaha*, with holy Ferahs. In *Beowulf*, happiness is expressed by saying that the Ferhð rejoices. The poem also says of prince Heremod that 'within his Ferhð grew a breast-hoard of cruelty' (l. 1818-9).

The Ferah is perceptive, aware and responsive to physical, social, and divine cues in the environment. This leads us to the meaning of the word *ferhð* in Anglo-Saxon, translated as 'mind, intellect, soul, spirit.' Ferhð is derived from the same root as feorh: Anglo-Saxon is odd in its tendency to split word-concepts that are unitary in other Germanic languages into two different words.

Usually *feorh* refers more to life-soul functions while *ferhð* refers more to wisdom-soul activities. It is often used in contexts implying wisdom and knowledge in worldly social interactions, as for example a wise member of a governing council or the advisor to a king. The Old Saxon *Heliand* gives a picture of a different kind of wisdom. There, a *feraht* person is someone who is deeply pious and devout, who focuses his or her life on the Divine, and derives from that attentiveness a more spiritual kind of wisdom.

Ferah, Law, and Priesthood

A number of people in the Old Saxon *Heliand* are described as *feraht*, and it is interesting to examine the context of this adjective. It is used to mean 'wise, pious, meticulous in following religious laws and obligations.' Though the *Heliand* is presented in an entirely Christian context, the words *ferah* and *feraht*, as I have shown above, are ancient Germanic words and obviously had a Heathen meaning long before they were used in Christian texts. By examining persons who were described as *feraht* in the *Heliand*, we can get at least a glimpse of what this word meant to Heathens.

The most detailed example of a feraht person is perhaps the Jewish temple priest Zacharias, the father of John the Baptist. Zacharias was described in the gospel of Luke (Ch.1) as being righteous and perfect, following all religious laws, serving a great deal of his time in the temple, a faultless man. These qualities were summed up by the *Heliand*-poet as *feraht*.

The connection between piety and law is very strong here. This brings to mind an ancient Germanic term for a Heathen priest: *Æweweard* in Anglo-Saxon, *Éwart* (rhymes with 'K-mart') in Old High German. This word means 'warder of the law,' and meant primarily religious laws and observances, though there were not strict boundaries between religious and secular law.

The Proto-Germanic word **aiwa*, and its descendants *ewa*, *æwe*, and *eu* meant 'law, religion, marriage'. It implied a covenant, a state of troth that has its lawful obligations and responsibilities. (Modern German still uses this word for marriage: *Ehe*.) The similarity between religious troth and wedded troth is very clear. So my understanding of the

The Ferah Soul

æweweard or *èwart* is a person who embodied and upheld Heathen troth, Heathen religious laws, customs and observances, and who mediated these values between the folk and the Gods in a trained, professional capacity. Such a person, based on examples in the *Heliand*, was called *feraht*, though the word was also applied to laypersons with the same kinds of personal qualities and spiritual strength.

This photo shows the oath ring attached to our Thor's Hammer. Oath rings of many different designs were used by Heathens in the past and are used by some modern Heathens. The ring is held while swearing an oath, and is considered to empower and enforce the oath. This ring was made by my blacksmith husband from an antique lightning rod, adding the power of Thor's lightning to the oath ring and Hammer. My husband and I swore our wedding oaths on this ring, and our marriage is still going strong, more than twenty years later.

So far, there may have been considerable overlap between *feraht* as used by Heathens and Christians. My guess is, however, that Heathens brought another dimension into the equation: for them, piety meant power. In the first place, pious practices tried to ensure that the Gods would not be angered, and luck would not be lost, due to human mistakes. More than that, piety was a way to tune oneself and one's folk into the patterns and powers of the Gods, as expressed in nature and in the occurrences of their lives. The better one could do that, the more luck, *hamingja*, and help one could expect to have. Feraht wisdom and power come from the Gods, from nature, from the ambient life-forces. They are gained through right action and right being, living in accordance with one's true nature and the patterns of Wyrd. While anyone could pursue such an aim, the priests and priestesses would have been expected to devote themselves fully to it.

The Roman historian Tacitus (p. 66) tells us that Germanic priests were the only ones who had the right to sentence a lawbreaker to fettering or any form of corporal punishment, including death; not even kings or chieftains had this right at that period of time. We also know of the powerful Cimbri or Ximbroz tribe, most likely Germanic, whose priestesses were responsible for sacrificial execution of war-captives. (Strabo, quoted in *Wikipedia* on the Cimbri).

Here I think we see one of the connections between priests, law, and the Ferah as a life-soul which suffers whatever the body suffers. In descriptions of Jesus' judicial torture in the Saxon *Heliand*, it is specifically stated that his Ferah (and his Aldr soul) are the actual subjects of the torture (ll. 5493-4). Law codes in all the Germanic languages throughout the Middle Ages used the term Ferah (fjǫr, feorh, verch, etc.) when referring to capital punishment. A criminal's Ferah was the *scyld* or debt owed for a capital crime, and it was stated specifically in those terms. For example, in the *Heliand* the phrase *ist thes ferahes scolo*, the Ferah is the debt owed, is used a number of times.

The Ferah Soul

I don't know all the reasons for the custom described by Tacitus, that only priests could apply corporal punishment, nor do we know how widespread it was. Certainly their knowledge of the law would have been a major reason, even though the scholar de Vries states that the Éwart was not the same person or function as the Ésaga, the secular Lawspeaker (Section 277 of *Altgermanische Religionsgeschichte*). But I speculate that the most ancient, primitive reason for having such a custom would have been that only priests could deal safely with the debt and punishment of people's souls. Only a feraht priest, with a powerfully developed and warded Ferah, might have authority over the dangerous, angry, desperate Ferah of a criminal or captive.

By being truly feraht, priests might protect themselves and their people from vengeful souls who considered themselves mortally wronged by execution or other corporal punishment. (This kind of thinking can be seen in the beliefs and customs of traditional shamans, in the emphasis they place on constantly protecting themselves through various arcane procedures from the dangers of dealing with the dying and the dead.) And if worst came to worst, if the priests were affected by the curses of the angry dying and dead, it would be less disastrous to the folk to have the priest's orlay and luck damaged than that of the king or chieftain who carried the luck of the whole folk.

Certainly, kings and warriors were the most common death-dealers with all their wars and feuds, rather than priests, and surely this had some effect on their souls. But I suspect that there was a significant difference, felt within the Ferah whose nature is to be pious, between a shameful execution as an outlaw or captive, versus more "normal" and even admired forms of death in feud or battle.

Ferah and Sacrifice

By being feraht, Germanic priests reduced the likelihood that they and their folk would be affected by the curses of lawfully punished and executed people, whether outlaws or sacrificial captives. But there is an even closer connection between Ferah and sacrifice: I think it is the Ferah soul and energy, specifically, which provides the benefits of sacrifice to the Gods and Goddesses. Whether the sacrifice consisted of people, or animals which were not eaten, or a feast of animal and plant foods and drinks, or even herbs, branches and flowers used in ceremonial practices and festive decorations, it would be the Ferah power within all of these that goes to nourish the Gods.

However, there is a radical difference between these practices and those of satanists and black magicians whose purpose is to raise power by causing agony and terror. Quite the contrary: if an animal sacrifice suffered and was terrified, this was a very bad omen. The most pure and powerful human sacrifices were also those who went willingly, for the wellbeing of the folk. I think it may be, that the Old Norse term for temple, the Fjarghus or Gods-house, was called that way not only because Fjarg was a term for the Deities who give us life and soul-power, but also because of the sacrifices and gifts of Fjǫr / Ferah which were given to them there.

For modern-day Heathens, I think that the most meaningful and true Ferah-sacrifice is the life-long effort to shape our own Ferah into a bridge that links the world of Nature and of human-occupied Midgard with the worlds of the Holy Ones. We do this by attuning our Ferah souls to the healthy life-force that flows through Nature and Midgard life, and at the same time attuning to the minds, the powers, and activities of our Deities.

The ongoing effort to attune to these wholesome, life-giving powers and offer a conduit between them leads our Ferah soul into a state of true Heathen piety, strength, and generosity of spirit, as well as benefiting all the beings involved in these transactions. This is a much more personal and powerful form of sacrifice than any 'sacrifice' of the life of other beings could possibly be, and should have far more powerful and meaningful results. I should say, though, that this description corresponds to the nature of my own Ferah's perceptions and activities. It may be that the Ferah souls of others have their own path to Heathen piety, power, and sacrifice, different from mine.

Here is another way to view our Ferah and 'sacrifice': we have the choice of making our own Ferah a great sacrifice to the Gods and Goddesses. I mentioned earlier that when a living thing is sacrificed to the Deities, it may be the Ferah within it that is the actual gift received by the Gods. We could spend our lives developing our Ferah to its highest extent, and then dedicating it to one or more of the Deities to receive as a sacred gift, whenever our death comes to us. We would thus give enriched spiritual energy, life force, and human wisdom to them, to use however they think best, perhaps expecting that they would either use it for their own strengthening or else for the good of Midgard.

The Ferah at Death

In the section "The Nature of the Ferah", I talked about how Ferah appears both as an etheric substance that confers life and bodily sensations, and as a soul-being with thoughts, emotions and character. Let's look at how these understandings of Ferah are expressed in the context of physical death.

Regarding the death of the beggar Lazarus, the *Heliand* author says that: "God's angels received his Ferh and led him forth from there (Midgard), so they could place the poor Siole (Saiwalo soul) in Abraham's breast (ll. 2353-4)." This is actually a very confused account: the Ferh is grammatically neuter, 'him' is masculine, and Siole is feminine. Grammatically, there are three different entities here: the Ferh is received by angels, 'he, Lazarus' is led forth from Midgard, and his Siole soul is placed in Abraham's bosom, presumably in the Christian heaven.

I interpret this confused passage as the result of early conversion efforts, when more narrow Christian soul-concepts and afterlife concepts were being translated with difficulty into broader, more prolific Germanic words and concepts rooted in Heathen understanding, and I analyze it in more depth in Chapter 15. Nevertheless, this passage does leave us with one item of information: that the Ferah was considered to exist at least long enough after death for angels to 'receive' it.

The description of Grendel's death in *Beowulf* is interesting: "Grendel laid aside his Feorh, Heathen soul; then Hel received him (ll. 851-2)." It was necessary for the Feorh to be removed or laid aside, before Grendel's afterlife could begin. This is somewhat reminiscent of the angels 'receiving' Lazarus' Ferh. Later in the story, as Beowulf lies dying, his oath-man Wiglaf cries out that he cannot hold or keep Beowulf's Feorh on Earth (ll. 2855-6). This hints that the Feorh is not destroyed at death, but goes 'elsewhere.' At

The Ferah Soul

Beowulf's death, his *feorh utgenge*, it went out, implying an entity or substance that may have continued after death, after it went out.

At the very end of *Beowulf* (ll. 3176-7), at the scene of his cremation, there is an intriguing phrase that can be translated in a couple of different ways. The poet says it is fitting to *freoge* Beowulf's Ferhð when he must be led forth from his lich-hama, his body. The word 'he' could refer to the Ferhð (a masculine noun), or to the person Beowulf. The word *freogan* can mean 'to think lovingly of, to honor,' which is how this is translated in the English version: the assembled folk are honoring Beowulf at his cremation. But *freogan* also means 'to liberate, to set free,' from the root *freo* meaning 'free.' We know that at least some Heathens considered cremation a blessing because it freed the spirit from the body immediately, rather than having to wait until the body decomposed. (See Ibn Fadlan's account of the Viking funeral, p. 9.) Thus the use of *freogan* in this phrase could mean that it was fitting to set Beowulf's Ferhð free by the splendid cremation they were giving him.

There are several examples of this kind of wording in the Saxon *Heliand:* when discussing people trying to kill other people, the terms *los, bilosian* are used, meaning to loose, release, set free the Ferah. This parallel in the *Heliand* tempts me to assume that *freoge* is intended to mean "release, set free" Beowulf's Ferhð in the cremation scene, as well. It also brings us back to the releasing of the Ferah-soul from trees at the time when the Gods transformed trees into humans. In both cases fire is the medium of release.

Here is another passage from the *Heliand:* "Christ gave Ferah to the fey, those who were ready to go forth, heroes on the Hel-way; the savior himself quickened them (brought them to life) after death" (ll. 4704-9, my translation). The word 'fey' is used in its Germanic sense: 'ready to die, knowing death is near, doomed to die soon.' This passage says that Christ gave Ferah-soul-substance to those who were dying and even to those who were already dead, the 'heroes on the Hel-way', and thus returned them to a state of life.

Völuspá vs. 41 (Poetic Edda) says that the Fjǫrvi of fey men "fall," as one of the signs preceding Ragnarök, though their fate after 'falling' remains a mystery. Note the important point that *Fjǫrvi* occurs here in the plural form, implying something like individual souls, rather than just a 'state of life'.

There is, however, not a great deal to work with here, in terms of gaining insights into earlier Heathen beliefs about the afterlife, if any, of the Ferah soul. Ferah is so strongly tied to life in Midgard, to physical life, to trees, Earth and sky-powers of Midgard, that I and other modern Heathens who have worked with Ferah believe its most likely afterlife fate is to return to the world of Nature in some form. Perhaps it is released by death to become a nature spirit, a landwight, a tree-spirit; perhaps simply to return to the ambient fields of life-energy circulating throughout Earth's swirling mantle of energies.

Powerful Ferahs may become the kind of guardian spirits reflected in the Germanic (and Celtic) Matronae of Roman times. They were place-based spirits or *genii loci* of rivers, cities, regions, clan and tribal domains, rooted in a specific area. This is reflected in the name of a group of Matronae or Nymphs called the *Alaferhviae*, the All-Ferh-Ones. Other Matronae names that may be related to Old High German *fereh-eih*, meaning tree / oak, include the

Alaterviae, Berhuihenae, and the *Dea* (Goddesses) *Vercana* (Simek p. 5).

These ideas link the Ferah soul with the Disir and Alfar ancestral spirits, which I believe are the Hugr souls of the ancestors, and with the spirits of the land. I think that one possibility, among others, for the Ferah soul after death is to accompany its partner Hugr soul, and perhaps one or more landwights as well, to form together a powerful ancestral or semi-divine land-warder spirit.

Alternatively, as I wrote above, we can make our own Ferah a deliberate gift to the Gods: growing our Ferah's strength, beauty and connections throughout our lives, and at the time our death comes to us, offering it to the Holy Ones with love and dedication.

Development and Psychology of Ferah

In my understanding, Ferah is the first soul that comes into being at conception, starting the processes of energy flow, cell proliferation and growth within the womb. At the right time, with the power of lightning, Ferah starts the heart beating and the nervous system operating. Just as the mother's Lichama (her living body) contains the baby's, so also the mother's Ferah contains and nourishes the Ferah of the baby within it.

The Ferah is a very prominent soul during childhood. In a healthy, happy childhood it provides the lovely innocence and lively, adventurous spirit, the child's love of animals, tree-climbing, cloud-watching, and many other aspects of nature, and the child's natural trust in the goodness of the Holy Ones. This inner innocence, trust and delight should be preserved within our Ferah-soul life-long, and should be regained if we have lost it. It provides a very great deal of our simple joy in life, and emotional, physical and spiritual wellbeing.

While a well-developed Ferah confers wisdom and power, a Ferah which has gone out of balance can become oversensitive, hyper-reactive, anxiety-ridden, fearful, phobic. It feels responsible for sensing and responding to environmental and social cues, yet it has lost confidence in its ability to do this, so it anxiously over-reacts or under-reacts. Modern life gives Ferah a double-whammy: on the one hand, our frenetic, overstimulated pace of life and information overload completely overwhelms the Ferah's response system. And on the other hand, most modern people's Ferahs do not receive enough nourishment from the traditional sources: time spent in nature, living with natural rhythms and patterns of life, and quality time with the Gods and Goddesses. Even in 'normal,' reasonably happy lives today, the Ferah is very stressed.

In an unhappy, abused child's or adult's life, the Ferah suffers even more from fear and injury, both physical and emotional. Its instincts can become distorted, leading it to develop cruelty, brutality, slyness and other subconscious defenses against fear and helplessness. The natural courage and strength of our Mod soul is the best companion and healer for a damaged Ferah, though in a person with an unhappy life history the Mod may need healing as well, or it may need to be 'dug out' of a retreat into subconsciousness.

A writhing, distorted tree mirrors the impact of harm to the Ferah. By Dale Wood.

Ferah and Magic

Our Ferah soul can provide impetus for fertility magic of all kinds, as well as natural magic associated with plants, trees, animals, stones, storms, lightning and bio-electricity. Ferah magic can support healing, health and wellbeing. Ferah strength and magic, if well developed, can protect against negative spiritual influences associated with death, illness and pain. Ferah knows, through its own experience, the power of transformation and therefore participates in all our processes of self-transformation throughout our life. Through its natural Heathen piety and connection with the Deities, Ferah guides us in right interactions with our Gods and Goddesses, whether they involve magical, mundane or spiritual purposes.

Summary

Ferah is the essence of life and vitality in Midgard, associated with trees, thunder, Thunder-God, Earth and Sky Deities, life-giving Deities. I think of it as the primal substance from which human Ferah-souls were shaped, drawn from powerful, living trees. Ferah is associated with the laws and patterns that govern natural life in Midgard, and govern the relations between humans, Nature, and the Deities. It is inclined toward a natural piety, and is a soul which supports the appeal and the practice of priesthood, formal or informal. Ferah-substance has been, through the ages, given as sacrifice to the Deities; here I have suggested new ways of performing such sacrifice. Ferah is lively and energizing during childhood, and ideally this Ferah-vitality and the childlike joy in life can be sustained throughout our lives. Significant terms are *firihi:* 'the folk, those who share Ferah together'; *feorhcynn:* 'the kindred of the living'; and *feraht:* 'devoutly wise, having a strongly developed Ferah'.

In Closing

Like trees, people are nourished and sustained by Gods of earth and sky. Like trees, we are sometimes struck by lightning / God-power, and if we do not burn to death, then we burn with life as conduits of God-power into the world. Great Yggdrasil is the backbone of the multiverse; the

The Ferah Soul

Irminsul pillar-tree unites earth and sky; Idunn sustains the Gods from her magical apple tree. Donar-oaks and other mighty Midgard trees sheltered assemblies and ceremonies of the folk through time immemorial. Ancient Greeks traveled many miles to hear Zeus Thunder-God whispering his oracles through the Oak of Dodona. Trees played the same central role in the worship and communal practices of Celts, Slavs, and Balts as they did with the Germans. The religions of the Pagan Indo-Europeans, past and present, would not be what they are without the holy presence of the trees.

Sunlight slanting through the solemn, silent forest shows us that even the greatest cathedrals with their stained-glass windows and carven columns are only pale reflections of the oldest temple of all. Beyond the logic of science and genetics, which are true in their own way, the human spirit knows its kinship with the trees.

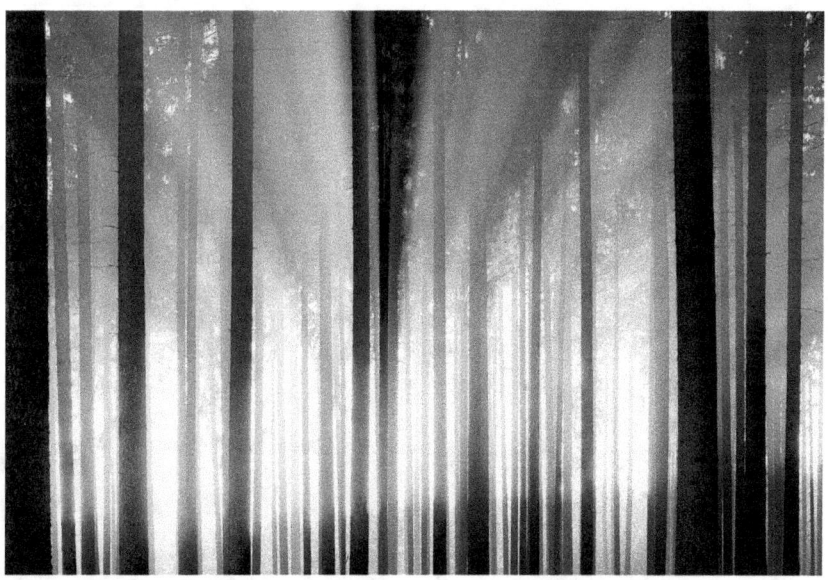

Heathen Soul Lore

Learning to know our souls allows us a glimpse of what lies behind the clouds that mask our perceptions.

Clouds are the breath of Earth, they are part of Earth's life and of our human lives in Midgard.

But when the winds of Ahma blow through the Worlds, all clouds are swept away from our vision, and Mystery becomes discernible to our souls.

Chapter 4

4. Ǫnd, Ahma, Ghost and Breath: Their Basic Nature

Ǫnd gave Odin........
(*Vǫluspá* vs.18, in the Poetic Edda)

In my previous chapter about the Ferah soul, I showed how the trees had their own Ferah souls before ever the Gods came to transform them into humans. But they had no breath as humans and animals have breath, nor did they have the Ghost / spirit who rides upon the breath. These things, breath and spirit (both meanings are contained within the word *ǫnd)* are the gifts of Odin. With these gifts our forebears took their first steps into the state of humanness and of kinship with the Gods. With the first breath the Ghost rides in and makes its home within the child: thus Ǫnd takes root within us.

This soul-complex: breath-spirit-ghost, is quite a complicated one, which I shall cover in two separate chapters. In this one I focus on the basic nature of spirit / Ghost and breath, its Indo-European roots and connections, and the radical differences between our real Ghost versus the stereotypes of the ghost that we come across in modern English. In my next chapter I discuss the interconnected activity between Ghost, breath and wode and the shamanic implications; the connections between Ghosts and Gods, and the source and afterlife of the Ghost.

The Breath

The Proto-Indo-European (PIE) language, as reconstructed by modern scholars, has six word-roots relating to 'breath' which are germane to our exploration here. I show these roots in Table 4, along with relevant words that are derived from them.

"Atmos": The Earth breathes.

Table 4: "Breath" Words

Proto-Indo-European 'Breath' Words	Derived Words	English Translations
*haenhmi, *an, *an-ah to breathe	Proto-Germ. *anadan Gothic us-anan Old Norse önd Mod. Icelandic andi	-breath, mind -to expire, breathe one's last breath -breath, spirit -breath, spirit, ghost, wight
*hehtmen, *et-men breath (et- or at- is derived from the an- root, see above. The -men or -man suffix indicates a noun of action.)	Old Indic atman Gothic ahma Anglo-Saxon æðm Old High German atum Old Saxon athom Greek atmos Modern German Atem	-breath, spirit, soul -spirit, wight -breath -breath, spirit -breath, spirit -breath, air, steam -breath
*haenhmos breath	Latin animus, anima Greek anemos	-soul -wind
*bhes to blow	Greek psyche	soul
*pneu to snort, sneeze	Greek pneuma	spirit
*dhues, *dhuesmi to breathe, to be full of wild spirits	Anglo-Saxon dysig Modern English dizzy Anglo-Saxon dwaes Mid. H German getwas Old Irish dasacht Lithuanian dvasia Old Norse dyr Anglo-Saxon deor Old High German tior Russian duch	-confused, dizzy -dizzy -foolish -ghost, foolishness -rage, fury -ghost, spirit -wild animal -wild animal -wild animal -breath, spirit

Anyone familiar with shamanism will note the last words in Table 4, *dhues,*dhuesmi, as being tied to pretty much all phases of shamanic practice: hyperventilating to bring on trance and soul-flight; the resulting dizziness, confusion, strange and hyper-excited behavior, ghosts and spirits, and wild animal powers. (These are subjects I will address in more detail in the next chapter.)

One also gets a hint here of the belief that animals too have spirits, since the words for breath, spirit, and animal are so closely related. In the same way, the Latin word *anima*, meaning 'soul', gives rise to our words 'animal' and 'animated,' meaning 'enlivened by having soul and breath'. The Latin root *spirare* = to breathe, belongs with this list as well. From this word we derive 'spirit,' 'inspire,' 'aspire,' 'expire' and 'respiration,' all relating to spiritual matters, breath, and life.

The special, sacred 'breath' word of the Germanic languages *(æðm, athom, ahma, etc.)* no longer exists in modern English, though it does in all other modern Germanic languages. In fact, Anglo-Saxon again shows its peculiarities here, because this language (a) adopted a different word for breath, unrelated to breath-words in every other Germanic language as well as in PIE, and (b) seems to have pulled a switch between the meanings of *æðm* and *bræth*.

Bræth meant 'odor, scent, stink, exhalation, vapor.' *Æðm*, as we have seen, descends from a PIE breath-spirit root, with implications not only of physical breath but of spiritual essence. Somehow in Anglo-Saxon, *æðm* came to mean not only breath but also "vapor, blast," and the verb *æðmian*, which should have meant "to breathe," instead meant "to fume, exhale, emit a smell." The original meanings of *bræth* = odor etc., and *æðm* = (pure!) breath, seem to have switched.

Eventually *æðm*, with its remnants of ancient sacred meaning, dropped out of English altogether, and we are left with 'breath,' which has no sacred connotations associated with the word itself–quite the contrary. Because of this peculiar word-history, I prefer to use Old Saxon *Athom* to mean the sacred breath, rather than A-S *æðm!*

Enter the Ghost

Overall, one can see from Table 4 that breath and spirit are intimately related. In some of the Germanic languages there is only one word that is used for both breath and spirit, and all such words are derived from Proto-Indo-European 'breath' words. But something strange happened in Old High German, Old Saxon, Frisian, and Anglo-Saxon. Though they retained the breath / spirit-derived words that I listed above, they also used a word for spirit that comes from an entirely different root:

Laxdæla Saga: Gudrun met the Ghost.

English *ghost,*
Old High German *keist, geist,*
Old Saxon *gest,*
Anglo-Saxon *gast,*
Modern German *Geist.*
Modern Dutch *Geest*

The old ghost-words were sometimes used to mean breath, but generally meant spirit, ghost, or otherworldly wight. Modern German *Geist* is also used the same way as the modern English word 'spirits' to indicate distilled liquor, or other distilled essences. Calling the results of distillation by the same word as a soul-entity gives us one clue to the nature of spirit: it is a distillation, an essence, a quintessential part of oneself. Spirit / ghost is something that must be refined and distilled from the more mundane portions of ourselves in order to reveal its true nature.

The words for ghost in the various languages I listed above are derived from the Proto-Indo-European (PIE) word root *gheis* meaning 'to be excited,' then from Proto-Germanic *gaista* = 'spirit, ghost', and *gaistaz,* meaning 'to be frightened, terrified.' A related word is Old Norse *geisa* = to rage, to terrify; this is also the name of a frightening Icelandic giantess. Gothic does have a few ghost-related words even though they consistently used Ahma to mean both breath and ghost/spirit. In these older Gothic words we can see how the meaning of ghost = spirit could have evolved. The Gothic words are:

~ *uz-gaisjan, uz-geisnan* = to frighten, to make aghast, to be beside oneself.

~ *uz-gheizan* = to be amazed, astounded, or aghast (aghast is linguistically the same word).

We can think of the word *uz-gheizan* as meaning 'to out-ghost' (*uz* = out) which is what happens when we are 'beside ourselves.' In the wake of terror, shock or extreme astonishment, our ghost becomes highly excited and flies out of our body upon our astonished gasp of breath. We can draw an analogy between the excited, energized molecules in a boiling pot of water, rising up out of the water in the form of steam, and the hyper-excited ghost-as-essence exiting like steam on the breath. This is also how alcoholic 'Geister / spirits' are produced. In the following chapter I discuss the importance of these ghost-phenomena in shamanic and spiritual practice.

Ond, Ahma, Ghost and Breath

In addition to the behavior of our own living ghost when in a state of fright or shock, there is the frightening, terrifying aspect of otherworldly ghosts, specters, apparitions and wights. So, through PIE **gheis* 'to be excited' and Primitive Germanic **gaistaz* 'to be terrified' to Gothic *uz-gheizan* 'to out-ghost due to amazement or fright,' and finally to the meaning of ghost as spirit-entity, we can approach an understanding of why the ghost-as-spirit word might have had preferential usage in some of the Germanic languages.

Old Norse language did not ignore the connection between the ghost and states of fear, terror, and threat. There is the Old Norse word *ǫndottr* meaning 'fearsome, terrible'. In modern Norwegian and other Scandinavian languages, *ond* means "evil, wicked," while spirit and breath are expressed by the word-root *and*. *Onde* and *ande* also appear in Old and Middle English, meaning 'fear, horror.' Thus, both the ghost word and the ond word have links to fear and terror, as well as to spirituality.

The Meanings of Spirit

Spirit-related words derived from PIE breath-words refer to five different but related domains of meaning:
a) the breath, both ordinary and divine;
b) the indwelling spirit or soul;
c) the human afterlife persona;
d) a non-human spirit-being or wight, such as a demon, guardian spirit, nature spirit, angel, etc., including the Christian Holy Ghost;
e) intellectual and creative faculties.
Table 5 shows how these different meanings are distributed in the various Germanic languages. I have included the

letters (a) through (e) in the table, as cross-reference to the list of spirit meanings, above. This table represents my best understanding of how these words were/are used.

Table 5: Distribution of Germanic 'Spirit' Meanings

Language	Spirit / Breath Words	Translation
Gothic	*Ahma*	(a) breath (b) indwelling spirit (c) afterlife persona (d) wights / spirits (e) intellectual faculties
Old Norse	*Ǫnd*	(a) breath (b) indwelling spirit (c) afterlife persona (seldom)
Modern Norwegian	*Ånd*	(a) breath (b) indwelling spirit (c) afterlife persona (d) wights / spirits (e) intellectual and creative faculties
Anglo-Saxon	*Æðm*	(a) breath
	Gast	(a) breath (seldom) (b) indwelling spirit (c) afterlife persona (d) wights / spirits
	And-giet	(e) intellectual and creative faculties
Old Saxon	*Athom*	(a) breath (b) indwelling spirit (d) Xian Holy Ghost
	Gest	(a) breath (seldom) (b) indwelling spirit (c) afterlife persona (d) wights / spirits

Ond, Ahma, Ghost and Breath

Old High German	*Atum, Atem*	(a) breath (b) indwelling spirit (d) Xian Holy Ghost
	Geist, Gheist, Keist	(b) indwelling spirit (c) afterlife persona (d) wights / spirits
Modern German	*Atem*	(a) breath
	Geist	(b) indwelling spirit (c) afterlife persona (d) wights / spirits (e) intellectual and creative faculties
Modern English	*Ghost*	(c) afterlife persona (d) wights / spirits - also images of objects such as a train, car or house.

In addition to the words in Table 5, there is also the Old Frisian *ethma*. I am not sure about how it was used in the ancient texts, but it remains in the modern Dutch *adem*, breath. Modern Dutch *Geest* is used much as modern German *Geist*.

This overall picture of ghost-words has important implications for us as English- speaking Heathens. Note, at the end of Table 5, how impoverished the English meaning of 'ghost' is, compared to meanings of the same word in other ancient and modern languages. There are only a few, old-fashioned usages of ghost in modern English that hark back to the older, richer meanings of the word, such as the Christian god-spirit called the Holy Ghost, and expressions such as "to give up the ghost," referring to our spirit's departure when we die.

Ghost and Mind

Several Germanic scholars I have read suggest that the meanings of ancient Germanic spirit words which relate to the intellect are newer acquisitions, which only evolved under the influence of Christian usage. They believe that pre-Christian Heathens did not make the connection between spirit and intellect. This conclusion is based on early Christian translations from Latin into Old Saxon and Old High German, where there are few indications that the Ghost possesses intellect *per se* as one of its characteristics.

There are several instances where, in contrast to *intellectus*, the Ghost is considered to possess *sapientia* or wisdom, which seems rather contradictory or confusing. Perhaps the distinction for them was that intellect is inherent, while wisdom is given by God, so that a Ghost could be given wisdom as a gift, in spite of not having inherent intellect. However, the spirit-intellect connection is very clear in the Gothic language, older by several centuries than the first writings in Old High German and Old Saxon.

The Goths were the earliest Germanic peoples in contact with Christians. The Visigothic bishop Wulfila developed a Gothic alphabet based on Greek, Latin and Runic characters, and translated parts of the Christian Bible from Greek into Gothic around 360 CE. In Wulfila's writings he used a number of words derived from Ahma (spirit) that relate directly to intellectual activities, and these are clearly not invented words or borrowed from Latin or Greek: they are long-established native words. (See Table 6.) If these intellect-related words already existed in native form in Gothic at the time of first Christian contact, this disproves the idea that spirit-intellect connections were unknown in

Ond, Ahma, Ghost and Breath

Germanic Heathen thought, at least among some branches of the Germanic peoples.

There are indications of a spirit-mind connection in Anglo-Saxon, as well. Two words of particular interest to Heathens are *gastgehygd* and *gastgemynd*. Both of these words refer to the faculty of thought. Gast-gehygd is a compound word, with *gehygd* or 'thought' stemming from the word Hyge or Hugi, another full-soul as I understand it. Gast-gemynd is the same: a compound with the word *gemynd*, which means memory, thought, consciousness, mind, intellect, and related meanings. Our modern word 'mind' stems from this root.

These two compound words seem to me of great significance for modern Heathens: they say to me that the Ghost-soul we each possess has its own reflection of Odin's ravens, Huginn and Muninn. The Anglo-Saxon words *gehygd* and *gemynd* are the same words, in noun form, as Huginn and Muninn ('Thinking' and 'Remembering') are in verb form, though in fact they include other meanings as well. As I mentioned above, *gemynd* is a word that covers a broad spectrum of intellectual faculties, and *gehygd*, in addition to meaning 'thought,' also means 'mind, reflection, and forethought.'

We can think of our Gast-gehygd, our Ghost-Huginn, as the one who 'thinks forward' in time and intentionality, while our Gast-gemynd, our Ghost-Muninn, 'thinks backward' in time and reflective memory. Both of these functions tie in with the ecstatic visionary and prophetic states of mind that the Ghost is capable of when inspired by wode, as I discuss in the next chapter. I believe that our strong Heathen Ghost-souls not only possess extensive mind-powers, but, like Odin, we have the potential to project hypostases or embodiments of those powers into soul-constructs like the Ravens.

Fledgling ravens coming into their power of flight.

This connection between Ghost and intellect does not exhaust the interesting clues we can find in Anglo-Saxon, however. In addition to *gast* and *æðm*, as I have discussed above, there are also words in Anglo-Saxon based on the *'and'* root that is related to ǫnd and ahma. *'And'* does not appear as a stand-alone word with a spiritual meaning in Anglo-Saxon, but it is part of compound words relating to intellect, perception, and skill.

And-wlita or 'splendor of *And'* referred to one's countenance, one's face, which reflects the beauty and strength of one's inner spirit. *Wlita* or *wlite* is the same word as Old Norse *litr*, one of the gifts given by Hœnir / Odin's brother to Ask and Embla *(Völuspá* vs. 18, Poetic Edda). *Wlite's* Anglo-Saxon meaning of 'splendor, beauty, brightness' as well as its meaning of 'appearance, shape, countenance' that it shares with Old Norse *litr*, enriches our appreciation for the beautiful gift of the human shape and appearance given by the Gods, which allows our spirit to shine through our form. The modern German *Antlitz* = countenance is a cognate of this. (For more about *Litr*, see Chapter 6.)

Anglo-Saxon *And-ribb* was the breast, the place where breath and spirit live. Interestingly, *And-weorc* meant 'matter, substance, material, cause,' implying that matter is something which is a 'work' of spirit-mind, or is worked by it. Someone who is skillful or expert is *and-wis*, wise in the ways of '*And*,' of spirit-mind.

In Anglo-Saxon, *and-giet* meant: 'understanding, intellect, knowledge, perception, senses, meaning, purpose'. *Andgietlic* meant 'intelligible.' The word *gietan* means 'to get', so this word-combination implies that understanding, perception and knowledge are what our *And*, our spirit-mind, 'gets' for us: get it?

There is a Sanskrit word which I think can cast some light on the deeper meaning of *andgiet*. The Sanskrit term is *atma-jyoti*. I have already noted the linguistic connections between *Atma* and *Ǫnd* / *And* in Table 1. *Jyoti* means 'light' in Sanskrit. A modern Hindu scholar (Ramakrishna Rao, p. 36) explains that the *atma-jyoti* is a glowing mental screen upon which the outer world is projected, and is then perceived from within by the inner self, the *atman*, which corresponds to Ahma, Ǫnd, And.

The *atma-jyoti* is thus, as I understand it, an intermediary between the outer, sensate world of objects, and the 'inner self who knows,' the atman. The *jyoti* is still part of our inner, subjective self, but is not as deep within us as the Atman-soul, the eternal, transcendent, cosmic Self. The *atma-jyoti* thus seems very much related to the *and-giet* as a faculty of perception and understanding.

I also see a connection here with the Anglo-Saxon *and-wlita*, our countenance and appearance, which is also a screen: our face and appearance project our inner self out into the objective world. Looking at our appearance and the expressions of our face and body, people can understand much about our inner self, our thoughts and feelings. Thus, the *andgiet* serves as a (mental) screen which projects outer knowledge inwards in the form of perceptions, to be perceived by our inner self, while the *andwlita* serves as a (physical) screen, our face and appearance, which projects our inner self outward to be perceived by others. These understandings of And-wlita and And-giet can form the basis for a Heathen practice of soul-based perception and communication.

Touching on the split between *andgiet* as spirit-mind versus *gast* as spirit-wight, we can look at what happens to a person who loses one or the other. The person who is *andgit-leas*, without andgiet, is foolish and senseless. The person who is *gast-leas*, or ghost-less, is dead. It is clear from this distinction that the Ghost is a life-soul, while the Andgiet is not, even though the Norse *ǫnd / and* is.

I believe that in prehistoric Germanic thought, the concepts of spirit, breath, intellect, afterlife-persona, and wights were all united as in Gothic Ahma. At some point in time, in some of the Germanic languages, a split gradually occurred between the Ahma-concept and the Ghost-concept, giving rise to many complexities. In modern English this historical development became further confused because Latin roots displaced native words: spirit versus ghost, intellect versus mind, and many other examples.

Table 6 shows examples of spiritual and intellectual word usage in two ancient and two modern Germanic

Ond, Ahma, Ghost and Breath

languages, representing the Ahma /And branch and the Ghost branch. I have also included some of the Anglo-Saxon 'and' words.

Table 6: Spirit and Mind Meanings

Gothic	Modern Norwegian	Modern German	Anglo-Saxon
Ahma spirit, ghost, spirit-being **Anan** to breathe out	**Ånd** spirit, ghost, mind, intellect, genius, morale **Ånd** breath	**Geist** spirit, ghost, essence **Atem** breath	**Gast** spirit, ghost, spirit-being, breath **And-ribb** breast (where the breath/ spirit lives)
Ahmeins spiritual	**Åndelig** spiritual, intellectual, mental, ghostly	**Geistlich** spiritual **Im Geiste** in spirit, in imagination	**Gastlic** spiritual, ghostly, ghastly
Aha understanding **In-ahs** wise, prudent **Ahjan** to think	**Åndelig** (see box above)	**Geistes-wissenschaften** (ghost-sciences) humanities, arts	**Gast-gehygd** **Gast-gemynd** (ghost-thought) **And-giet** understanding, intellect, knowledge, perception, senses
Ahmateins Inspiration	vaere í ånde be inspired	**Geistes-blitz** (ghost-lightning-strike) inspiration **Geistes-flug** (ghost-flight) flight of the imagination	**Gastan** to meditate **Gast-brucende** (ghost-usage / enjoyment) spiritual practicing
Uz-anan (out-breathe) to expire, die	Oppgi åndan to give up the ghost, expire	Geist abgeben give up the ghost	**Gastgedal** (what is dealt out to the ghost) death

The connection between the Ghost and the Mind / Intellect also comes across clearly in words relating to mental illness and mental health in modern Germanic languages other than English. Table 7 shows some examples of such words in German and Norwegian, with a couple of Anglo-Saxon interpolations.

Table 7: Illness or Health of Ghost

Modern German	Modern Norwegian	English translation
Geistes-gestört (ghost-damaged) Geistes-verwirrung (ghost-confusion)	--	mentally disturbed mental derangement
geistige Gesundheit (ghostly health)	ånds-friskhet (spirit-health)	sanity, soundness of mind
Geistes-schwach (ghost-weak)	ånd-svak (spirit-weak)	cognitively disabled
Geistes-abwesend (ghost-absent)	ånds-fravaerelse (spirit-absent)	absent-minded
Geistes-los (ghost-less)	Ånd-las (spirit-less) note also Anglo-Saxon: and-leas (spirit-mind-less)	spiritless, shallow, foolish foolish, senseless
Geist-reich (ghost-rich)	Ånd-ric (spirit-rich) also Anglo-Saxon: and-wis (spirit-mind-wise) and-gitol	witty, ingenious, brilliant, highly intellectual expert, skillful intelligent, sensible

The Impoverishment of the Ghost

As the preceding discussion and Tables 6 and 7 show, the connection between our Ghost-soul and our highest mental, creative, and spiritual capacities is clear in various ancient and modern Germanic languages, with modern English being a rather glaring exception! Our English term 'ghost' implies only the category of 'spooks,' things that are generally not taken seriously and which are severely limited in scope and stature compared to true Heathen meanings. Ghosts, as they are commonly envisioned today, are generally stupid or pathologically single-minded, emotionally uncontrolled, lost, distraught, pathetic even in their (sometimes) dangerousness. This is a far cry from the real, fully-developed stature of our Ghost-souls. However, the connection between our living Ghost-soul and afterlife ghosts, spooks and wights is important and will be touched on in my next chapter.

The connections I have described here are ones that healing and exorcising shamans, priests, and other Heathen spiritual practitioners must deeply understand, yet the path our English language has taken makes it difficult to grasp the connections unless we burrow more deeply into these matters.

Summary of Meanings, and Modern Heathen Usage

As I have shown, the concept of the spirit / spirits in ancient and modern Germanic languages is complex. We need words for modern Heathen English usage, that can refer to all the complex aspects I have discussed. Modern speakers of the Scandinavian languages, German, and Dutch, all have native words that can serve the purpose reasonably well or very well, but we are not in as good a position. In general conversation, of course there is no need to use much in the way of technical jargon. At times, however, Heathens who are interested in soul lore, and especially those who are dedicated spiritual practitioners, might want to use more specific, technical vocabulary which distinguishes between the five aspects of meaning that I listed above, without using the cumbersome, Latinized terms in my list. I don't mean to impose anything here, but for those who find my approach to soul lore useful, here is a list of suggested terminology.

Note: Modern English-speaking Heathens (and perhaps Scandinavian and other Heathens as well; I don't know) often use *ǫnd* to mean an ambient spiritual energy that can be accessed through magical and spiritual practices. I think this is similar but not identical to ancient usage. In any case, it seems best not to propose the word *ǫnd* for general English-speaking use regarding the whole complex spirit-entity I have discussed here, so as not to cause confusion with its other common use as a modern term in magic. Here are my suggested usages:

1) The divine breath of life: **Athom**. (The "th" sound is voiced as in 'them;' the 'a' is long, as in 'father.' Thus: AH-thom.)

2) Indwelling spirit: Ghost or **Athom-Ghost**. The latter term is more specific, indicating the Ghost's living status because of its linkage with Athom, breath.

3) Afterlife persona: **Ghost**. The indwelling spirit and the afterlife persona are obviously the same entity; the

distinction lies in their 'in-life' or 'not-in-life' status. This in turn depends on the presence or absence of Athom-breath.

4) Non-human spirit-beings: **Wights**, and of course more specific terms such as wood-wife, skogs-ra, heinzelmann, nixie, etc.

5) Intellectual and creative faculties which are part of the Ahma soul, as opposed to similar intellectual faculties seated within Hugi, Mod, and other full-souls, can be referred to as **Andgiet** (pronounced AHND-yit). Note that although several other full-souls possess strong intellectual powers, the Ghost / Ahma is the most creative of all of them because it is the one through which Wode flows, in my understanding. (See discussion in the next chapter.) Our Ghost-Huginn and Ghost-Muninn are integral here, as well: **gastgehygd** and **gastgemynd**.

In Closing

When our Ghost is fully functional and stable, and connected with our other Souls and with the Holy Ones, it provides us with many of our greatest human traits: brilliance of intellect, spiritual power and presence, creative talents, ecstatic abilities and insights, the ability to perceive and to shape our world. Our Ghost directly receives divine communications, inspiration, and *wode*: the inspired frenzy or ecstasy sent by divine powers (see next chapter). When we nurture our creative, intellectual and spiritual powers, we are nourishing our Athom-Ghost. This is why it feels so good, so personally rewarding, when we do that! We are expressing, developing and fulfilling our Ghost-self.

When we feel no urge to learn and create, or fear that we cannot, our Athom-Ghost is either not fully present in us, or is being suppressed in some way, often due to unfortunate life circumstances. A psychologically unhealthy upbringing can cause severe damage to our Athom-Ghost and stunt its confidence in its abilities and gifts, until this condition is overcome.

Having here discussed the basic nature of Ahma, in the next chapter I will move on to look at the interconnected activity between Athom, Ghost and wode, and the kinds of practices and ecstatic states that arise from this. I discuss the relationship between Ahma and Ghost, whether they are one soul or two, touch on the relations between our human ghosts and non-human spirits, explore the connections between Ghosts and Gods, and the source and afterlife of the Ghost.

A ghostly eclipse of the moon.
Such scenes lure us into pondering what might lie behind outward appearances, calling to something deep within us.

Chapter 5
5. Ghost Rider: Athom, Ghost, and Wode in Action

Dhuesmi: Wild Spirits, by Dale Wood.

*Ǫnd gave Odin,
Óðr gave Hœnir....*
(*Völuspá* vs. 18, in the Poetic Edda)

The first gave ǫnd and life, the second consciousness and movement....
(*Gylfaginning* in the prose Edda)

*Ullr's grace (hylli), and that of all the Gods,
He has, who first seizes the flames;
The Worlds will open over Asa-sons,
When the kettles are heaved up.*
(*Grimnismal* vs. 43 in the Poetic Edda, vs. 42 in Larrington)

In my previous chapter I began the attempt to put the complexities of our Ahma / Ghost full-soul into some sort of shape that would be useful for modern Heathens. In case I have not already made this clear, I will note again the impossible task of describing a concept of the Ghost or spirit (or any of the other souls) that is consistent across time and place for all Germanic Heathen peoples.

As all modern Heathen loremasters have experienced, developing a modern body of soul lore means imposing some consistency and clarity even where it did not always exist in the historic record. My purpose is to contribute to a systematic modern Heathen theory and practice of all activities involving our souls, using historical evidence as source material. In all of my writings I try, however, to show why and how I draw the conclusions that I do, so that you, the reader, can judge them for yourself.

Origin and Afterlife of Ghost and Ahma

Whether or not our Germanic forebears believed in an abstract, transcendent, pure consciousness-being-soul, a question which is difficult to answer based on the little evidence we have of their beliefs, this is a belief which is held by many people today, including many Heathens, I think. It is part of the modern landscape of belief. This transcendent, eternal, abstract consciousness, this Spirit in its ultimate sense, I am calling *Ahma*, the Gothic term for "spirit." It corresponds closely to the Hindu Atman, which is very ancient in origin and could well reflect, in part, an ancient Indo-European understanding of Spirit. Certainly, the words *Ahma* and *Atman* are closely related, as I discussed in my previous chapter.

What is the relationship between our Ahma-Spirit and our Ghost? Are they one and the same, or different from each other? I believe they parallel the nature of our Gods and Goddesses, in the following way. Ginnungagap, the Gap of Magical Potential, contains within it the proto-energy-matter that has not been actualized or materialized in any way. We can call this the Godhead or the Source, something that is beyond any attempt to characterize or describe. As this Ahma-source wells up and overflows from Ginnungagap, it gradually takes on the characteristics of energy and matter as we know them.

Thus are formed the Gods and Goddesses, the Worlds and the elements of matter, of souls and bodies. The Gods and Goddesses have personal characteristics, they are beings who can be described and known to some extent by us, and to whom we can relate in a personal way. Yet they are also shapes—Hamas or soul-skins—of the Godhead / Source / Ginnungagap-outflow.

Our Ahma-soul corresponds to the primal source, with its lack of personal characteristics and its limitless nature. Our Ghost, on the other hand, corresponds to our Gods and Goddesses as personal, individualized entities. Our Ghost relates to our Ahma in the same way that the Holy Ones relate to the Source within Ginnungagap. They are one in substance, but have different characteristics; or rather, the Ghosts and Gods have characteristics, while the Ahma and Ginnungagap cannot be defined by characteristics.

We can think of Ahma as the steam or mist rising up out of Ginnungagap, based on the common Indo-European word-roots for spirit, breath, wind, steam (Greek *atmos*). As I understand it, this is the same mist that rises to fill Niflheim / Mist-Home and coalesces into Hvergelmir, the Roaring Cauldron of World-Energy.

The Gods shape or distill our Ghost out of this spirit-steam and blow it into us at the moment we take our first breath. In some cases, it may be that the Ahma forms its own Ghost, without the action of the Deities. When a person feels connected with some abstract form of Spirit, but feels no connection with any personal Deities throughout their life, it may be because of an autonomous formation of their Ghost.

Because our Ghost-soul is shaped from Ahma / Source, we can call it a shape-soul and understand it as the hama or shape of our Ahma-soul. But the Ghost is a being in its own right, not simply a shape of something else, just as the Holy Ones are beings in their own right and not just sacks of Ginnung-power. Although Ghost comes from the spirit-steam hovering over Ginnungagap, once it is shaped into the Ghost it has a different life and fate, with natural ties to the Gods and Goddesses if we choose to pursue and honor them. Our Ahma, on the other hand, remains essentially connected to the Ahma hovering over Ginnungagap. I am thus considering Ahma and Ghost to be two distinct souls in the tally of Full-Souls that I am exploring.

One can, by certain kinds of spiritual practices, reunite one's Ghost with the Ahma spirit-steam of Ginnungagap. This path bypasses or passes through our connection with the Gods as personal beings, breaks open the soul-skin of the Ghost, and returns our personal portion of Ahma to the primal spirit-steam. This path is described in other religions and spiritual practices as Nirvana, union with the Godhead, disembodiment into Pure Bliss, and other efforts to describe the indescribable. Certain religions, Eastern in particular, hold this as the aim of all their spiritual efforts and development: in Heathen terms, to burst open the Ghost's skin and release the impersonal Ahma to return to the Source.

My impression of Heathen belief, past and present, is that most Heathens prefer to keep their Ghost whole and (if all goes well) dwell as a personal Ghost-being with the Holy Ones in the afterlife. The connection between Ghost and Ahma still remains, both in life and after death (I will describe this below), but so does the distinction between them. However, nothing prevents Heathens from choosing to follow the kinds of spiritual disciplines that break down the Ghost and return Ahma to the primal source in Ginnungagap.

This dissolution of the Ghost into pure Ahma can be a path for those who feel no attachment to any Deities during their lifetime, and thus may feel no benefit to staying in a personal shape, the Ghost, which can easily interact with personalized Gods and Goddesses after death.

Among other things, Ghost forms the bridge between abstract, impersonal Ahma, on the one side, and personal Gods, Goddesses, humans, and other personal beings on the other. An individual can choose whether this bridge, the Ghost-soul, is meaningful to retain after death, or whether to dissolve personal Ghost into impersonal Ahma-spirit.

Athom and Ghost

The previous chapter about the Ghost showed how closely Ghost / Spirit and breath are tied together. Our Ghost consists of Ahma-Spirit encapsulated in a soul-skin, a hama. The Ghost is thus like a pod (but a pod with personality!) existing within a wider field of Ahma.

Ghost pulsates within this Ahma-field, drawing Ahma, the steam from Ginnungagap, into and out of its skin in a nourishing bath of spirit-power: this is what keeps it strong and living, and sustains the vital ties between our Ahma-soul and its hama, our Ghost-soul. When our body, our Lich, breathes, it is mirroring the pulsations of our Ghost. In other words, our Lich breathes because, and only because, our Ghost is pulsating within the field of Ahma. As our Ghost expands and contracts, so do our physical lungs and our *andribb* or chest where our ribs enclose our ǫnd.

This understanding of the relationship between Ghost, Ahma, and Athom or breath makes clear many spiritual and physical phenomena. Effective meditation requires mindful breathing, which involves tuning our physical breath-pattern to the pulsations of our Ghost, thus opening a way for our awareness to touch Ahma-Spirit in a transcendent experience. People who are in a very deep meditation or trance, or who are in a coma or unconscious, experience a loosening of the Ghost from the Lich. When the Lich is not fully connected with the Ghost, breathing becomes very slow, and consciousness, which is tied to the Ghost, is located elsewhere in an out-of-body experience.

In a Lich which is slowly dying, the Ghost is simply drawing more and more distant from the Lich, taking with it both breath and consciousness. When the final breath flows out, the Lich has "given up the Ghost," just as we take in the Ghost during our first breath of life after birth.

Heathen mothers and other Heathens who attend a childbirth should be fully aware of the wondrousness of this moment: not only is a child physically born, but the Gods and Goddesses are present as our Ghost-Givers, and many good Ghosts are gathered around to attend and honor the Ghost-Giving.

Regulating the breath is a time-honored way of regulating consciousness or awareness, aiming toward various kinds of experiences ranging from simple meditation to ecstatic visionary journeys and paranormal activities.

Some traditions emphasize calming and slowing the breath to achieve these experiences; the Eastern traditions such as Zen Buddhism and some forms of Yoga are examples. Breath regulation is often achieved by whatever form of galdoring is customary in that tradition, such as the chanting of Tibetan monks and the plainsong used in Christian monasteries. One example is the full, chanted Eastern Orthodox Christian liturgy for the Holy Week preceding Easter, which lasts for eighteen hours a day; one can imagine the powerful effects this can have on the Ghosts of those who chant and those who listen mindfully. And of course, in our tradition there are many creative possibilities for using rune-galdor or runic chanting to energize our Ghosts.

Slowing the Athom is only one way of activating our Ghost, however; the opposite action of speeding and exciting the breath is also effective. Our Ghost can be excited inadvertently, with no spiritual intention or control; the results are often negative in these cases. Examples are hysteria, panic, shock, injury or pain. Germanic words for these states show the Ghost-connection: Anglo-Saxon and Modern English aghast, Gothic *uz-gheizan* (out-ghosting), and others that I listed in the previous chapter. Our Ghost is temporarily shocked loose from our Lich. Depending on the severity of the shock and the degree of loosening, our reactions range from panicky breathing and gasping (when we gasp, we are instinctively trying to draw our Ghost back into our body, before we faint) to fainting or coma.

In cultures around the world people are often concerned about sneezing and yawning, and we are taught to cover our mouths when we do this. We might consider this to be due simply to courtesy and hygiene, but the practice is deeper and older than such considerations. It is meant to prevent the inadvertent breathing out of the Ghost when yawning or sneezing, as well as avoid breathing in any ghosts that are floating around "out there." Note that the Greek word for spirit is *pneuma*, which comes from PIE **pneu*, to snort or sneeze. (This is really rather an amusing 'life history' for this word which later, under the development of Greek philosophers and Christian theologians, became the word for the transcendent human spirit!) Presumably, the ancients would not have called 'spirit' and 'snort, sneeze' with the same word unless they believed that the spirit could be inadvertently set loose from the body by explosive breath.

If you look at photographs or drawings of native people present at a shamanic healing ritual or an exorcism, you may notice that some cover their mouths or turn away to avoid breathing in the expelled ghost or evil spirit. I have seen some pictures where mothers in these circumstances are covering their babies' mouths to keep them safe, while themselves turning their faces to the side so as to be out of direct line with the escaping ghost.

Some cultures also cover their mouths when laughing or weeping, for the same reason, especially because these excited states arouse one's own and others' Ghosts. Recall, from the previous chapter, that the word and concept of 'ghost' relates directly to a 'state of excitement or arousal.'

I must point out here that the Ghost is not closely involved in our everyday emotions, which are more the domain of other souls. Ghost does not so much feel or cause emotions; rather, Ghost is activated and energized by strong, sudden emotions or physical states similar to the way that water molecules are energized into steam when heated. Unusual breathing, like sneezing, laughing, sobbing, singing, shouting, gasping, screaming, and so forth, is likely to excite or alert one's own and other people's Ghosts, as well as any non-human ghosts / spirits hanging around. It is these kinds of 'excited breathing' situations, reactions to sudden, strong emotions or physical states, that can lead to ghostly entrances and exits on the breath.

Shamans and other spiritual technicians use this tie between Ghost and breath, and the excitability of the Ghost, both to elevate their own Ghost to paranormal levels of activity and sometimes to manipulate the Ghosts of other people to bring about healing or cursing. I would say that shamanic healing and bewitchment more often involve other souls of the patient / victim than that person's own Ghost, but sometimes Ghost-work is needed in the process. And regardless of which soul of the patient is being healed, any shamanic work that involves excitation of the shaman's breath, heating of the body through dancing, singing, sweating, and so forth, and especially loss of consciousness, likewise involves the Ghost of the shaman. (Others of the Shaman's souls, such as Hugi and Mod, are generally involved, and perhaps associated spirits such as the Hamingja, Fylgja and Gandr.)

I'll repeat here the verse I quoted from *Grimnismal* at the beginning of this chapter, which may have several layers of occult meaning that relate to our subject here: *Ullr's grace, and that of all the Gods, to him who first takes away the flame; the worlds will open to Asa-sons as the kettles are heaved up.*

On the surface, the verse applies to Odin's situation of being tortured by being placed between two fires in Geirrod's hall. It also implies a form of spiritual initiation or training, since that is Odin's purpose in speaking the poem: to instruct young Agnar about the mysteries of the Gods and prepare him for sacral kingship. (See the prose introduction to *Grimnismal* in the Poetic Edda.) This initiation is not simply one of endurance and courage, however. 'Steaming' a person between two fires is an image of distillation, of refining and distilling a substance down to its essence.

Ghost Rider

Odin is being 'distilled' between two fires, while Agnar attempts to give him comfort. (W.G. Collingwood.)

I mentioned in my previous chapter that the terms 'spirit' and 'alcoholic spirits' (German *Geist* is used for both meanings) are not just coincidentally related. Our Ahma rises like steam from Ginnungagap and is distilled by the Gods into our personal essence, our Ghost. Once our Ghost has been refined by the ordeals of life under the tutelage of the Holy Ones, we become a son / daughter / child of the Æsir and receive the grace *(hyllir)* of Ullr and all the Gods.

When the 'kettle' is lifted off the fire, our body is removed from the boiling fire of life (that is, our physical body dies), our Ghost rises like steam from our Lich, and the Worlds lie open to our Ghost's perception. This is what I see as the life / afterlife meaning of the verse. It can also be seen as a reference to *seiðr* or shamanic practice. Being heated by the fire can refer to the body-heating exercises often used in shamanism, such as violent exercise and / or steam-bathing. The kettle may contain herbal or alcoholic steam that has psychogenic effects, leading to a trance state where the

Ghost can come forth and act. (See Larrington's note 42 on page 290.)

In summary, our Ghost can extend itself outside the body, as long as there is still an Athom-tie between it and the body. Athom-work is the way to bring this about, and it can be achieved by two opposite techniques. The breath and body can be quieted (along with the mind and the other souls), allowing the Ghost to release itself from mundane ties and enter otherworldly realms. This is the approach of mystics and other spiritual seekers, as well as some forms of artistic creativity such as composing music.

Conversely, the breath and body can be brought to an extreme state of excitation, thereby arousing the Ghost to paranormal action: this is the path that most shamans take, as well as berserkers and some kinds of artistic performers. When the Ghost is fully extended, while still tethered by Athom, the practitioner is in a very deep state of trance or even unconscious. Extreme examples are Yogis who can enter a state of suspended animation, or legendary shamans of different cultures who could survive for long periods underwater or who fall deeply unconscious while in the shamanic state.

Ghost-Runa, by Dale Wood.
The architecture of the World Tree serves as a wind-tunnel to funnel Ahma-Athom, the sacred breath, to the Ghost contemplating the Runar: the mysteries of the Worlds.

Wode

Once we move into the realms of Ghost-excitation, we are dealing with the phenomenon of *Wode* (Anglo-Saxon) or *Oðr* (Old Norse). In the Old Norse sagas, oðr is generally presented in the form of battle-madness, as shown in the berserker and other warriors in an exalted state of consciousness. In Old Norse poetic literature *oðr* appears more often in the context of inspiration toward poetry or wisdom. An *oðar-smith* referred to a poet. *Oðrœrir*, meaning 'oðr-stirrer' is the name of one of the three cauldrons from which Odin drank to gain poetic power. It is also the source of his gift of poetic wode to humans, as is told in *Skaldskarpamal* of the Prose Edda.

The Anglo-Saxon language split the concept of wode into two words, spelled almost the same. One word is *wod*, pronounced as 'wode.' The other word is *woð*, with a voiced "th" rather than the "d" at the end, rhyming with "loathe." *Wode* meant madness, fury, raging, paroxysms. It often applied to illnesses, poisoning or spirit-possession of both humans and animals that resulted in fits and frenzy, such as rabies, epilepsy, mania, hallucinations, intoxication, and the like. Anglo-Saxon had the same expression as Oðrœrir: *mid wodnysse astyrod*, 'stirred by wode.' But instead of the sacred stirring of poetic, prophetic frenzy it applied to a person afflicted with madness. The connection between wode and Ghost is strengthened when we see the A-S word *astyrod*, meaning 'stirred up, excited,' applied both to wode and to Ghost in various writings.

Woð, on the other hand, referred to voice, song, poetry and eloquence. A *Woðbora* or woð-bearer was an orator, singer, poet or prophet. Clearly we have here a split between what the Anglo-Saxon Christians would have seen as the 'bad' wode versus the 'good' woð. Woden was specifically associated, by them, with the 'bad' wode, while having nothing to do with the 'good' woð. Since the other Germanic languages did not split the wode-concept, and included all of the meanings in one word, I must suppose that the Anglo-Saxon split was a late one, motivated by a changed, Christian world-view. They were happy to believe that Woden brought the curse of madness, but could not credit him with prophecy and eloquence.

The ghost of Tiresias prophesies for Odysseus. (Johann Heinrich Füssli.)

It is useful to look at the root and cognates of *wod*. The Proto-Indo-European root is **uehatis* meaning 'god-inspired.' Related words are the Welsh *gwawd* = poem, Gaulish *ouateis* = ovate, one of the ranks of the druids, Latin *vates* = seer, prophet, and Old Indic *api-vat* = to inspire. Mallory points out that this word-root is widespread in the Indo-European languages, and notes Odin's role as inspirer of both battle rage and poetic inspiration. He also comments that the Gothic word *wods*, which is used to mean 'demon-possessed' in the Gothic translation of the Christian Bible, shows a distinct change of perspective resulting from Christianization. (Mallory p. 493.) We see the same in Anglo-Saxon: a wode person is supposedly demon-

Heathen Soul Lore

possessed rather than god-possessed as was earlier understood.

At the beginning of this chapter, I quoted the *Völuspá* poem of the Poetic Edda, telling us that when Odin, Hœnir and Loðurr found the trees and turned them into humans, Odin granted them *ǫnd* while Hœnir gave *oðr*. In my second quotation above, from Snorri Sturlusson's *Gylfaginning* in the prose Edda, Snorri retells this event but says that while the first of Bor's sons (Odin and his brothers) gave "ǫnd and life," the second gave "vit and movement." *Vit*, related to wit, means consciousness, sense, intelligence. This is a very different thing from *oðr* as it is used everywhere else in Old Norse lore, and also different from any meaning of *wod*-cognates in every other Germanic language and other Indo-European languages. Although some modern Old Norse dictionaries give *oðr* the meaning of "consciousness," this interpretation seems to me to be based on Snorri's retelling of the story and his substitution of *vit* for *oðr* in his version.

The prominent Germanic scholar Jan de Vries, in his etymological ON dictionary, does not give the meaning of "consciousness" to *oðr*, and in the modern Icelandic dictionary *oður* means furious, mad, not wit and consciousness. The same is true for the Faroese dictionary, which has many compound words with *oðar*, all relating to fury and wildness. It includes the interesting word *oðar-hugur* which means 'violent or intense passion.' See also the reference I made to Mallory, above, with Indo-European meanings of *wod*-words relating to god-possession, divine madness and poetic inspiration. Using the concordance to Eddic poetry, I don't find any instances of *oðr* in the Poetic Edda that could indicate 'wit', unless one interprets the gift of Hœnir in this way.

Ghost Rider

Diana Paxson, in her book *Odin: Ecstasy, Runes & Norse Magic*, quotes the Cleasby and Vigfusson Old Norse dictionary, saying that the noun *oðr* is different from the adjective *oðr*. The adjective means 'wild and furious', as mentioned above, while the noun means 'mind, wit, soul, sense.' They compare it to Icelandic *æði*, meaning sense, wit, manner. I realize these scholars have expertise that I do not, yet I still have to wonder how solid this interpretation is, at least from a spiritual-practice standpoint, which is where I am coming from. I might also note that 'manner, behavior, conduct' were given to Ask and Embla by Loðurr's gift of *Læti*, (see Chapter 6), while 'consciousness' comes from Ǫnd, so it seems superfluous to give these things twice.

Cleasby and Vigfusson translate the name of the mead / cauldron Oðrœrir as 'inspirer of wisdom', whereas every other translation I've seen for this name is along the lines of 'ecstasy-stirrer', which is a more characteristic name for an alcoholic drink than 'wisdom-stirrer', I would think. Though, considering that this mead was brewed from the blood of the wise Kvasir, perhaps this does make sense.

Looking at the etymology of this word *oðr*, its common usage in the lore, and the interpretation of some scholars, we reach one conclusion that it means something like 'divine ecstasy, inspired madness.' Looking at some other scholars and Snorri's interpretation of the divine gifts, we reach a different conclusion, that *oðr* can mean 'mind, wit, soul, sense.' In order to proceed with this study of Ghost and Wode, I need to choose an interpretation to go forward with. To me, the preponderance of the evidence falls on the side of considering oðr / wode to mean 'divine ecstasy / inspiration / frenzy, madness'. This is the interpretation I choose to follow as I pursue the study of soul lore for application to modern Heathen spiritual practice.

Based on the linguistic evidence and discussion that I presented in the previous chapter about "Ǫnd, Ahma, Ghost and Breath", I conclude that the sacred gifts of consciousness, intellect and spirit are all included with Odin's gift of Ǫnd, the sacred breath which carries consciousness and spirit with it. If that is the case, then Hœnir giving 'mind, spirit, sense' would be rather superfluous.

This leaves room for the other interpretation: that the gift of Óðr is really the ability, treasured and respected in many cultures and religions around the world, to reach divine ecstasy and inspiration, a holy gift from the Gods to humankind.

The seeress Veleda sings in ecstasy.

This is my understanding of these two gifts. Ǫnd is the gift of our Ghost, our personal spirit which enwraps pure Spirit, Ahma, within its shaping hama or soul-skin. Ǫnd / Ghost includes our creative and intellectual abilities along with our spirit, and includes our breath, both mundane physical breath, and the divine Breath of Life. Oðr is the gift of divine inspiration and ecstasy: a capability that is granted by the Holy Ones to our human Ghost.

    I see oðr / wode as a bridge between humans and Deities, a channel through which divine power can flow into humans and into Midgard, bringing inspiration and creativity into our own world through the Gods' gifts. Wode or oðr flows through our Ghost-soul, in my understanding, and triggers Ghost's creative and prophetic abilities to their highest level. Other abilities may be triggered by wode as well, especially the berserker-ecstasy that gives warriors great power, fearlessness, and delays the physical effects of wounds and injuries until the warrior has exited the trance.

    Other people besides warriors can sometimes enter the same kind of ecstatic, super-charged state, especially during dire emergencies when someone needs to be rescued, or needs to rescue themselves, from fatally dangerous circumstances. Under these circumstances, people can accomplish amazing deeds, not normally possible for them, thanks to the raging torrent of wode that powers through their Ghost and breath, and into their body to achieve such deeds.

    Because wode is the divine madness that is linked to an experience of the Gods and the power of holiness, I believe that it is Odin's brother Ve or Wihaz, whose name means "sacred," who gives us the gift of oðr / wode. It seems odd to all of us at first glance, I think, that Oðinn / Woden is not the giver of wode, yet it does make sense that he gives us ǫnd / ghost / spirit. He is associated with wind and storm, and spirit rides the wind and rides the breath within us. He is a God of consciousness, awareness, wisdom, all associated with ǫnd. Odin's brother Ve, so closely related to him, adds his own unique element to the mix: the capacity to transcend the Lich and all the ties of Midgard, and to enter the sacred realms of the Gods on a tide of wode.

Who knows—perhaps long ago, before the tales we know of, it was Ve who gave us our sacred Ghost, and Odin / Woden who gave us wode. These days, some Heathens regard Odin and his brothers as sort of a three-in-one proposition, so the distinction is perhaps not vital, anyway. It is something I like to pursue in my own meditations, however!

When our Ghost is in a full-blown state of wode, our normal faculties of judgement, rationality, self-control and so forth are not operational. We are consumed by our inspiration or frenzy, and 'normal' is the last word one would use to describe us! We may well speak great wisdom, poetry, and prophecy, but the wisdom we grasp and communicate in this state of being comes from the Otherworlds, not from the mundane here and now. We are 'other,' 'elsewhere,' and outside of 'this-time.' Wode takes us out of ourself into a non-ordinary realm of consciousness and action.

This can be a good or a bad thing. Like many of the born berserkers who are described in the Icelandic sagas, a removal of our awareness to a non-ordinary state can result in our abandoning ordinary rules of conduct. A person with a berserker personality may be very exploitative and predatory toward others, and show no restraint, compassion, or respect for customary law and behavior. Their wode carries them beyond these boundaries.

Wode which expresses itself in creative, intellectual, or mystical passion generally does not lead to deliberate mistreatment of other people, but often causes the wode-filled person to neglect and be uncaring about everyday obligations such as one's family and job responsibilities.

Uncontrolled wode, unbalanced by the strengths of our other souls and the considerations of Midgard life, can lead to ethical carelessness, the wrecking of relationships, jobs, finances and other everyday necessities, serious illness and outright madness. Yet, controlling wode is a real challenge for a person whose Ghost is prone to wodeness.

By its nature, the wode-filled Ghost is basically out of control. In traditional cultures there are experienced elders who can teach the wode-prone person—whether warrior, seer, artist, shaman, or whatever—to manage their condition. In our culture we have neither the proper respect and value for the benefits of wode, nor the social traditions and structures that could help us manage it. Instead, we medicate it away, and / or punish or marginalize those who give way to wode. As a result, most of us learn to suppress and deny that facility in ourselves. This tactic helps us lead a 'normal' life but closes us out from transformative, otherworldly experiences that would inspire all the powers of our Ghost, that could benefit both ourselves and others.

This whole subject area is large and deep, and certainly I am not qualified to address all aspects of it. Genuine shamans, mystics, martial artists, artistic or intellectual geniuses, and others whose Ghosts are open to wode, go through rigorous, years-long training and discipline. The training process is a necessity not only in order to develop their art, but to remain somewhat balanced and in control of one's life in spite of the demands of wode.

This often involves living an unusual lifestyle, perhaps somewhat withdrawn from 'the world,' and perhaps without many of the social and material amenities of ordinary life.

In some cases, one must struggle with the ill-health that can be part of a wode-filled life. The "shaman's illness" is often considered a necessary indicator of a real shaman's calling, and it is not always cured by becoming a shaman. Neurological malfunctions such as dizziness, fainting, fits and seizures often accompany a powerfully wode-filled Ghost.

In my previous chapter I mentioned the Proto-Indo-European word *dhuesmi which developed, in different Indo-European languages, into words expressing various facets of shamanic and berserker experiences. The original word may have meant not only 'to breathe,' but also 'to be full of wild spirits.' It led to words meaning: dizzy, confused, foolish, ghost, rage, spirit, and wild animal. (Mallory & Adams p. 82.) The words that stem from *dhuesmi encompass not only the experience of entering into and enacting a shamanic or berserker trance, but also entering into a true state of madness.

Our English word 'giddy' is also relevant: it comes from the Anglo-Saxon *gydig* meaning "possessed by a spirit, insane." The word *gydig* comes directly from the word 'goddess' *(gyden)* or 'god', showing the original sacred Heathen connotations of this state, as someone whose Ghost is being stirred by a Goddess, God or a spirit.

"Wode," by Dale Wood.

Experiences of our Ghost are reflected in our Lich, often as symptoms that today are regarded as illnesses. The discipline and focus required to live a wode-filled life, while still functioning in Midgard and maintaining health and sanity, may shape a life that is quite different from the ordinary, sometimes painfully so.

Wode is not always an all-or-nothing affair, however. It can come out of nowhere and overwhelm a person, but it can also, to some extent, be invited and nurtured in a controlled and measured way, though there is always a risk involved. These measured invitations to wode can form part of the spiritual-mental practice of a Heathen life. We must recognize that an important aspect of this practice is to maintain healthy ties with other people and with Midgard life, and in particular to cultivate wise Heathen friendships where we can help each other with reality checks and thus maintain some control over how wode expresses itself in our lives.

The big question for us is: does wode ride our Ghost, or does our Ghost ride the wode? The former can lead to Ghost-madness both during and after life. The latter can lead to disciplined, inspired spiritual practice. Essential to this process is the training of Athom, the sacred breath, which energizes our Ghost, and controls the degree of wode and its mode of expression. A strong, disciplined, inspired Ghost is one who is a trained Ghost Rider, one who can ride both Athom and wode to other Worlds, achieving deeds and experiences there that reflect into Midgard in many ways.

Athom is not simply breath and breathing, as I have described above: it is also our link to our transcendent Ahma-spirit and its energy-field. Adams (Mallory & Adams p.82) notes a very interesting suggestion that has been made regarding the meanings of *dhuesmi and *haenhmi (another PIE breath-word that is the root of Gothic *anan* and *ahma*, Latin *anima*, and other Germanic and non-Germanic words meaning breath, wind and spirit—see previous chapter).

Adams suggests that *dhuesmi refers to breathing in, inhaling, which under some circumstances can mean breathing in wild spirits. *Haenhmi (root of the Greek *anemos* = wind), on the other hand, refers to breathing out, exhaling, and can sometimes involve releasing or sending out our Ghost. With a good deal of care to prevent breathing-in spirits one does not want to breathe in, and to deal safely with Ghost-travel, this understanding could provide some guidance for Heathen ghostly practice.

Before leaving the subject of wode, I should mention that it is not only Gods-sent wode that can excite our own Ghosts. Wode can also be passed between human Ghosts, both living and after life, and between other spirits and humans. Any person who is inspiring enough, who has strong enough charisma, can pass wode from himself / herself on to other people. This can be a beneficial or a dangerous phenomenon. Hitler is an example of the latter: he worked himself up into a wode-filled frenzy during his public speeches, and assisted by stunning effects of music, lighting, parades, etc., he incited enormous wode-frenzy in most people who attended his performances.

Other public performers can cause wode in different forms to arise, such as rock stars and athletic champions, great artistic performers, as well as great teachers, political and spiritual leaders. Alfar and Disir (ancestral spirits) may be able to infuse us with inspired wode: witness tales from Old Norse lore that tell of sleeping on a grave mound or making an offering on a grave mound and gaining poetic inspiration or wisdom. Various non-human wights can also stimulate our Ghosts to wode, usually with ill results unless we are very firmly in control of the process.

The Otherworldly Nature of the Ghost

In the ancient Germanic languages, the ghost-words and *and*-words applied not only to human spirits but to various kinds of non-human beings and wights, as well. Although in modern English we think of a ghost as being quite immaterial and ethereal, Anglo-Saxon usage shows us that the word *gast* was frequently applied to otherworldly entities which had a very physical presence. A good example is the monster Grendel in the *Beowulf* epic. Grendel is very frequently referred to as a *gast* or ghost (our word 'ghastly' comes from gast). Yet there is no question that Grendel has a physical presence: he not only tears apart people and eats them, but he himself is killed by Beowulf ripping his arm off, causing him to bleed to death. The dragon which kills Beowulf is also called a gast.

Old Germanic language usage, as well as folklore, lumps in with 'ghosts' and *'ande'* many other kinds of otherworldly beings, beings which are physical in their own worlds, such as dwarves, elves, dragons, wights of many kinds, but whose physicality in our world is less than or other than our own. For example, they can appear and disappear, slip through portals into other worlds that we usually cannot, have more power or less power than we do over events in the physical world, and so forth. The Grendel monster, in spite of physically bleeding to death as a human would, lived deep under an otherworldly lake within a fen or marsh, as a human could not. Here we can see an example of a ghost's combination of physical and otherworldly / non-physical characteristics.

I want to insert an anecdote about the Grendel episode in the *Beowulf* saga because it relates to ghosts, and the usual translation is a pet peeve of mine. The *Beowulf* poet tells us that the dwellers in Heorot, tormented for years by Grendel's ravages, prayed to their Gods to save them. The poet here is speaking as a Christian, and inserts a little sermon about Heathen ignorance, referring to the God to whom they are directing their prayers (presumably Woden) as the *gast-bona*, the ghost-bane.

Ghost Rider

All translators I've come across, including the Anglo-Saxon dictionary, give this word in English as "soul-slayer." This is both inaccurate and ridiculous! Who would petition to a Deity who slays souls – how would you know your own soul would be safe? It is very clear from the context – the people are being bedeviled by a gast/ghost, as Grendel is constantly described – that the folk are beseeching the ghost-bane, the godly ghost-slayer, to save them from the ghost. What they are asking for is a ghost-buster, not a soul-slayer! If a soul-slayer had been meant, then the word would have been *sawol-bona*, not *gast-bona*. They are not the same thing at all.

This is what happens with such sloppy soul-terminology as we are stuck with in modern English, and this is what I am trying to remedy through further development of terms through my soul lore work. To wrap up the tale here: the Christian *Beowulf*-poet primly points out that their Heathen Gods fail to save the folk from the Grendel-gast. But Beowulf, having previously slain a strange and powerful water-wight in his early youth, comes to slay Grendel for them. Beowulf is of mysterious, divinely inspired descent, his life shaped by a strange wyrd. Any Heathen would realize that Beowulf is, indeed, the Gods' answer to the prayer, and that the odd circumstances of his life were brought about by the Gods to prepare him for that role.

What lies in common between the idea of an immaterial human ghost, versus a non-human wight which might be quite physical? To us, they don't seem very similar. The common factor between them is that all—both human Ghosts and non-human wights—are native to worlds other than Midgard. They appear in Midgard, attached to our Lich in the case of humans, and in various non-ordinary contexts in the case of wights, but this is not their home-base and there is always something otherworldly about them. All are eldritch and uncanny, none are completely bound by the physical laws of Midgard, all feel pulled Elsewhere even when they are located in Midgard.

Our elder kin even recognized that Gods appear as ghosts to us. The old Germanic Christians wrote often about "God's ghost," and I get the impression that they did not necessarily mean the third person of the Christian Trinity, the Holy Ghost. They recognized the Holy Ghost as an independent entity, mysterious and distant from the world, but also believed (this is my impression) that the Christian God had his own personal ghost which visited people.

I think this early Christian perception was influenced by a prior Heathen understanding that Gods appear as their own Ghosts to people. Gods have Ghosts as part of their makeup, just as we do. Early Germanic Christians also referred to the Christian Father-God's Hugi, Mod, and other souls or soul-parts, as well as those of Jesus. This is only logical: Gods cannot be less than we are, and we are supplied with a richness of souls and soul-parts. How could the Gods not have them, too?

I think this idea reflects a very Heathen perception of the physical nature of Gods. An interesting example of this thought process occurs in the *Heliand,* regarding the conception of Jesus in Mary's womb. The familiar tale we are told in the Gospel of Luke is that at the Annunciation, the angel Gabriel appeared to Mary and told her: "The Holy Spirit will come upon you, the power of the Most High will overshadow you." (Phillips p. 109.) This is how Jesus' conception will occur: through the power of the Holy Ghost, caused by the Holy Ghost.

However, in the Old Saxon *Heliand,* remarkably, "the Helago Gest *became* the child in her womb" (ll. 291-2). From the perspective of Heathen soul lore, the Holy Ghost here has taken on a Hama, a soul-skin, in the form of a physical human body, just as human spirits do. (See Chapter 6 about the Hama.) This is not how it was presented in the original versions of the Gospels.

I'll follow this thought a little further, and guess at something about the old Heathen-based understanding of the first Pentecost, when the Christian Holy Ghost descended on gathered crowds of the faithful and inspired them. This happened after Jesus had departed Midgard and ascended to heaven, fifty days after his resurrection. I'm guessing that a Heathen-based understanding of this event required that Jesus no longer be present in his physical body, in order for the Holy Ghost to descend to Earth.

As long as the Holy Ghost was enwrapped in its Hama, Jesus' body, the Holy Ghost could not perform as a Ghost, a disembodied being, by inspiring multitudes of people all at once. Only after Jesus' ascension to heaven would the Holy Ghost, in this conceptualization, be free to act, unfettered by the flesh. (Unfortunately, the final pages of the *Heliand,* which would presumably have described the Pentecost, are missing, so we lose any clues there might have been in that part of the text.)

This whole understanding, of Jesus in the flesh being the *embodied* Holy Ghost, is not in accordance with Christian doctrine, which regards the Holy Ghost as a distinct third person in the Christian trinity, not as Jesus' own Ghost or spirit. The *Heliand* poet would not have gotten the idea of the Holy Ghost becoming the child Jesus in the womb from his Christian sources. In the *Diatessaron*, the primary source for the *Heliand*, the description of Jesus' conception is simply that Mary "was found with child by the Holy Spirit" prior to her marriage to Joseph. (Section II 2:2.) I think we see here another clue to how Heathens understood the nature of the Ghost, buried beneath the Christian mythology.

Returning now to my original point: we are physical beings in Midgard, but when any of our soul-selves travels outside the physical dimension, they appear ghostly, as apparitions or pure-energy bodies. By the same token, the God/esses can take physical form in their own worlds if they wish, but can seem ghostly to us when they visit here in Midgard, though they also have the ability to take on solid form if they choose. Many tales and lore from the Heathen lands tell of the Holy Ones appearing in physical form in Midgard, and in the foregoing paragraphs I described how this understanding may have shaped the Christian tale of the incarnation of Jesus for the old Saxons.

Overall, my point is that when any being native to one World moves into a different World, this being will appear as a ghost in the World it is visiting. It may be strong enough, and / or its native world and Midgard may be close enough together, to appear and behave as a physical being in Midgard, but there will always be some uncanny difference in their being.

After we die and our Ghost moves permanently to the God-realms, then our Ghost is in its natural element and can exist as a physical being in that World (Asgard, Vanaheim, etc), as can the Gods and Goddesses. I believe that this physicality is, for all of them, an optional form of existence, and that non-physical modes are also open to Deities and Ghosts.

It is very important, in understanding and developing our Ghost, to grasp the implications of the Ghost's otherworldly nature. Our Ghost is honestly not very body-friendly, nor is it usually all that interested in the concerns of Midgard except as an arena where its talents can shine. The stronger our own Ghost is, the more likely it is that we neglect the care of our Lich-Hama, or even reject the Lich altogether, unless our other souls such as our Hama, Ferah and Mod are strong enough to balance the Ghost.

I mentioned earlier that people with wode-prone Ghosts often suffer from poor health. Religions or religious sects which see the Ghost / Spirit as the only human soul have often been notably hostile toward the body, limiting or denying needs such as sexuality, the enjoyment of food, bodily comfort, and Midgard pleasures generally. Their rationale is that our Spirit is here in Midgard in unwilling confinement, and that it can only be released and be its true self by denying and rejecting the Lich and Midgard, longing only for death and Heaven or the realms of Ahma.

To me, this view emphasizes the unhealthiness of believing that we have only one soul or spirit. For those who hold this belief, the one soul they believe in is the Spirit / Ghost who, in truth, is not native to Midgard nor particularly attached to Midgard. So it is no surprise that these world-rejecting religious practices arise, when only the Spirit is real. I find a Heathen perspective to be much healthier, with our multiple souls which can balance one another with their varied attachments to different Worlds, Midgard very much included, and different modes of being.

But in rejecting other world-denying and body-denying religious beliefs, we must not lose sight of the fact that our Ghost, with all its wonderful gifts and strengths, is not truly a friend to our Lich or to Midgard life. We should pursue all of its rich talents and abilities, and prepare our Ghost well for an afterlife in the God-realms by following the lead of the Holy Ones while we are in Midgard life. But we also must develop our other souls with equal strength, and strike a healthy balance to honor the richness of the Gods' gifts of Midgard and our own Lich-Hama, our ensouled, living body.

The conflict between the Ghost and other more Midgard-oriented souls, as well as a confirmation that Gods themselves have these souls, is poignantly shown in a passage in the *Heliand* (Chapter 57, Jesus' prayer on the Mount of Olives, in the version on the Hieronymus website.) This is the scene of Jesus' agonized effort to accept his fate of crucifixion, and the poet presents the scene, very intriguingly, as a dramatic conflict between several of Jesus' souls.

His Ghost is firmly committed to his father-god's mission; it is focused on the Otherworld and eager to set forth out of Midgard even at the cost of the body's pain and humiliation. Jesus' other souls, however, are much less willing. The opposition party is led by his Likhamo (lich-hama), his Hama-soul. Partnered with Likhamo are Hugi, Mod, and 'flesh,' his Lich. Eventually his Mod-soul crosses over to the side of the Ghost, and their combined weight leads to acceptance of the crucifixion. (See Becker's discussion p.19-20 and p.42-43.) (I discuss in Chapter 8 my thought that our Mod-soul does indeed join our Ghost as a partner in the afterlife.)

This fascinating Germanic representation of Jesus' inner struggle clearly shows that the Ghost is not closely attached to Midgard concerns, and naturally prefers the divine realms, while many of our other souls are more heavily involved in, and attached to, our Midgard life.

Ghost, I believe, normally goes to the God-Homes after death, to the Deities it was closest to during its lifetime. There, our Ghost associates with other human Ghosts and with the Deities, and perhaps other spiritual beings as well. As I understand it, the afterlife Ghost has the option of involving itself with the works and activities of the Holy Ones. For example, Ghost may undertake training with the Einherjar warriors in Odin's God-Hall, Valhalla / Valhöll, or help with the work of Alfheim or Vanaheim under Freyr or Freya, work with Njorð as the God of seafaring and wealth, participate in the many domains of action of Frigg and her Ladies, or Frau Holle, or may work with Thor or Tyr, in their different ways, on warding the well-being of Midgard.

Ghost likes to use its talents, and likes to associate with the Deities. Ghost's partner Mod likes to achieve and be active. Keep in mind that, as I described earlier, the Ghost can take on a quasi-physical nature, which gives it a spiritual body and spiritual strength for these activities. As our Mod-soul accompanies Ghost in the afterlife, it adds its own strength, abilities and Will to these endeavors.

Summary

I envision Ahma as primal, unchanging Spirit arising from the foundations of the cosmos, while our Ghost-soul consists of Ahma enwrapped in a soul-skin which gives it shape, coherence, boundaries, and individual personhood. In this, I see these souls as being parallel to the Deities, who have the natures of both unbounded Spirit / Ahma, and of individual, personal divine beings.

Our Ahma and Ghost work together to maintain us in physical life, and are at the same time connected to unbounded, eternal spiritual being. They do this through the process of breathing: as our Ghost rhythmically draws Ahma-energy into and out of its permeable soul-skin, our Lich-Hama (living body) breathes air in and out, following the rhythm of our Ghost's breathing.

The power of wode flows through our Ghost-soul, in my understanding, and is both energized and controlled by various methods of breathing, including galdoring or chanting. Wode can express itself in ways ranging from mild inspiration to highly-developed forms of genius; from battlefield trance to extraordinary physical abilities and emergency reactiveness; from religious ecstasies and shamanic states, visions and prophecy, to mob behavior, hysteria and frenzy, or to full-blown mania and madness. Athom-work (breath-work) and other disciplines and training can control and direct wode into beneficial channels.

In Closing

The original shaping and final destination of our Ghost are generally in the hands of the Gods. During our Midgard-life our Ghost is directly linked to the Gods and Goddesses and their realms of power. This link is powered by wode, and the fully developed Athom-Ghost learns to ride wode, athom and ǫnd to the height and breadth of human spiritual capacity. After our Midgard life is over, if all is well, Ghost moves on to dwell with the Gods and Goddesses, to share with them consciousness and experience, activities and purposes.

Alternatively, people with a strong sense of Spirit but no significant attachment to personal Deities may find that after death their Ghost dissolves its shape and releases the Ahma within it, to return to the formless fields of Spirit hovering above Ginnungagap.

If all is not well, Ghost will be in trouble after physical life is over (and probably during physical life, as well). It may get stuck or wander – lost, confused, angry, despairing – as a haunt within the Midgard-realm, until / unless it is able to reestablish an appropriate connection with the Deities. It may wander off into other, less savory realms, giving up its original, Gods-given nature and distorting itself into some lesser form of being: perhaps evil, certainly less worthy than its true nature calls for. Some Heathen spiritual practitioners have the kindness, courage and skill to come to the aid of these lost Ghosts and try to guide them, at least to a homely place in Hel, even if not to the God-realms.

If we wish our Ghosts to grow and mature, and end up with the Gods and Goddesses as is their nature, then it behooves us to keep our channels of understanding, trust and troth clear between us and the Deities to ensure that all happens as it should. The Holy Ones are not forced, after all, to accept our Ghosts as their friends. They offer their gifts, their friendship and aid for our use. It is up to us to make the most of these and grow to be worthy of their true friendship and companionship during and after life.

The friendship of the Holy Ones.
(Relief from Mother Hulda / Frau Holle Fountain, Eschwege.).

Chapter 6
6. The Shape of Being Human: The Hama Soul

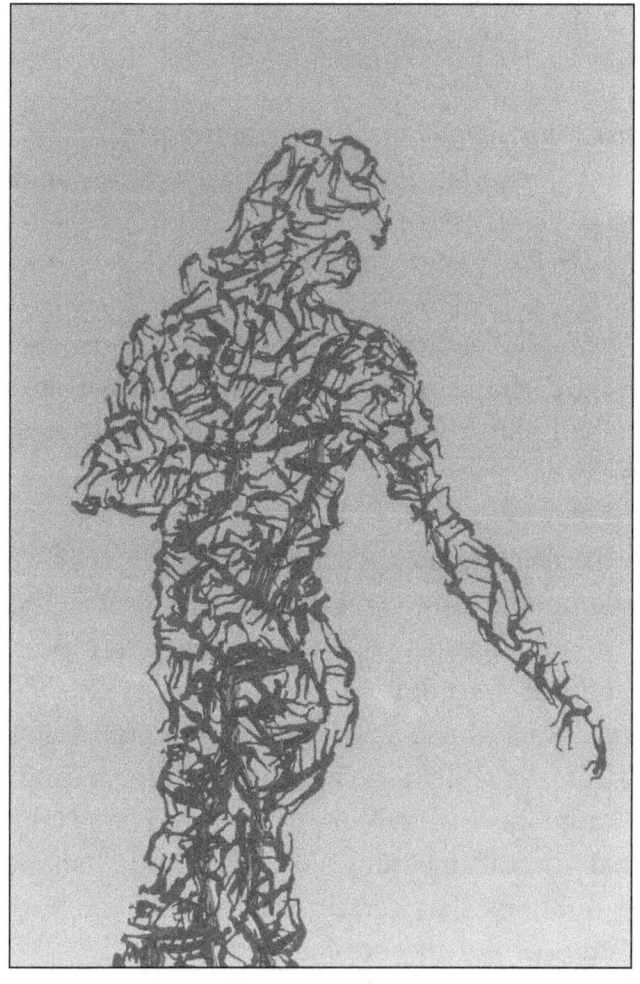

The Hama takes shape.
The tiny human figures within this shape can be seen as ancestral influences on the Hama.

Ǫnd they had not,
Oðr they had not,
Neither la nor læti nor litr godas.
Ǫnd gave Odin,
Oðr gave Hœnir,
La gave Loðurr, and litr godas.
(*Völuspá* vs. 18 in the Poetic Edda)

Odin said:
I gave my clothes, along the way, to two tree-people.
They thought themselves heroes when they were so clothed:
The naked person is ashamed.
(*Havamal* vs. 49, Poetic Edda, my translation.)

Proto-Germanic **hama(n)* = shape, physical form; ON *hamr* = skin, slough, shape, form; A-S *hama* = covering, womb, slough (shed skin of a snake); OS *hamo* = covering; OHG *hamo* = skin, covering, net.

The word *hama* (rhymes with mama) appears in all of the ancient Germanic languages, and a number of other Indo-European languages as well, tracing back to a proto-Indo-European root meaning 'a covering.' In the Germanic languages, *hama* is used to indicate an item of clothing: a simple dress or shift, a shirt or cloak, depending on the specific language. In Old Norse, the word Hama takes on an additional, occult meaning: it refers to a 'shape' with physical qualities that certain individuals can take on as shapeshifters or during soul-journeys.

Hama also means the caul (birth membrane) and the afterbirth in Scandinavian usage, meanings which are important in magic involving the Hama. 'Womb' is a related

The Hama Soul

Anglo-Saxon meaning of Hama. In several of the Germanic languages Hama also means the 'slough', the shed skin of a snake. All of these are clearly in the domain of 'a covering.' As I shall show later, there is also a different word in Anglo-Saxon, *hiw* (hue), which is used in a similar way as Hama in the domain of soul-lore.

As with many of our other souls, our Hama soul is a complex one, sometimes consisting of more than one Hama-form per person: a human-shaped Hama, and another shape our Hama can take on, such as an animal form or other non-ordinary-human form. Often, in Scandinavian lore and folklore, the Hama seems to be interchangeable with our Hugr soul and with the Fylgja guardian spirit that accompanies each of us. There is also a luck-bringing spirit called the *Hamingja*, a word related to Hama, which may or may not be the same being as the Fylgja.

The word *fylgja* seems actually to be a broad term that is often applied in folklore to any accompanying spirit or externalized soul, such as the Hama, Hugr, Hugham, Hamingja, Dis (female ancestral spirit), *Vörðr* (warder), Gandr, or spirit animal. (See de Vries *Altgermanische Religionsgeschichte*, p. 224 ff. and Grimm vol. 3 p. 874 ff.) This realization can help to reduce our confusion somewhat when reading through the lore! Often the context of the word *fylgja* in the text can help us discern more about what kind of being it is.

The concept of Hama is further confused by the understanding that a *hama* can refer to a covering or a shape taken on by another of our souls, as well as being one of our souls in its own right. Ancient Hindu lore tells of complex systems of 'soul sheaths,' much like Hamas, with souls enclosing and shaping other souls or soul-parts within them, sometimes in multiple layers like onions (see Walker's entry on the soul). I think that something similar may be present in the Germanic concept of the hama, though in a much less complex and systematic form.

In Chapter 5, about the Ghost and Ahma souls, I discussed how the Ghost can be understood as the hama or soul-shape of our formless Ahma soul. Our Hugr soul is also capable of taking on a visible or tangible shape, called a *hugham* (hoog-hahm) in Scandinavian folklore (see Chapter 11). Our personal 'world,' or *Werold*, our perception and experience of our own lifetime, is in my understanding the hama or cocoon spun by our Aldr soul (see Chapter 7). I will try to preserve the distinction by using the capitalized form of Hama for our Hama soul, and the lower-case hama when referring to shapes or coverings that our other souls may take on for themselves, such as our Hugham and Werold.

I will make a further distinction, as well, between our primary, human Hama soul which shapes and supports our physical body, and the secondary or alternate Hama which some people have or develop, which is an animal shape or a human-seeming shape with non-human abilities such as flying. Occasionally it might also take on the shape of a non-human being such as a troll, water-wight or some other wight. An example of a witch faring aloft in her 'other-hama' can be seen in the following verse from the *Havamal* in the Poetic Edda:

I know a tenth (spell or rune):If I see a tun-rider (witch) playing aloft in the air, I can cause her to fare astray from her home-hama, from her home-hugr. (Verse 155, my translation.)

The Hama Soul

Here we can see that the witch's Hugr soul also takes part in this astral faring-forth, in the form of a hug-ham or Hugr-shape. It is not clear from folklore whether people who are 'shape-strong' or *hamrammr* in any of these ways  possess two completely different Hamas, or whether their own human Hama can shift its shape and roam abroad under the right circumstances. I incline toward the latter perception: that our own Hamas can take on a different shape and sometimes travel and take action in that shape.

I am calling the non-ordinary, potentially out-faring Hama soul-form the *Ellor-Hama* (EL-lor hama). *Ellor* is an Anglo-Saxon word meaning 'elsewhere,' with a strong connotation of other-worldliness. The *ellor-sith* is the journey into death, into another world. *Ellor* was also a prefix used to denote otherworldliness; for example, the monster Grendel in the *Beowulf* saga was called an *ellorgast,* an alien or otherworldly ghost. In the same sense, I am proposing the term Ellor-Hama to denote a non-ordinary / non-human shape that our Hama may be able to take naturally, or that we may acquire through esoteric practice.

Here I focus on our primary, human Hama, rather than on any manifestations of the Ellor-Hama. We must first understand the great gift the Gods gave us, our human Hama, before pursuing an understanding of the more arcane forms of Hama.

The Gifts of Loðurr

When the ancient trees were first transformed into human beings, in the persons of Ask and Embla, in my understanding the following events happened: Thor released our ancient Earth-given Ferah soul from the Trees, to spring out into human-ness; Odin gave us our Ahma and Ghost souls along with our breath, and Hœnir gave us the power of wode that can serve as a bridge between humanity and divinity. Another set of gifts was given at this time by Loðurr; these gifts are named in the *Völuspá* (vs. 18, Poetic Edda) as '*La, Læti,* and *Litr godas.*' I believe that these gifts comprise our human-shaped Hama Full-Soul.

To clarify: La, Læti and Litr are mentioned in the *Völuspá* poem of the Poetic Edda, which describes the coming-into-being of humans. 'Hama' is not used in this context, though it does appear elsewhere in the Eddic poems, and is frequently mentioned in Scandinavian folklore. The definition of the Hama as consisting of the La, Læti, and Litr, and the link between Loðurr and the Hama, are my own interpretations of these two different strands of information.

(I am indebted to the Swedish scholar Viktor Rydberg for aspects of the material I cover in my following sections about the La, Læti, and Litr. *Teutonic Mythology*, Vol 3, section 95, "On the Anthropology of the Mythology.")

1. The Gift of La

La or *Lö* is a mysterious word that occurs only in the verses of the *Völuspá* quoted above. Modern scholars variously interpret it as 'blood,' 'warmth,' 'hair,' and occasionally even 'water,' related to the Laguz rune. (See de Vries' dictionary.)

These seemingly disparate substances have something in common, however: they each carry powerful vital force. Blood is synonymous with life, warmth and strength, as well as carrying distinctive characteristics from one generation to the next. Before the discovery of genes, and often even now, blood was / is considered to carry genetic inheritance. These generational characteristics are seen not only as physical features (she looks just like her grandma), but also as family culture or disposition (they're all a hot-headed bunch). By mingling blood in a sibling-ceremony, two people are considered to share the power and characteristics of each others' 'blood.' Blood is also connected with female fertility and hence with the power of life.

In Indo-European cultures, and others as well, hair was thought to carry a particular potency within itself. It carries the strength of a warrior, the charisma of a chieftain, the mysterious power of a magic-user, and the allure of a beautiful person. The condition of our hair reflects our health and our self-esteem. Hair is often the first thing we note when we describe a person. In the past, thralls' hair was cut very short to emphasize their disgrace and powerlessness, even the fact that in some ways, such as certain legal rights, they were 'dead.'

Thus, *La* can be understood as life force, carried in blood and in hair, not only in the individual but also passed down in characteristic ways within families. Both of these, blood and hair, are also powerful ingredients in magic that is intended to influence other people, usually by imposing illness or death through use of the victim's hair or blood in charms.

2. The Gift of Læti

Læti refers to two different things: one is 'noise, cries, voice' the other is 'disposition, manners, conduct.' It is related to the Anglo-Saxon word *gelætan* meaning 'to conduct oneself, to behave.' In the disciplines of philosophy and psychology, the quality of volition or will is the necessary precursor to behavior; in other words, one first wills, then acts. Though I think this can sometimes be an oversimplification, it does illustrate the connection between Læti and Will, supporting my belief that it was Odin's brother Vili (will), under another name, who gave us these gifts. His gift gives us the vehicle through which we can enact our will into the world. Will is also deeply inherent in the life-force, La, expressing itself as the will to live and thrive, the most fundamental of all forms of will.

With the gift of Læti, Vili / Loðurr gave us the ability to move and to act, from the most simple to the most complex actions. On the more complex end, we have human behavior and disposition, manners and personal conduct. I must emphasize that the gift of Læti does not mean that specific, time-and-place dependent manners and social customs were given to us: the Gods know well that we must be able to adapt and evolve behaviorally as well as physically. Rather, Læti is the inborn capacity to learn and express patterns of behavior that:

~ identify us each as a unique individual;

~ identify us as members of a particular social group (family, tribe, culture) that has characteristic behavioral customs and speech patterns such as accents and dialects; and

~ enable that group to function well and support the well-being of its members, by promoting such things as reduction of strife (through good manners, avoiding insults and rude behavior,), cooperative efforts (through coordinated actions with others), and the maintenance of physical and mental health and safety (through cooperative care and social stability).

Along with these behavioral patterns comes the 'voice, noise, cry': the power of speech and other vocal expressions. Each of us has a unique voice that others can recognize as ours. Accents, dialects and languages all identify us as members of a particular group or culture, and enable us to communicate and interact.

As reported in a recent evolutionary science research article, scientists found 407 genetic variants that showed changes in expression between archaic humans and modern humans. A preponderance of them were concentrated, not on the cognitive parts of the brain like the neocortex, as might be expected, but on the vocal tract and the cerebellum. The cerebellum is the part of the brain that controls voluntary movement: walking, coordination, balance, speech, etc. The findings suggest a rapid evolution of these organs on a path specific to modern humans.
(https://www.sciencedaily.com/releases/2021/04/210426154805.htm)

In other words, the main difference between modern and archaic humans looks to be speech and unique ways of walking and other movement. Here is Loðurr at work! Speech and voluntary movement, leading to conduct and behavior: these are his gifts. And note the 'voluntary' nature of the movement here, as opposed to automatic action such as heartbeat and breathing. 'Voluntary' or 'willed action' points us toward Odin's brother Vili, whose name means 'will'.

Læti is not unique to human beings; all animal species, even insects, have behavioral patterns, and vocalizations or other sound effects, that are essential to their species' identities, interactions and survival. But, each species has its own Læti, its own ways of moving, behaving, vocalizing. In our mythology, it is Loðurr (perhaps Vili) who provided these patterns for humans.

3. The Gift of Litr

Loðurr's final gift was *Litr godas* (LEE-ter GO-das). This is usually translated as 'good appearance' or something similar. Viktor Rydberg makes a different assumption: this gift is actually the 'appearance or form of the Gods.' This interpretation is entirely consistent with the mythology of Indo-Europeans and most other peoples: the idea that in physical form we are modeled after the Gods and Goddesses. I take this view as well: our appearance was created to be both 'good' and 'godly.'

As Rydberg describes, our Litr is an actual form, made from a very refined or etheric substance which he calls *efni* from the Norse term for 'substance.' This *efni* is imprinted with a holy image and serves as a template for our physical form and our behavioral 'shape.' By using the expression 'behavioral shape,' I am suggesting an analogy between our physical shape and the way it occupies physical space, and the 'shape' that our behavior creates in the space-time continuum of social interaction and other individual actions. This behavioral shape is just as real as our physical one, and holds a place in space and in time.

The Hama Soul

Consider, for example, that it is not usually a person's physical shape that gives them a 'place' in history, but rather their actions and behavior, along with subtle aspects of their appearance such as their charisma: the subtle glow of their luck and personal power. Social space is just as real and has just as much impact on us as does physical space, and to act in social space means that we need a suitable body to do it with. This body is our human Hama, comprising our Litr / appearance, our Læti / behavior and voice, and the life-force of our Hama-soul: our La, which expresses itself especially in our blood and our hair.

The concept of Litr is a very rich one, going far beyond a simple physical description of our appearance. Litr lies behind our physical form, and gives it liveliness, magnetism, attractiveness or repulsiveness. Litr draws out our emotional reactions toward someone's appearance, and our social responses to this appearance. This can be in response to negative or positive ethnic or cultural stereotypes, emotional reactions to the appearance of celebrities, etc.

As an example, many people respond in an endearingly silly and affectionate way toward babies, even completely unfamiliar babies irrelevant to our lives. Babies have a powerful Litr, in the form of irresistible 'cuteness,' that draws the attention and affection of adults. In this way, the baby's Hama soul ensures that the baby receives the care it needs in order to live and thrive, and ensures that the negative behaviors that are part of being a baby, such as crying and dirty pants, are met with affectionate tolerance rather than hostility. The baby's Hama soul knows exactly what it is doing in presenting its appealing Litr to the world, even though the baby's conscious mind is not capable at this point of conceiving and enacting this survival strategy.

Our outer, physical appearance depends on the condition of the inner *efni* or substance of the Litr. Joy and health shine from the Litr out through the physical body and create a great attractiveness emanating from our whole person. A person with charisma, with subtle power and luck that draws other people to him or her, shows forth that charisma through a magnetically attractive Litr. The Anglo-Saxon cognate to Litr gives us additional understanding: *wlite* (wlee-teh) means 'brightness, appearance, form, aspect, countenance, beauty, splendor, adornment.'

For each of us, whatever our degree of purely physical attractiveness, the Gods have given a Litr which is meant to shine and glow through our physical body, to project into the world our spiritual health, strength and beauty, and a deep and powerful joy-in-life, all as reflections of the same qualities embodied in our Gods and Goddesses.

Think, for example, of the heady power of life and beauty emanating from Freya, ranked with the power of the Sun and Moon, coveted by the giants: this is her Litr shining forth. Shining Heimdal, with his golden teeth and gold-maned horse, his great horn that echoes through the worlds, surrounded by the shimmering light of Bifrost, also shows forth a stunningly powerful Litr. Thor's literally 'magnetic' power, expressed through lightning and thunder, through his iron Hammer and his great voice, his might and main, and his hugely exuberant personality, is another example of a mighty Litr. Each of the Holy Ones can give us such examples of what a Litr can and should be.

The Hama Soul

Freya's shining Litr. ("Freja" by John Bauer.)

The Gift-Giver

These, then, are the gifts of Loðurr:
~ our Litr, the appearance of our subtle energy body that both shapes and shines through our physical form;
~ our Læti that shapes our speech, actions and behavior as physical and social beings;
~ and the La, the life-force of our Hama-soul, that expresses its power through blood, warmth and hair, and through all the appearance and actions of our Litr and Læti.

In my understanding, these gifts together comprise our Hama soul. Our Hama is our persona, which gives us the ability to act in, and be a part of, this great world of Midgard. Without Loðurr's gift of the Hama, we would be simply disembodied spirits.

There is not a full agreement among scholars as to the derivation of Loðurr's name. Some maintain that it could be Loki; others disagree. One interpretation is that Loðurr stems from a root relating to Gothic *liudan* = to grow, ON *loð* = fruit, yield, and *ljoðr* = people, community. This would make Loðurr possibly equal to Freyr, or another God with similar qualities. (See discussion under Loðurr in Simek, and Waggoner 2021, pp. 405-408.)

My own idea is that Loðurr is a byname of one of Odin's brothers, most likely Vili, and that the name Loðurr could stem from an ancient term for skin, hair or covering, just as the word Hama does.

In Anglo-Saxon we have the word *loða* = cloak, while in Old Norse we have *loða* = furry cloak, and the famous Ragnar Loðbrokk, Ragnar Hairy-breeches. Modern Faroese, which retains many words from its ON forbear, has the words *loðin* = hairy, shaggy; *loðskinn* = furs, and *loðær* = sheep which have not shed their wool. There is also the related modern English 'leather' and German *Loden* = coarse woolen cloth. These meanings comprise hair, skin and covering, which relate directly to the La and the Hama.

The suffix *-urr* in Loðurr's name is interpreted by Polomè as an alteration of 'verr', meaning 'man' (pp. 30-54. My thanks to Dr. Ben Waggoner for this lead.) Thus the name can mean something like 'shaggy man'. I interpret all this as leading to the meaning of Loðurr as 'a man wearing

The Hama Soul

a shaggy, furry cloak.' This fits with the image of Odin and his two brothers, presumably all cloaked as Odin usually is.

There is also the quotation from the Havamal, where Odin says that he "gave his clothes to two tree-people" (*tremönnum*, v. 49; note that *man / mönnum* means 'person / people' and can refer to either gender). Though there are other interpretations of this verse (see Waggoner's *Havamál*, note 20), to me it makes sense as a reference to the shaping and clothing of Ask and Embla by Odin and his brothers. My understanding is that Loðurr, the one with the furry cloak, gave us our 'cloak' in the form of our Hama with its power of shaping our body, skin, hair, warmth, appearance, and also our behavior and social 'shape.'

I envision Loðurr walking with his brothers in a furry cloak shimmering with La, life-power. I see Thor releasing the Earth-born Ferah souls from the Trees, Odin breathing breath and Ghost into these souls, and Hœnir / Ve striking the fiery spark of wode that arcs between the souls of the Gods and the souls of humankind, magnetically drawing them into divine communication.

Then I see Loðurr / Vili swirling off his furry cloak, each hair vibrating with life force, and wrapping the two new spirit-beings in it, thereby granting them the Hama soul with its power to create living physical forms out of subtle energy. What overwhelming marvels these are! Our physical body and its powers may sometimes seem so mundane to us, yet it is a wonder that is equal to the other amazing gifts of the Gods.

Modern clairvoyants and energy healers perceive auras or energy waves that surround the human body (and other bodies as well). These are usually seen as patterns of light or felt as warmth or pressure to the touch. I am not able to perceive auras clearly in these ways, though I can sometimes do so indirectly in a spaeworking (trance-work). But I do sometimes get a sense of very fine, light, short fur lying over my skin or others' skin, which perhaps are tendrils of auric energy.

'Light' is a very popular metaphor these days for many people, including those with New Age and various religious perspectives. We tend to perceive non-ordinary things as metaphors that are especially meaningful to us, so it is no surprise that today auric energy is perceived as colors and intensities of light. This is, I believe, an accurate, detailed and useful way to perceive and work with auras. It is not confined to modern perspectives, since we so often see images of saints, ancient Gods, and heroes with haloes or rays of light emanating from them. But I think that in the past, such energies were perceived in other ways as well, and that 'fur or hair' was one of them, as well as 'antlers or horns,' which were probably an interpretation of tendrils and rays of energy emanating from the body and the head.

When we have three Gods shaping modern humans out of something else, it would not be surprising if the one who is granting life-energy, La, expressed in blood, warmth and hair, and who is granting the power to create and maintain a physical shape, is represented as someone clothed in energy-rich hair or fur: one who is 'Loðurr' in my understanding of the word.

The Lich-Hama

In all the Germanic languages, there are two words that are used to mean the body, both living and dead: Lic / Lik / Leik, and Lichama / Likama / Leikhamo, and variants thereof. The latter set of words comes from adding 'Hama' to Lik or Lic

The Hama Soul

(pronounced Lich). I believe that originally these word-forms were not synonyms for each other, even though they often appear so in the old texts. Languages do not invent two different words to describe identical things; rather, words which originally had different meanings sometimes evolve into synonyms when the concepts they originally described change their meanings.

I think that originally Lich / Lik / Leik described the physical body separate from its Hama soul, whereas Lichama described the compound entity of the Hama and its creation, the Lich, together. This assumption would be strengthened if we see that Lik / Lich words apply to the corpse, while Lichama words apply to the living, Hama-ensouled body.

These distinctions do exist in some languages, though they are not fully consistent. Modern Icelandic *lik* means a corpse, while *likama* means the (living) body. The same is true in Faroese: *lik* is the corpse and *likam* or *likamur* is the living body. Words relating to the living body, such as 'physical strength,' use the form *likam* rather than *lik* in their construction. In Old Norse, the *lik* was a body either living or dead, while *likamo* was the living body.

Old Saxon and Anglo-Saxon used the words pretty interchangeably, but the word *lych* still survives in relatively modern English terms relating to the dead. Examples are the lych-gate to the cemetery, through which a corpse is taken to be buried, and place-names like Lychfield or Lichfield which indicate that there was once a graveyard there. The same meaning shows up in the modern German word *Leiche*, meaning corpse, though they also use *Leichnam*, perhaps derived from *Leik-hama*, to mean a corpse as well.

While the linguistic evidence is not completely consistent, there is enough to suggest that there was an original distinction between the living, Hama-ensouled Lichama, versus the Lich, the corpse from which the Hama has fled. Thus, I suggest that when we want to speak technically in our discussions of soul lore, we preserve the distinction between Lich and Lichama. Lich can best be used for a corpse, or else used when discussing the Hama and the Lich of a living person separately, as I do in following discussions about how the Hama forms the Lich in the womb, and how healing the Hama can cause healing of the Lich.

Anglo-Saxon Hiw

In Anglo-Saxon, at the time it was written down by Christians, the word *hama* meant a) an item of clothing, b) the womb, and c) the slough or shed skin of a snake. Though there are some traces of connections here with Scandinavian magical concepts relating to the Hama, there is another Anglo-Saxon word whose meaning correlates more closely with the Scandinavian Litr and Hama. This word is *hiw*. It is pronounced 'hue' and is the ancestor of our modern word 'hue' meaning a shade of color.

The first set of meanings for Hiw are: 'appearance, form, species, kind, hue, color, portrayal.' A *hiwbeorht* (hue-bright) person is radiantly beautiful. *Gehiwian* means to shape, fashion, transform or transfigure something. *Hiw* is also the basis for words meaning: to feign, pretend, and dissimulate; and hypocrisy and irony; in other words, putting a different shape on something. (Interestingly, the word Lic or Lich was also the root for the same kinds of words relating to deception, hypocrisy, etc.) These sets of

The Hama Soul

meanings are clearly in the same domain as the godly gift of Litr and our Hama, our shape-soul that defines our form, kind, and species, among other things.

The word *hiw* (but not Anglo-Saxon *hama*) also applies to occult and magical shape-changes, showing a definite parallel between it and the Scandinavian Hama. For example, the Anglo-Saxon cleric Ælfric wrote in one of his many homilies that someone encountered a devil *on mannes hiwe*, in a human Hiw or Hama (2.2.5-6). In other words, the devil shapeshifted in order to deceive his victim.

Ælfric also wrote that the Christian Holy Ghost had two Hiws: the shape of a dove, and that of a pillar of fire (2.3.168-9; 2.3.72-3). These were Hiws that the Holy Ghost made for itself in order to act on Earth. In the form of fire it led the Hebrews out of Egypt, and in the form of the dove it descended on Jesus at the time of his baptism. Without a Hiw, this spirit could not act directly in Midgard, just as we could not act ourselves without our Hama and the Lich that it produces.

The modern Anglo-Saxon scholar J.R.R. Tolkien also used the word 'hue' in its modern spelling, but with the ancient meaning, when he had Gandalf describe his fellow wizard Radagast as "a master of shapes and changes of hue" (*The Fellowship of the Ring*, Book 2, Ch. 2, "The Council of Elrond").

A phantom or spectre is called a *scinnhiw* in Anglo-Saxon: a 'shining Hiw' or sheen-hiw: a shining shape. The scinnhiw was handled or dealt with so much by shamans and magicians that very common terms for these practitioners were *scinnere* (m.) or *scinnestre* (f.), and *scinnlac*.

Interestingly, there is a second set of meanings belonging to Hiw that I find to be relevant in practical soul lore applications. A *hiwen, hiwisc,* or *hiwscipe* (hiw-ship, as in 'relation-ship') refers to a family, household, or other group which lives together with close ties, such as a religious community. Words formed from Hiw refer to 'household, domestic, family, familiarity, and marriage' matters. *Hiwgedal,* the dread blow of fate against Hiw, means 'divorce'. I find this concept of Hiw, as a close relationship between beings, to be very relevant to my understanding of the Hama soul, and the interactions among all our souls together.

Firstly, I see such a close *hiwscipe* or domestic relationship between our Hama soul and our living physical body, our Lichama. As I understand, our Hama actually creates our Lich within our mother's womb, as I will discuss further, below.

Secondly, all our souls which have personalities or qualities to express into Midgard, which is most of them, reflect these things through our Hama or Hiw: our appearance and our shape through which we act in Midgard. Our Hama is like a lens through which our other souls shine into Midgard. Our other souls express themselves through our actions, appearance, behavior and voice, which they could not do without our Lich-Hama.

Some of our more abstract and ethereal souls like our Ahma / Spirit need to be tied to Midgard by the strength of the Hama in order for us to be well-balanced and healthy while in Midgard. When there is close partnership or Hiwship between our souls, this is reflected powerfully and beautifully through the shining of our Litr, the actions of Læti, and the life-force of our La. When there is conflict or lack of relationship among our own souls, this damages our Hiwship, our soul-household, and shows forth in

The Hama Soul

disruptions to our Hama / Hiw, which in turn affects our health, luck, personal power and well-being at all levels.

Thirdly, there is the interesting phenomenon of the Hugham, where the Hugr soul takes the shape (hama / hiw) of one's own Lich and walks abroad as a Doppelgänger (see Chapter 11). This is an example of Hiwship or close relationship between our Hama / Hiw soul and our Hugr.

The Hama in the Womb

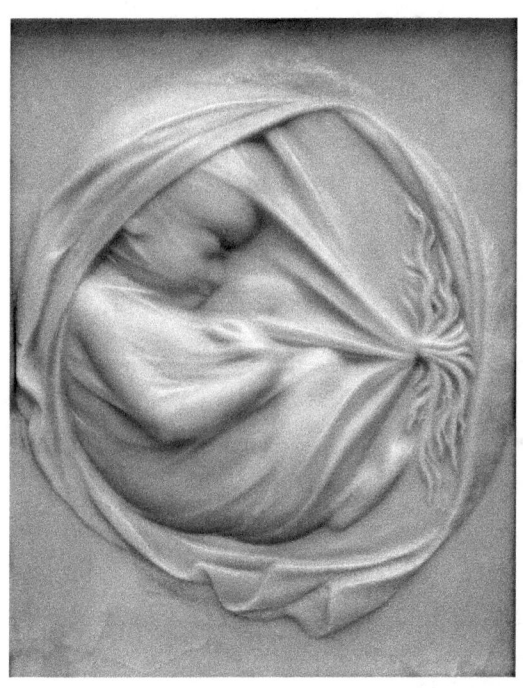

In Anglo-Saxon, one meaning of Hama was 'the womb,' the covering which protects, nourishes and shapes the growing baby. In Scandinavian usage up until modern times, the word Hamr as well as Fylgja applies to the afterbirth and/or the caul of a baby. Logically, the word Fylgja, which means 'follower', should apply to the afterbirth which follows the baby out of the womb, while the word Hamr, which means a covering or skin, should apply to the caul, but they seem fairly interchangeable according to what scholars write about them. Perhaps the old midwives, speaking quietly among themselves, showed more verbal accuracy; I like to think so, anyway!.

The caul is the birth membrane which normally opens and slides off the baby while it is going through the birth canal, and becomes mixed with the afterbirth. Occasionally this membrane does not split open, and the baby is born enveloped by part or all of it. Many cultures, including the Germanic ones, believed that this is a sign that the baby is especially lucky and/or has magical powers. In modern German, the caul is called the *Glückshaube,* the luck-cap or luck-cowl. The caul used to be dried and carefully saved for the child.

Many customs also surrounded the afterbirth in Germanic lands, including the common practice of burying it under an existing tree or a new sapling, which became the life-tree of the baby, holding strength and luck within it. Some modern Heathen parents take the trouble (it is not always easy) of getting their newborn child's afterbirth and burying it under a tree. The idea is to treat it respectfully so that any spirits associated with it are friendly to the child, and also to create a place of power for the child.

In general usage it seems that Hamr and Fylgja are used fairly interchangeably for the afterbirth and the caul. Both of these physical objects are understood to contain significant power and luck, which in turn are known to be given by the Fylgja or Hamingja spirit. This is especially true for those who have an animal Hama-form as well as the human one. This blend of power and luck is called *hamingja* in Norse, a word which is used both for a luck-bringing spirit, and for a type of luck-power itself.

All three of these terms: Hamingja, Hamr, and Fylgja, were mixed up together in general usage, all were considered to be luck-bringing, and to be involved in the processes of gestation and birth. According to some sources,

The Hama Soul

the caul / Hama / Hamingja actually contains the baby's soul or part of it, and must be kept and protected with that in mind. This further validates the idea that the Hama is actually a soul.

(References for the above paragraphs about folklore: de Vries sections 161-162; Grimm vol. 3, p. 874 ff; Erich & Beitl entries on *Nachgeburt* and *Geburt*.)

Birth and afterbirth.

The power inherent in the caul and afterbirth is not a passive or abstract process of life and luck; it is brought about by spiritual beings that are linked with these objects. More specifically, the physical objects are manifestations of the spiritual beings. The Hama and Fylgja are present with the child in the womb and are involved in its safe gestation. Norwegian folklore gives evidence of terrible things that can happen if these entities escape from the womb (of both humans and domestic animals) during gestation or after birth.

In an extensive collection of Norwegian spells and charms from the late Middle Ages onward, Anton Bang includes a number which are used to 'lay' such spirits by returning them to the womb or otherwise disposing of them. (For more about this, see my article "The Kindly Gods Go Wandering".) These entities are variously called Afterbirths *(epterbyrd / efterbyrd), bølen,* and *barne-mora* ('baby-mare', parallel to 'night-mare' meaning 'haunter of the night', not 'female horse'). All of these terms seem to be synonymous with one another. The Afterbirth is definitely seen as a spirit-being which can escape from the womb, wander around, and cause a lot of trouble. Even worse, whole troops Afterbirth-entities can be captured by evil sorcerers and magically sent out to wreak harm.

In Bang's collection of spells there are a number showing 'three maidens' (clearly they are Norns or Goddesses) who bind the Afterbirth-entity of a human or a domestic animal and lay it in its right place in the womb. Some of the spells call on the ability of these beings to spin or to utilize bands of gold and silver for binding the *barne-mora* and returning it to the womb. This image of the golden bands with magical powers is reminiscent of Freya's necklace or girdle, Brisingamen, and of Frigg's treasured ornaments, warded by her sister Fulla.

I believe that among their other sacred powers, these Goddesses hold the power to ward the Hamas of infants and keep them safe in place, thus helping to prevent miscarriage and developmental problems that could occur if the Hama went missing during gestation.

The Hama Soul

This flexible wrought-gold belt or band looks like something that could be wrapped across the abdomen to magically hold a baby in the womb. I don't suggest that this item was used that way, but the 'bands of gold and silver' used by the Goddesses in the charms might look something like this.

There is a term *hamstolinn* or Hama-stolen, that is used to describe a person addled in their wits (de Vries p. 221). This can happen if the soul called Vörðr or Vårðr (warder), which can be the Hama or the Hugr soul, is traveling while the person is asleep and is prevented from returning before the person awakens. Being deprived of these souls will seriously affect a person's wits and behavior. But I suspect the term *hamstolinn* might also be used if a baby's Hama wanders away from the womb for long enough to hamper the baby's mental development.

One of the terms used in these spells for the Afterbirth-entity, the *bølen*, is intriguing. One meaning of this word must come from *bøl*, meaning evil, ill, harm or destruction, related to English 'baleful.' This clearly applies to the harmfulness of this entity when it gets loose. The Faroese dictionary lists another, very different set of meanings of this term which show the role of the Hama in gestation, as I understand it.

The word *bøla* means 'to make a nest or bed, to warm something, and to brood', as in a hen brooding her eggs or a mother animal curled around her young. This meaning must surely apply to the physical afterbirth, which comprises the placenta, umbilicus and other structures of the womb that protect and nourish the baby while it gestates. I think it also describes the role of the Hama in brooding the baby's Lich: the body-soul gestates the physical body within itself, condensing and ordering energy into matter. This idea is consistent with the belief, in modern energy-body theory, that energy bodies create and sustain the physical body, rather than the other way around. (For more discussion of these topics, see my article "The Kindly Gods Go Wandering.")

The Hama as Healer

It is not only during gestation that the Hama can guide the physical body in its growth. There is a very interesting anecdote in the Icelandic *Laxdæla Saga* (ch. 48, 49) that exemplifies the importance of the link between the Hama and the Lich. A man called An the Black was sleeping, along with his companions, on the night before a deadly attack was planned. An was extremely restless during his sleep so his comrades woke him, whereupon he related his nightmare to them. A horrible old woman with a huge knife had dragged him to the edge of his bed, slit his gut and pulled out his entrails, and stuffed brushwood into their place. She left, carrying a wooden trough with her.

An's comrades thought this hilarious and nicknamed him An Brushwood-belly, but An had the last laugh. The following day most of his comrades were killed, and An himself was taken up for dead, having been disemboweled during the skirmish.

During the wake for the dead the following night, An severely startled everyone by sitting up and announcing

The Hama Soul

that he felt much better. He said that he had actually been aware during most of the time since his injury, but had briefly gone into a swoon, and during that time the old woman had returned to him, emptied the brushwood from his belly, and returned his entrails to their proper place. An Brushwood-belly made a full and rapid recovery, an astonishing outcome for someone who had been disemboweled.

My understanding of this event is that the old woman, surely An's Dis (a female ancestral spirit), foresaw that An's injury was wyrded for the following day. Foresight is a function fully consistent with many tales of the Disir and Fylgjur. She took action to save her kinsman by operating on An's Hama, removing his Hama's entrails, and keeping them safe from injury in her wooden trough. When his physical entrails were damaged, apparently beyond repair, she returned the unharmed Hama-entrails to his Hama. An's Hama, restored to health, was then powerful enough to heal his Lich from the deadly wound.

Another mention of a similar phenomenon, lacking any detail in the account I read, said that a sick person's 'soul' (read Hama) would wash itself during a dream, and the sick person would then be restored to health (Chesnutt p. 155). Modern energy-healing techniques operate on a similar understanding about the role of our energy bodies in illness and healing.

The Hama After Death

Here is my understanding of what happens to the Hama when our Lich dies. Under normal circumstances, the Hama is closely linked to the body both during life and after death. If the body is cremated, then the Hama dissolves and its energy returns to the ambient pool of natural energies. If the body goes through the process of decomposition, then the Hama's energy gradually decomposes along with the flesh, but some of the energy will remain as the 'soul of the bones.' Some necromantic and shamanic practices make use of this soul-energy lingering in the bones of people, and of animals.

However, just as can occur with the Hama in the womb before birth, the Hama after death can occasionally roam abroad and cause harm. In Norse sagas and folklore, one often reads creepy tales of the *draugr*, a re-animated corpse that has supernatural strength and endurance, usually a savage, ferocious, but otherwise pretty mindless character. Sometimes the draugr remains in its burial mound, defending its burial treasures from those who seek to steal them. Other times the draugr will roam the neighborhood where it once dwelt, harassing and frightening its former kin and neighbors, sometimes even killing them.

Sometimes, in the tales, a draugr is created by necromantic practices, but more commonly it comes into being because the person during life had a very strong and malignant Will, focused on greed, malice and revenge. This Will can sometimes be strong enough to re-attach Hama to Lich after they have separated in death, so as to continue the person's desired assault on their community. Occasionally, there are instances of more friendly or neutral draugrs. (Hilda Ellis (Davidson) *The Road to Hel* has many examples of draugrs and similar beings.)

It's my belief that the soul which re-animates the draugr is the Hama soul. Draugr-corpses usually show signs of morbidity in the tales, and in my view the actions and character of the draugrs show that their original Hama soul with its human qualities of speech, behavior, and good appearance, is also undergoing a process of rot and decomposition. As the draugr-corpse becomes more decomposed, so also its re-attached Hama soul becomes more and more incoherent and degraded, less human in any way, until at last the Hama and Lich can no longer function at all, and both of them fall apart.

I want to emphasize, for modern readers, that the likelihood of any of us becoming draugrs is vanishingly small! The normal course of events after death involves either a rapid return of our Hama-energy to the ambient pools of natural energy after cremation, or the quiet and peaceful process of natural decomposition in the grave.

Examples of Hama Words

The Faroese language, a descendant of Old Norse, has retained some interesting words and word-usages that relate to our subject here, many of which I don't find in other Scandinavian dictionaries. Most of these words refer to occult phenomena and magical practices, and it is useful to show them here in order to round out our understanding of the Hama as a multi-faceted soul. Interesting Faroese words are:

~*Hama* = "to conjure up something (esp. ghosts) in order to haunt someone." [Compare to the 'Afterbirth' and Bølen as used by sorcerers.]

~*Hamfarin* = "an ecstatic feeling of the glory of life." [Any ecstatic state is clearly soul-related.]

Heathen Soul Lore

~*Hamferth* = an absent person's form; seeing such a sight means that the person seen will die within a year. [Compare with the idea of the Fetch.] Note that the second part of the word, *ferth*, is related to *ferah*-words in other languages.

~*Hamfriðr* = having a handsome appearance. [Relating to the Litr.]

~*Hamskifti* (Hama-shifting) = (1) sloughing of skin (e.g. a snake); (2) transformation, change. [Relates to shapeshifting.]

~*Hamskiftur* (Hama-changed) = terror-stricken, paralyzed by terror. [Our Hama is subject to this damage as well as our Ghost-soul. But in this case, apparently some kind of substantial change occurs in the Hama itself, a phenomenon worthy of further exploration for soul lore and healing purposes.]

~*Hamskotin* (Hama-shot) = "as in another world," one's mind is elsewhere, amazed, preoccupied. Similar to some of the symptoms of 'elf-shot, hag-shot' in other Germanic cultures.

~*Hamur* = a sloughed skin, an item of clothing (archaic usage), or a ghost, apparition or specter. [Picture the Bølen and the Scinnhiw.]

Summary

Hama is a covering and a shape. It forms in the womb, with the womb itself providing a covering, and the Hama providing the shape for the infant. Hama is related to Hamingja, which is both a spirit-being, and the power of

The Hama Soul

luck that the spirit brings with it. It is associated with gestation and the structures of the womb. The Hama's power of shaping extends to its ability to heal the body and return it to its original shape and proper functions after injury.

Our Lich is our physical body, and our Lich-Hama or Lichama is our body ensouled with our Hama: our living, spirit-powered body. In my understanding, the three gifts given by Loðurr to Ask and Embla are the components of our Hama: the La, Læti, and Litr. La is the life-force of Hama, contained especially in the blood and warmth of the body, and in the hair. Læti is our speech and behavior, ability to move and take action, and our personal mannerisms. Litr is our spirit-infused appearance: not only our physical shape and traits, but the essence of all our souls that shines through our face, expressions, movements, and our whole appearance. It is the power of our presence.

Together, these qualities give us each a personal identity, and the ability to recognize each other as individuals. These gifts also enable the behaviors and abilities that make human social life possible. A strong Hama soul brings us luck and charisma, and smooths the path of life for us.

The Goddess Sif's long hair cloaks her beauty and shows the power of her Hama. When Loki cut off her hair and damaged her beauty, her Hama and her luck were damaged by this malicious act as well. Sif's Hama-power was restored when the Dwarves made magical, living hair of gold to replace what had been stolen.

("Sif" by John Charles Dollman.)

Aldr, Orlay and Werold

Chapter 7

7. Aldr and Orlay: Weaving a World

These maids shape / make people's aldrs (skapa mönnum aldr); we call them Norns. (Gylfaginning in the prose Edda.)

Then came three Gods, potent and loving Æsir from their homes. They found on land Askr and Embla, capable of little, ørlög-less. (Völuspá vs. 17, Poetic Edda.)

Urðr one is called, Verðandi another – scoring the tines – Skuld the third. There they lay laws, there they choose life for Aldar-children, speak ørlög. (Völuspá vs. 20, Poetic Edda.)

The wise lack for little: now Oðrœrir has come up to the rim of Aldar Ve. (Havamal vs. 107 (106 in translation), Poetic Edda.)

(All are my translations.)

With the Aldr soul we are dealing with some very large themes. Aldr is our interface between Time and Eternity, between our Midgard lives and deeds, and the work of the Norns who weave the strands of orlay and wyrd into the fabric of the Worlds. Aldr defines our mortality and the parameters of our humanity, and ties us to the power and poignant beauty of the tides of time as they wash over our beloved Midgard, bringing everything with them, taking everything away, eternally changing, always renewed.

In previous chapters I wrote of the Ferah soul, born of trees and thunder, and the gifts given by Odin and his kin: the souls called Ahma and Ghost, the capacity for divine inspiration and ecstasy called Wode or Óðr, and the La, Læti, and Litr, which in my understanding comprise our human Hama, our shape-soul.

Now we come to our Aldr Soul and the cocoon or hama that it weaves for itself: the personal Werold or World that defines the circumstances of each of our lives. This is the last of the souls that are given by the Holy Ones at the mythical moment in time, as described in the *Völuspá*, when pre-humans were transformed into fully human beings, or the moment when the Gods transformed trees or non-human substance into humans, however one understands this event.

While Thor and the Goddesses and Gods of Earth and Sky are the patrons of the Ferah soul, and Odin and his brothers give us Ǫnd / Ahma, Ghost and Hama Souls, it is the Norns who give the gift of our Aldr Soul. This is made clear in the passage quoted above from *Gylfaginning*: we are told that the Norns shape people's Aldrs.

The verb used here is *skapa*; it means not only to shape but to make or create something. This and the related words in the other Germanic languages were used to translate the Judeo-Christian myths about the creation of the world and human beings into Old Norse and Old English. Interestingly, the same words also mean fate and destiny, linking us again with the Norns.

The verses quoted above from the *Völuspá* tell us first that Odin and his kinsmen encountered two trees, or beings with the names of trees, on land near the sea, and then list the things which they lacked. The passages go on to tell us that the three Gods gave Ask and Embla everything they were listed as lacking, except for one thing: ørlög or orlay, roughly translated as 'fate'. The verses immediately following in the *Voluspá* then go on to tell us about the Tree, the lake which stands under the Tree, and the three wise maidens who live there, who are understood to be the Norns. Then their gifts to humans are somewhat obscurely mentioned: the laws they lay, scoring on slips of wood (perhaps these are runes), the lives they choose, the ørlög they speak for the children of Aldr.

Frey's messenger Skirnir, in the *Skirnismal* poem of the Poetic Edda, was surely referring to these actions of the Norns in his dialog with the giantess Gerda's watchman. When Skirnir arrives on Gerda's land, the watchman is astounded at his presumption and wonders whether he is fey (doomed) or dead already, that he would risk his life there. Skirnir calmly tells him that "in one day was my Aldr shaped, and all my life laid down" (vs. 13). He means that his wyrd is what it is; he does not fear threats because he cannot change his wyrd. He acts as his duty lays out, and his death will come when it comes.

There is a balance between verse 17 of the *Völuspá*, which tells us that the trees / Askr and Embla were "without ørlög", and verse 20 about the Norns which imply that these beings are involved in some way with the gifts of ørlög, wyrd, fate, destiny to the children of Aldr: human beings. It is clear in the *Völuspá* verses that the original lack of ørlög/orlay in Askr and Embla meant that they were not truly human, not in possession of human lives and the metaphysical power that such lives should command. I will return to the subject of orlay and its relation to human-ness later on, but first want to explore the Aldr soul.

Nourisher and Life-Span

Aldr in Old Norse and Gothic means 'age', both a person's age and an age of time, and lifetime, life-span or generation. *Aldar* in Old Saxon also means age and life-span, as does Anglo-Saxon *ealdor*. Old Saxon *eldi* means 'people' and *eldibarn* means 'human beings.' Anglo-Saxon *ealdor* also means an elder or noble person, but most significantly here it means 'life, vital part.'

These words also are used to mean 'forever, eternity.' ON *aldr-lag*, OS *aldar-lagu*, and AS *ealdorlegu* all mean 'destiny, death'. Death is what the Aldr-soul 'lays' or 'sets down' for us at the fated time, the end of our life-span. Another translation for this term is 'specified time (duration) of life', and the Old Saxon dictionary links it with the modern German word *Lage* ('what is laid, layer') meaning 'situation, place, condition'. Here we see again words meaning 'layers, lay down,' as we do with ørlög, the 'primal layers'. These 'layers' refer back to the actions of the Norns who lay laws as layers of fate in the Well, and plaster layers of mud upon the World-Tree to nourish it. (*Gylfaginning* in the prose Edda, p. 19.) Their actions of laying various layers influence the situations and conditions of our lives.

The word *Aldr* comes from the Proto-Indo-European root **al* = to nourish, related to *alan*, with the same meaning, a word found in Gothic, Anglo-Saxon and other Germanic languages. **Al* is also the root for words relating to age in the various Germanic languages, including English 'old.' The connection between nourishment and age is clear, especially when we think about the circumstances during

Aldr, Orlay and Werold

the millennia of human existence, when the availability of food, or lack of it, determined a person's health and longevity. Aldr nourishes our souls and body so we are able to achieve a long life-span.

There is a lovely term for the World Tree Yggdrasil in verse 57 (Jonsson's Old Norse Poetic Edda) of the *Völuspá:* it is called *Aldrnara*, which I interpret as being the 'nourisher of the Aldr', the soul which itself nourishes life. Some translators present this term as the *Eldrnara*, the 'nourisher of the fire', since this verse is describing the events of Ragnarök and the burning of the World Tree. Jonsson interprets this term as referring to the fire itself as the 'life-nourisher' (p. 18), which I find a bit forced, given the context here of a world-destroying conflagration.

I incline toward Simrock's translation of *Aldrnara* as the 'all-nourishing World-Tree' (*allnährenden Weltbaum*, vs. 56). The World-Tree is the supporter of all life, rooted in the Well whence the Norns draw life-nourishing water and mud to sustain it, and shelters the Norns and the life-giving Gods. Under the Tree is the home of the Norns, who 'shape Aldr' for *Aldar beornum*, the 'children of Aldr / humankind'. Aldrnara / life-nourisher seems a most fitting name for this great, world-supporting Tree.

The idea of nourishment holds as much relevance to a person's non-physical or metaphysical health as it does to one's physical health and ability to reach old age. Among the most important functions of our souls is the ability to absorb, metabolize and transport subtle energy throughout our body-soul system. I believe that our various souls work with energy from various levels or frequencies, and that the Aldr and Ferah souls process energy very close to the physical spectrum. As I will show here, a primary function of the Aldr soul is to nourish and support our physical life and all the achievements and experiences of this life.

To be designated as a full-blown soul, the Aldr must fit into one or more of the three criteria that I identified in Chapter 1: 1) a life-soul which confers physical life by its presence and whose absence means immediate physical death; 2) a wander-soul or shape-soul which can temporarily leave the body during life and act as an independent entity without the body; and / or 3) an entity which has an independent, self-contained afterlife. According to my understanding, the Aldr is a soul based on the first criterion: its presence is necessary for physical life, and its absence means imminent death. Farther on I will also discuss my thoughts about whether the Aldr has an independent afterlife.

The Anglo-Saxon language offers some useful words for understanding Aldr / Ealdor: there is a word for the physical body, *ealdorgeard*, which means 'yard or enclosure of the ealdor / aldr.' One of the words for 'murderer' or 'killer' in Anglo-Saxon is *ealdorbana* or Aldr-bane. These words give us a picture of the physical body as an enclosure which contains and protects the Aldr. Someone who breaks in and destroys this enclosure is the bane or murderer of this soul, allowing the Aldr to spill out of its protected boundary and be lost.

Lines 55-6 of the poem *Beowulf* tell us, concerning Beowulf's father: *fæder ellor hwearf, aldor of earde*; that is, his father had died and his Aldr was "elsewhere gone, Aldr (away) from the Earth." Toward the end of the poem, Beowulf's Aldr departed, that is, he died (l. 2624). The absence of the Aldr on earth indicates that death has occurred.

The function of the Aldr as a life-soul shows clearly in other expressions from *Beowulf*, for example in line 2599 where Beowulf's companions fled in terror from the dragon in order to protect their Aldrs (*ealdre burgon*). During his fight with Grendel, Beowulf sought to rob Grendel of his Aldr (*aldre beneotan*, l. 680). There is a parallel expression in the *Reginsmal* poem of the Poetic Edda, where the sons of Hunding are described as Eylimi's "Aldr-snatchers" (*aldrs synjuðu*, l. 15), that is, his killers. The relatively physical nature of the Aldr shows up in a dramatic scene in *Beowulf*, where a Geatish spearman shot at a sea-serpent and the spear actually "stood in the aldr" of the sea-serpent (*him on aldre stod*, ll. 1433-5).

A Greek Soul-Cognate: the Aion

Pre-Classical Homeric Greek ideas about multiple souls show some fascinating parallels with Germanic concepts, although by several centuries later, moving into the classical period of Greece and the philosophies of Plato and Aristotle, concepts about the soul had greatly changed. There are several archaic Greek (Homeric period) concepts of souls which have particularly close and clear cognates with Germanic souls; one of them is the *Aion* which parallels the Aldr.

One of the most striking parallels between Aion and Aldr is that they both began with meanings concerning both life-force and the related aspects of a person's age and span of life. Then, both eventually lost the sense of 'life-force' and became solely related to time: the age of a person, an age of time, everlasting, eternity. We can see the parallel usage in the final words of the Christian Lord's Prayer ("for ever and ever") in the different languages: in Greek it is "from aion to aion," in Anglo-Saxon, "from ealdre to ealdre."

The word and concept of 'Aeon' is an important one in Gnostic philosophy, which reaches back into pre-Christian or early Christian times and continues today, and also in the writings of the great psychologist, C.G. Jung. To them, Aeon is 1) an age of time, 2) a finite, created world (both inner and outer), and 3) the godly spirit indwelling or embodying that time and world. As we shall see here, these meanings overlap very interestingly with Germanic Aldr and Werold.

The Greek word *aion* derives from Proto-Indo-European **ayu* or **yu*, meaning 'life force, vitality, vital force of animated beings'. It is related to other Greek words: *aiolos* = 'nimble, changeful of hue,' and *aiollein* = 'to shift rapidly to and fro'. (Claus p. 12.) These words suggest the fluttering, pulsating energy of the human aura, which constantly changes color, shape and size in response to thoughts, emotions, and other internal and external influences. Understanding a little more about the Aion soul reinforces some of the understandings about the Aldr.

The Greek Aion shows itself as a life-soul in many instances in the Homeric poems where it leaves a person at death, and its going equates to loss of life. In the *Iliad*, the Greek Achilles speaks of a dead warrior, fearing that flies, worms and rot will enter the corpse "now that the aion is slain therefrom." (Onians p. 200). Clearly, it was understood that the presence of the Aion preserves the living integrity of the body, while its loss leads to corruption.

Its quasi-physical nature shows up in a hymn to the God Hermes, describing him slaughtering his sacred cattle whom he "pierced in their aiones" (Onians p. 205): here he can fairly be called an Ealdorbana, an Aldr-bane! This usage is identical to the line in *Beowulf* I mentioned above, where the spear thrown by a warrior 'stood in the Aldr' of the sea-serpent.

The Footholds of the Aldr / Aion

Aion is 'shed' as tears, sweat, semen, and cerebrospinal fluid (Claus p. 13, Onians p. 201ff). Hippocrates, the famous Greek physician known as 'the father of medicine,' and others referred to spinal marrow as *aion* (Onians p. 206). Some modern scholars think that Homeric Greeks believed Aion is actually marrow, or dwells in the marrow, or is otherwise related to marrow and to certain bodily fluids. Fluids must be held in some kind of container in order not to be lost, hence the Ealdorgeard or Ealdor-yard, the place where these Aldr-containing fluids are held and protected.

This still-living plane tree, on the Greek island of Kos, is said to be the tree under which the physician Hippocrates taught (460-375 BCE). However old this tree actually is, it is certainly an exemplar of an Aeon, a great age of time!

The Aion as marrow reminds me of an Old High German healing charm which commands "the Worm and nine grandchildren-worms" to crawl out from the marrow, through the veins, flesh, skin, and into an arrow, which I assume was held so as to prick the skin as the charm was chanted. (Barber p. 83 & note p. 158.) Presumably, once the worms had crawled into the arrow, the arrow would be shot far away where it could do no more harm. The 'worms' (in a shamanic sense these are energy intrusions, in a scientific sense they act as germs or viruses) are considered the cause of pain and illness, affecting the Aldr soul and through it the body. They are laired in the marrow where the Aldr / life-force is strongest and their effects most severe.

In my understanding, our souls have what I call footholds in our physical body and its life-processes: places where that soul interfaces most powerfully with our physical life. Aldr's foothold lies in our bone marrow and in the many fluids of our body, which are held within the body by our Ealdoryard, the Aldr's boundary that coincides with our physical exterior.

Many of our body fluids are regulated by cycles of time: the rise and fall in levels of hormones, neurotransmitters, digestive, reproductive, immune-related fluids, the fluids that bathe our brain, spinal column and bone marrow, and many others, influenced by diurnal, lunar and seasonal cycles and by our age and stage of life. These are among the means by which Aldr influences our physical body and our body-in-time; they are Aldr's foothold in our body. The fluids ruled by Aldr symbolically mirror Aldr's source in the waters of the Norns' Well.

Aldr-Wita: Holistic Health Practice

India is still home to a form of health practice that is one of the oldest recorded medical practices in the world, called Ayurveda. The term itself is very telling: *Ayu* means 'life-span, life force'. The word root is the same as that of aion: *ayu* / *yu* = 'life-force, vitality, vital force'. *Veda* means 'knowledge, science' in Sanskrit. It is directly cognate with Anglo-Saxon *wita* = knowledge and Old Norse *vit* = consciousness, intelligence, knowledge, etc.

Thus, Ayurveda means "science / knowledge of the life-span, life-force". This connects directly with Aldr as 'life-span, life force." Whether or not our elder kin actually used the term *Aldr-wita*, it would be a perfect word for modern Heathens to use to indicate a Heathen perspective and practice of holistic health and healing. And there is, I believe, much we could learn from the ancient Indian practice, some of which goes back to prehistory and times when the Indo-European groups were still in contact with each other.

An Ayurvedic practitioner in India is known as a *Vaidya*, 'one who knows.' This is cognate to the Anglo-Saxon *witega* (m) and *witegestre* (f), terms for wise people, counselors, elders; and also the Old Norse *vitki*, a wizard. 'Wizard' itself is a related term. So a nice title for a practitioner of Aldr-wita would be an *Aldr-witega* (WIT-eh-gah) or *Aldr-vitki* for a man, *Aldr-witegestre* or *Aldr-witegess* (WIT-eh-guess, being easier to pronounce), or *Aldr-vitka* for a woman. Or, for that matter, they could be called Aldr-wizards!

Another nice term for modern use is *Alveig* for a health-giving potion, whether herbal or rune-magical. The word *al-veig* means 'nourishing drink'. The practice of noble women giving nourishing and magical drinks is very widespread in the Old Norse lore, including especially the drink filled with magical power that Sigrdrifa gave to Sigurd in the *Lay of Sigdrifa* in the Poetic Edda. Our modern Aldr-wizards can prepare an alveig to strengthen and heal the Aldrs of those they are helping.

Rig-Heimdal enhances the Aldrs of the great-grandparents. Here, he appears to be empowering the alveig in the kettle. (W.G. Collingwood, artist.)

In the *Rigsthula* of the Old Norse Poetic Edda, we see a fine example of a Heathen Aldr-wizard. It tells how the Heathen God Heimdal, in his guise as the wandering teacher and progenitor Rig, taught his grandson Konr about *ævinrunar ok aldrrunar*, runes of eternity and runes of the Aldr. The verses go on to say that Konr could, among other things, help in childbirth, deaden sword blades, quiet the ocean, quench fires, soothe and comfort men, allay sorrow. Konr himself had the strength and vigor of eight men, showing his powerful Aldr. (*Rigsthula* vs. 43-44, in the Poetic Edda.)

One of the most interesting things about these verses, to me, is the pairing of *ævinrunar*, 'everlasting-runes' with *aldrrunar*. I mentioned earlier that I see parallels between the Greek aion and Germanic Aldr souls. Greek *aion*, which evolved to mean 'an age of time,' and is used in the sense of 'forever,' is linguistically related to Gothic and Proto-Germanic *aiw* and *aiws*, meaning 'ever, age, eternity, an age, the age of the world.' From these words evolved ON *ævin*, along with English 'ever' and German *ewig*, meaning eternal, forever.

The Rigsthula verse links *aevin* and Aldr together, in the same way that the meaning of the Greek word evolved. It links the Aldr soul, the life-force that represents humanity and the human life-span, with the concept of eternity or everlastingness. The poem tells us that Heimdal-Rig has power over these mysterious runes, that he taught them to Konr, and that Konr developed them further on his own, to the point where he outdid his divine grandfather in skill (v. 45).

To me, these are important verses for understanding the Aldr and the art of Aldr-wita. Konr was able to use Aldr-runes to protect people from Aldr-banes, things that would otherwise shorten the lifespan or make a person's life unhealthy from a holistic, soul-deep perspective of health. By helping in childbirth, and counteracting the dangers of sword blades, fire, and ocean, he extended people's lives. By soothing anger, frustration, sorrow, grief, and distress he removed the kind of stress that brings on heart disease, depression, anxiety, and other states that afflict people's health and life-span.

With regard to the ancient Greek Aion, the poet Homer often described a person's tears of grief, yearning, and despair as the outflow of the life-soul Aion itself: tears were the actual physical expression of Aion. Following the analogous nature of Aion and Aldr, we can assume that grief and related emotions actually cause a slow, creeping loss of the Aldr-soul, showing the great importance and need for methods of emotional as well as physical healing in order to keep our Aldr hale.

Although I don't know which runes Konr used for his Aldr-wita work, there are a few that especially stand out as related to the Aldr and Aldr-wita. One is Raidho, relating to rhythm and the movements of time, things coming about at the suitable or wyrded time, step by step, stage by stage in our lives. Another is Perthro, representing the Well of Wyrd and the 'lots' or portions of fate dealt out to us by the Norns.

Jera governs the harvest, again related to time and the events in time which bring about other events, leading to harvest and to the growth of our Werold. One of the forms of the Jera rune, a diamond crossed by a vertical line, looks like thread spun onto a spool, resembling the image of the Aldr spinning our Werold around us. (See discussion of the Werold, below.) Finally, Uruz is considered an important rune for healers, with the mighty aurochs representing the life-force within us, fiercely defending its territory, its Ealdorgeard or Aldr-yard. A little meditation will show that there are other runes as well, with more subtle connections to Aldr and Aldr-wita.

Aldr and Orlay

Orlay (Anglo-Saxon) or ørlög (Old Norse) is a large and complex subject which has been worthily discussed by many modern Heathen writers. Many, myself included, have been influenced by Paul Bauschatz' brilliant book *The Well and the Tree: World and Time in Early Germanic Culture*, a doctoral dissertation that examines the early Germanic concepts of time and fate, with special focus on the *Beowulf* poem.

In his chapter "Action, Space, and Time" Bauschatz discusses the roots of the word ørlög: *ør* or *ur* meaning 'primal, first, original,' and *lag* meaning both 'law' and

Aldr, Orlay and Werold

'layer.' Law, both mundane and metaphysical, is that which was laid down by past actions; it accretes in layers like the geological strata of sedimentary rocks, and forms the foundations for that which is now coming into being. Thus, in the *Völuspá* passage quoted at the beginning of this chapter, we see the Norns 'laying laws,' bringing the present into being out of the layers of the past.

Bauschatz uses the imagery of the Well and the Tree to picture how life is lived within the space-fabric of the Tree. Humans, living in Midgard upon the Tree, enact deeds which form like dew and drip down toward the Well below, the fabric of time. Insignificant deeds and events fall outside the rim of the Well and are gone, while significant ones fall into the Well itself and form the basis of ørlög. In turn, water / ørlög from the Well is sucked into the roots of the Tree to nurture new layers of deeds in the life and worlds of the Tree. The Tree and all it carries builds up in rings through this nourishing action: thus ørlög underlies the structure of space-time. Bringing this perspective to my view of the Aldr-soul: as the Norns nourish the Tree with water and mud from the Well, so our Aldr, the gift of the Norns, both nourishes and is nourished by our deeds and orlay.

Bauschatz also uses the image of constriction and containment of a spring or well-structure, which encloses the water and forces it powerfully upward instead of letting it spread out weakly as a thin flood of water over the landscape. This illustrates the actions of constraint, necessity and ørlög in powering the heroic life. His vision of ørlög is much more profound than that which regards ørlög simply as fate, or even as a Heathen equivalent of Karma, though the latter is also a useful view in some contexts.

Heathen Soul Lore

There isn't space here to go into a lot of detail about ørlög, but I need to note why it is important in the makeup of the human 'soular system' and why I think it is the link between the actions of the Gods and those of the Norns in the mythic deed of bringing humans, Aldr-bairns, into being. To me, it's very significant that verse 17 of the *Völuspá* says that Askr and Embla, before the Gods' gifts, were without ørlög.

Wooden carving of Ask and Embla: at first they are without ørlög. As the Norns carve on slips of wood, they shape the Aldrs of humankind.

I see this on two levels. One is that they, as individuals, lacked the driving and shaping force of orlay. It would be lovely to think of ourselves as completely free to do and be as we wish during every minute of our lives, but this is not the Heathen heroic vision. Ancient Heathen philosophy / world-view saw people as being constrained by many things: their own past history, their kindred's history, circumstances and deeds, their social position, gender, and duties, the decrees of the Norns, the death that awaited them and the name they wished to leave after them.

Aldr, Orlay and Werold

In fact, the greater and more heroic a person, the more severe these constraints were. It was, indeed, the pressure of these constraints that drove people to heroic deeds, or to despicable ones, depending on their character. "Necessity is the mother of invention"; it is the goad of difficult circumstances that drives one to rise above them. When everything is easy, we often don't accomplish all that much.

In all of this we see the action of the Nauthiz rune, a primal container for the active force of orlay, as the Perthro rune is a container for the wyrd set in motion by that force. The Anglo-Saxon Rune Poem tells us that Need / Nauthiz is a constriction or constraint on the breast (where most of the souls are housed), but becomes a help to us if we heed it at the right time. Thus, when Askr and Embla had no ørlög, we can understand that they were in a pre-human state of primal innocence, unshaped, unconstrained, not answerable for themselves.

Another level of orlay that I see is in the metaphysical definition of a species. Each species has its own orlay. As well as individual orlay, humans have the 'orlay of being human' as an important shaping factor. At the moment of conception, the fetus is already genetically determined as a human, or a cat or eagle or bull. This is the first layer of our orlay, and it shapes all the rest that come after. Before the Gods gifted Askr and Embla, or pre-humans, with human souls, there was no human species in the sense of modern *homo sapiens*. For those who don't believe in the existence of souls, the previous sentence is nonsense. For those who do, it points to the essence, quite literally, of our human-ness.

With the gift of the Norns, Askr and Embla first became *aldar-beornum, eldi-barn,* children of Aldr, the term most often used in the lore to indicate a human being. In the

Old Norse lore, the word 'man (person)' can indicate not only a human man or woman, but also a giant, God, dwarf, or other sentient being, but 'Aldi-barn' or 'child of Aldr', always means specifically a human being.

Although the Hama soul gives each being its characteristic shape, I see the Aldr soul as being the metaphysical link between an individual and the species it belongs to, each species having its own characteristic Aldr, its own unique expression of the life-force. Our human Aldr contains within it both the potential and the constraints of our species as well as of ourselves as individuals. For example, we humans cannot naturally fly nor live underwater, but we have the inborn capacity for complex language and reasoning.

Werold: Our World as Aldr's Soul-Skin

Our word 'world' comes from the Anglo-Saxon *wer-old* or *wer-eld*, meaning 'man-age'. The same word was used in Old Saxon, and Old Norse had an equivalent word, probably borrowed from Anglo-Saxon: *ver-aldr*. Werold was used in a very personal way in these old languages. To us, the world is 'everything out there', but to our elder kin, each person had a world, their own world. The Old Saxon *Heliand* offers many examples of this personal use of *werold*. The poet said that John the Baptist would never taste wine 'in his weroldi' (l. 127). Mary said that she had never 'in my weroldi' been with a man (l. 272-3). An old widow was 'four and eighty winters in her weroldi' (l. 513-4).

A more modern example of this ancient usage appears in the writings of the Anglo-Saxon scholar J.R.R. Tolkien. He wrote of King Aragorn telling his wife Arwen, when his death was approaching, that "my world is fading."

Aldr, Orlay and Werold

(*The Return of the King*, App. A(v), "The Tale of Aragorn and Arwen".) Even though Aragorn's health, strength, and kingly honors were still with him, he could tell it was time for him to go (the choice was his) because he perceived his Werold fading.

When the aged Beowulf set out to face the dragon, he did not know how his *worulde-gedæl* would come about (l. 3068). This phrase is strong poetry, because it holds a powerful double meaning. *Gedæl*, on the one hand, means 'separation, cutting off'. The audience, familiar with the tale, knows that Beowulf's world will be cut off, come to an end, he will be killed by the dragon. The word *gedæl* or *gedal* is often used poetically as a synonym for death-orlay, the timing and nature of one's death, the blow of fate that is dealt by Wyrd or the Norns.

Gedæl, in second meaning, is like our modern English 'to deal'; it refers to the fate or wyrd that is dealt out to a person and brings about the moment of death, the end of their world. In parallel phrasing, the poet speaks of the monster Grendel's death as his *aldor-gedal* (*Beowulf* l. 805), showing the connection between werold and Aldr: both are subject to the fate dealt out by Wyrd. Gedael is thus dealt to us at the beginning of life, setting wyrd in motion, and cuts off our Aldr at the end of life when our wyrd finally comes due.

It is clear, when reading how werold was used in context, that it referred to the space-time each person occupies and shapes during their lifetime. Their world was measured in years and characterized by the events, deeds and experiences that shaped their lives. Another way to understand this is to recognize Aldr as the soul which can see and grasp our life as a whole, our past, present, and possible futures in this world of Midgard: the soul which gives meaning and power to this life-span, this Werold.

Aldr is our body-in-time, as our Lich-Hama, our living body ensouled with Hama, is our body-in-space. Remember how I wrote at the beginning of this chapter that the Norns 'shape' orlay. Orlay itself gives a person 'shape' within the dimensions of Time and Wyrd. 'Shape' is a concept relating to Space, but its analog within Time is 'continuity'. Orlay provides continuity: the deeds which inevitably lead to other deeds, events leading to other events; the webs of fate co-woven by ourselves, the Norns, and others with whom we closely interact.

Because of ørlög, the human experience is not random; it is patterned. Events happen because other events happened, deeds build on deeds, and life builds on lives gone by. Each lays down layers in the Well of Wyrd, which together with the World-Tree forms the fabric of Space-Time. Orlay anchors us in Time, as our body anchors us in Space, and the web that is woven to hold us in Time is our own Werold.

In the previous chapter, I wrote about my idea that some of our souls have their own soul-skin, their hama or covering. I believe that our Aldr soul has its own soul-skin or spiritually-tangible shape, and that this is our Werold, our personal world that we create through the process of living our life. I envision the Aldr as being like a caterpillar and the Werold as the cocoon it slowly spins, using the years and events of our lives. In the end we shall each have a soul-garment to show as proof of how we lived our lives. We can think of it as a great tapestry that we weave and embroider throughout our lives, picturing all we have done and experienced. What does your tapestry look like? What do you want it to look like?

Godly Patrons of Aldr

There are several Holy Ones who are closely associated with the Aldr. I've discussed the Norns' role at length here: they are the actual bestowers of our Aldr. A beautifully-expressed example of their actions appears at the beginning of the *First Lay of Helgi Hundingsbane* in the Poetic Edda. It speaks in dramatic tones of the circumstances surrounding Helgi's birth, with eagles shrieking and sacred waters pouring down. The Norns arrive and "shape his aldr" as a hero and chieftain, "twining with great power the ørlög-strands". The Norns secured these strands in the east, west, and north, establishing the lands that Helgi would rule (Verses 2-4).

Three Norns bestowing a baby's Aldr.

Aldr, ørlög, fate, destiny, life-span, circumstances of life and death: together they are all associated with the Norns throughout the lore and the experiences of Heathens, past and present. We see this also in folklore and fairy tales from all the Germanic countries, in the tales of fairy godmothers and the fateful gifts (and curses) they give to newborn children. Fairy godmothers are the latter-day guises of the Norns of old. See Grimm's good discussion of the Norns for more (vol. 1, pp. 405 and following). Grimm mentions a folk belief that babies come from *Frau Hollen Teich*, the pond or well of Frau Holle, a German Goddess: another echo of the Norns, their Well, and their gifts of soul and fate (Grimm vol. 4, p. 1368).

Another patron for the Aldr-soul is Heimdal-Rig. His role in this matter, as shown in *Rigsthula* (Poetic Edda), is to foster physical and cultural evolution of humans and human society, including the ability to live well and live long. I showed him and his grandson Konr as Aldr-wizards, above. We can add the Goddesses Eir and Idunn as matrons of Aldr, as well: Eir as the Healer-Goddess of Scandinavia, and Idunn as the one who, with her sacred apples, keeps the Aldrs of the Gods and Goddesses themselves young and hale.

Frey was known as Veraldr-God (*Ynglingasaga* and *Olafs Saga Tryggvasonar*, both in the Heimskringla). This title is often translated as "God of This-World." With a better understanding of the concept of Werold / Veraldr and the Aldr soul, we can see a lot of connection with Frey. First there is the connection between Aldr / *alan*, meaning 'to nourish', and Frey as the God of harvest and plenty, as well as a God of the great powers of nature that underlie fertility in all its forms.

Aldr, Orlay and Werold

Then, with the concept of Werold as the cocoon of life that is spun by our Aldr soul, we enter into the life that we each live and weave, every day. Frey is a God who has much to do with our everyday lives, a God who was and is prayed to for *ar ok fridhr*, harvest and peace, that we all desire. We each have our own Werold, and together they form collective Werolds of kin, groups, nations, species, the world as a whole.

Freyr, by Johannes Gehrts.

Frey is a great patron of frith, which means not only 'peace' but the whole fabric of trustworthy relationships that is woven and maintained between people and forms the basis of peaceful interaction. It is frith that weaves individual Werolds into collective ones that have strength and durability in space and time. Without frith, everyone's Werolds scatter in all directions, unconnected, or else form harmful, oppressive bonds that strangle people and groups.

Odin is called *Aldafaðir* or *Aldaföðr* in *Vafthrudnismal* of the Poetic Edda, vs. 53, which is translated as "father of men / mankind." As a patron of specific, individual souls, I see Odin as being more connected to our Ghost and Ahma. His role as Alda-father, as I see it, is more in the sense of his patronage of human beings, Aldr-bairns, as a whole. However, there is certainly a connection between Aldr-wita and Odin's healing power over injuries and illnesses of humans and animals.

To me, the connections between these Deities, in fact all our Deities, and our Aldr and Werold are significant and profound, and offer excellent seeds for Heathen meditation exercises.

The Afterlife of Aldr

Does the Aldr have an afterlife? I take three approaches to this question for each of the souls. 1) What can I find in the elder lore? 2) What makes sense based on the nature of the soul itself? 3) What can I discover about souls' afterlives through my own meditations and experiences? Here are my findings about the Aldr based on each of these approaches.

I find very little that would hint at an afterlife for Aldr in the elder lore. The little I've found is in *Beowulf*, some of which I've quoted above, to the effect that Beowulf's and his father's Aldr "went elsewhere, was gone from the earth." We must keep in mind that although the *Beowulf* poem is rooted in Heathen oral lore, it was composed in written form by a Christian and does show some Christian influence. If I had found any other hints along these lines in other lore, I'd consider a Heathen interpretation here, but so far I have not. As I will discuss farther on, I do believe that our Aldr-soul 'goes elsewhere' for a little while, but does not remain for long in its familiar form.

I was very intrigued when I came across a phrase in Old Norse, the verse from the *Havamal* that I quoted at the beginning of this chapter: "The wise lack for little: now Oðrœrir has come up to the rim of Aldar Ve." A *Ve* is a sanctuary, a temple or other sacred space, and here was a reference to the sacred space of the Aldr. The verse refers

Aldr, Orlay and Werold

to Odin's theft of the mead of poetry and wisdom, when he drank it out of the giant's vats, escaped, and flew back with it in eagle's form to Asgard. At first I thought that somewhere in the Asgard plane must be a holy afterlife place, a heaven, for the Aldr soul. After more thought, however, I realized that Aldar Ve must mean Midgard itself, the sacred enclosure of humankind and the life-force in all its forms. Odin brought the mead to Asgard, but he also gives a taste of the mead to the wise and poetic living human from time to time, thus bringing Oðrœrir to Aldar Ve.

So, much as I'd like to, I don't think this is evidence for an Aldr afterlife. Nevertheless, this is an important and beautiful image of Midgard as Aldar Ve: the sacred enclosure of the life-force that fills all mortal beings. On the world-level, this is the same idea as the Ealdorgeard or Ealdor-yard, our physical body which encloses our life-force soul, our Aldr. The Earth itself is Aldar Ve: the sacred enclosure of all mortal life, and deserves to be honored as such.

The nature of the Aldr is really rooted in Midgard life, in the vitality of the body and the mundane Werold our Aldr makes for us. This makes it more likely, based on its nature, that it does not long survive the end of physical Midgard life as an entity in itself. What would be its function, if it was no longer associated with a body and a Werold?

Aldr does have a function outside of Midgard: it feeds our deeds, as strands of orlay, back to the Norns for their action of weaving the ever-growing fabric of space and time. But Aldr performs this role specifically while living in Midgard. Midgard is Aldr's realm of action, the place where orlay, fate, wyrd play out in human lives, interacting with all other life forms, physical and spiritual. One of the profoundest insights I feel I've gained in studying and meditating on the Aldr-soul is the realization that our Aldr souls are active agents of the Norns in Midgard. Input, feedback, and throughput between the Norns and Midgard flow through the Aldr-soul dwelling within each of us, weaving the orlay of This-World.

There remains the connection between Aldr and Eternity, as I discussed earlier. This would seem to point toward an eternally-existing soul who does not die with the body. This interpretation, however, depends on what one understands by 'time and eternity.' Bauschatz and others have shown that Time, and hence Eternity, was understood quite differently by Pagan Germanic peoples, versus Christians and the Hellenistic philosophy that influenced them, and that influences us today.

This is a far larger subject than I can cover here, in a chapter already filled with complexity. But very briefly, for an ancient Heathen 'eternity' would have been more real in terms of the past, rather than the future. The past is real, it happened, and because significant deeds and events which have happened enter into the Well of Wyrd, they continue to influence the growth of the World Tree and the unfolding of space-time. They cannot be erased or undone: their influence is eternal in this sense, though their impact or outcome can sometimes be reshaped by new input. This understanding is embodied in this verse from the *Havamál* of the Poetic Edda:

> *Cattle die, kinsmen die, just so self will die.*
> *One thing I know that never dies:*
> *The doom of each dead person (domr of dauða hvern).*
> (my translation; vs. 76 in Jonsson, vs. 77 in Larrington.)

Aldr, Orlay and Werold

The term "doom / domr" here is often translated as 'reputation,' but 'doom' is really much more apt when we understand it properly. It means the judgement that is passed and spoken, and that cannot now be changed. It is the final word, spoken by the ultimate authority, on the life of a person. In the ancient lore, the Gods are often described sitting on their 'doom-stools,' their seats of judgement where they 'speak doom'. These seats are placed at the Well of Wyrd, in the presence of the Norns, under a root of Yggdrasil (see *Gylfaginning* in Edda, pp 17-18). What the Holy Ones speak here enters into the Well and thus becomes everlasting reality.

When 'doom' is translated as 'reputation' then we get the impression that each person's earthly reputation "never dies." While we may like to believe this is true, I think we're all clear that it is not! And I doubt that our ancient kin really believed this either, even though they too would have liked it to be true.

But this is not really what the verse says: it does not speak of our human, earthly reputation, which sooner or later will fade for almost all of us. It speaks, rather, of the judgement that the Holy Ones pronounce about us, about the way we have lived our lives and woven our Werold. This is the doom that lives on after us, and our hope and desire is that it is a worthy one, words spoken that reflect the Holy Ones' appreciation and even honoring of what we have done with our lives. (For an interesting discussion of one perspective on our souls and the doom-stead of the Gods, see Rydberg's chapters 69-75.)

After death, when our Werold is finished, I envision our Aldr soul dressed in its completed Werold-hama coming to the Well and the Doom-stead of the Gods. The 'doom' that is spoken here, I believe, is not so much a 'judgement' as we think of it today, influenced by Christian ideas of 'judgement day' resulting in eternal reward or punishment. What our Gods do at the Doom-stead is more a divine observation and acknowledgement of 'what is.' Our life and Werold are now complete: the lifetime achievement of our Aldr and of all our souls working together. Aldr comes to this Doom-stead to display to the Holy Ones what it and our other souls have achieved together, for the Holy Ones to observe, acknowledge, and hopefully to bless.

In my understanding, what the Norns and the Deities are doing here does not involve the 'damnation or salvation' of any of our souls. Rather, they are attending to the right functioning of cosmological processes, in particular the processes of wyrd and ørlög, which are the foundations of continuity in Time, and of the way that Time influences all life in Midgard. Our Aldr-souls, the Holy Ones, and especially the Norns, all participate in the process of weaving Time and Space together, maintaining the cosmological environment where Midgard life can thrive. This, I believe, is what is going on at the Doom-stead of the Gods and Norns.

Once the Gods' doom has been spoken, their acknowledgement of our Werold, Aldr says farewell to its soul-mothers, the Norns, and slips back into the Well from whence it came. There it dissolves and gives back all it created during life, as its Werold-hama gently spreads out to become another one of the endless layers of orlay within the Well. The words, the acknowledgement, the 'doom' or deeming of the Gods and Goddesses go with it, and fasten its load of orlay into the Well. Thus are the Well and the Tree,

Aldr, Orlay and Werold

Time and Space, enriched by each of us and our worthy lives.

The Norns attend to the right functioning of the cosmological process called ørlög: the basis for continuity in Time.

I think that Aldr has two connections to a Germanic conception of eternity. One is the doom that is spoken by the Holy Ones about one's life / Werold at the Well of Wyrd, which encapsulates that life and carries it into the ever-growing fabric of time and reality in the Well and the Tree. The other is that our Aldr, as I see it, connects us with our human species and with the life-force inherent in all beings in Midgard, which continues on after our individual death. Our individual Aldr / life-force arises out of the collective life-force, and sinks back into it at our death. The life-force itself is considered to be everlasting.

Summary

Our Aldr governs our life-span, and nourishes and protects our health in order to maximize the life-span. It is seated especially in our bone-marrow and the fluids of the body, contained within our Ealdor-yard, the physical boundary of our body. The spiritual nourishment Aldr draws in flows through these areas especially powerfully. Aldr is given to us by the Norns, along with our ørlög and wyrd, and it serves as an agent of the Norns in Midgard by feeding strands of ørlög back and forth between us in Midgard, and the Norns with their Well.

Aldr can be considered our 'body in time', as our Lich-Hama is our body in space. Instead of creating a physical shape or Lich-Hama in space, as Hama does, Aldr creates a 'time-shape', which is our Werold. Our Werold or 'world' is the totality of our deeds, experiences, thoughts, memories, years, that we weave thread by thread, day by day throughout our life. When our life is over, Aldr, dressed in its Werold-hama, proceeds to the Doom-stead of the Gods and Norns. There, our lifetime's experience and deeds, our Werold-tapestry, is observed and acknowledged by the Holy Ones, and, if deserved, is blessed and fastened into the Well of Wyrd, to become one more layer of All-That-Is upon the Tree of Worlds.

In Closing

Aldr seems to be a soul with few personal traits. Though it shapes our life-time, our Werold, it does not play a significant role in our personality, nor does it provide general capabilities such as thought, emotion or will, though it does communicate through intuition. Aldr sensitizes us to issues of timing in our lives: biological, social and spiritual aspects of Wyrd. It sets into motion physical changes such as puberty, menopause and aging. It gives us a sense of the right or wrong moment for our actions and words, sends us hunches or gut feelings about a wyrd-filled moment or opportunity.

Aldr gives us the capacity to sense Time itself, to understand and work with it, at least on a practical and everyday level. It enables us to view our own life-time as a whole: as a weaving that extends through time, where we can look backwards, and to some extent make projections forward in time, in our quest to understand and shape our Werold.

Aldr is our 'body in Time', as our Lich is our body in Space, and it governs our relationship with Time. In my understanding, Aldr does not survive for long as an entity after death, though some of the work it does during life returns to the Well and the Norns, and thus continues on past this life.

How do we connect with this soul, or shift into an awareness of it? Is there anything there to be consciously aware of, or is it simply an important but mechanical process: life force programmed to do its tasks by the Norns, by orlay and circumstance and biological imperative?

I can only answer these questions by reference to my own experience, which may be similar or different from the experiences of others. As with each of the Heathen souls I am writing about, once I learned about the Aldr soul I spent a lot of time looking within myself and back over my life, to see if I could identify traces and evidence of this soul in my own experience. Not surprisingly, with the Aldr and Werold this effort has brought many, many hours of life-review and coming to terms with orlay and wyrd in my life. But aside from my Werold, my Veraldr, I have perceived the Aldr-soul as a vague but aware entity within my 'soular system.'

Ever since early childhood I've had the eerie and beautiful experience, when the wind blows in a certain way, of perceiving the wind and the dust it carries as Time itself. I lived many years in Greece, during childhood and adulthood, and I would often think: "perhaps this dust blowing past was once a part of Socrates, or part of an ancient city or a temple." And the same in all of the other places I've lived and traveled....traces of time and history blow past us on subtle winds, everywhere we go. Even if we are not aware of this, our Aldr knows, and feels itself linked to others, Time, and World.

Aldr shows itself most of all, I believe, in the sense of ephemeral beauty and meaning we find in this ever-changing world, our feelings of nostalgia and surprise when we suddenly realize that time passes, that each moment we experience will never come again, and our knowledge that one day our own dear and unique life, our Werold, will be over. Our Aldr is the one who knows, on the profoundest level, that everything including itself passes.

The mature knowledge and acceptance of this forms the root of an inner philosophy and sense of poetry, expressed or unexpressed, that shapes a life of wisdom and meaning. Sometimes these insights can be so painful that we avoid thinking about them or allowing ourselves to experience them fully, but by doing so we miss out on a profound dimension of life and of our Werold. We thus fail to fully acknowledge and honor our Aldr in this world of Midgard.

Aldr, Orlay and Werold

Many forms of philosophy and religion, East and West, regard Truth, Beauty and Reality as being perfect, eternal and unchanging ideals. They urge us to turn away from fleeting and imperfect worldly phenomena and ponder eternal verities. Heathen philosophy, expressed among other ways as ancient poetry, celebrates the opposite: the wyrd-filled moment in time, never to come again; the powerful, cathartic sadness and longing when we think of time and change, and the deeply meaningful imperfections of all our striving and living in this world. Without this sense of ephemeral beauty, of the ever-changing tides of time, what would the poet sing, and how would our hearts answer?

Raddusch aurochs.

The Aurochs is steadfast and mightily horned,
A bold beast, it fights with its horns,
Famed strider on the moors: that is a mody wight!
(Anglo-Saxon Rune Poem: "Ur"; my translation.)

Chapter 8

8. Dances with Daemons: The Mod Soul

With discussion of the Aldr Soul in the previous chapter, I finished the list of souls which were given by the Powers of Earth and Sky, by Odin and his brothers, and by the Norns; the latter two as described in the *Voluspà* of the Poetic Edda. Now I will turn to two souls whose origins are less obviously divine, more earthly but also more mysterious in origin, and which are very active and powerful in our everyday, earthly lives: the Mod and Hugr Souls. (Note that Mod is pronounced "mode," and Hugr is "who-gr". The Hugr is covered in Chapters 9, 10 and 11.)

There is a great deal of overlap in the nature of these two souls, and in fact a good argument can be made that they are really one soul with two different names given by different branches of the Germanic peoples. I see both similarities and differences between Hugr and Mod; I will compare and contrast these two souls as I discuss their respective natures.

The Mod as an actual soul-being is not much developed in Gothic writings or in Old Norse lore; there, it appears primarily as an emotional state of anger, rage or fury, which can reach ecstatic levels similar to wode (see Chapter 5 for more about wode.) In Old Norse lore and folklore, in contrast, the Hugr stands out so strongly as a full-blown soul that some scholars have concluded it is the original, "pure" soul of Norse belief, before it was influenced by Christianity. On the other hand, the Hugr does not clearly appear as a full-blown soul in Anglo-Saxon belief at the time they became literate, while the Mod does so strongly.

In Old Saxon, both Mod and Hugi are strongly developed. In Old High German writings the word *mod* frequently appears; though its usage is often heavily influenced by Christian thought, there are still a number of instances useful for our explorations here. Thus, for discussion of the Mod as a human soul I rely primarily on Anglo-Saxon, Old Saxon and Old High German, but draw on Norse lore and folklore for some limited but important aspects of Mod's nature and evolution, as I shall show.

A fascinating idea is put forth by Meyer, and further discussed by Eggers, Becker and other academic scholars. According to some of these scholars (others debate the idea but are not convinced), and I agree, Mod seems to have begun as an undifferentiated natural power or energy and then gradually developed into a nature spirit, a *daemon* (Greek) or *genius* (Latin) that became associated with, and eventually incorporated into, the human "soular system." Daemons and geniuses refer to a guiding, protective, tutelary spirit that influences a human being. One of the most famous daemons is the one that guided the philosopher Socrates. Christians later turned "daemons" into "demons," who lead people astray through temptation and deception: here we see a form of detrimental rather than helpful guidance. Christians substituted guardian angels for the helpful function of daemons.

The Mod Soul

As I will show here, Mod appears in several forms. It is an individualized spirit / soul being, which I am calling the Mod with a capital M. It is also an undifferentiated force which permeates Nature, animals and humans, and can be drawn upon by the Gods and otherworldly beings, that is closely related to the form of power / energy called *megin* or *mægen*. Finally, it is a state of being similar to wode, involving any of the following: natural or supernatural strength, courage and determination; great intelligence and wisdom; battle rage; savagery, cruelty, vengefulness and capriciousness. The latter two forms of mod (undifferentiated force; state of being) I refer to with lower-case 'm,' and depend on context to differentiate them.

I am coining a word for modern Heathen use, namely *mody* (mode-ee) to translate the adjective / adverb made from Mod (*modig* / *modags*). It is used very frequently in the ancient languages, is a useful word, and saying "having a lot of mod, done in a mod-filled way" is awkward, especially when trying to translate poetry. Likewise, much meaning is lost if we try to use only one modern English word to translate *modig*, such as "courageous" or "angry", rather than leaving the deep and complex word 'mod' to stand on its own, untranslated. Hopefully after the explorations I present here, we will be able to take *mod* and *modig* on their own terms, without translation.

Basic Meanings

In 1926, Elisabeth Meyer published a very useful doctoral dissertation entitled *The Evolution of Meaning of Germ. *moda- (Die Bedeutungsentwicklung von Germ. *moda-)*, meticulously researched and thought-through, which was drawn on by many later scholars. She begins with a list of meanings of the word from both ancient and modern Germanic languages, according to various scholars in those languages, most of which I give here with the meanings translated into English and the terms for the languages (e.g. Old Icelandic instead of Old Norse) as given by Meyer. (A few of the words I was unable to translate.)

~ Gothic *moths* = fury, rage.

~ Old Icelandic *moðr* = wrath, moodiness, heart's grief, courage, fury.

~ Old Danish *mod* = mind, senses, *hu* (hugr, frequently used as synonym for mod).

~ Old Swedish *moð* = mind, senses, mind/senses in an uproar / disturbed; envy, pride, overconfidence.

~ Meanings in the modern Scandinavian languages include fury, courage, bravery, boldness, daring.

~ Anglo-Saxon *mod* = 1) the inner man, the spiritual as opposed to the bodily part of a man; 2) courage, high spirit, pride, arrogance; 3) greatness, magnificence, pride – applied to inanimate things.

~ Middle English *mod* = mood, mind, courage.

~ Old Saxon *mod* = mind, disposition, inner person, soulfulness, feeling, the inner person, heart, character, bold courage, the ability to enact one's intentions effectively.

The Mod Soul

~ Middle Low German *mot* = thinking, sensing, emotions, disposition.

~ Old High German *muot* = mind, soul, spirit, heart.

~ Middle High German *muot* and Middle Dutch *moet* = strength of thought, sensation, feeling, sentiment, will, senses, soul, spirit, mind, disposition, emotions, overconfidence, high spirits, longing, desiring, pondering a deed, decisiveness, courage, selfish, self-seeking, hopeful. (Note that if we look at kennings (synonyms) for the word *Hugr* in the *Skaldskarpamal* of the prose Edda, we will find most of the same words or very similar ones listed.)

~ Old and New Frisian *mod* = courage, mind, disposition, inner person, will, independence. (Meyer pp 9-10)

~ Note also the modern German descendants of mod: *Mut* (moot) meaning courage, bravery; and *Gemüt* meaning mind, disposition, inner person, soulfulness, feeling.

Meyer observed that other scholars drew these all together into a consolidated meaning of "strongly moved emotions / soul; high excitement / stimulation; stirred-up *Gemüt* / inner person; lively feelings." But her sense is that these meanings are too abstract to be completely true to the ancient Germanic culture and languages, and reflect more of a modern psychological understanding than of older, more concrete perceptions.

She emphasized the importance of looking at the word in context with others that frequently accompany it, namely *mægen* (main), *mægencraft* (main-craft), and *miht* (might), all of them Anglo-Saxon words denoting power and strength, both natural and supernatural. Especially in Anglo-Saxon, where the word-meanings are highly developed, Mod very frequently appears paired with one of these other words for power. The context shows that not only physical strength and power are meant, but also mental and spiritual power.

As one among many examples, Meyer quotes a verse from the Anglo-Saxon poem *Elene*, where "the wise among you who have the most *mægen* and *modcræft*" are called into council to develop a clever strategy for saving their people from a foe that is physically stronger than they are (p.13). Queens and wise counselors are very often described with mod and mægen words in Anglo-Saxon, denoting both wisdom and virtue in the sense of a good character powerfully applied for the good of the folk.

Gods (Heathen and Christian), Heathen heroes like Beowulf, Christian saints, Queens, wise folk: all were seen as being gifted with *mod, mægen, miht, modcræft*, and related terms, which distinguish them from the ordinary and the every-day. The Latin word *virtus*, the root of 'virtue', was translated into the ancient Germanic languages using the words 'mod and mægen' together (Meyer p. 14-15).

We gain a sense of the same meaning when we speak of the 'virtue' of an herb, a potion or a magical object, its special power that sets it apart from the ordinary. An example of such virtue is found in *Fjölvinnsmal*, vs. 15 (Poetic Edda). Svipdag, seeing Menglöd and her ladies sitting under the great Tree that bears mysterious healing and life-giving fruits, asks "What *moði* has this famous tree, that it can be felled neither by fire nor by iron?"

The Mod Soul

Powerful animals also have these characteristics: think of the aurochs described in the Rune Ur, in the *Old English Rune Poem* that I quoted at the beginning of the chapter, called a *modig wiht*, a mody wight. Uncastrated stallions and bulls were called 'mod' to distinguish them from geldings and oxen (Meyer p. 20). Weather, too, could be referred to by this word, as in *Grimnismal* 42 in the Poetic Edda which describes the hard-mody sky / cloud-cover that was created from Ymir's brains *(heila)*.

The power of the sea was seen as an expression of mod. Anglo-Saxon poetry, for example, contains several references to *merestræmes mod*, the mod of the streaming sea; Old Norse and Old Saxon have similar expressions. Even a good beer was considered to have mod: Meyer quotes an old German Brewer's Guild document from Hamburg that refers to a beer's "modes, smacks (flavor), und krafft (*sic;* strength)" (p. 27).

Merestræmes mod: The Mod of the streaming sea.

Our modern English 'mood', descended from mod, also refers to a powerful state of being; that is, moods can be powerful, though sometimes they can also weaken us.

Moods can overwhelm us, fighting our best, most reasonable efforts to overcome them and put them aside. Moods are primitive, powerful, springing from hidden roots, and are much affected by our environment: the weather, our surroundings, the moods of people around us, and by conditions such as mob mentality and group-think. We can be swept up not only by our own moods, but by group moods, into anything ranging from fads and fashions, to political or religious movements, to mass hysteria, panic, and mob violence.

The Mod soul underlies our moods and is integrally connected to, and reflective of, mod and mægen in our environment and in others around us. This close connection between moods and environment is another clue pointing toward Mod-soul's daemon nature, its nature as an independent being rooted in the flows of energy that surround us all in Midgard.

Meyer's conclusion is that the root meaning of *moda* is based in the concept of *Macht*, of might, strength, virtue in the sense of special power, that sets one above the ordinary and can even reach to supernatural and divine levels. The scholar Becker agrees with Meyer on the connection of mod with supernatural spiritual might or Macht (Becker p. 158).

Turning to another source, de Vries' *Old Norse Dictionary* postulates that mod stems from the Proto-Indo-European root *ma*, meaning to be emotionally stirred, excited (*gemütserregung*), as well as meaning 'striving.' He suggests related words in Greek that mean to strive, to yearn or wish for, to rage; also a Tocharian word meaning strength.

In previous chapters I noted the connection between our Ghost soul and the root of the word Ghost meaning 'to be excited, stirred up.' There is certainly some overlap between the state of wode, a characteristic of the Ghost soul as I understand, and the state of mod, a characteristic of the Mod soul (see Meyer's discussion of these similarities, p.44-5). Here, in seeing similarities between Ghost-states and Mod-states, we begin to move into the idea of Mod as a Daemon, a spirit-being who has a certain independence from us and influences us through urges, longings, and various strong emotional states that seem like they come upon us out of the blue.

Mod as Daemon

Numerous scholars of southern and western Germanic literature have noted that the Mod-soul or Mod-faculty within a person has the ability to drive, urge, incite that person to action. The Old Saxon *Heliand*, which retells the Christian gospels in heavily Germanicized imagery and vocabulary, states at the very beginning of the poem that: "many were those whose Mod incited / urged them (*iro mod gespon*) so that they began to spread God's word". Here we see clearly that Mod was envisioned as something belonging to oneself but also having its own volition and identity.

Another example of Mod acting separately from the person is in the *Beowulf* poem. Lines 720 through 735 describe Grendel entering into Heorot hall, filled with sleeping warriors, and exulting at the opportunity for violence and bloodshed before him. This sense of exultation is expressed as "his Mod laughed (*his mod ahlog*)." It is clearly Grendel's Mod, not Grendel 'himself' who laughs here. In others of these lines, we see phrases that indicate he has entered into a supernatural state of strength and rage, showing the exaltation of his Mod-daemon-soul: he burst the iron-bound door open with a touch, in his eyes was an ugly light like fire, he was *yrre-mod*, his Mod in a state of rage, of ire.

Likewise, Thor's Hugr soul laughs and exults within his breast when his stolen Hammer is brought out of hiding, at the end of the *Thrymskvida* poem (Poetic Edda). And it's interesting to compare this with another moment of triumph / exultation in Greek mythology, when Zeus's *Htor* soul laughs within his breast during (what he thinks is) his seduction of his previously-angry wife, Hera, though actually she is seducing him using Aphrodite's magical belt (Claus p. 24). In each case, we see a soul acting as a separate entity within a person, energizing them toward what they consider a great deed and triumph. Energizing, inciting and motivating are major functions of the Mod soul at all levels of being.

In the Old High German poems of Ottfrid we see more examples of the Mod acting as a separate person inside oneself. "My Mod (muat) informs me that you are a foreseer," he writes. He also describes in several places how the envious Muat hates and rejects the good (that is, the Christian God and his teachings). (Eggers p. 7-8.) Eggers notes that the verbs used to describe the Muat's actions are used only in the context of persons or people, showing a personal construction of the word *muat*. In King Alfred's Anglo-Saxon translation of the Psalms, like Ottfrid he uses the expression "my Mod tells me...." (Ps. 51:21). This is just the same as the phrase that comes up in the Norse sagas: "my Hugr tells me...."

The scholar Eggers, looking at the passage from *Beowulf* that I quoted above, sees Grendel as being possessed and driven by his Mod-daemon (p. 6). He and other scholars

The Mod Soul

studying the continental Germanic literature note that Mod is the only soul-entity or soul faculty that is used with transitive verbs, where Mod itself takes action as a person would (Eggers p. 4-5). (In Norse lore, it is the Hugr that has this same characteristic, but not the Mod.) Meyer, Eggers, Becker, and other scholars see this characteristic of Mod, the way it is used with transitive verbs of action, as well as the archaic syntax of Mod word-usage, as a possible indication of a very ancient understanding pointing back to Mod as an independent nature-spirit which would at times possess and overwhelm a person and drive that person to act in accordance with the Mod-spirit's desires.

The Norse Hugr does something very similar, though with some subtle but significant differences. In particular, the Mod generally acts upon the person from within, affecting their own behavior, while the Hugr may act upon others outside oneself through magical means, a flowing or bursting outward of occult power. (See Chapter 11 for more about this.) However, the ON word *moðr* can occasionally be used to mean "sorcery" (*trolldom*), and in these cases it is much the same as Hugr in this context (Meyer p.26).

Eggers (p. 14 f), drawing on Meyer, sees our ancestors conceiving of Mod as originally being an external Daemon spirit, not very personal, but more in the nature of barely-personified energy, force, power. This power can be expressed through humans, Gods and Goddesses, Jotnar, animals, weather, and other natural phenomena like ocean waves (much like the magical concept of Elementals).

In the second stage, Mod wandered or was drawn into the soul-realm of human beings, but was not yet fully incorporated therein. It expressed itself as urges toward certain actions, as well as strength and will, generally, but

Heathen Soul Lore

was still quite distinct from the "person." This is the level of development that appears in the few Gothic uses of the word, as well as in Old Norse, mostly used to mean enormous rage, fury, overwhelming desire to win, to conquer, to have one's own way against all obstacles. The Norse expression *jotunmoði* describes such a state, comparing it to the Jotnar, the Giants, in a state of rage. Thor can enter a state of *asmoði*, the rage-power of the Æsir, in the same way.

Thirdly, Mod internalized itself into the inner person of human beings, expressing itself as more sophisticated emotions, desires, motivations, as well as more primitive eruptive impulses and moods.

And finally, as we see especially in Anglo-Saxon writings, Mod becomes the entire Inner Person, the persona, ego, living soul, of human beings, without overt implication of an external force acting on the human. The Anglo-Saxon dictionary defines *mod* as: heart, mind, spirit, mood, temper, courage, arrogance, pride, power, violence.

Notice in particular that the primary meanings in Anglo-Saxon are heart, mind, and spirit. If we look at the list of mod-words given by Meyer that I quoted earlier, we can see this expanded meaning of mind and spirit carried forward into Middle High and Low German, Middle Dutch and other languages of that period. In the process, according to Eggers, Mod displaced the "original inner self of humans," the Hugi soul. (Eggers p.14 f).

For myself, I see this question of "which was the original soul in ancient Germanic thought" (a question also discussed by other authors based on Old Norse lore) as off-base. I don't think the Germanic peoples, any more than any other 'primitive' tribal peoples that I am aware of through

The Mod Soul

anthropological studies, saw humans as having only one soul. Thus, an argument as to which soul was the 'original' one is rather a waste of energy, in my opinion. Instead, we should be focusing on understanding all of the souls and soul-parts as understood in Germanic thought, without prejudice toward one or the other.

In fact, if we were going to look for original Germanic souls, I would point to Ferah / Fjǫr and Ahma / Ǫnd / Athom as being the oldest soul-words, going directly back to words meaning 'soul, spirit, vital principle' in Proto-Indo-European, and appearing with the same meanings in all the Germanic languages as well as other Indo-European languages, in contrast to Mod and Hugi which are somewhat more ambiguous. There is quite a difference between these various entities: Ferah (vital principle), Ahma / Ǫnd / Athom (spirit), versus Mod and Hugi (daemonic, separable from the body), differences which are difficult to discuss in modern English if we call everything by the same word 'soul.'

I want to make it clear that, in my understanding, while the humanized Mod-soul inserted itself and evolved as described above, the original mod-force and Mod-daemons or elementals which inhabit nature still continue their own existences. Some Mod-spirits decided to join or were drawn into the human soul-orbit, while others remained nature spirits, or joined with Deities (especially Thor and his children), Jotnar, Dwarves, natural phenomena, animals, and other beings of the Worlds.

So if we accept, even just for the sake of discussion, the ideas presented above, how might the Mod-daemon have accomplished this intricate process of incorporating itself into the human soular-system? To address this intriguing question, I will turn in an unlikely direction: the role of the Mod in illness.

Mod as Daemon of Sickness

(Sjuk Lapp Studie, Anna Nordlander.)

There are two ways to consider the role of the Mod in illness. One is that mod in its simplest form is strength and power, intimately connected with might and main. When people or animals lose their strength, this is the cause and / or the result of illness. In a tale about the deeds of St. Cornelius, *modstuhlin* or mod-stolen was used to translate into Old Swedish the Latin word *paralitica*; that is, a person or animal whose Mod has been stolen or lost becomes physically paralyzed. The same translation occurs in medieval medical texts (Meyer p. 19). (If you are interested, the remedy for this condition is hedgehog meat.)

I suspect that the phenomenon of war-fetter, the paralysis of warriors in the midst of battle by rune or galdor magic, is in effect the paralysis or theft of their Mod soul that deprives them of strength, courage, will, and motive force. Note here that the loss of the Mod does not necessarily result in immediate death, showing that the Mod is not a life-soul according to my criteria. Rather, it is a wander-soul which

The Mod Soul

can be removed from the living body unwillingly, with severe consequences to one's health.

This is certainly a logical consequence of the understanding that the Mod was not originally part of the Gods-given human soul-complex, so its loss should not lead directly to death. Rather, theft, loss, or damage to the Mod-soul leads to a decrease in the inflow of mod and mægen (power, strength, energy) from the environment. Without this inflow, people and animals become lethargic, depressed, weak, paralyzed, lacking the strength and will to act or even to live, depending on the severity of the condition.

Many of the magical spells in Anton Bang's Norwegian compendium of *Hexeformularer* are designed to restore mod to an ailing person or domestic animal. Note that these spells are directed more toward restoration of health and energy through the ousting of afflicting spirits, rather than toward what would today be called 'soul retrieval'.

The other connection between Mod and sickness brings us back to the interesting question of how Mod-Daemons and humans became connected in the first place. Meyer (p. 34-7) discusses examples of words meaning 'mod-sickness' from a variety of Germanic languages (*e.g. modsott, mosott, modseoc, mossuen, etc*. Note that Germanic language dialects often drop the last consonant from both Mod and Hugi, so that Mod becomes Mo and Hugi becomes Hu or Hei.) These terms can apply to both humans and animals. As she discusses, it is difficult to tell from the old texts what specific illnesses are meant by these terms, and modern scholars have made a number of different suggestions, including jaundice, heart ailments, and stomach pains and ailments. Many instances indicate more of a psychological state rather than a physical illness, such as the Geatish warriors who wait, *modes seoc* or Mod-sick, by the swamp for Beowulf to return from fighting Grendel's mother. He has been gone so long that they are heartsick and hopeless, sure that he is dead. (l. 1603)

Modes-seoc: Beowulf's comrades wait, their Mod-souls sick with fear, beside the marsh where Beowulf has gone to fight Grendel's mother. (George T. Tobin.)

There are, however, some indications that all these kinds of illnesses can be caused by wights: Meyer quotes a Danish saying about the 'evil Mo' in this context, and give examples of afflictions caused by something like the 'evil eye'. She further describes afflictions just like those called 'elf-shot, hag-shot, troll-shot' etc. in the various Germanic languages, which are attributed to the Mo or Mod. In some cases, this seems to be caused by a sorcerous person's Mod-soul, but more often it seems to be associated with a free-ranging evil spirit, or with the Christian idea of devils. These afflictions

The Mod Soul

resembling elf-shot include sudden onset of nausea, tics, trembling, pains, and various other symptoms I have not been able to translate.

It's interesting to compare this with what can happen to the Greek *thymos* soul, a soul which has strong similarities with both Mod and Hugr. Snell (p. 18) describes the *thymos* as greatly affected by pain: eaten away, torn asunder, feeling it to be sharp, heavy, immense. The examples of mod-sickness describe both physical and emotional pains that could fit those descriptions well. In Homer's *Iliad* Book 16, the healing-god Apollo answers the prayer of wounded Glaucos by soothing his pain and casting strength in his thymos (Snell 19-20).

Meyer notes the confusion I have experienced myself, in that the various 'mod' words in Old Norse and the continental Germanic languages frequently refer to 'tiredness, fatigue' rather than to a spirit or soul of any kind, though she also notes that the words 'mod-as-spirit' and 'mod-as-fatigue' are at root related to each other, deriving from the idea of might and strength, and hence the lack thereof. She goes on to say that there are countless examples of states of fatigue, depression, etc. called 'mod' and attributed to the afflictions of evil spirits (p. 37), and Bang also gives many examples of this.

So, although the specific details are somewhat unclear, overall the evidence is suggestive of the idea that Mod-wights are involved in certain human and animal illnesses, and especially involved with illnesses that affect a person's or animal's Mod-soul and disrupt its physical and psychological functions. This is very consistent with the beliefs of shamanic cultures around the world which personify the cause of illnesses as spirits or wights.

The anthropologist Herrera, in his book *Microbes and Other Shamanic Beings*, offers an interesting perspective on this, though he is working with a different (Amerindian) culture and time-frame. He argues that the phenomena that religiously-oriented Christian missionaries interpreted as belief in harmful, non-material 'spirit-beings' can be more effectively viewed as real-world microbial entities which indigenous shamans are able to perceive and interpret through shamanic methods. "Since the earliest accounts, Amerindian shamanic notions have shared more in common with current microbial ecology than with Christian religious beliefs" (referring to 'evil spirits'; p. ix).

Let's look at modern evolutionary theory for a moment now. Viruses and bacteria are thought to have actually incorporated themselves into human (and other species') DNA and molecular processes. For example, the mitochondria that power our cells with energy were once independent, parasitic bacteria that evolved into a symbiotic relationship with early multi-celled organisms. Now we provide these originally independent organisms with nourishment and a place to live, they provide us with energy. Interestingly, they come with their own separate DNA, called mitochondrial DNA.

Here is a fascinating report: "...findings suggest an astonishing 30 percent of all protein adaptations since humans' divergence with chimpanzees have been driven by viruses. ....this constant battle with viruses has shaped us in every aspect."
(https://www.sciencedaily.com/releases/2016/07/160713100911.htm.)

There is an enormous amount of recent research available on the internet, showing how various microbes, including those in our own gut, skin, and other personal

The Mod Soul

microbiomes, have affected human adaptation and evolution. I view this as 'the will to thrive, succeed and win' in action, showing a vital characteristic of the Mod soul.

There is also the well-understood situation of the bacteria in our gut being vital to our life and health, providing not only for our digestion but producing many of our most important biological substances such as neurotransmitters, hormones and vitamins. This is another example of something that is within us, vital to our survival, but not exactly 'us,' and integrates potentially disease-causing organisms (bacteria) into our own body's strength and health processes, including support of our immune system, our defender. Moalem's book *Survival of the Sickest: The surprising connections between disease and longevity* (as well as many other current writings on this subject) shows how some diseases carry adaptational advantages along with them, like the well-known example of how the gene for sickle cell anemia carries with it a resistance to malaria infection. I recently read a news article about discoveries showing how intestinal parasites may confer resistance to certain diseases as a 'gift' to their hosts.

So, modern evolutionary theory is now looking at a situation where agents of illness - bacteria, viruses, parasites - incorporated themselves into our body and influenced our human DNA, and over a period of evolutionary time become useful, indeed essential, parts of our own being. Yet still they retain traces of their original separateness, and in the case of our gut bacteria, they really are separate. Doesn't this provide a nice parallel model for how the Mod, as a daemon or wight that often expresses itself as a spirit of illness, could have incorporated itself into our soular system?

I think that our microbiome, especially in the gut, is a part of the physical foothold of our Mod soul, in the same way that our heart and chest are the physical foothold of our Hugr soul, and the breath is, of our Ghost and Ahma. Ferah and Alder 'fill' our body, our Ealdor-yard, with subtle energy bodies very close to the physical level, to the point where they can feel the torture or sickness happening to the physical body. Hama's physical foothold is the shape and the abilities of our physical body. All our souls, with the possible exception of Saiwalo, have physical footholds while we are alive in Midgard, and Mod is no exception.

Mod's foothold is not only our microbiome, but all the body systems and processes that are integrated with it, such as our digestive system and our immune system. These systems provide us with physical strength and energy, energy for powerful thought processes and will power, and strength to resist what needs to be resisted (our immune system), all of them characteristics of the Mod soul who gives us the 'power of the gut'! At the same time, these physical characteristics of Mod also provide avenues for illnesses and disabilities to take hold.

Indeed, it might be possible that certain illnesses, in evolutionary terms, are simply the by-product of efforts by our body-soul complex to adjust to the presence and energies of the Mod daemon, much as in tribal cultures shamans may go through a long and terrible period of illness as part of their calling by, and integration with, their tutelary spirits. Many cultures say that the shaman's body itself must be radically changed, most often through illness, in order to accommodate and work with the spirits. Something like this could be the case, too, during an evolutionary period of human / Mod-daemon integration.

The Mod Soul

The Implications of Human-Mod Co-Evolution

Here is my interpretation of these ideas, in a nutshell. Microbial entities (viruses, microbes etc.) very clearly possess, in a non-conscious way, these fundamental qualities: the 'will' to survive, multiply, take over the 'territory' that they are invading, alter that territory to their advantage, and 'make the world their own.' These qualities are very similar to the state of *jotunmoði* that I described earlier: the primitive, powerful rage and will to conquer, to overcome, to get what they want, that characterizes the Jotnar in a state of *moðr*. If we look at primitive Mod itself, regardless of what kind of being it is expressing itself through, whether microbes or giants, the qualities and characteristics are much the same.

My theory of Mod's evolution is that Mod-wights began as very primitive spirit-beings which could attach themselves to, and work through, physical Midgard beings. (I believe that the Mod-power within otherworldly beings such as Deities, Dwarves, Jotnar, Landwights, develops in a different way, through being absorbed directly from their own natural environment.) These Midgard Mod-wights brought with them their powerful, though unconscious, 'will' to survive, thrive, multiply / increase in strength, and take over. They also brought with them the strategic adaptability that microbes and viruses are famed for.

I think that in physical Midgard the primary trajectory for this development is through Mod-microbe symbiosis, keeping in mind that microbes are the largest, most widespread and adaptable category of beings on Earth, and play a major role in the evolutionary and ecological processes of life on Earth.

Once a Mod-wight, attached to a microbial population, was settled within another type of being such as a human, through symbiosis and evolution they adapted to each other, and Mod took on other qualities characteristic of that type of being, whether human, animal, whatever. My thought about 'where our Mod comes from' is that during our life and as death approaches, Mod grows 'buds' from itself and releases them as a tree releases its seeds. These Mod-buds float around in the environment and attach themselves to infants of the same type of being that they were released from.

This sculpture can be seen as a representation of the Mod-soul / microbial-elemental spirit. It can be seen as beginning its union with the human soul-complex, represented by a tree, or as a Mod-spirit budding from that tree. I envision that the Mod-spirit eventually becomes fully integrated within the human soular-system.

As a parallel development, keep in mind that baby humans, animals, birds, etc. pick up the microbes of their mother during birth and from the nest / den / environment, and pick

The Mod Soul

up those of other close family members as well. These microbes establish themselves as the infant's microbiome, the foothold of their Mod.

The Mod-buds, likely to come from someone in the infant's close environment, carry with them something of what the Mod-soul of the originating person or other being has developed and learned throughout their lifetime. Thus, with each generation, the Mod-buds of humans become more human-like, while the Mods of bears become more bear-like, and so forth. These connections affect not only the development of species, but the development of family characteristics as well, such as temperament and attitude.

I like to interpret this cave painting as the hands of human ancestors passing down the powerful Mod of the ancient beasts, the mody wights, through ages of evolutionary time. The black spots, which are not only upon or within the animals, but also above and below them, I view as spirits of the microbial Mod-collectives that harbor the evolutionary will to survive, adapt and thrive. (Pech Merle cave.)

Here are the implications of these ideas, relating to the everyday conduct of our lives. The symbiosis of ourselves as humans with embedded microbial populations offers adaptational advantages, as I discussed earlier, but also comes at a cost. The same can be said concerning our Mod soul. Our Mod soul confers many advantages, all relating to strength, willpower and outstanding capability as these express themselves through our body, mind and souls. The gifts of the Mod can indeed reach supernatural and even divine levels of development.

However, Mod also can plague us with moods, unwise impulses, knee-jerk reactions, selfishness, capriciousness, bad temper, rage, cruelty and savagery. All of these meanings come across very clearly when reading the word in context of the oldest Germanic literature. The word *mod / moðr*, used as an adjective about a person in all the Germanic languages, often signified a person who was angry, cruel or savage, as well as other times signifying courage and bravery. The primitive nature of the Mod-daemon can express itself in unthinking reactiveness like mob violence, domestic abuse, hair-trigger temper, and social injustices.

The Mod (as with the Hugr) is very much a soul that needs to be trained and cultivated, and brought into harmony with our other souls. Mod carries great physical and mental power and ability, but to my way of thinking it shows its non-human origin by its natural lack of great human gifts like compassion, foresightedness, self-control, and the willingness to compromise one's own desires for the greater good of one's communities, from one's family on up. These considerations are not natural to the primitive Mod soul, and we can easily see this in the innocently selfish behavior of small children until they have been guided toward more of a sense of empathy and of how humans can beneficially interact with one another to keep family and community ties strong.

I would say that many of the social / political / economic problems in today's world (as well as many other periods in history) could be an example of mass Mod-daemon-possession, leading people to pursue power, selfish advantage, and their own aims without awareness or concern for the greater long-term damage that occurs to everything from the environment to the social processes necessary for living together and collectively solving problems. This is the kind of thing that can happen when our daemon souls are out of balance with our other Gods-given souls.

The Afterlife of Mod-Soul

The word Mod was often used to translate the Latin term *anima*, meaning 'soul' (only when referring to the soul within a living person; the afterlife *anima* was translated with the word *sawle, seola* or 'soul'). This shows the central role that Mod played in their conception of the human soul-body complex. King Alfred, in his translation of the Psalms into Anglo-Saxon, went so far as to cry out for salvation not only for his Gast (his spirit) and Sawle (his anima / soul), but also for his Mod (also anima) to be saved and taken to heaven, showing that he conceived it to be a true soul (for example, in Psalm 15:10, O'Neill).

He used the word *mod* more frequently than *gast*, and at least as frequently as *sawle* in his texts, when referring to the 'soul'. This illustrates a more evolved form of Mod, not simply a mood or state of being but an actual soul. (See further discussion of this in Chapter 15.)

In fact, after years of exploring and struggling with the question of Mod's afterlife, I'm inclining toward Ælfred's view, though I'm coming at it from a different direction. There isn't much to go on, concerning this topic, in the old literature. In *Beowulf*, a person's death is described by saying "nor could his restless / wavering Mod remain within his breast" (ll. 1150-1). That's about the extent of what I've found, in terms of Heathen-oriented material on the Mod at the time of death! It would certainly be logical to conclude that Mod returns to some sort of existence as elemental energies in Midgard. Yet, I don't believe this is the case, at least for human Mod.

Mod shows too much development, too much shape, coherence, complexity and strength of will in living humans, to assume that this all falls apart after the separation of our souls at death. Not to mention Mod's great degree of energy, strength, and determination. All of these point toward an entity that should be able to maintain its coherence, even when it is disembodied.

Yet, my sense is that there is no particular Mod-place where human afterlife Mod-spirits congregate, on their own. I'm coming to believe that Mod actually remains in partnership with our Ghost after death, and gives Ghost the power and energy to pursue the kind of active afterlife that we see in the portrayal of Valhalla and the Einherjar, Odin's chosen warriors, as well as the warriors in Freya's Folkvang, and Thor's Bilskirnir. Not necessarily active in warlike ways, but active along the lines of whichever Deity or Deities they associate with after death.

The Mod Soul

One confirmation of this idea comes from the account in the *Heliand* that tells of Jesus' agonizing inner conflict on the Mount of Olives, as he struggles to accept his mission of crucifixion. The *Heliand* -poet presents this inner conflict as an argument among his souls, as I describe in Chapter 5. Jesus' Ghost accepts his mission; his Likhamo (Lichama), Hugi, Mod, and 'flesh' (Lich) are resistant to it. Eventually the Mod decides to join the Ghost, and the other souls are outvoted or overpowered by these two together. (*Heliand* Chapter 57; also see discussion in Becker pp. 19-20 and 42-43.) The *Heliand*-poet, at least, recognizes an affinity between Ghost and Mod souls, and I am coming to see it that way, myself.

Our afterlife Ghosts are drawn toward the God-homes or divine realms that they are closest to during life. I think that our afterlife Ghost has the option of becoming very involved with the aims and activities of whichever Deities they are closest to, and that its partner-Mod can add Will, strength, energy and ability to these efforts. The whole idea of an active, goal-oriented afterlife is one that would appeal to the active, goal-oriented Mod-soul.

If Mod began, in an evolutionary sense, as energy associated with microbiological communities, needing a host to develop further, then we can see this affinity for partnership with the Ghost as a natural progression. Mod is hosted within a human and the human environment, and becomes more human-like. This process occurs especially through its association with the Sefa-soul and their mutual creation of our Modsefa, discussed in Chapter 12.

Then after Mod's evolution within this living environment, it may be hosted with our Ghost after death. Mod then participates in, and contributes to, all the spiritual growth, activity and spiritual evolution available to Ghost in the God-realms, and thereby reaches its own evolutionary pinnacle. This understanding of Mod's trajectory is very consistent with its signature powers of Will, determination, drive, achievement, and strategic adaptation.

Another factor that weighs in favor of this close connection between Mod and Ghost is the similarity between Ghost's ability to enter or be thrown into a state of wode (see Chapter 5), and Mod's tendency to enter into an ecstatic state called 'mod', as I discussed earlier. The characteristics of these two states are very similar. It is easy to see that Ghost and Mod could mutually inspire and energize each other through their own natural ecstatic states.

Mod's Potency and the Holy Ones

Mod appears in Gothic and Nordic lore as a state of high energy and raging emotion, much like uncontrolled wode. Thor is described as being in *jotunmoði*, in a state of powerful energy and rage like the Jotnar. *Asmoði*, the mod of the Æsir, is another phrase used. This is Mod in its elemental form: powerful, raw, unsubtle, motivated by Will but not necessarily by Wisdom. On the opposite end of the spectrum, Mod appears in Old Saxon and Anglo-Saxon writings as a fully developed Inner Person, the Persona, the Ego, who urges and motivates the person into powerful actions and deeds.

A key thing to understand about Mod is that within each of us, it is both primitive and elemental, and evolved and complex, but always powerful and potent. Mod is rooted in the Will, and one of its main characteristics is that it motivates, urges, and incites us toward action. 'What kind of action,' however, is open to question! The word *mod* in

The Mod Soul

the old Germanic languages frequently meant 'savage, cruel, enraged, hot-tempered, vengeful' and the like. On the opposite end was the word *modcræft* which meant 'intelligence.' This word was used to describe wise queens, councilors and elders, people of experience, knowledge and strategic wisdom.

Mod, when combined with the word 'mægen', meaning power, strength, energy, was used to translate Latin *virtus* or 'virtue' in the sense of special qualities or powers inherent in an object. It can be confusing to understand the difference between *mægen / megin /* main, versus mod-power, with both of them meaning forms of powerful energy. I view these energies as coming from the same source, except that mod-power is shaped by the mood and character of the being who is accessing it, while mægen is sheer strength and power. Thus, we have *asmoði* and *jotunmoði:* states of Mod which involve great main or mægen, but these flows are channeled through different beings with different moods and motives, taking on the flavor of their respective Mod-souls.

The mod and mægen of Thor's great Hammer.

(Shape seen in campfire.)

Heathen Soul Lore

Although, as I believe, Mod and our other Daemon souls are not given to us by the Deities, the Holy Ones also possess Mods of their own and can serve as guides and role models for us in developing our Mod. Thor, his sons Magni (Might) and Móði (Mod-y, having great Mod), and his daughter Thrúðr (Strength) are the most obvious examples. Any or all of them can be mentors of great value when we want to train and develop our Mod in the areas where their powers lie.

Mod's power of 'virtue or potency' is exemplified in Thor's mighty Hammer, with its power to crush and conquer, and its power to confer life, fertility, blessing, protection and hallowing.

Frigg, wise and competent Queen of Asgard. ("Odens Hustru," Jenny Nyström, 1893.)

Frigg and her Ladies exemplify a different arena of Mod. Queens, in Anglo-Saxon writings, were honored for their modcraft and wisdom, and were praised as *mode gethungen* (for example, Queen Wealhtheow in line 624 of *Beowulf*). *Gethungen* translates to "excellence, virtue, goodness, perfection." An

The Mod Soul

exemplary queen developed her Mod in this way and applied its powers for the good of her people and land. Frigg is the 'queen of queens', well known for her wisdom and the sense of strategy she brings to her contests of wit with her husband Odin!

Frigg's Mod, and those of her Ladies, can serve as examples and guides for those of us (men and women both) who want to develop modcraft: power which is expressed as subtle wisdom, strategy, wise rede, and the kind of noble comportment and behavior that draws respect, honor and trust from others. Frigg's distaff, spindle and loom, and her box of adornments guarded by Fulla, are also mod-filled objects of great potency and virtue.

There was once a princess named Modthryth, meaning 'glory of Mod'. Unfortunately, she glorified all the problematic aspects of Mod, including savagery, cruelty, selfishness and capriciousness; in fact, she was a really terrible person! Neither her parents nor anyone else in the kingdom could control her. Eventually she was married to the great king Offa, and once she became queen she changed greatly. She "Held high love for the heroes' lord," and "Fame she found there for generous gifts from the throne...she used her fortunes well." (*Beowulf* ll. 1931-1955, Rodriguez version.) This presents a nice little allegory of Mod's evolution within a person: from basically a savage beast, a wild elemental uncaring about human values, into a gracious and generous queen worthy of her name: Modthryth.

In Closing

My own sense is that Mod is rooted in the concept of 'Will.' All Mod's expressions of power, virtue (in the sense of special qualities), strength, rage, moods, and all the rest are at root expressions of the individual willpower of the Mod daemon striving to gain the object of its will. At a primitive level, the object of Mod's will is likely to be selfish and often even destructive from a humanistic perspective. When Mod is well integrated and balanced with a person's other souls, then Mod's enormous will, power, and determination can be harnessed to achieve great, beneficial deeds and purposes. Our Sefa soul is a major player in this process of integrating our Mod soul, resulting in the creation of their joint soul-space: our Modsefa, as discussed in Chapter 12.

My gut feeling ("my Mod tells me....!") is that here lies the clue to explain why both the Mod daemon and the human soul-complex would be drawn to associate so closely with each other in the first place. Mod daemons can and do exist independently in nature. The original human soul-body complex has its own sources of power and strength. Why would they need or want each other, especially if their symbiosis or coexistence was associated with physical and emotional frictions such as illnesses, states of moodiness, inner conflicts, and increased vulnerability if they lose connection with each other?

The answer, I think, is that both the Mod daemon and the original human soul-body complex have much greater potential for power, self-development, and self-expression when they work together than when they are separate. And, as I am coming to believe, some of this connection, along with its mutual benefits, continues after death as our Ghost and Mod-souls continue in an afterlife partnership.

The rune Ehwaz, illustrating the mutual power and benefit gained from a well-managed partnership between horse and rider, has much to teach us as we ponder the

The Mod Soul

possibility that our own total soular system includes a powerful daemon within it. We need to act on the understanding that our Mod is the horse, our mody wight: powerful, beautiful, willful, temperamental, full of great potential. And we—our Gods-given human soul-complex—are the rider who must deeply understand the horse, train it well and care for it, value it and make good use of it, but always retain the mastery over this powerful being.

Heathen Soul Lore

Horse and rider: together, they form a mody wight, indeed! Notice that the rider uses neither reins nor stirrups. He and the horse are in rhythm together, amplifying their mutual power.

Chapter 9

9. Hunting the Wild Hugr

Dale Wood.

I know a fifteenth (spell-song) that the dwarf Thjóðrœrir (Folk-Stirrer) galdored before Delling's door: potency to the Æsir, progress to the Alfar, hyggju (the action of Hugr) to Odin. (Havamal vs. 160, my translation.)

There is so much material – ancient poetry, lore, folklore, scholarly studies, and modern Heathen lore – concerning the fascinating Hugr soul that I will present several chapters to cover different aspects of it. In this first Hugr chapter I will explore the mysterious roots of Hugr's deepest past, using a technique that I liken to the creation of bind-runes.

Bind-runes are created for esoteric purposes by combining (binding) several runes together into an artistic shape, to guide powerful meditations and insights, or as the foundation for a magical spell. They are meant to be highly evocative and to stimulate intuition and insight. Instead of runes, here I use the roots of words, their connections and implications, to stimulate deep thought and intuition, and thus explore the mysterious roots of this soul.

Modern Heathens often think of Hugr as a soul-part which provides the capacity for rational (left-brain) thought, or for 'thought' in general. Evidence from lore and folklore amply shows that Hugr also encompasses emotions, temperament, disposition, character, occult and magical abilities, and can leave the body as our double or in other forms and take action on its own. Our Hugr also serves us as an advisor and warder, and as a harbinger, bringing forebodings of things to come. Hugr has its own mind and thoughts, emotions and feelings, temperament and moods. It is not just a function or capacity within us, a soul-part. Hugr is a full-blown soul-being or spirit in its own right, a powerful entity within our overall 'soular system'.

In the next chapters I will explore all of these aspects of Hugr. Here, I will focus on the *daemon* nature of Hugr, its existence as an independent spirit, where this spirit might have come from, its relationship to our ancestors, and what happens to it after we die. As usual, I will base my exploration on ancient words and where their implications might lead.

I have not found any firmly attested word roots for Hugr; its origin seems to be something of a mystery – a Hug-runa! But there are a number of suggested roots and related words in other languages that lead in seemingly different

Hunting the Wild Hugr

directions, converging on a very interesting and relevant set of meanings. For what it is worth, my own Hugr advises me that these word roots offer spiritually valid associations (whether or not these associations are proven linguistically) that lead toward greater understanding about the nature and source of Hugr.

Jan de Vries, in his Old Norse etymological dictionary, provided several suggested roots and related words for the word Hugr. I have taken each of these and followed them up using Mallory & Adams' *Encyclopedia of Indo-European Culture*, taking us back to reconstructed Proto-Indo-European (PIE) roots of the words and their cognates.

In the process of this exploration I have also followed intuitive branches and connections that expand each meaning. I've taken the scholarly approach as far as I can, but even though there is a great deal of material about Hugr generally, when it comes to understanding where the root and original concept of Hugr come from, it is more like following a scanty trail of linguistic breadcrumbs through the dark forests of the past, rather than zooming along an information superhighway! This trail is complex and difficult to follow, formed of interweaving branches, but I hope you will find that the end result is inspiring and enlightening, as I do.

Each 'root-complex' shown below takes one of the suggested roots or cognates of Hugr from deVries' dictionary and expands it. They can be thought of as 'verbal bind-runes,' which I distinguish with italicized phrases.

Please note that in the process of language evolution, the 'k' sound often transmutes into the 'h' sound, which is why these PIE words beginning with 'k' could be roots of 'hug / hugr / hyge / hu' words in the various Germanic languages.

Root-complex #1: 'Shining'

Old Indic *socati* (de Vries) from PIE root **keuk* = shine, burn. *Socati* = shines, glows, burns, and related words meaning light, flame, bright, white. Related Greek word *kyknos* = swan. (Mallory p. 514.) An unrelated word meaning 'white, bright' is *albh*, which is the root of alf, elf, Elbe (Mallory p. 177) and is also, I believe, the root of 'Alps', the white, elf-inhabited mountains of Europe. Words coming from *albh* include Old High German *albiz* = swan, and Hittite *alpa* = cloud, shining one.

Implications and connections #1.

Hugr is a shining, shimmering being, which is how elves are described in Anglo-Saxon: elf-sheen is the word used for their unearthly beauty. Anglo-Saxon has the word *scinnhiw* (sheen-huc) meaning 'shining shape', a 'specter, illusion, or phantom,' and a word for sorcery or magic is *scinnlac*. Lac means 'play, sport, strife, battle, sacrifice, offering.' An Anglo-Saxon sheen-laca (*scinnlæca*) is a sorcerer or shaman who deals with specters, shining shapes, otherworldly spirits in any of the ways described by *lac*. The white swan is a shape taken on by swan-maidens in Germanic lore, who are shapeshifters and otherworldly beings.

    This is the first clue on our path: *Hugr is a shining, glowing, unearthly-white otherworldly being*, and may be associated with other beings described in this way, such as the Alfar.

Hunting the Wild Hugr

Root-complex #2: 'Mounds and Wights'

Lithuanian *kaukas* = kobold, ghost of an unbaptized child (de Vries). The PIE root is **keu-k* meaning 'curve', and related to various Indo-European words for 'hill, hump, female breast, high ground, boil' (a swollen, infected lump under the skin) and the word 'high' in Germanic languages. The second set of related words includes additional meanings of Lithuanian *kaukas* = boil, goblin, gnome; Old Prussian *cawx* = devil; and Latvian *kauks* = hobgoblin. (Mallory p. 62.)

Implications and connections #2.
As noted in Mallory, the connection between a hill or mound and otherworldly beings is very common in European myth and folklore, especially associated with burial mounds. Hills and mountains with their caves and crannies are considered to be the abode of many kinds of wights. The fact that Baltic words for ghosts and goblins actually derive from the PIE word for curve makes a very tight connection. De Vries' use of the word 'kobold' (a type of wight) to translate *kaukas* is further explained in his book on old Germanic religious history, where he suggests that 'kobold' relates to Anglo-Saxon *cofgodas* or household-gods, both terms coming from the word for 'room, chamber'. He relates these beings to (a) the hearth and home, and protection thereof, and (b) to the

practice of honoring and relying on the family ancestral spirits (p. 176).

A name for the (still active) spirit of a dead person dwelling in a burial mound is *haugbui*, the 'dweller in the mound or howe.' De Vries' dictionary gives the older form of the word *haug* as **hugila*. I have not seen these words suggested as actual roots of 'hugr', yet certainly both the sound and the meaning-context are very close. The sound and meaning of haug also seem to me to be very close to *kauks* and other words listed above. Another, unrelated term for a mound-dweller is *odaldraugr*. *Odal* means 'the original owner of the property' and by extension the ancestral founder. *Draugr* is a ghost or a revenant. Though *odaldraugr* is unrelated linguistically, the concept of the mound-dweller as an ancestral figure ties in with our exploration here.

Borre Mound Cemetery, Norway

In this root-complex we have meanings of 'curve, hill, hump, the female breast', which lead on by implication to the curve or hump of a pregnant belly, sometimes leading to the ghost of an unbaptized child (unable to rest in peace, according to

Christian doctrine), then the burial mounds of the ancestors, and the ancestral spirits that are associated with all these things. All of these meanings point to the *cycle of life and death, and to a soul that moves around within this cycle.* As I shall develop further, I believe that both reincarnation, and service for a time as an ancestral spirit, are two of the choices or fates of the Hugr soul after death of the body.

The Kaunaz Rune

If we juxtapose the meaning of 'light, burn' from root-complex #1 *(*keuk)* with the meaning of 'boil', an abscess or infection under the skin, from #2 *(kaukas)*, then we have the strange pairing of meanings for the Kaunaz / Kenaz rune. In the Anglo-Saxon rune-poem, it means 'torch', while in the Norse rune poems its meaning is 'sore'. I see this juxtaposition as offering another clue to the ancient nature of Hugr.

    The A-S rune poem tells us: *Cen / Torch is, by every living being, known by its fire. Pale and bright, it burns most often where æthelings (nobles) rest within* (my translation). This imagery can apply not only to a feasting hall lit by torches, but to the noble child growing within the mound of the mother's belly, lit by the bright aura of growing life, the fire that is 'known by all living beings'. The word for 'living being' in this poem is actually *cwicera*, the 'quick' (compare the phrase: the quick and the dead). When an unborn child first is felt to move within the womb, this is called the 'quickening'. (See root-complex #3 for more connection with the fetus.)

    The Old Norwegian and the Old Icelandic rune poems both refer to the Kaun rune as a sore, the curse or bale of children, a scourge and source of grief, and a 'house of rotten flesh'. All of this, along with *kaukas* = boil or sore, ghost, goblin, adds up to the process of infection, sickness, death, decomposition, and haunting, and again, connects with children.

So here we have the paired image of the 'quick and the dead'. On one side are æthelings in the feasting hall and the babe quickening in the mound of the womb, full of life and joy. On the other side are decomposition and the grave-mound, complete with deathly wights. The two are linked by fire and light *(*keuk)*. The light of the feasting torches and the auric light of the growing babe are balanced by the flame of the funeral pyre, the burning pain of sore infections, the dim, strange corpse-light said to be seen on occasion around a burial mound, and the white, shimmering figures of ghosts and other wights.

Here is the next clue on our path, reinforcing the first: *the Hugr spirit or daemon appears as a ghost or an otherworldly being such as a kobold or hobgoblin. It is associated with mounds and burial sites, and with the mounded belly of the pregnant mother.* These associations again indicate its involvement with human cycles of life, death, and rebirth.

I have a theory as to why ghosts of (unbaptized) children figure so prominently in Germanic folklore, and it is not only because Christian priests tried to terrify parents into baptizing their children. I think the Hugr soul is drawn toward reincarnation as one of its afterlife options, and this is particularly so for the Hugrs of children who did not have the chance to continue developing during their lifetime. The hauntings by a child-ghost are its Hugr's attempt to reincarnate.

Hunting the Wild Hugr

The Goddess Frau Holle with her troop of Heimchen, the spirits of deceased children she has gathered into her care.

Root-complex #3: 'The Unborn, Swelling'

In this branch I am not following any suggested word in de Vries; rather I am following up on Root-complex #2 with two additional connections: 'curve / boil' leading to 'swelling', and 'ghost of an unbaptized child' leading to 'fetus'. As it turns out, these two words (swelling and fetus) have a single PIE root that sounds very much like the hu-root of hugr / hyge / hu, namely *keuh = 'to swell (with power), grow great with child.' Words derived from *keuh include Greek *kuos* = fetus, and *engkuos* = pregnant, as well as Germanic words *hunn* / *hun* meaning 'young one', Old Indic *svayati* = 'swells, becomes powerful', and Welsh *cawr* (intriguingly similar to OPrus. *cawx*, devil, above) = a giant, a being swollen with power. (Mallory p. 560.)

Implications and Connections #3
There is a bizarre instance in the Poetic Edda, relating the Hugr to the swelling of pregnancy and the birth of powerful ogre women / trollwives / witches (ON *flagð*):

Loki ate the heart, half-burned by linden wood, the hug-stone of a woman; then was Lopt (Loki) pregnant by an ill woman; thence come all the flagd of the world. (Old Norse version: *Voluspá hin skamma* vs. 11; *Hyndluljoð* v. 41 in translation.)

Here the burned heart of a woman (some think it was the heart of Gullveig, burned by the Æsir) is called her hug-stone. In Chapter 10, I will show how very closely Hugr is connected with the heart. But it is clear that the physical heart alone could not impregnate anyone; it is the spirit associated with the heart, the Hugr, that had this capability. After eating the hug-stone, Loki swelled with power and gave birth to powerful, otherworldly women skilled in evil magic.

There is another type of power associated with the fetus in Norwegian folklore. Bang's compendium of *Hexeformularer* or magical spells gives a number of spells intended to deal with 'afterbirths' or *bølen*, which are spirits associated with unborn children or with the placentas or cauls of newly-born children. These spirits are supposed to remain attached to the child as their soul, but they sometimes get loose, wander off, and cause harm to people and domestic animals (and harm to the development of the abandoned fetus). Even worse, evil sorcerers can call these spirits from their proper places and send them out to enact the will of the sorcerer.

'Swollen with Power and Wind'

'Being swollen with power' (**keuh*) leads us through its meaning (not linguistically) to the Sanskrit root *brh* or *brah*, the root of Brahma, the Hindu supreme God who dreams the world into being. *Brh* means 'to grow or increase, to

Hunting the Wild Hugr

fatten', and Hindu Deities are described as being 'fattened, swollen, puffed up with power' using words with the *brh-* root. The word also means 'to roar', which is sending out power on the breath and voice, as one does when chanting or galdoring runes. The word 'brahman' also refers to the expansive power that emanates and sustains the cosmos.

Brhaspati, 'lord of brh', a brahmin priest-magician or God in Hindu lore, embodies "the very quintessence of the highly developed intellectual faculties of the Hindu genius" (showing the swelling of his Hugr-mind), and is able to wield enormous power (Zimmer p. 76). The use of this magical power is described as 'building up, swelling with power' as the long, complex process of the magical spell progresses. Then the power bursts out and affects the world. (See Zimmer's sections 4 "The Dying round the Holy Power" and 5 "Brahman", beginning p. 66.)

This swelling and bursting-out of power well describes actions of the Hugr: a kenning or synonym of Hugr is 'wind of the troll-wife,' a magical wind of power (Prose Edda p. 154). In German folklore witches, sometimes called *Windbraut* or wind-bride, are known to fare about in a magical whirlwind. Wodan may have been originally a god of storm, and the souls he leads on the Wild Hunt are sometimes called 'wind-souls' *(Windseele)*. (Erich & Beitel p. 891, 896.) Wodan, witches and troll-wives are beings with powerful Hugrs, and the power they wield often takes the form of wind-bursts, or it rides upon the breath and voice in spell-songs. (See Lecouteaux pp. 161-164 for interesting connections between spirits and wind in Baltic traditions; many examples can be found in other cultures as well.)

Our word 'bosom', comprising our chest, heart and lung area as well as the breasts, comes from the PIE root *bhou* / *bhu*, meaning 'to swell, to grow' (Berr, p. 63). Note that the root of *brahma* that I described above, **brh*, has the same meaning: to swell, to grow, expand, enlarge. I must assume these words are related. Our bosom is the seat of our expansive, swelling emotions and our breath. It generates the power behind our voice and vocalizations, and it houses the Hugr.

If a human's Hugr is strong, and especially if it is motivated by ill thoughts toward others, it can burst or flow out of the person as wave of power, even without the person's conscious intention, as is described in Dag Strömbäck's article on "The Concept of the Soul in Nordic Tradition." As de Vries points out, the Hugr can move out of the body as breath or wind. The more dangerous a person's Hugr is, the more powerful the wind (p. 220, *Altgermanische Religionsgeschichte*).

The ancient Hindu sacro-magical tradition of building and using *bhr*-power is far more sophisticated and detailed than anything we find in Germanic lore, but I suggest that the actual mechanics of the process may correspond closely with the capabilities and nature of the Hugr, as I discuss further in Chapter 11.

The Hugr is unique among the Heathen souls I've studied, in that it is associated with a specific physical sensation in the chest, where the Hugr is located in the body. This is a wallowing, whelming, churning, upwelling sensation when the person is moved by very strong emotion, as is shown in ancient poetry. I will go into this upwelling sensation, and the location of the Hugr within the chest, in more detail in the next chapters. But I suggest here that this feeling is caused by the process of power swelling within the Hugr and seeking a way out, whether it is simply a strong emotional power such as anger, love, or grief, or explicitly a magical power.

So, our third clue on our hunt for the wild Hugr is that the *Hugr has the capacity to swell with power, and seeks a way to express it.* This power to swell is analogous to the amazing power of life within an unborn child, which grows and differentiates from a single cell into a complex human being in only nine months. The swelling of one's Hugr can be a gradual process, building up over time: a long, complex enterprise involving the Hugr, whether magical, intellectual, a life plan or strategy, a plot or a hidden activity, or simply the growth and training of Hugr's power due to life experience and our cultivation of it as Heathen spiritual practitioners. Hugr can also swell up suddenly with powerful emotions and burst out in reaction, in appropriate or inappropriate ways, to powerfully release that emotion. This release can be an emotional or physical expression, an occult or magical act, or a burst of genius, depending on how we develop and use our Hugr.

Root-complex #4: 'An Eldritch Cry'

PIE **kau(k)* means to 'cry out, cry out as a bird.' Descendants of this word include Old High German *huwo* = owl, and words for owl in other languages; Lithuanian *kaukiu* = howl, and a bird *kaukys* whose call foretold the harvest (Hugr is also a foreteller); Latvian *kaukt* = howl; Greek *kukuo* = cry, lament; Armenian *k'uk* = sighing, Groaning; Middle English *hulen* = howl, and others (Mallory p. 66). These words are not specifically suggested by de Vries as Hugr-roots, but **kau(k)* is so similar in sound to *kaukas* as discussed in root-complex #2, and so well-related in meaning, as I show below, that I include it in our explorations here.

Heathen Soul Lore

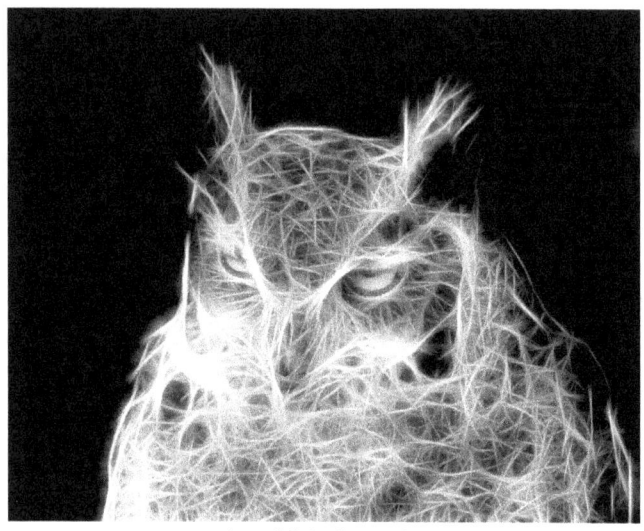

An eldritch wight.

<u>Implications and connections #4</u>
Owls in cultures around the world are considered to be associated with the dead, the otherworlds, the uncanny, and hidden knowledge. Their calls send a shiver of foreboding when we hear them. They are also considered birds of wisdom, making them suitable 'Hugr-birds' along with the raven. And of course, many owls have the typical "huu-huu" cry, giving us the very sound-root of Hu-gr.

One of the things Hugr does in Scandinavian lore is serve as a *hugboð*, a harbinger or foreboding of something yet to come (Strömbäck p. 11). Ghostly beings of various kinds, associated with burial mounds and graveyards, are often reported to howl, groan, or cry out in eldritch voices, and sometimes give forebodings of ill news. The cry of a newborn baby can sound like the cry of a bird, as well, linking birth with the sound of crying out.

An obvious connection between calling birds and Hugr is Odin's raven, also a bird of the dead, named

Huginn. Odin's wisdom is linked both to his Hugr soul and its embodiment in Huginn, and to his ability to speak with the dead, who groan and protest about this disturbance, as we read in saga accounts of necromancy and in *Baldr's Dreams* (Poetic Edda) where the seeress has much objection to being awakened from the dead.

Odin himself let out a great cry after nine days hanging on the Tree, when he finally grasped the runes of wisdom and fell down. Perhaps this was the triumphant birth-cry of Odin's own Hugr as it arose within or took root within his newly-expanded soular-system and swelled with power and life. Perhaps, also, this was the moment when the raven Huginn came into being, or when it joined with Odin. (If Odin's ravens did join him or come into being at specific points in time, then I suggest that Odin giving his eye to the Well was the act / time when Muninn joined him or arose from him.)

In this root-complex we have more associations of elements already discussed: eerie sounds associated with burial mounds and with the otherworlds, crying out of the newborn or the newly-empowered, and expressions of deep emotion that can come from an upwelling of the Hugr. This root-complex deepens the aura of meaning around the ancient Hugr, and adds a sensory dimension of sound to our holistic perception of what Hugr is.

Root-complex #5: 'Excitation, Stirring up the Soul'

De Vries suggests two other words possibly related to Hugr which add much to the picture of the ancient Hugr we see developing here. One is Greek *kukao*, meaning 'to stir up, to excite.'

Implications and Connections #5
This connects closely in meaning (but not linguistically) with the PIE word **gheis* = 'to be excited', which is the root of many Germanic words relating to 'ghost, fear, terror, astonishment', including in modern English. Of particular relevance here is the Gothic word *us-gaisjan* or *us-gaisnan*, 'to terrify, to make aghast'. This word literally means 'to out-ghost': a person is so terrified or worked-up that their Ghost exits from their body. (See Chapter 5 for further discussion of this phenomenon.) A stirred-up Hugr, excited with strong emotion, leads to the wallowing, whelming sensation in the breast, and sometimes to a bursting-out of Hugr-power, as I described earlier.

At the beginning of this chapter I quoted the *Havamal* (Poetic Edda) vs. 160:
I know a fifteenth (spell-song) that the dwarf 'Folk-Stirrer' (Thjoðrœrir) galdored before Delling's door: potency to the Æsir, progress to the Alfar, hyggju (the action of the Hugr) to Odin.
(my translation)

Notice the name of the dwarf, 'Folk-Stirrer' in relation to this root-complex of being 'stirred up.' When I meditate on this verse I get the image of Thjoðrœrir standing on a mountain ledge at dawn, bursting out with a deep, roaring, vibrating song of power, calling to the folk to bestir themselves, to awaken. He *stirs our Hugrs to swell and dwell within the mighty flows of power that run between us and the holy tribes of the Æsir, the Alfar, and the deep and broad Hugr of Odin himself.*

Root-complex #6: 'The Watcher; Magical Force'

The last related word that de Vries offers for Hugr is Czechoslovakian *cihati* meaning 'to lurk, to lie in wait, to watch for.' I do not know if this is correct, but I link this word to the PIE root **keuh* = 'pay attention to', which is discussed under Mallory & Adams' entry on 'Magic'. Other words from this root include Latin *caveo* = be careful (be watchful, wary); Germanic words for 'to hear', and Old Indic *kavi* = wise man. Even if the linguistic linkage is not correct, the meanings certainly hang together, and the root **keuh* gives rise to words for 'magical force, wonder, miracle' in other languages (Mallory p. 361), tying it closely to Hugr's abilities.

Implications and connections #6.
The 'magical force' aspect of Hugr comes from its powerful rooting in manifestations of life, growth, death, decay, and rebirth—the deep soul-powers of Nature and Earth-life. The watchfulness, the careful attention to these deep powers and their manifestations in both embodied and disembodied life-states, is the hallmark of Hugr's potential wisdom and power.

The set of meanings – 'to lurk, to watch, to pay attention to'—leads to many of the most prominent characteristics of the Hugr as we learn from early Germanic writings and from folklore and word usage continuing up to the present day. These will be covered in detail in the next chapters, but as a couple of examples, Strömbäck says that the verb *hugsa* in Old Norse means 'to think' but also 'observe.' In Norwegian dialects it means 'watch, observe, wish, have a strong desire for' (p. 12).

I believe these meanings form the bridge which takes us across from the more 'primitive' associations of Hugr—lurking ghosts and wights, eerie cries and burial mounds—to the more developed and sophisticated meaning of Hugr as *a being who expertly perceives, observes and thinks, who has access to hidden knowledge and serves as an advisor, warder, and harbinger* within our own complex of soul-beings, our soular system.

De Vries tells us that another word for a Hugr that is outside of the body is the Old Norse *Vörðr* or *Vårðr*. He uses the German word *Wachter* to translate these terms (p. 221).

Wachter means both 'warder, guardian, caretaker' and also 'watcher, watchman, lookout'. In the next chapters I will give examples of how Hugr undertakes these duties.

The Watcher.

De Vries describes the Greenlandic *spåkona* or oracle, Thorbjorg Litilvolva, who asked for the *Vårðrlokkur* to be sung for her during her oracular spaeworking session. The word *lokkur* is the same as the German word *locken*, which means 'to bait, decoy, attract, allure, coax, tempt.' De Vries writes that the *Vårðrlokkur* song is intended to coax or lure the Vårðr or Vörðr, the Watcher spirit, which he interprets as being the Hugr-soul of Thorbjorg herself, disembodied from her, with whom she needs contact in order to perform her spaeworking (p. 221, *Altgermanische Religionsgeschichte*).

Modern Heathen practitioners of this skill interpret the Vårðr as spirits of the land, nature, and ancestors, who have knowledge of hidden matters and can answer the questions asked of the oracle. In my view, there is no contradiction between these interpretations; either way the *Vårðr* refers to Hugr-souls, among others, whether embodied or disembodied, who are lured to attention by the singing of the Vårðrlokkr.

Afterlife and the Ancestral Connection

As we have seen so far, there are many clues linking the Hugr with ancestral spirits and with unborn children. Here are my thoughts about this connection. Hugr's main focus, as I show throughout my writings about the Hugr, is on human interaction and the challenges of human life in Midgard. (I am speaking of Hugrs associated with humans here, as opposed to those within Deities, Alfar, or other beings.)

Our Hugrs are much engaged with all our endeavors throughout our lives, and when we die, that engagement, that interest, usually continues. Thus, the disembodied Hugr after death usually wishes to attach itself to the lineage of people that it was associated with during life, to continue the story, the engagement, and to use the skills and wisdom it has accumulated during its embodied life in Midgard.

A Hugr after death has several options for doing this. It can become an ancestral spirit, a Dis if it had been associated with a woman in life, or an Alf if it had been associated with a man. I believe that all the Disir and Alfar spirits are the Hugr souls of the ancestors. (I am referring to 'Alfar as ancestors', rather than necessarily to 'Alfar as a divine tribe associated with the Æsir', though there are likely overlaps between these categories.) The Germanic Matronae, in cases where they are ancestral figures rather than Goddesses or nature spirits, fit into this category too.

Another option for the Hugr is to reincarnate, either within the family line (the traditional Germanic belief), or farther afield if the Hugr wishes to experience life in a different way, expand its horizons (consider modern scientific studies, and anecdotal accounts, of evidence for reincarnation). (See *Our Troth 2nd Edition*, pp. 508-510 for a discussion of Heathen reincarnation beliefs.)

The Hugrs of folks after death are not necessarily all benevolent, however. During life, people's Hugrs can be quite malevolent and cause a great deal of trouble. It's only logical to suspect that many of the spirits (for example, the 'hags' that cause 'hag-shot') which haunt and afflict people with illness, nightmares, bad luck, or damage of various kinds are the afterlife Hugrs of people of ill-will, who did exactly the same things during their lifetime. (See Chapter 11 for more discussion of this.)

By the same token, if an ill-willed Hugr reincarnates into a new life in Midgard, this will give rise to a very difficult person in life, who may carry over feuds and grudges. This is the big opportunity provided by reincarnation, however: life in Midgard offers a reincarnated Hugr the opportunity to learn a new path of life and change its ways.

Afterlife Hugrs may also be the source of other spirits in our lore such as the 'lesser norns' or fairy godmothers (those who give good luck, and ill luck); the *anses*, revered and powerful ancestral spirits; *Vörðr*, *Vårðr*, and other 'watcher, guardian' spirits; *kinfylgjur* (womanly guardians attached to the head of the family or clan), and perhaps some of the *fylgja* or personal guardian and luck-spirits. In general, I would say that if a spirit is human-like, it could well be the Hugr soul of a departed human. Hugrs are very active and engaged with human life, whether they are embodied or disembodied!

Origins and Evolution of Hugr

In my understanding Hugr, like Mod, was not one of the souls originally given to us or shaped for us by the Gods and the Norns, as I described in earlier chapters about the Ferah, Ahma, Ghost, Hama, and Aldr. I believe that the human Hugr is an ancestral soul that, unlike Mod with its source in nature-energies, is at root based in human life in Midgard. Its role and purpose is to engage in human Midgard life, whether Hugr is embodied within a living human, or whether it is disembodied, serving as an ancestral spirit, an independent warding and guiding spirit, or awaiting rebirth.

I believe that Hugr has undergone a gradual, evolutionary process of development. Unlike some of our other souls which have more 'timeless' natures, the various paths or strands we've explored here hint that Hugr has changed over time. It has evolved from an eerie, otherworldly spirit lurking around the dead, to a soul within us that embodies a great deal of our sense of who we are, deeply involved in our thoughts, emotions, character, personality, temperament, and behavior.

I think that this evolution took place through the process of Hugr's lives, afterlives and rebirths. Each time a Hugr is attached to a living human and experiences

Midgard life, it grows in knowledge, experience, skill. Sometimes this growth is minimal, sometimes great leaps of growth are taken, depending on how that person lived his or her life. The Hugr can grow and expand through the pursuit of worthiness during life. Or it can grow in ill-will, envy, spite and anger, and develop the skill to express those urges in harmful ways. Likewise, the afterlife activities of the Hugr can be helpful and beneficial, or harmful. Through all of this, the Hugr grows and learns, and over time and generations becomes more powerful, more complex, more skilled.

So, how did Hugr originate? I've suggested that after death, Hugr can reincarnate, or serve as an ancestral spirit, or a guiding spirit to a living person, and it may do all of these things in turn. But how did the first Hugrs begin, and how do new Hugrs arise to meet the needs of a growing human population?

I think that the earliest proto-Hugrs arise from the spiritual wetlands of Hel as floating wisps of imagery and longings relating to that imagery (see Chapter 16 for more about the Saiwalos and imagery, the transformational processes of Hel, and the arising of these proto-Hugrs). At this stage, the Hugr-ling has no power or knowledge of how to attain its desires; it is simply a wisp of longing. But the energy of its longing is enough to draw it up toward the Midgard-plane, the source of the imageries that the Hugr-ling is formed from.

When the Hugr-ling reaches the spiritual-energy planes of Midgard, it encounters other, more developed Hugr-spirits, who have already lived human lives, once or many times. Through association with these disembodied but experienced Hugr-souls, the Hugr-ling is 'apprenticed', so to speak, and begins to develop its powers. Ancestral, experienced Hugrs guide the new ones into association with parents-to-be, spurring their desire and love for each other, and their desire for a child. Thus, a new home is created for the Hugr-ling: a child with its full household of souls, and Hugr begins its long journey toward experience, wisdom and power.

An image of Hugr-wisps arising from the wetlands of Hel. (Dale Wood.)

I think that this is how Hugr souls originally arise, but I think it is also possible that sometimes a disembodied, formerly-living Hugr will help to gestate a new Hugr developing within a young child, and that this can relate to memories of reincarnation. I have discussed here how gestation, and 'swelling and growing with power' are important aspects of Hugr's nature. When we read academic studies about apparent cases of reincarnation, it's clear that in the great majority of cases, the memories and influences of reincarnation appear in very young children, and slowly fade as the child grows toward young adulthood.

This evidence would support the idea that a disembodied Hugr could join with a baby's soul-household and stay for several years, gestating and supporting the growth of a new Hugr in the child, and while doing so, it may (or may not) share memories, experiences and influences from its former life (or lives). Then, as the new Hugr grows into its full powers, the reincarnated Hugr will move on. Some of the past-life memories and experiences may stay with the child and continue to exert their influences on this person's life, though they may be far less intense once the reincarnated Hugr has left. Another way of expressing what I describe here, is to say that a Dis or an ancestral Alf involves herself / himself in establishing a new Hugr within a child.

In many cases, the Hugr simply chooses to reincarnate and remain with the person throughout their life, in order to experience Midgard life again. In this case, it would not gestate a new Hugr, but simply join with the baby's 'soular-system' and remain there for life. Hugrs of other sentient beings such as the tribes of the Alfar may occasionally be inherited into a family line if matings have occurred between them and humans. Thus, there are a number of paths whereby new Hugrs can arise and join with living humans.

The Tale of the Hugr

There was a time far back in human history, not long after humans had received their souls given by the Holy Ones, when an eerie song arose. This song began within the souls of the strongest and wisest folk back then, the ones with the greatest desire for themselves and their kinfolk to thrive and prosper in the challenging environments they lived in. The song was strengthened and built up when all gathered around the fires at night to sing and worship and tell tales together. These songs of longing and of knowing, of dreaming and desiring, called to the Hugr-lings forming like wisps in the dreaming lands of Hel, and the wisps floated up to hover around the singing humans.

These wispy, infant Hugrs were primitive, undeveloped. They needed to be in contact with the living. They congregated around burial sites, crying and calling to attract attention, and clung to people who neared the graves with open, grieving hearts and prayers to the ancestors for help. The loose Hugrs attached themselves especially to fertile women and men, drawing them into desire and love for one another, and encouraged conception and gestation of infants as new homes for themselves.

If a person came to a gravesite to pray for a gift from their ancestor—a gift such as skill in singing and tales, skills for hunting, gathering, toolmaking, medicine, strength and wisdom for a child in the womb—the ancestral Hugr might well join the soul-complex of the petitioner or the newborn child, temporarily or permanently, and pass on the gifts that Hugr had accumulated during life. Hugrs from other races of beings: Alfar, Vanir, Æsir, Giants, Dwarves, drifted into the pool of human soul-complexes occasionally when matings took place between them and humans, and a clan of humans gained an otherworldly ancestral Hugr to empower them.

Over the generations Hugrs became more powerful, more diverse and complex, more skilled, wise and subtle. They became more embedded within the human soul complex and had less need of the ploys they used when they were weak and young. Working together with the other evolutionary daemon-soul, the Mod, the Hugr became greatly skilled and powerful in all the abilities needed to thrive and succeed in everyday Midgard life, and evolved new skills and powers as human society became more complex and challenging. Today, they are primary actors among our souls in all the domains of Midgard life.

"Harbinger" by James Blalock.

Chapter 10

10. Who is Hugr?

The Hugi / Hugr / Hyge is often considered a soul-part which provides our capacity of thought. This is undoubtedly true, but it is only part of the picture. For one thing, as I have explored in other chapters, there are other souls in addition to Hugr which have powerful intellectual capabilities, including the Ghost and the Mod. Thus, Hugr is not the sole source of these abilities. And for another, when we look at the elder writings and the folklore, we can see overwhelming evidence that Hugr encompasses also the emotions, most of our everyday traits of personality, character and temperament, as well as many paranormal phenomena like our alter ego or double, our spirit-warder, our inner voice of wisdom, and more.

It was in studying the Hugr in lore and folklore that I first became aware that Hugr is not just a soul-part but a full-blown soul person in its own right, a full-soul as I call it. This led me to ask whether we have other such souls, and set me on the path of these years-long explorations.

Hugr is a true soul, in my understanding, based on the second and third criteria that I developed in Chapter 1. It does not match the first criterion: it is not a life-soul that causes death if it leaves the body. On the contrary, Hugr leaves the body more readily than any other soul – its departure may not even be noticed by our conscious mind –

and it is the most active and versatile of the souls as an independent entity. Thus it fits my second criterion: it is a soul which can leave the body and act independently of it, with its own awareness. I also believe it meets the third criterion of having an independent, self-contained afterlife, as I discussed in the previous chapter.

Basic Meanings

Please note that I use *Hugr, Hugi, Hyge,* and other word-forms interchangeably, depending on the language source I am discussing. I'll begin with showing how broad Hugr's characteristics are, looking first at the *Skaldskarpamal* of the prose Edda. The 13th century author, Snorri Sturlason, wrote this compilation of *kennings,* which are words or phrases that can be substituted for one another, like synonyms, with the purpose of deepening and enriching the expressiveness and symbolic overtones of Old Norse poetry. According to Snorri, the following words can be kennings or synonyms for Hugr: *mind, tenderness, love, affection, desire, pleasure, disposition, attitude, energy, fortitude, liking, memory, wit, temper, character, troth, anger, enmity, hostility, ferocity, evil, grief, sorrow, bad temper, wrath, duplicity, insincerity, inconstancy, frivolity, brashness, impulsiveness, impetuousness* (Anthony Faulkes' translation, p. 154). (There is also a kenning for Hugr: 'wind of the troll-wife', which I discussed in the previous chapter and will return to in the next one about the occult activities of the Hugr.)

These kennings for Hugr, taken all together, really add up to a complete personality, not just a part of a person such as rational thought alone. In fact, rational thought may play little role in many of the characteristics listed above! We can also see how limited the standard modern English

Who is Hugr?

translation of Old Norse *hugr* as 'thought' is. The English translator of the list of synonyms for Hugr does not use the word *hugr* in his translation: he lists these words as kennings or synonyms for our word 'thought'.

Read through the list again, and ask yourself how many of these words can possibly be stretched to be synonyms of 'thought' as it is understood in modern English? Although 'thought' plays a role in the actions and capabilities listed, these words do not really mean 'thought' as it is understood today. 'Thought', while being a valid translation of one important meaning of *hugr*, cannot cover the full range of meanings of Hugr itself. Other Old Norse meanings for Hugr include 'mind, mood, desire, wish.'

Let's take a look now at how *Hugr / Hugi / Hyge / Hugs / Hu / Hei* is defined in other old Germanic language branches. The Anglo-Saxon dictionary defines *hyge* as 'thought, mind, heart, disposition, intention, courage, pride.' There are a great many compound words formed with the *hyge* root in Anglo-Saxon; I count 38 word forms and compound words beginning with *hyge*, and there are many more scattered throughout the dictionary with the hyge-root at the end or middle of a word.

Together, the meanings of all these compound words provide a similar grouping to the ones Snorri listed, above. They include characteristics such as wisdom, folly, heedlessness, prudence, courage, and so forth. The compound words using hyge show that the Hyge is considered to be the source, the site, the locus within our soul-body complex, of these various characteristics, emotions and reactions. As in Old Norse, translators of Anglo-Saxon often use the modern word 'heart' to translate hyge, as well as 'mind', depending on the context.

Heathen Soul Lore

In the <u>Old Saxon</u> *Heliand* (a poetic retelling of the Christian gospels written around the same time as the *Beowulf* poem) *hugi* is the most frequently used word relating to soul-functions (Becker p.159-60), occurring 188 times in this poem (p.180) and has forty different adjectives formed from it (p. 51). It is also widely used in other OS texts. Overall, *hugi* refers to sense, perception, mind (*Sinn*); thought (*Gedanke*); mind, soul, heart, disposition, temperament, spirit, feeling (*Gemüt*); and heart (Becker p. 22).

An interesting compound word is sometimes used: *hugiskefti* or *hugiskaft*. This word literally translates to 'hugi-ship' – the state of being in one's Hugi, in the same sense as we would use the word 'apprenticeship' to denote the state of being an apprentice, or 'friendship' as the state of being friends with another person. Anglo-Saxon has this same word, *hygesceaft*, translated as 'mind, heart.'

<u>Old High German</u> *hugu* means 'mind, heart', and word-forms of the hugu-root include words for 'to remember, to think, sense.' Becker (p. 97-8) notes that *hugu* is not as widely used in OHG texts as it is in Old Saxon, and has a more focused meaning: hugu is involved primarily with intention, with focus, with thought oriented toward a particular goal such as the understanding of Christian writings and teachings. On the other hand, the words for 'heart' and 'breast' are widely used in places where *hugi* would be used in Old Saxon. Below I discuss the close connection between Hugr and the heart and breast. Another connection between heart and hugu comes in the OHG words *gihuct* or *gihugd* meaning not only 'thought' but also 'joy', and *hugelich* meaning 'gladdening'.

The <u>Gothic</u> dictionary shows the following meanings:

Who is Hugr?

hugs: intelligence, thought, understanding;
hugjan: to think, imagine, believe; and *ga-hugjan*: to deem, consider;
ga-hugds: a thought, mind, conscience;
af-hugjan (to remove the *hugs*): to make senseless, stupefy, bewitch.

These meanings are more in line with the modern idea of the Hugr as primarily rational thought. Did the Gothic language not have the other, more emotional meanings and implications of Hugr listed above? Were these perhaps later developments in the other Germanic languages? Or is the more limited meaning of the word due to the subject matter of the few Gothic texts we have? These texts are not poetry; they are translations of portions of the Christian Bible and a brief biblical commentary, part of a calendar, and a couple of title deeds (Skeat p. vi-vii). If we had examples of passionate, deeply felt Gothic poetry, would the meanings of Hugs be more expansive? Who can say?

Other <u>Germanic language</u> meanings: Faroese *hugur* = 'understanding, mind'; Old Frisian *hei* = 'mind'; modern Dutch *hoge* = 'mind, spirit, courage', and *heug* = 'desire'; Middle High German *hüge* = 'mind, spirit, memory.'

Hugi has dropped out of modern English and German, with only a few dialectical remnants. It's useful to look at the Hug-word in a modern language derived from Old Norse that has retained much of the 'flavor' and character of that language, namely Faroese. In the Faroese dictionary there are many words and compound words based on *Huga*; here are some of the meanings of these various words: *to think of, to recollect, mind, temperament, temper, disposition, wishful or desirous of something, eager, keen, zealous, interested, attentive, whole-hearted, thought, idea, that which brings delight or sadness, envy, strong desire for what another has,* and other meanings. The latter meaning – the Hugr as the source of envy and what results from it – shows up in dialects of other modern Scandinavian languages and is a subject I will return to in the next chapter about the Hugr's involvement in magic and occult phenomena.

Hugr and related words are still widely used in modern Scandinavian languages. You might find it enjoyable to look into the modern Danish and Norwegian term *hygge*, a popular concept of comfort, coziness and soulful living that you'll find all over the internet (in English, too), as well as in lovely little books. It's interesting to compare this term to one with essentially the same meaning in modern German, namely *Gemütlichkeit*. The base-word here, *Gemüt*, is descended from the old German word for Mod. This is another example of how similar the concepts of Hugr and Mod are, and how they were preferentially emphasized in different languages.

Three Domains of Hugr

Hugr functions as a human soul-being in three large domains. One of them is intrinsic, fully within ourselves and feeling like our 'self.' It is much involved in the soul-functions that are attributed to the heart, such as love, grief, anger and other emotions. It also has a strong influence on our character, temperament, behavior and moods, a function shared with our Mod soul. And Hugr forms the mental framework for our thought processes, doing a lot of our thinking as well as shaping the thoughts that come to us from our other souls, influencing them with its 'matters of the heart' and its concerns relating to its warder functions.

Who is Hugr?

The second great domain where Hugr operates is on the borders between our 'self', and the world and beings outside our self. Here Hugr functions as a rede-giver, an advisor and counselor, a warder of the heart and mind, and a *hugboð* (hoog-bodh) or harbinger who delivers forebodings about future events. This second domain is where Hugr's access to knowledge hidden from our conscious minds comes into play, including knowledge of the hidden motives of other people, 'gut feelings'(which it shares with Mod), intuition, hunches about some future event on the horizon, knowledge of other Worlds and beings, and understanding about matters of orlay, wyrd, luck, and other obscure threads running through the fabric of reality. In my experience, Hugr plays a primary role in oracular spaecraft as well.

Hugr's facility in this second domain, as warder of the boundary between Self and outside worlds, depends in part upon its own maturity and development over lifetimes of ancestral service and reincarnation, and in part upon our willingness and ability to 'hear' our own Hugr, to enter into our own *Hugiskeft* or *Hygesceaft*, our Hug-ship: the state of bringing our awareness fully into our Hugr-soul for a period of full communication. Hugr and the conscious or 'everyday' self can work together to improve this process of trust and communication throughout our lifetime.

Concerning Hugr's third domain of action: it is sometimes capable of moving entirely outside the compass of our self, either as a shapeless flow of power, or by taking on a shape called a *hugham*, which may be a double of our physical body, or an animal shape, and in either case often possesses paranormal powers such as flying, bilocation, or supernatural strength. The Hugham or the unshaped flow of Hugr-power can operate independently at a distance from us, sometimes entirely without our awareness that this is happening. I discuss this phenomenon in the next chapter.

And of course, the other large part of this third domain occurs after death of the physical body, when the fully independent Hugr may become an ancestral or warding spirit for a time, before reincarnating.

So these are Hugr's three domains of action: 1) inner self, enclosed within the body; 2) on the border between self, outside world and otherworlds, and 3) fully independent of the body.

Hugr and the Heart

The Old Saxon *Heliand*, a poetic retelling of the Christian gospels that provides a rich trove for understanding how words relating to soul lore were used, frequently links the Hugi with the heart, both in terms of location of this soul within the body, and in terms of the emotional functions of this soul.

The Hugi is described as being "within the breast, with the heart, around the heart, near the heart" in many places in this epic-length poem. The breast and the heart are 'containers' for the action of Hugi within. Eggers gives several examples of *an herton huggian*, meaning "to think within the heart" (p. 9-10). Another way to understand this is to see Hugi as a being who thinks, and resides in and around the heart.

The same connection with the heart is seen in Old Norse lore, and shows up in many places in the Poetic Edda. Verse 95 of the *Havamal* says that "Hugr alone knows what lies near the heart; Hugr alone knows Sefa." (The Sefa is a soul much involved in our emotions, and closely linked to

Who is Hugr?

both Hugr and Mod, as discussed in Chapter 12.) This *Havamal* saying is a very significant one, in my opinion. It points to one of Hugr's most important functions: it is a warder, a protector, of the integrity and independence of our heart-mind functions, and of our Sefa soul that resides in the heart. Here is another telling verse from the *Havamal* that clearly illustrates this point:

I know a sixteenth (spell-song or rune): if I wish to have all of a woman's mind (geð) and play, I turn / cast away the Hugi of the white-armed woman, and turn all her Sefa (toward me). (Vs. 161.)

Along with this, let's look at another *Havamal* verse:

Fickle are men's Hugrs toward women; when we speak fairest, that is falsest hyggjum (action of Hugr; intention); that entraps the (woman's) clever Hugi." (Vs. 90.)
(Both are my translations.)

Both of these verses clearly show that the woman's Hugr naturally protects her heart, her feelings, her tender Sefa soul. The only way a man can seduce her against her will is by turning away or distracting her inner warder, her Hugr, with its power of discerning the hidden motives of others, and its power of speaking or acting in self-defense. Note that the man's own Hugr is involved in this endeavor: this is, at root, a contest between Hugrs!

In the first example, the woman's Hugr is turned away by rune-magic. Her Hugr, in this case, must be very strong to require such powerful intervention. In the second example the woman's Hugr is weaker. Its instinct is to defend her heart and Sefa from disappointment and betrayal, but this Hugr is subject to distraction and misdirection by fair words and promises.

The Hugr has a strong instinct toward self-protection, but also toward love and friendship, and it can be difficult, as we probably all know from experience, to balance between these two important impulses! Because Hugr enjoys the play of minds and words, enjoys being clever and interacting with witty people, it can be distracted from both of these greater impulses of self-protection and of trust and love. This tendency toward distraction results in a weak Hugr, unable to ward us fully.

Gunnloð's Hugr failed to ward her from Odin's wiles, as he seduced her and stole the mead of inspiration. Odin himself regretted the necessity: "A poor reward I gave her, for her hale Hugr, for her sorrowful Sefa." (Havamal 105, artist Lorenz Frølich.).

Some people's Hugrs are eager to exploit and manipulate others. These manipulators see relationships of any kind, including work, social, and familial relationships, as a contest they intend to win, rather than as a give and take of goodwill and mutual benefit. These are the people our Hugr needs to ward us from, alerting us to the situation and coming up with good ways to deal with it.

Who is Hugr?

Some spirit-beings have the same manipulative attitude, whether they are hostile after-life Hugrs, or any of a variety of other hostile or exploitative beings. Our own Hugr is needed for protection from these beings, too, partnering with Mod and some of our other souls, and with Deities, ancestors, and other spiritual beings willing to help. Though we may be fortunate to have many others to aid us, our Hugr plays a central role here because of its ability to discern the hidden motives of others, and its rede-giving wisdom leading us in the best direction to deal with the problem.

This illustrates the importance of *hlutro hugiu*, a 'clear or clarified Hugi', which can observe a situation without distortions, assumptions, hang-ups and other baggage, and thus produce wise, clear-minded rede for us to follow. This phrase, *hlutro hugiu*, is often urged as a desirable state in the Old Saxon *Heliand*; I shall discuss it further, below.

Continuing with examples from the Poetic Edda showing the close connection between Hugr and the heart, in *Hyndluljoð* v. 41 we are told that Loki found and ate a woman's burned heart, called her *hugstein*, her Hug-stone. *Havamal* (Poetic Edda) vs. 119 says that "sorrow eats the heart if you never tell anyone your whole Hug," showing the importance of trustworthy friendship to the Hugr.

Hugr is so much involved in the emotion of love, as described in Old Norse, that the word *hug* is often used to mean 'love and / or desire,' without further mention of the latter words. When Frey is overwhelmed with desire and love for Gerda, so deeply that he becomes ill, this is referred to as *hugsott*, meaning "Hug-sickness" (*Skirnismal* introduction, in the Poetic Edda). No mention is made in the ON text about 'love or desire'; Frey's state is simply summed up as *hugsott*. When Sigurd is greatly distressed after hearing Gripr's prophesy that he will forget and betray the Valkyrie Sigrdrifr, he expresses his love for her as *alls hugar*; all his Hugr belongs to her (*Gripismal* v. 32, Poetic Edda). He does not see how it could be possible to turn his Hugr away from her. Again, the word 'love' does not appear here, only the phrase *alls hugar*. Saying 'the whole Hugr' is the way they expressed the experience of love, in these ancient poems.

Helgi and Sigrun, by Johannes Gehrts.

The tale of the hero Helgi and the Valkyrie Sigrun in the *Second Lay of Helgi Hundingsbane* (Poetic Edda) offers some interesting clues on the nature of Hugr and its role in love and in reincarnation. The preceding poem, the *First Lay of Helgi Hjorvardson*, shows the death of Helgi at the end, and the tragic parting between him and his beloved Valkyrie Svava. That poem closes with the statement "it was said that Helgi and Svava were reborn."

Near the beginning of the second Helgi poem it is stated that the heroine, the Valkyrie Sigrun, was Svava reincarnated. Sigrun went to meet Helgi II for the first time in that life, and immediately took his hand, hugged and kissed him. She said that she already loved him before she ever saw him. In Old Norse, the verb 'loved' does not

Who is Hugr?

appear in the text. Again, there is simply the phrase *ollum hug*, all-hug, to indicate her wholehearted love.

So, the poem is implying that Sigrun's Hugr was the soul reborn within her, since her Hugr knew and loved Helgi before she ever saw him in that life. This familiarity and love, carried over from the previous life, led her to greet him with hugs and kisses the first time she saw him. In response, Helgi's Hugr immediately turned toward the woman, responding to her with love.

Next, Sigrun took counsel with her own Hugr (*nama Högna mær of hug mæla*), and concluded she wanted Helgi's protection, meaning she wished to wed him. She was concerned, though, because her father had previously betrothed her to another and she feared her father's anger. Helgi responded that she need not fear the 'ill Hugr' of her kinsmen when she came to live with him. (ON: *Volsungakviða hin forna* v. 16-20; in translation: *Second Poem of Helgi Hundingsbane* v. 14-18.)

Here we see Hugr acting in several distinctive capacities. It is the 'one who loves' within ourselves, so much so that the word *hug* is used where we would expect to see the word 'love'. It is at least one of the souls which was reborn in Svava / Sigrun and Helgi, and remembered their former beloved ones, so it is 'the reincarnated one' and 'the rememberer'. It is Sigrun's rede-giver, counseling her to propose marriage to Helgi by asking his protection. And finally, Helgi promises to protect her from the 'ill Hugr' of her deserted kinsmen. In one brief tale we can see the wide-ranging nature of Hugr: lover, reborn soul, rememberer, rede-giver, and the angry one of ill-will. Unfortunately, none of this information about the Hugr is apparent when we read these poems in translation!

Hugi 'Wallows' Within the Breast

The Hugi exhibits a strange physical feeling within the breast, around the heart, when it is strongly moved; a description which is very seldom used about any other soul. (It is used a few times about the Sefa soul, closely connected with the Hugr.) This phrase is found in Anglo-Saxon and Old Saxon texts, and the word exists in Gothic but I have not read it in context. The term, with its variations, is *wallan, weoll, well, wylm*, related to modern English "up-welling, wallow, whelm / overwhelm." Additional translations include 'to bubble' and 'roil.' This ancient word is used to describe motions of water, or of people or animals in the water, and also to describe the movement of flames in the fire.

Here are some examples from the Old Saxon *Heliand* where it is used about the Hugi soul. When King Herod heard from the three wise men about Jesus' birth and became angry and afraid, "then was Herod, within his breast, harm around his heart; his Hugi began to *wallan*, his Sebo (welled) with sorrow" (ll. 606-8). On Palm Sunday when Jesus entered Jerusalem, he foresaw Jerusalem's downfall and felt grief within him: "Then *welled* him within, his Hugi around his heart, though he did not show outer weeping...his Hugi was sorrowful (ll. 3687-9)." When Jesus, accompanied by his disciples, was arrested by the Roman soldiers, "then his swift sword-thane Simon Peter was enraged, his Hugi *welled* within him so he could not speak a word, so much harm was in his heart" (ll. 4866-7).

Similar expressions are used in the Anglo-Saxon *Beowulf* poem. Deep emotion caused an overwhelming wallowing sensation in old King Hrothgar's breast when

Who is Hugr?

Beowulf bade him farewell. Beowulf was so beloved to him that Hrothgar could not prevent his *breost-wylm*, the whelming within his breast, and within his chest *hyge-bonds* tightened, causing a deep-felt longing for the dear man, burning within his blood (*Beowulf* ll. 1877-1880). When Beowulf heard about the destruction caused by the dragon, "then the good (man) was anguished in his chest, great *hyge-sorrow*....his breast *weolled* within, with dark thoughts he was unaccustomed to thinking" (ll. 2327-2332). (All the preceding translations are mine.)

Here we see how closely strong emotions and thoughts are connected within the breast, around the heart, causing a physical sensation. In the previous chapter, I described how Hugr 'swells' with the power of strong emotions and desires. In some cases this can result in a magical bursting out of power ('the wind of the troll-wife'), or even the production of a Hugham, an astral or etheric body, which can leave the physical body and act independently of it. My impression is that the wallowing or upwelling sensation within the chest is a physical sign of the Hugr building power, which could simply result in a powerful emotional expression such as sobbing or shouting, or could lead to more arcane magical expressions of the Hugr.

The Roots of Hugr

In Chapter 8 about the Mod soul, I concluded that the fundamental root-source of the Mod is the Will, or otherwise stated, the Mod-Daemon is the root of a powerful Will within us. This root-source gives rise to all the characteristics of the Mod as ways of expressing and achieving the Will, including strength, courage, mind-craft, skill, fury, potency, power, etc.

My study of lore, scholarship, and folklore regarding the Hugr coagulates into a similar root-source of the Hugr, namely Desire / Wish / Longing. The scholar Jan deVries gives the meaning of Hugr as "spirit, mind, intellect, soul (*Geist*) and thought (*Gedanke*)"; but also as "wish, desire (*Wunsch*); and longing (*Verlangen*)" (p. 220, *Altgermanische Religionsgeschichte*). Again, it may be more accurate to say that our Hugr soul is the root of our own desires, wishes and longings.

Hugsott (Hug-sickness): Frey is entwined in the bonds of desire, longing and love-sickness, after seeing Gerda from the High Seat. Though he holds a sickle to cut the grain, he cannot cut himself free of his Hugr-bonds.
(Frederic Lawrence, artist.)

In the same way that I think all the characteristics and abilities of the Mod soul arise from the root of Will, so I think that all the characteristics and abilities of the Hugr soul arise from the root of Desire / Wish / Longing. We can see examples of this in the role of Hugr in love and erotic desire, in its tendency to manipulate others to achieve its desires, and in another strong attribute of Hugr, namely envy. Envious thoughts and feelings are a major driver of

Who is Hugr?

Hugr's magical activities as seen in Scandinavian folklore, which I discuss in the next chapter.

Desire, wish, and longing also, I believe, play a deep role in Hugr's afterlife choices: whether to become a helpful, protective ancestral spirit supporting the family line; or to be reborn into familial and other relationships that were important in the previous life; or to enact its feelings of hostility and vengefulness as an afflicting spirit such as a hag or a murk-elf. The Hugr's desires, born of love, hostility, envy, engagement, wanting to stay involved, drive such afterlife choices.

Why do I not conclude that the root of Hugr is Thought itself? I suggest that 'rational' Thought is not the root of Hugr, but rather its blossoms, the result of all the foundational workings of the Hugr soul that build roots, trunk, branches and leaves out of all the stuff of our lives before it reaches the epitome of the blossoms of Thought. Hugr is indeed an intelligent soul, and has learned over lifetimes that 'Thought' can be the most powerful of tools, enabling Hugr to clarify, understand and communicate its desires, and to achieve and maintain them.

Let us stop and think about Thought for a minute. How many of us spend most of our time thinking abstract, emotionless, intellectualized thoughts that have no relation to our own lives, interests, problems, challenges, memories, experiences, fears, and desires? I would say, very few! 'Thought' is in no way a detached, abstract faculty most of the time. Rather, it is a faculty that is driven by, and placed in the service of, all of our desires, emotions, habits, needs, fears and longings.

Modern neurological studies show that memory is dependent upon emotion, and the stronger the emotion, the stronger the memory. Rational thought depends on memory to structure and sustain it, which in turn depends upon emotion motivating the whole process. Thought, emotion and memory are not separate processes, but rather complex interweavings of our multifaceted souls, from which our Mind emerges and acts.

We do not have to become free of emotion in order to pursue rational thought. Rather, it is important to consider which emotions support the rational thought process and which ones disturb it, in each individual context. Fear can destroy rational thought in some cases; in others, it can motivate a brilliant, rational solution to address the cause of the fear.

Emotions of depression and self-pity damage clear sight and rational thought; if they are replaced by courage, determination, and desire for change, those emotions will power rational thought with strong energy to create a new path. The Hugr is much involved in all of these processes, not only the process of rational thought. Hugr is not a tool or a skill; it is a complex, multifaceted soul-person.

Clarifying the Hugr

I mentioned earlier that the phrase *hlutro hugiu*, a 'clear or clarified Hugi', occurs a number of times in the Old Saxon *Heliand* poem. Of course, in that context the meaning is to purify the Hugi so as to make way for the Christian teachings that the poet is trying to convey. Obviously, our Heathen purposes are not the same. But if we understand how Hugr shapes our opinions, beliefs, behavior, motivations, and so forth, we can see the value of clearing and clarifying it.

Who is Hugr?

Hugr constructs within us a 'framework of thought', made up of all the factors that Hugr is involved with in our inner life and our contact with the outer world. Our thoughts and feelings, perceptions, judgments and reactions, are all filtered through this conceptual framework, being shaped and influenced by what Hugr has made out of our life experiences.

Our aim can be to make our Hugr, and the thought-framework it constructs, less of a clouded, roiled, confused, obstructed mash-up of thoughts and feelings, and more of a mental-emotional patterning of transparency, brilliance and power, channeling the best of what we can be, rather than the worst. Clarifying the Hugr may involve re-evaluating not only our present life experiences and the assumptions and thought-patterns they have generated, but possibly past life experiences as well.

One of the many reasons why clarifying our Hugr is a valuable undertaking, is that often our other, more obscure and occluded souls can only communicate with our conscious minds by going through the Hugr's framework. These soul perceptions may be channeled through the framework until we have reached a certain level of development in recognizing and consciously communicating with our other souls and are able to be in touch with them directly. The relative clarity or cloudedness of our Hugr will thus affect how well we can perceive and experience our other souls. This in turn affects our whole being, our spiritual growth, and everything about our life and afterlife.

When our Hugr is clear (even just temporarily during meditation or 'zoning out', for example) it's interesting to notice that the thoughts or the consciousness of our other souls have quite a different flavor than our Hugr's thoughts. For example, true, profound artistic creativity and higher, abstract intellectual thought, both of them taking us 'out of this world', are the province of our Ghost / Ahma souls, as is the experience of wode. Sensing and engaging with the energies and spirits of Nature come through our Ferah soul, and so does childlike, open-hearted playfulness and delight. So do piety and sacrifice.

Our Hama soul can give us a vital and accurate sense of our body and its many needs, processes and abilities. Contact with our Aldr soul can give us a sense of timelessness and of the play of wyrd and orlay in our lives, placing our everyday concerns into a different context. All of our souls are many-layered, complex, subtle, very individualistic and even contradictory – just like people! We need to spend a lot of time consciously experiencing them in order to get to know them and grow them, and to do that, our Hugr needs to have enough clarity to facilitate our awareness, or at least to get out of the way of our perception.

In my experience, our various souls are often more attuned to one God or Goddess than another. Some of this is because of the nature of each soul and each Deity. For example, our Mod souls have a special affinity with Thor and his children, and for different reasons, with Frigg and some of her maidens. Our Ghost and Hugr souls are drawn to Odin; our Ferah souls to Thor, Erda, and the Vanir; our Aldr to the Norns, and so forth.

There are also, for each of us, personal affinities between each soul and a given Deity or other spiritual being, based on our own character, life history, practice of our faith, and our relationship with that Deity. As we become more familiar with our various souls, we may be pleasantly

Who is Hugr?

surprised to discover that they have close relationships with Deities of our pantheon whom we previously assumed were not close to us or not well known to us.

The same discovery of connections or attunements can happen with beings of other worlds, such as the Alfar, Dwarves, Jotnar, Landwights, Ancestors, etc. There can be whole unexplored worlds within us, that we are unaware of until we come into more shared consciousness with all our souls. And, just as we do in Midgard, we need to be aware of our connections, make sure they are healthy and desirable, and attend to them if they are not.

Thus, it's important to keep these channels clear between our souls, the Deities and spirits, and our conscious mind and everyday life in Midgard. If we are stuck within a Hugr-framework filled with worries, anxieties, resentments, anger, distractions, stereotypes, and so forth, we block this essential communication among all our souls and our Deities. Then it is difficult to live fully in our faith, and have it reflect in all the doing-and-being of our Midgard life.

As we begin our journey of soul exploration, Hugr serves as the gate-keeper between our conscious, everyday mind and our other souls, on the one side, and the warder between our inner self and the outside world, on the other side. When it comes to the outside world, Hugr needs to be wise in the ways of the world, weighing the need to open up for human relationships and Midgard activities, but also needs to ward our inner selves from anyone untrustworthy and from unhealthy situations. The same is true when dealing with spirit beings. When it comes to the innermost world of our own 'soular-system', however, our Hugr gate-keeper needs to be fully clarified and transparent, and facilitate the vital interactions among all our souls.

Summary

Hugr, like Mod, carries with it much of our character and temperament, our capacity for thoughts and emotions, including the desires for love and friendship. It can operate in all three domains of our personal environment: within our inner self, as a warder and advisor on the border between our self and the outside world, and sometimes can extend beyond ourself entirely, and act independently at a distance. Hugr is likely to reincarnate after death, and may to some extent remember people it held strong feelings for during the previous life. Hugr creates within us a framework of thought, which shapes our perceptions, reactions, and understanding of the world around us and our interrelationships with it.

A Meditation on the Hugr's Power.

The photo on the next page is an unusual stele or grave-marker from Niederdollendorf, Germany. It was found in an empty grave in a Frankish cemetery dating from 600 or 700CE, but could be older, and its meaning remains unclear.

Here is my own interpretation. I consider this ancient figure to be an illustration of the Hugr and its power. The Hugr itself is represented by the circle on the chest of the warrior, over his heart. The swelling and emanating power of his Hugr is represented by his hair standing on end and the forceful lines and shapes radiating out from his body. His spear is a symbol of his power to focus his Hugr's will and desire.

Compare the idea of the Hugr directing a spear's power with this description of a sword in the Lay of Helgi Hjorvardsson: "There's a ring

Who is Hugr?

on its hilt, hugr in the middle, and terror on the point" (verse 9; Poetic Edda). Why is 'hugr' in the middle of the sword? Hugr is the force of direction, of intention, of courage and action, and forms the supporting structure of the sword, and of the spear.

I interpret the braided lines that the warrior is standing on as a representation of the interwoven strands of human life, culture, society, from which we all arise and which support all our interactions and achievements in life.

Finally, I see the zigzag lines at the bottom of the stele as representative of powerful waves of ancestral forces, influences, and support, that underlie and empower us in Midgard life. These ancestral forces are the Hugrs of the departed, sinking down and rising up like waves, influencing our Midgard lives.

There are many runes to be seen in this carving, especially Kenaz, Ingwaz, and Gebo. These, along with the interpretations I offer above, provide a fruitful context for meditation on the Hugr and its role in our life.

Reference: https://www.megalithic.co.uk/article.php?sid=37144

Oden som Vandringsman.
(Georg von Rosen, artist. 1886)

Odin the Wanderer:
His Hugr drives him to pursue deep wisdom
and the mysteries of the Worlds.

Chapter 11

11. The Occult Activities of the Hugr

Part 1: The Actions of the Hugr in Nordic Folk Beliefs

"I know a tenth (spell-song): If I see tun-riders (witches) playing aloft, I can make it happen that they wander astray from their home-hamas, from their home-hugrs." (Havamal vs. 155, my translation.)

In this chapter we'll begin by looking at a particular perspective on Hugr, namely its role in the folk beliefs of Nordic peoples in past and recent times concerning uncanny, occult, and 'magical' occurrences and activities. My purpose is to continue our exploration of the Hugr soul's nature by looking at traditional understandings of this soul's behavior and abilities, focusing on the very rich lore of Scandinavian folk belief.

I will make frequent reference here to an article, "The Concept of the Soul in Nordic Tradition," by the Swedish academic and folklorist, Dag Strömbäck. This article is one of the most useful and interesting writings I've found, and very relevant to the study of soul lore as I conceive it. One thing to note is that Strömbäck describes folk beliefs about various soul-beings as though they were all one soul with different names: Hugr, Hugham, Fylgja, Hamr, Vörðr or Vårðr, even Draugr as it is colloquially used in some regions. As he describes in his article, the same tales and descriptions are told about the activities of souls given these different names, depending on where and when the tales were collected. A story told about the Fylgja in one instance, for example, is told with the same details about the Hugr or Hama in another instance.

All of them have this defining characteristic, however: these souls can all emanate or externalize themselves under certain circumstances. They each belong to a living human and normally dwell within that human or very close to them. Under various circumstances, which I shall describe, the souls can exit the body, or emanate their power, acting independently at a distance from their human's body, sometimes independently of the conscious awareness and intention of the human.

The Occult Activities of the Hugr

Strömbäck is not concerned, in this article, about firmly distinguishing between different soul-terms, but in my soul lore studies, I am! Nevertheless, it is clear to me that the distinguishing boundaries between our different souls are very porous and fuzzy, with a good deal of overlap and interconnection between them, but also distinctive differences. Along these lines, I agree with the interpretation of *fylgja* as being any disembodied soul or spirit which 'follows' or accompanies a living person, since that is the literal meaning: fylgja = follower (see DeVries p. 224f, and Grimm p. 874f). This follower can be an animal fetch, a kinfylgja, Dis or guardian ancestress, a Várðr or watcher / guardian spirit, a doppelgänger, a form of disembodied spirit-energy giving intuitions or forebodings, or whatever.

Thus, following Strömbäck, descriptions of what a Fylgja does can relevantly be applied to the Hugr soul as well as to other types of daemon or disembodied spirits. A number of scholars, in addition to Strömbäck, find very little if any difference between the Vörðr or Várðr and the Hugr, including Jan DeVries, whose thoughts I described in my previous chapters about the Hugr. One of the root-complexes for the word 'Hugr' that I discuss in Chapter 9 comes from a Proto-Indo-European word meaning 'watchful, wary, careful', showing the relationship between the Hugr-spirit and the Várðr or Vörðr spirit, whose name means 'ward / warder'.

I will begin by describing several types of occult activities of which the Hugr is capable, according to traditional Nordic beliefs. These include the following: 1) The occult behavior of the Hugr when motivated by desire, longing, envy, hatred and revenge. 2) Hugr as a fore-runner, harbinger, and warder: running ahead of the person, bringing forebodings and warnings, and serving as a protector. 3) The Hug-ham: the Hugr exiting the body as an independent entity and performing actions at a distance. This includes the Hugr as a troll-wind, witch-wind or outflow of sorcerous power. Another area where the Hugr is involved is in rune-work and spell-casting, which I will cover in the next section of this chapter.

Desire, Longing, Envy, Hatred

In the previous chapter, I concluded that the root of Hugr within us, its defining impulse or motive, is Desire / Wish / Longing, rooted in the Heart, which bears the desire for love and friendship, and sometimes also desires related to envy, hatred and vengefulness. The power of Thought, which is so characteristic of the Hugr, is the primary mode that Hugr uses to act upon and achieve its desires.

Consider this: in all older traditional societies I am aware of, the activity of Thought was assumed to occur in the heart, not in the brain. The philosophical / scientific idea of thought and emotion being strictly separate activities, one in the brain and one in the heart, is a relatively modern one which held sway for a few centuries since the Enlightenment, but is now, through modern neurology, being shown to be a highly oversimplified assumption. Thoughts and emotions are intertwined and involve chemical and electrical (and microbiological) activity over large areas of the body, including the heart and the gut as well as the brain, nervous, and endocrine systems. So both traditionally and scientifically, the Hugr's characteristic mixture of strong thought and strong emotion makes sense.

The Occult Activities of the Hugr

Having discussed in the previous chapter how Hugr is involved in the desires of love and friendship, I will now move on to describe examples of how desirous thoughts result in uncanny and occult expressions of envy, a powerful motivator of people's Hugrs generally, and especially those living in small, close-knit, insular, resource-constrained societies. The following paragraphs are summarized from Strömbäck's article, except as otherwise noted. I include my own comments in square brackets.

In Norwegian dialects *hugsa* means 'to watch, observe, wish, have a desire for' (p. 12). [Envy arises from observing that others have something which you lack, and want. The Faroese dictionary expands these meanings: *hugadr* means 'wishful or desirous of something, eager,' etc., while *hugbit* (hug-bite) = 'a strong desire for what one knows, especially sees or hears, another person has; envy with unfortunate effects for the possessor.']

In Dalarna district *hugsa* means 'by strong thoughts to cause somebody to feel ill.' This hugsa was not necessarily intentional ill will. An anecdote tells of a grandmother watching a young girl eating something good, and simply thinking to herself how delicious it looked. The girl immediately became ill. A little while later when the grandmother realized that her thoughts had unintentionally made the girl ill, then the girl quickly recovered. (p. 12.) [Here we see a phenomenon where observation and intention change the outcome of an event, mirroring the 'observer effect' in quantum mechanics. It has clear implications for some forms of modern magic.] If one suffers from depression and low spirits, lack of energy and ability, this is attributed to the Hugr of someone who does not like you and sends bad wishes your way. (p. 13-14.)

Heathen Soul Lore

Traditional accounts from folklorists in this area associate *hugsa* with 'strong thoughts or heavy thoughts' combined with a 'firm look from a person's eyes', together called *hugsning*. This can result in animate objects losing their power and effectiveness, and inanimate objects stopping their proper functions. (p. 13). In the Sogn-district of Norway, they spoke of a person's Hugr being so strong that it could do great damage to things at work. For example, if such a person came near brewing beer, or milk in the dairy shed, their Hugr could cause it to spoil and the vats to leak. If a Hug-strong person eagerly desired an alcoholic drink, the keg would bubble and splash as they approached it (p. 14). (End of summary.)

It's interesting to compare this phenomenon with the Saxon and Anglo-Saxon idea of *Hugi wallan*: the Hugi upwelling or wallowing within the breast, around the heart, when it is powerfully moved (see previous chapter). In one case we have the 'inner whelming or wallowing' within the breast where Hugr resides, and in the other case it is external containers of liquid doing the same thing when someone with a powerful Hugr approaches.

Some of these are examples of unintentional harm caused by people who have strong Hugrs but basically good characters. But outright envy, anger and related negative emotions, rooted in the Hugr and leading to occult or magical phenomena, apparently played a heavy role in traditional Nordic society.

I will note here that when I lived in Greece for many years during the 1950s, '60s and '70s, I observed many convincing instances of actions of the Evil Eye, generated by envy, which involves beliefs very similar to the Nordic ones. In particular, I was cautioned that since I have blue eyes, and

The Occult Activities of the Hugr

blue-eyed people are especially prone to cause the Evil Eye even if they don't intend to, I should be careful how my actions were construed by others. This required me, among other things, to be restrained about how I admired other people's possessions and circumstances, and especially their babies and children, since admiration could be construed as envy and thus cause the Evil Eye (severe headaches, illness, bad luck, loss). Babies are particularly sensitive to the Evil Eye, and ill-intentioned people apparently cover up their envy over another person's lovely baby by pretending to admire it, but covertly causing it to fall ill. I have read that many other traditional cultures around the world have similar beliefs about envy causing bad luck and illness through occult means, so traditional Nordic cultures are not alone in this!

Here are some examples of envy / *avund* or *ovund* in Nordic cultures and the harm it can cause. First, another summary from Strömbäck. In ancient Scandinavia *avund* was considered to be something with real physical power, emanating from the Hugr of a malignant person. This is called *ovundhugen* in old records, and there was a folk-saying that it was so powerful it could consume stone. This is illustrated by the following anecdote.

There was an old woman known for her *ovundhug*, and one of her neighbors decided to test its power. The neighbor woman chose a time when the *ovundhug*-woman was watching her from a distance, then stooped and picked up a pebble. Pretending it was something valuable, she quickly tucked it into her pocket and hurried home. There, she put the pebble secretly into a chest, and took it out to look at it from time to time. Eventually, the pebble was eaten away by the *ovundhug*. Strömbäck proposes that behind a

Norwegian spell such as *ek snui uppa thik heipt ok ofund* (I turn upon you hatred and envy) lies the terrible threat of turning loose an ill-intentioned Hugr upon that person, a threat that could lead almost to death by occult means (pp. 15-16).

This brings to my mind a scene from the *Greenlandic Poem of Atli* (Poetic Edda), which takes place after Atli has brutally killed Gudrun's brothers, and she has taken revenge by killing her and Atli's young sons and serving them to Atli for dinner, unbeknownst to him. (Vs. 81 in Old Norse, vs. 88 in translation.) Not surprisingly, Gudrun and Atli are consumed by hatred for each other, and the poem describes them sitting together in the same building, "sending *far-hugi*, throwing *heiptyrdi*" at each other. The word *far* means 'dangerous, inimical, damaging', and *heiptyrdi* means 'hateful words'.

These two people, Gudrun and Atli, were known as *ulf-hugr*, having wolf's-hugrs, and *hard-hugr*, meaning strong, courageous, determined, but also cruel and ruthless. Gudrun was described as *stor-hugud* (vs. 71) or strong-hugr'd. Compare this description of their behavior with Strömbäck's summary that I discussed above, where Nordic folklore informants described *hugsa* as 'strong thoughts or *stora tankar*' combined with a 'firm look' and believed this was the cause of *hugsning*, the Hugr having an effect on other people and objects.

Gudrun and Atli were not simply sulking and insulting each other like grumpy kids in this scene of the poem: they were directing their powerful Hugrs with laser-like intensity at each other with the firm intention (*hyggjum*) of causing severe harm. In the rest of the poem Gudrun conspires with her nephew Hogni to bring about Atli's death, and later tries (unsuccessfully) to kill herself. These dire outcomes were shaped, I am sure, while these two inimical spouses 'sent *far-hugi*' at each other, thus setting grim ørlög in motion.

The practice of turning the *ofund / avund*, the envious and corrosive form of the Hugr, against someone is attested to in Bang's compendium of Norse spells and charms, which gives at least eight magical spells against *avund*, dated from the late 1700s to the mid-1800s. Avund, in most of these spells, is treated as a being, an evil spirit, which ties in with Hugr's daemon nature and with the Hugham, the externalized Hugr in a shape of its own. This Avund-spirit is very likely to be the envious Hugr of a person, living or dead; as Strömbäck stated, above, the term for a person with such a Hugr is *ovund-hugen*.

Envy can drive one to evil deeds. (John Bauer, artist.)

Two of Bang's spells mention the *Avundmand* or *Avindsmænd*, the 'envy-man' (e.g. #104), which is another term for an 'enemy.' I am not clear whether this refers to a living human, in the same way that Strömbäck described the old woman with *ovundhug*, above, or whether it is another way of naming the Avund-spirit or externalized Hugr, separate from the person, which is clearly referenced in the other spells about Avund.

Some of the spells seem to be intended to protect against a person wielding Avund, while others are against a wandering spirit apparently not associated directly with a human. Spell #73 works to protect a cow from the *avund* of both *onde* or wights, and from *mennesker* or humans. Both of these perceptions of the Avund fit well with my understanding of the Hugr soul, which can be strongly motivated by envy, and is a daemon-soul which can operate either from within a person or independently of the person it is associated with. The Avund-spirit or ovund-hugen, in these spells, afflicts domestic animals and humans with illness, loss of productivity, malaise and misfortune.

Strömbäck describes the Danish Valby amulet with the runic inscription *viðr ofund*, 'against envy', which offers another example of magical defense against the envious Hugr (p. 15).

Hugr as Fore-runner, Hugboð, and Warder

Summarizing again from Strömbäck: the Hugr flying ahead of a visitor, or ahead of an enemy who is approaching, is recognized as a very common phenomenon in Nordic folklore (also told about Vörðr or Vårðr, Fylgja, Hama, and Draug). This fore-runner or foreboding aspect of Hugr could express itself in many ways: an itch, a sneeze, a noise caused by no one present, yawning, severe sleepiness. One of my favorite terms is *nasehug* / *nesehau*, or 'nose-hugr', where the visitor's Hugr flies up the nose of the host, ahead

The Occult Activities of the Hugr

of the person's arrival, causing sneezing or itching. (I'm not sure my Hugr really wants to do this, though!)

Another strange aspect of the Hugboð (Hugr-foreboding) is that it can cause a severe itching sensation, about a day prior to a person's death or injury to the part of the body which had been itching; for example, on the nape of a person who is decapitated the next day. Strömbäck suggests that the famous line spoken by the three witches or wyrd-women in Shakespeare's Macbeth: "By the pricking of my thumbs, something wicked this way comes," is another example of the same phenomenon. (pp. 8-11.)

"By the pricking of my thumbs, something wicked this way comes." (Henry Fuseli, "Study for the three witches of Macbeth".)

I see all of these examples, trivial though they may seem, as efforts of the Hugr to communicate through the Hama—the soul which constructs and maintains the physical body and its actions. (See Chapter 6.) Considering the very close connection, even overlap, between the Hugr, Hugham, Hama, and the Hamingja as a luck-bearing spirit, this would make a great deal of sense. Most of us, most of the time, are more aware of what our body, our Lichama, is telling us through annoying messages like itching or yawning, than we are aware of vague 'forebodings' somewhere underneath our everyday attention level.

The Hugr is a watcher, a lookout, a keen observer, and among other things it is aware of the shifting and turning of 'luck' or hamingja, and the effects this may be bringing our way in the near future. As our Warder or Vårðr, it tries to make us aware and to mobilize us toward action by triggering the Lichama to grab our attention. If we are wise, we then 'take counsel' with our Hugr: listen to our Hugr's rede and act accordingly.

If we take the Vårðr or Vörðr spirit to be essentially the same as the Hugr, as understood by both Strömbäck and by DeVries (p. 221-2), then we can add more anecdotes and descriptions to expand our grasp of Hugr / Vårðr, such as the following from Strömbäck. The Vårðr could sometimes be heard, but not seen, as footsteps or the closing of a door, when apparently no one was there. After a little while, the visitor or the absent householder would arrive and make the same sounds that had previously been heard. The forerunner spirit that causes this phenomenon is variously called *Vårðr, Vale, Vårsel, Forbö* (foreboding), and other names. Strömbäck mentions that the same phenomena are recognized, under different names, in England and Scotland. (p. 9.)

Strömbäck quotes another famous folklorist (Gunnar Olof Hylten-Cavallius, 1864): "The Vårðr (literally: the guardian) is a being attached to an individual, a spirit who accompanies a person wherever he goes, and sometimes reveals itself either as a glimmer or in the form of a person as a second self (*hamn*), a phantom. The presence of the Vårðr can even be felt, both by other people and by the individual himself when he is out of doors at night. The expressions used for this are: .... 'he has the glimmer with him', 'he has the Vårðr with him'" (p. 17). I'll discuss the 'glimmer' and the 'second self' later in this chapter.

The Wind of the Troll-wife

Trolls attack with magical wind and water. (John Bauer, "Troll Trouble.")

This evocative phrase comes from the 12th Century *Skaldskarpamal* of the Prose Edda, presented by Snorri Sturlason as a kenning or synonym for 'hugr' (p. 154). The troll-wife is another word for a witch or sorceress. I take this phrase to refer to the Hugr bursting invisibly but powerfully out of a person and acting at a distance, usually in a damaging way. DeVries writes that the Hugr could exit the body as breath or wind, and the stronger a person's Hugr was, the more dangerous the wind. He compares this to the folk-belief, up until recent times, that witches travel around in a whirlwind (p. 221).

Here is a summary from Strömbäck's article describing this phenomenon. A strong Hugr is considered capable of *fljuga å* or *laupa å*, to 'fly at, or attack' something. People may find that their Hugr does this even without their intention. This uncontrolled Hugr activity was considered disgraceful, and those who were basically good-natured but possessed such Hugrs had to be especially careful about their thoughts and desires, and how their neighbors were affected.

A tale is told of a man who was known to have a such a *hugham* (a Hugr that takes shape outside a person), on his way to visit a farm. Before he arrived (here is Hugr as a forerunner), his Hugr 'flew at' the farmer's only cow. When the visitor arrived he found them hauling away a dead cow. The farmer, apparently aware that the visitor did not intend this destruction, said nothing, but the visitor knew his Hugr was responsible and handed over money for a new cow. (p. 14)

Hugham: The Hugr Takes Shape

This is perhaps the most dramatic magical act of the Hugr as seen in Nordic lore, and as far as I can tell from my reading, it is not the result of a magical ritual or spell, or often, even a magical intent. The extrusion of a personal double or a person's soul in animal form seems to 'just happen' when circumstances warrant it, among people who are shape-strong or *hamrammr*.

There is conflation, overlap, or confusion of soul words in the old tales of shapeshifting, with different terms applied to the shapeshifted being in tales from different times and places, even when the details are pretty much identical. This shape can be referred to in the tales and anecdotes as the *hugr, hugham, mannahugr, Vǫrðr or Vǫrðrøgr, hama, gongham* ('walking shape'), *fyreferd, or fylgja*, in different accounts. Sometimes it is even called the draugr, as Strömbäck mentions, though modern Heathens generally think of the draugr as a revenant, a re-animated corpse,

The Occult Activities of the Hugr

which is not the Hugr's domain. (The draugr, in my understanding, is a phenomenon of the Hama / Lichama, discussed in Chapter 6.) This many-named etheric shape can sometimes be visible to anyone, other times is only visible to those with second sight. It can take action at a distance from the originating person, sometimes with their conscious intent, but often without their knowledge. (Strömbäck p.16-17.)

The Hugham may take an animal shape. By Dale Wood.

If a person's thoughts were evil they could hurt others by making them objects of intense hatred, envy or discontent. One could activate the Hugr in this way, sending it in specific directions with specific intentions. One resulting phenomenon was called *re-hug* (riding-Hugr) or *re-ham* (riding Hama). The Hugr would be sent to a stable or barn and choose a horse or a cow to ride upon, goading it on for hours and leaving it exhausted and unproductive. (p. 17-18)

Strömbäck discusses at length the first documented witch trial in Icelandic history, told in the *Eyrbyggja Saga* (ch. 15, 16), and dating from sometime during the 9th to early 11th centuries. The protagonist, Gunnlaug, is invited by the witch Katla to spend the night with her, but he refuses her advances. Later he is found unconscious from exhaustion, bloodstained over his shoulders and legs. Katla is known as a *kveld-riða*, an evening-rider, and Strömbäck mentions other women in the sagas and folktales known as *kveldriður*, *myrkriður* (darkness rider), or *trollriður* (witch / sorcerer-riders) who would likewise ride men against whom they bore a grudge, causing injury, exhaustion and illness. They were able to let their Hugr take on *hamr* or shape, and thus materialized, able to do harm to humans and animals by this night-time spirit-riding. (pp. 17 ff.)

A troll-ridden horse. ("Trollritten" by John Bauer.)

Strömbäck provides a discussion of the *Havamal* verse I quoted at the beginning of this chapter, where Odin says he knows spells to confuse flying witches—*tunriður* (fence-riders)—causing them to lose their way when attempting to return to their own Hugrs and Hamas, their own ordinary minds and shapes. Strömbäck explains this phenomenon as something that occurs while the physical body is sleeping, allowing the Hugr (or other soul / spirit) to exit the body and act independently (pp.18-21).

A similar phenomenon occurs in various sagas when observers see a night-time battle taking place between two spirit-animals, who are later discovered to be the *manna-*

The Occult Activities of the Hugr

hugur or *hug-hamur* (or *fylgjur*) of sleeping humans pursuing their feud by occult means (p. 6).

I will now summarize another scholar, Jan DeVries, on the subject of the Hugr. He defines Hugr as not only thought and spirit, but also as wish, desire, and longing, as I have discussed in the previous chapter. This 'Wish' (*Wunsch*) can be so strong that it condenses itself into a magical being, which can exit from a person and take visible or audible form. The expression for this is *hugen tok ham på*, 'the Hugr shaped a form for itself'. As an example: a farmer badly needed another horse for his busy harvesting operation, but his only available horse was in a mountain pasture some distance away. The farmer was too occupied with the harvest to be able to leave and get the horse, but his wish took form as an invisible but audible being who was heard moving around the herder's hut and mountain pasture where the horse was. (p. 220-1, *Altgermanische. Religionsgeschichte*).

Part 2: Hugr's Involvement in Magical and Esoteric Practices

In Part 1 of this chapter, I focused primarily on the innate abilities of the Hugr-soul to undertake certain occult actions, whether or not the whole person intended these actions, or deliberately developed these abilities. Here, I will focus more on the Hugr's involvement in deliberate esoteric and magical practices. In essence, the previous section covers the 'wild' Hugr, while this one takes a look at the 'trained' Hugr: the situation where the Hugr and the ordinary or

Midgard-mind of the person work consciously together, developing mutual experience, skills and trust.

Keep in mind: this is a very brief overview of broad areas of esoteric and occult activity that our Hugr is capable of, and—importantly—that it is also subject to, when wielded by the Hugrs of others. I'll start with the Hugr as an inner rede-giver, a counselor and guide, because this is the basis for building mutual trust and skill, and then I'll link this with what one might call 'ancestral magic.' Then I'll discuss my understanding of the Hugr's involvement in spellcraft and runecraft, and touch on the subject of the 'double' or doppelgänger. A discussion of Hugr in *seiðr* and spaecraft follows, which includes not only oracular work, but also traditional witchcraft. Then I'll move on to its role in Anglo-Saxon *scinnlac* or sheenlock, a form of shamanistic magic, and close with a discussion of Hugr's ability to swell with power.

Rede-Giver

I see this aspect of the Hugr as the foundation for all of its more thoughtful and deliberate esoteric abilities. Understanding the Hugr as a trusted counselor, advisor, rede-giver, means that we recognize Hugr as a soul-being in its own right: a being who knows what our conscious mind doesn't know, and can see farther into the future, the past, and the complexities of the present than our rational minds are capable of. In my understanding, our Hugr is our inner partner in active magical work of all kinds. (Others of our souls are likely to be involved as well, depending on the type of working.)

The more developed our Hugr is, and the clearer the communication is, between our Hugr and our conscious

The Occult Activities of the Hugr

mind, the more effective is our esoteric work. As I outlined in the previous section, the Hugr is quite capable of acting on its own in an occult capacity, sometimes in ways we might not want or agree with. The key to occult work that is both effective and ethical is to bring our Hugr into full consciousness and work consciously with it and our other souls together, as a team.

Here are some examples from Germanic lore that illustrate the Hugr's rede-giving abilities.

~ "He bore a wise Hugi (*spahan hugi*) within his breast." *Heliand* ll. 173-4.

~ Here are two quotations from *Hymiskviða* (Poetic Edda): "(Thor's) Hugr did not speak encouragingly to him"…when he saw the power of the giant Hymir. (v. 14.) Hymir tells Thor to go off to the herds of oxen to get bait for a fishing expedition, "if you trust in your Hugr." (v. 17.) Here, Hugr is both the provider of courage to Thor, and his advisor who is telling him how to manage the menacing Hymir.

~ Near the end of chapter 19 of *Egil's Saga*, Kveldulf receives a *hugboð*, a Hugr-foreboding, that Thorolf will die before he does. Later, Skallagrim says to Thorolf: "one thing my Hugr tells me: if we part now, we will not meet again" (ch. 38).

~ "We come through friendly Hige to seek lord Hrothgar," meaning 'by reason of, by the agency of' the advice from a friendly Hyge or Hugr. (*Beowulf* l. 267.) Note that it does not say 'with' a friendly Hige, but 'through' a friendly Hige, that is, the Hige is the cause of their action to visit Hrothgar.

~ Verse 69 in Old Norse, 74 in translation, of the *Greenlandic Lay of Atli* (Poetic Edda), says that Gudrun, who was described many times as having a strong and fierce Hugr, 'knew how to take counsel with her Hugr' in order to take strategic action.

Showing that our source of trust, as well as distrust, comes from our Hugr:

~ Sigurd and Gripir speak 'heart to heart': "as we two *hugat mælum*" or speak Hugr-to-Hugr (v. 10). Gripir later says "the shining king, Gjuki's heir, trusted you, prince, with all his Hugr". (v. 47; *Gripismal*, Poetic Edda.)

~ Verse 46 of the *Havamal* (Poetic Edda) says that when dealing with a person you don't trust and who has ill intentions, go ahead and laugh with him, but take counsel with your Hugr (*of hug mæla*) and consider how to return the same 'gift' that he is giving you.

Ancestor-Work

The first step for working consciously with our Hugr is to recognize it as a being with its own thoughts, intentions, emotions, knowledge and power, and develop an aware and trusting relationship with it. This path expands into the field of interactions with our ancestors (whether actual genetic ancestors, or 'ancestors of the spirit'), because, as I believe, ancestral spirits are actually the Hugr-souls of the ancestors. In addition, my understanding is that when reincarnation occurs, it is the Hugr soul which reincarnates, bringing with it knowledge from past lives which links it with ancestral knowledge. When your Hugr gives you rede and

The Occult Activities of the Hugr

knowledge, it is likely coming from ancestral sources as well as Midgard and other sources that Hugr taps into.

When we work with the ancestors and other departed folk, we are working Hugr-to-Hugr; hence the value of developing our awareness of, and communication with, our own Hugr so as to facilitate this process. When we wish to contact our ancestors through spaecraft / seiðr and in other ways, and when we desire help or knowledge from them, this work is done through our Hugr, reaching out to their Hugr-spirits and powers. Then, once contact has occurred, it is our Hugr who processes the full meaning of what was shared, and who evaluates the intentions, wisdom, and the execution of any actions that may arise out of this communication. It is important to 'bear a wise Hugi within our breast' when undertaking such activities!

There is an Anglo-Saxon charm against miscarriage, which instructs the mother to step over a grave while reciting a charm, and then to step over her husband in bed, speaking another charm to strengthen her child and make it live. (Storms pp. 196-8.) I interpret this as a form of Hugr-magic which calls on the Hugr-spirits of the child's ancestors, both deceased ancestors and the living father, to keep the child hale and whole. When the mother steps over something, she is opening the passage for power to enter her womb and her baby.

Another form of ancestral magic that is mentioned numerous times in the ancient writings is sleeping or meditating on a burial mound, while asking for healing, inspiration, or ancestral knowledge, often accompanied by a sacrifice or gift.

Our Hugr is also our inner warder, and advises us when it detects possible harm or risk as we consider an action we might take. Not all ancestral spirits are friendly and helpful, and forays into the afterworld of the ancestors entail various risks and dangers. An aspect of ancestral magic that I strongly advise, is to move your consciousness into your Hugr-soul with its powers of discernment and subtle thought, when contacting the world of the ancestors. In other words, enter your *Hugiskeft,* your 'Hug-ship.' That way you will have real-time awareness of dangers, opportunities, insights, precautions, that might not be available, or might be delayed or misinterpreted, if you rely entirely on your conscious mind. (My article "Disir, Hama and Hugr as Healing Partners" offers one approach for entering your Hugiskeft.)

Consider the powers of Odin. He is the exemplar of Hugr-powers: deep thought, powerful intentions and desires, galdor-father, Wish-father, advisor to heroes, subtle strategist, pursuer of hidden knowledge and wisdom, source of Huginn and Muninn. His ability to speak with the dead is a great source of his arcane knowledge. This kind of ancestral contact, and ancestral wisdom and knowledge, flow through our Hugr soul. Developing the ability to perceive, hear and trust our Hugr, to enter our Hugiskeft, is a great step in any quest to work safely with the ancestors, with other spirit-beings including Deities, and with past-life experiences.

Spellcraft and Runecraft affecting the Hugr

It is clear from the anecdotes I wrote about in the previous section of this chapter, and many other examples, that the Hugr can be an actor using occult powers to affect others, whether intentionally or inadvertently. I offer some examples here that show that the Hugr can also be the *subject*

The Occult Activities of the Hugr

of deliberate magical spells. This is something that the careful practitioner should be aware of; these manipulative spells can come from otherworldly beings, as well as from living humans, who are not always fully aware of how their own Hugr is acting.

Skirnir threatening Gerda with runic spells, to persuade her to accede to Frey's desires. Gerda holds her fist over her heart, seeking to protect her Sefa soul. (Lorenz Frølich, artist.)

Here are two examples of how Hugr can be affected by spells.

I know a sixteenth (spell-song or rune): if I wish to have all of a woman's attention (geð) and play, I turn away (hverfi) the Hugi of the white-armed woman, and turn (snyk) all her Sefa (toward me). (Havamal vs. 161, in the Poetic Edda, my translation.)

The *Grógaldr* (Poetic Edda) tells of how young Svipdag goes to his mother's grave and asks her help as he prepares to set out on a dangerous quest. Her afterlife Hugr-spirit responds by giving him magical spells to protect him. Verse 9 describes one of these spells: *If a foe stands before you, ready on gallows-way, turn (hverfi) his Hugr toward the other side, and turn (snuisk) until his Sefa is reconciled.*

These two spells take the same actions and use the same words for these magical actions. First, the subject's Hugr is *turned away*, using the verb *hverfi*. Then the subject's Sefa, a heart-based soul which is greatly involved in our relationships (see Chapter 12), is also 'turned', using a different verb, *snui*. This 'snui-turning' involves *turning toward* the spell-caster, rather than away, as with the Hugr. In both cases, it is clear that the subject's attitude is one of resistance or enmity, as long as their Hugr is on guard within them. Once their Hugr is turned away, then the spellcaster works to move the subject's Sefa soul into a more accommodating attitude, giving the spellcaster what they want.

This verb *snui* is used again and again in the Norse languages when referring to magical action, and is worthy of further examination. I see it as meaningfully (not linguistically) related to our modern expression of '*turning* something into something else' through magic.

As one example of magical usage, forms of *snui* are used multiple times in *Egil's Saga* (chapter 60) when describing the famous scene where Egil uses runecraft to create a *nithing-pole* or cursing-pole topped with a horse's head, for the purpose of vengefully driving out the king and queen from the land. Egil first turns the head toward the king and queen, then turns it toward the land, then turns it on / against the landwights to disorient them and make them

The Occult Activities of the Hugr

feel lost, with the intention of harassing the landwights until they have driven out the rulers. All of these 'turns' use forms of the word *sny, snui*. (See discussion in Mitchell, p. 68 and p. 102.)

Another of the spells that Gróa gives to her son Fjölsvin is used to 'turn / *snuisk*' the dangerous rivers (or beings) Horn and Ruðr back toward Hel, when they are threatening his path (vs. 8).

Gudrun offers Sigurd the rune-spelled potion, brewed by her mother Grimhild, that will turn his Hugr and his memory away from the Valkyrie he loves. He will forget the Valkyrie, and turn his Hugr toward Gudrun.

The verb *hverfi*, used in the spells to 'turn away' the watchful Hugr, is related to 'warp', and stems from Proto-Indo-European *werp meaning 'to turn, wind, bend.' I find that the meaning of 'warp' fits well in the context of these magical spells: the natural intention of the Hugr to guard the Sefa is warped out of shape through manipulative magic.

Here's another act of magic that can be similarly interpreted. Odin boasts to Thor that "I considered Hlebard a hard Jotun. He gave me a *gambantein* (a magical staff, wand or twig), and I 'rolled or rotated' (*velta*, related to 'revolve') his wits." Thor replies "An ill Hugr you rewarded him with, who gave you good." (*Harbardsljoð* vs. 20-21, Poetic Edda.) Here, the use of 'Hugr' can mean several things: it can mean a mood or attitude, or an intention, all of which fit well in this context. But I interpret it that Odin actually changed or overturned Hlebard's Hugr, warping and roiling his wits and the other powers of his Hugr, perhaps through use of the *gambantein* itself.

I think that working with runes and spells, and working with Odin in magical endeavors, all require strong involvement of our Hugr, interacting with Odin's Hugr. Here is another magical work of Odin's:

I know a tenth (rune or spell). If I see tunriders (witches) playing aloft, I can work it that they wander astray from their home-Hamas, from their home-Hugrs. (Havamal vs. 155, Poetic Edda, my translation.)

Here, Odin can use rune-craft to prevent witches, in their out-faring Hughams, from returning to home-base in their bodies. This provides us with a segue to the next phenomenon: the Hugr as a double, doppelgänger, or as a spirit in animal form.

The Double and Animal-Double

The idea of humans having a spirit-double, either in their own form, an animal form, or some altered form such as a flying witch, is common among all the Germanic and other European lands, and among many other cultures as well. As I discussed in the previous section of this chapter, this double is given many different names. One of the names is Hugr, also Hug-ham or 'Hugr-shape'; and others of the names, such as Fylgja and Vårðr, may in some cases be alternate names for the same entity.

The Occult Activities of the Hugr

A dramatic scene where two lovers meet their own doubles, causing great shock. (Henry Treffry Dunn, after Dante Gabriel Rossetti: "How they met themselves.")

As one example, in *Hardar Saga Grimkelssonar*, ch. 30, a woman dreamed that eighty wolves surrounded the house, and they were interpreted as being the Hugir of their enemies: spirit-forerunners who were surrounding the house preparatory to an attack (DeVries p. 221). Another example is given in the quotation from the *Havamal*, above: the flying witches are able to go aloft because they are in spirit-form or Hug-ham, a shape (hama) that their Hugr can take on through magic in order to fare abroad from their body.

The ability to walk as a 'doppelgänger' or double of oneself is known in folklore around the world, going back many years and into the present. Lecouteaux describes an instance of a doppelgänger from a Nordic medieval compendium of 'miraculous' works by Christian priests. A man named Snorri was under the spell of a troll-woman, who pressed upon him with her spells, trying to force him toward the mountain where she lived. During an attack, Snorri called for help from his bishop, Father Gudmund, whereupon Gudmund appeared as a light-form, sprinkled the giantess with holy water, and caused her to melt into the earth. As this was happening, the physical Father Gudmund had fallen asleep (or gone into trance) against the shoulder of his assistant, while he was praying. The assistant said that for a little while, he could not feel the weight of the bishop against his shoulder, corresponding to the time the bishop's double was out of his body. (pp. 32-3.)

Lecouteux uses this anecdote to make the important point that people's Hugrs can be in close and instant communication with each other, even when in our conscious minds and the physical world, this instantaneous communication would not be possible. Snorri, in great danger, called upon his bishop, the bishop's Hugr heard his need, and his Hug-ham, his doppelgänger, was there instantaneously to help.

Many times the doppelgänger appears to a relative or beloved one of a person who is dying or passed into death, even when the two persons are separated by many miles. There are so very many examples of this type of phenomenon, and so many ways and terms for describing it, that I will not go into more detail here. The main point, aside from the existence of the doppelgänger, is the ability of instant communication from Hugr to Hugr through visions, calls for help, counsel, insight, awareness. This is how and why the Hugr is so good at anything that involves communication unconstrained by time and space, such as seiðr and spaecraft, and communication with the ancestors, Deities, and other spirits.

(Those who are interested in further reading on this subject may enjoy Claude Lecouteux' *Witches, Werewolves and Fairies: Shapeshifters and Astral Doubles in the Middle Ages*. He focuses on the Germanic concepts of the Hugr (witches), Hama (werewolves) and Fylgja (fairies), and offers a multitude of examples from many sources, primarily from Germanic cultures, but also Baltic, Saami, Roman, and others.)

Seiðcraft

Seiðr and spaecraft are, I believe, large and powerful domains of action for the Hugr soul. Spaecraft refers to oracular trancework, second sight, and related skills. Seiðr ('say-thr') includes these skills, but also many others that fit within the fields of 'witchcraft' and shamanistic activities, depending on how one defines them. Modern Heathens tend to use these terms interchangeably, and focus on the oracular or wisdom-seeking aspects of this craft, such as communicating with the departed, with Deities, Landwights, and other spirits, and for seeking counsel about important matters in their lives. These are all areas where Hugr's skills and knowledge serve us well.

The seeress Gróa.

Older references to seiðr show that it could be used for malicious magic, or to stymie the efforts of others to engage in malicious magic. There are also expressions showing the involvement of the Hugr in these matters, including examples that I quoted, above.

There's an intriguing line in the Voluspà (Poetic Edda) that says of the *seiðkona* or witch-woman Heiðr: *"seiðr, hvars kunni, seiðr hug leikinn"* (vs. 22 in ON, 23 in translated edition). The first phrase says that Heiðr knew seiðr; the second has been interpreted in various ways. *Leikinn* means 'to play', also 'to skip or hop'. A *leika* is a toy or game. It occurs in the other Germanic languages as well, for example Gothic *laiks* = a sport, a dance.

Strömbäck interprets this phrase, *hug leikinn*, as moving into the ecstatic state of outfaring, soul-faring out of the body (*Sejd*, p. 19). An example of this meaning may be shown in this quotation from *Fostbrœðra Saga* ch. 20: "I took a *gandreið* (magical ride, outfaring ecstatic state) to many places this night, and I learned with certainty things I did not know before" (quoted in Lecouteux p. 29-30).

Many others interpret *hug-leikinn* as 'playing with people's minds / Hugrs', generally for malicious or selfish ends. The spells that I quoted above, about turning / *hverfi* / warping people's Hugrs and 'rotating their wits', are good examples of this interpretation. In my view, *hug-leikinn* can have both meanings: the playfulness and delight that can come from faring out of our body on magical flights, as well

The Occult Activities of the Hugr

as manipulating and toying with people's Hugrs, minds, perceptions, and feelings.

Either way, this word *hug-leikinn* associated with seiðr shows that seiðr does involve working with Hugrs: using one's own Hugr for seiðcraft, and affecting the Hugrs of others in various ways through seiðcraft. This is further confirmed by the *Havamal* verse I quoted above, about Odin knowing a rune-spell to block witches, faring out in their Hug-hams, from returning to their ordinary shapes and minds. The witches he is referring to are practicing a form of seiðr, and they are doing it in their Hug-hams, their outfaring Hugr-forms.

Let's use this word hug-leikinn as a bridge toward another form of magic that may be related: Anglo-Saxon *scinnlac* ('sheen-lock'), with *lac* being the Anglo-Saxon equivalent of *leikinn*.

A Glimmer of Anglo-Saxon Magic

The Anglo-Saxon language had the word *hyge* or *hige*, cognate with Hugr, which was widely used and richly compounded with other words, but I have not seen that word applied to magical and occult phenomena in Anglo-Saxon in the way that Hugr was used in the Scandinavian languages until recent times.

However, let's consider this. In Chapter 9 I noted that one proposed word-root and cognate words for Hugr meant 'shine, burn, glow, bright, white'. Anglo-Saxon has the word *scinn* (sheen), from which come our words 'sheen, shining'. *Scinan* meant 'to shine, flash, illuminate', and *scinnes* meant 'radiance'.

Scinn and *scinnhiw* (shining shape) meant 'specter, illusion, phantom, evil spirit, magical image.' Interestingly,

Heathen Soul Lore

scinn also meant 'skin' (conceptually relating to shape, Hama, Hug-ham or Hugr-shape). Very common terms for 'magic' in Anglo-Saxon used this word *scinn* in their construction, and one of the most common was *scinnlac*, with a *scinnlæca* or *scinncræftiga* (masc) and a *scinnlæce* (fem) being a magician, wizard, sorceress, witch. Now let's compare this with a description I quoted previously, from 1864 by a Swedish folklorist:

> The *Vård* (literally: a guardian) is a being attached to the individual, a spirit who accompanies a person wherever he goes, and sometimes reveals itself as a glimmer or in the form of the person as a second self (*hamn*), a phantom. The presence of the *Vård* can even be felt, both by other people and by the individual himself when he is out of doors at night. The expressions used for this are: 'It is with him', 'he has the glimmer with him', 'he has the *Vårðr* with him'.
> (Quoted in Strömbäck, "Concept of the Soul", p. 17.)

As I discussed earlier, the Vårðr seems to be much the same as the Hugr, and I suggest that with the *scinnhiw* or 'shining shape' we are dealing with the same sort of phenomenon: a warding spirit who can appear as a sheen or a glimmer in the night, or as the double of a person. My own thought is that the Anglo-Saxon *scinn* or *scinnhiw* can refer to an afterlife Hugr, and to a Hugr disembodied from its living human, as well as perhaps some other types of phantom phenomena such as ghosts and dwimors.

Now let's look at the other part of the word *scinnlac*. '*Lac*' in Anglo-Saxon had a great many meanings, including 'play, sport, strife, battle ('sword-play'), sacrifice, offering'. The verb *lacan* meant 'to move up and down, leap, jump,

The Occult Activities of the Hugr

swing, fly.' The verb *gelacnian* meant 'to heal, cure, treat, look after, dress a wound,' and *lacnung* was a 'healing, cure, remedy'.

A number of those meanings are the same as Old Norse *leikinn* that I discussed earlier, with reference to the effect of seiðcraft on the Hugr. Here we have the same word associated with the Scinn or Scinnhiw, the shining shape, to create the word Scinnlac which refers to magic, as does Seiðr. I think it's reasonable to assume that we are dealing with the same class of phenomena here: a form of magic that deals with phantom shapes which may be the Hugrs of people, living or dead, as well as possibly other types of phantoms.

Phantoms were also called *scinngedwola* (shining phantom). A person could be *scinn-seoc* or sheen-sick: haunted by a phantom, which sounds similar to phenomena I described earlier, concerning the effects of an envious or inimical Hugr. The Anglo-Saxon translation of the Greek Elysian Fields, the beautiful afterlife abode of those blessed by the Gods, was *scinfeld* or sheen-field: the abode of shining beings. Clearly, these are souls.

It's unfortunate that the Anglo-Saxon texts I have read that refer to the *scinnhiw* etc. are not very enlightening for our purpose of understanding Heathen souls. They mostly talk about Christian miracles overcoming the evil phantoms and practitioners of magic, dressing up Christian sermons and homilies to make them exciting for their listeners, and to make points about Christian morality. There's lots of stuff about 'evil' phantoms and magicians, and judging from Scandinavian and other folklore around the world, this is true enough: there was plenty of evil stuff going on. But not only evil stuff. The Elysian Fields, abode of the Blessed Spirits, would presumably not have been translated as *scinfeld* or sheen-field unless *scinn*-beings could be considered 'good' or 'neutral' as well as 'evil.'

Like so much else in Heathen lore, I think that the understanding of scinn / sheen' and scinncræft / sheencraft' was transformed from a rich and complex set of concepts and practices into a parody of itself due to Christian efforts to demonize Heathen understandings and practices.

Finally, I want to note the wide scope of the Anglo-Saxon word *lac*, including not only play, battle-play, sport, dance, etc., but also 'offering, sacrifice', and meanings relating to leechcraft, to medicine and healing. If we combine all these meanings and activities with the activities of dealing with spirits in various ways, we end up with a broad description of shamanistic practice. Shamans give offerings and sacrifices to spirits, work with them for healing, cursing, and bewitching, hold contests and battles with them (often while in spirit-form themselves), and dance, leap, play music, etc., during their rituals for calling the spirits and entering into alternate states of consciousness.

To me, Scinnlac (which I modernize as Sheenlock) carries the meaning of an Anglo-Saxon form of shamanistic practice, and also links up with Norse seiðr practice. I believe that Hugr souls are deeply involved in all of these practices. This includes the Hugrs of the practitioners, of those they practice upon, and the disembodied Hugrs of the departed.

Swelling of the Hugr

This is a composite photo showing successive stages of a tornado's development. For our purposes, we can regard it as a depiction of the Hugr progressively 'swelling with power', and also as the 'witch-winds', the whirlwinds that witches ride in, and the 'winds of the troll-wives'. While our human Hugrs may not be able to cause actual tornados, an ill-intentioned Hugr, swollen with malign or selfish power, can cause similar levels of disruption in the human social and psychological domains. This is especially true when it concerns the Hugrs of persons in positions of authority or leadership.

When shamans, rune-magicians, seiðr and other magic practitioners prepare to do their work, they must undertake some form of raising inner power. Practitioners, and types of magical practice, tend to have their own preferred ways of doing this, and these ways often differ greatly. But the purpose is the same: raising, focusing and directing magical power to achieve their purpose, and to protect themselves, and perhaps others, as necessary while they are doing this. Thus, we arrive at the Hugr's propensity to swell with power and burst out as the 'wind of the troll-wife', as I discussed in previous chapters about the Hugr.

I wrote in Chapter 9 about the idea of 'swelling with power' as it is understood in Vedic (Hindu) sacro-magical tradition, a very ancient tradition rooted in Indo-European culture. Here I want to expand a little upon this belief, because unlike the European Pagan traditions which were interrupted and damaged, Vedic lore about souls and magic has been preserved and grown through the centuries. Though of course there are a great many differences between Vedic and ancient Germanic beliefs, I find that there are also some remarkable similarities, which can expand our understanding of aspects of our own traditions.

Brahma in Hinduism is not only a great Deity; *brahmana* is also a term for magical power expressed through spells and sacred ritual formulas: basically, this is galdor (magical chanting or singing). Compare this description of *brahman* with the totality of all that I have written about Hugr:

> *Brahman* "is capable of assuming the form of any specific emotion, vision, impulse, or thought. It moves our conscious personality by premonitions, flashes of advice, and bursts of desire, but its source is hidden in the depths, outside the pale of sense-experience and the mind-process... Brahman properly is that which lies beyond the sphere and reach of intellectual consciousness, in the dark, great, unmeasured zone of height beyond height, depth beyond depth." (Zimmer p. 79; see also his discussion beginning on p. 74.)

This description can very easily be applied to the Hugr as well. The root of *brahma* is *brh* or *brah*, meaning 'to grow or increase, to fatten', and it is used to describe Deities 'swollen with power'. *Brh* is also the root of the Sanskrit word 'to roar', which I associate with the power of rune-galdor: swelling with rune-power and bursting out with the deeply vibrated roar of power as one utters the galdor.

I think that some of these Hindu ideas about brahman-power practices could be enlightening for those who are interested in pursuing Hugr-magic as expressed in galdors, rune-spells and the like. In particular, these ideas relate well to the practice of building Hugr's power within the chest, swelling until it bursts out in galdor like the 'wind of the troll-wife.' We may not actually want to behave like a troll-wife! But this is a poetic way of expressing the great power of the Hugr and how it can burst out into the world. It is up to us, to ensure that the power is used for worthy goals, and not for harm.

Summary and Closing

I want to close by referring again to Chapter 9, "Hunting the Wild Hugr." There, I explored a number of word roots and related concepts to help us comprehend the complex being that is the Hugr. I'm just going to touch on the six 'root-complexes' I discussed there, and show how they relate to what I have discussed in this chapter.

"<u>Shining</u>." This relates to the 'glimmer', the Scinnhiw or sheen-hue, the shining shape, that is sometimes perceived when the Hugr is disembodied and roams in Midgard. This subject-area expands into the shamanistic domain of scinnlac or sheenlock, as well as seiðr-work.

"Mounds and Wights" relates to ancestral magic and the ability of our living Hugr to communicate with the Hugr-spirits of the dead. It also refers to Hugr's involvement in the cycle of birth, death and rebirth.

"The Unborn, Swelling." This relates to powers of conception, generation, and regeneration, and to swelling with power, whether it is the power of growing a child within, or the power that swells within us and is born forth from us through galdor, spells, and other deeds of magic.

"An Eldritch Cry." This connects with the previous root: the calling-out of galdors and spells, songs of enchantment, powerful poetry, heartfelt emotion, the birth-cries of mother and baby, or the birth-cry of new powers and enlightenment bursting forth from our Hugr. The eldritch cry is also what we sometimes hear, loudly or faintly, calling us to pursue the mysteries and powers of all our souls.

"Excitation, Stirring up the Soul." This is what occurs as we pursue first the lore of the souls, and then again during the many ways each soul can grow and take action in our lives. More specifically, this is part of the process for building power and preparing our Hugr for shamanistic and other forms of magic.

"The Watcher; Magical Force." I've discussed magical force throughout this and other chapters, and this is one of many areas where Hugr links up with Mod and its powers and abilities. The Hugr is our warder, our lookout, our fore-runner, our scout, our rede-giver or advisor, our hugbode, in the otherworldly domains of magic as well as in our everyday-world. All of these domains of action are filled with challenges, decisions, and need for wise judgement and action.

Our Hugr has the potential to be a wise and powerful soul-being within us, able to promote and protect our well-being, our relationships, and our goals in life, whether magic is one of those goals, or not. Hugr can also lead us astray if its powerful negative emotions and selfish desires are allowed unrestrained action in our lives, and the consequences are even worse if we pursue magical activities motivated and powered by a Hugr in this state. It's up to us to work together consciously with our Hugr, to promote the wisdom, goodwill, and beneficial power that we are all capable of. The soul who can guide us in this direction is the topic of the next chapter.

Like the shining white swan, the Hugr knows how to ride the turbulent, swelling winds of the world, flying high and strong to achieve its desires.

Note that swans are faithful mates. This one is leading us toward the Sefa soul, who promotes strong relationships.

Chapter 12

12. Sefa: The Soul of Relationship

Anglo-Saxon *sefa, seofa*; Old Saxon *sebo*; Old Norse *sefi*; all of them with the meaning of 'mind, spirit, understanding, heart.' The Old Norse word *sefi* also has the meaning of 'a relative'.

Shaping our Understanding of Sefa

Related words:
~ Gothic *sifan* = to rejoice, be glad.
~ Anglo-Saxon *sifian, seofian* = to sigh or lament (also modern German *seufzen* = to sigh or groan).

~ Old Saxon *aseffan*, Old High German *intseffan*, Anglo-Saxon *anseffian* = to grasp, to understand, to be aware of. Eggers considers that the original meaning of *sebo* was 'to use one's senses to establish what is real' (p. 10).
~ Old Saxon *af-sebbian* and Middle High German *beseben* = to notice, perceive, observe.
~ Old Norse *sefa* = to quieten, to calm down, soothe, reassure, set one's mind at rest, also to bring into awareness.
~ Old Norse Goddess name *Sjöfn*.

Possible Roots:

I haven't found a definite root for *sefa*, but I believe that the etymology of 'sib' gives us some clues. In particular, the Proto-Indo-European (PIE) root **s(w)e-bho* as an "enlargement of the word 'self'" (*Online Etymology Dictionary* for 'sibling') brings us very close to Old Saxon *sebo* (the 'b' is crossed and indicates a 'bh' sound). DeVries suggests a possible linkage between the Goddess-names Sjöfn and Sif, and the word *sefi* (p. 479, 467), while at the same time, the Goddess-name Sif / Sippe / Sibbe is known to stem from the same root as 'sib' or relative. Simek says that Snorri in his Gylfaginning derives the name and meaning of the Goddess Sjöfn from *sefi* = which means both 'sense' and 'relation' (p. 286).

In Old English, *sibb* meant 'kinship, relationship, love, friendship, peace, happiness'. (Basically, the same meanings as the rune Wunjo, which we'll return to later.) Proto-Germanic **sibja* meant literally 'one's own', a blood relation. Sib-related words indicating 'relationship' occur in all the old and modern Germanic languages (though interestingly, our modern word and meaning of 'sibling'

Sefa

was coined less than 100 years ago, according to the *Online Etymology Dictionary*.)

Considering the soul-like nature of Sefa: 'mind, spirit, understanding, heart', it seems very logical to me to trace the roots of this word back to PIE **s(w)e-bho*, a word extended from the personal pronoun **s(w)e*, the root of 'self' as well as 'that which belongs to oneself', namely one's relatives, friends and beloved ones. The Old English and modern word 'swain' / Norse *sveinn*, comes from this root as well, meaning basically 'the man belonging to someone'. Thus, a swain is a suitor or boyfriend, and in older meanings a page, squire, manservant. In a looser sense, 'swains' was a term used for young men belonging to a group or cohort of some kind. Relationships and belonging are the domain of the Goddesses Sjöfn and Sif / Sippe / Sibbe.

The basic meanings I derive for Sefa are thus *(1) our Self, with its abilities to sense, notice, perceive and understand, and (2) that which is connected to our self through relationship, love and affection.* The meanings related to awareness, noticing, paying attention to, as well as soothing and quieting, which I listed above, are all faculties of our Self that are needed to promote strong relationships between people who understand one another well, pay attention to and care for one another.

I associate the word 'caring' in all its meanings with Sefa, along with the perceptive insights that are gained from sincerely caring about others. A nutshell-meaning of Sefa, to me, is 'the one who cares' within ourselves, whether that caring is related to people or other beings or things, or to any kind of situation or idea that one may care about. This includes the meaning of 'cares' as 'worries, sorrows, concerns,' as well as the meaning of caring *for* someone or something, and caring *about* anything. Sefa-soul includes the energy and the link between our self and whatever we care about, whether concrete (like another person, or the environment) or abstract (like the ideas of justice, beauty, kindness, honor).

Frigg is concerned for Odin's safety, as they discuss his visit to the Jotun Vafðrudnir. (Lorenz Frølich.)

Some Examples of Sefa in Old Texts

Rigsthula 44: Rig knew runes that could 'soothe and pacify Sefa, lay sorrows (to rest).' (Jonsson p. 163, my translation).

Gylfaginning: In the tale where Thor visits a peasant family and slaughters his goats for a meal for all of them, the son, Thjalfi, cracked one of the bones for the marrow. In the morning, Thor raised his Hammer over the goats, hallowing them and bringing them back to life, but when he saw that one of them was limping he became furious or *moðr*, his Mod cast into a state of rage. But when he saw the terror of the family, "he left off his moðr and *sefadiz*": he entered into his Sefa with its kind and soothing nature; he calmed himself and accepted compensation. (Prose Edda pp. 37-8.)

Sefa

Heliand l. 582: When the angel Gabriel announced to Mary that she had conceived Jesus, she understood him "in her own *Sebo*." Mary entered into a state of heart-deep perception and profound caring. Joseph *afsuof* or 'perceived' that Mary was pregnant (l. 93).

Havamal v. 57 (56 in translation): "Moderately wise a person should be, never too wise; he who wishes a carefree Sefi should not know his ørlög (fate) beforehand."
~ Verse 104 (105 in translation): Odin gave Gunnloð ill repayment for her hale Hugr, for her sorrowful Sefa, when he stole the mead of poetry after seducing her away from her guardianship of the mead. (Poetic Edda.)

Beowulf ll 49-50: 'He experienced grieving Sefa, mourning Mod.'
~ Ll. 277-8: 'That I may through (my) broad / spacious / abundant Sefa offer rede to Hrothgar."
~ L. 473: "It is sorrow to me to say from my Sefa...".
~ Ll. 1841-2: "The wise drighten (the Christian God, according to the poet) has sent these words into your Sefa."
~ Other places in *Beowulf* describe people's Sefa as grim or savage.
~ Ll. 489-90: Hrothgar says to *Beowulf*: "Sit now to sumble (feast), let go of constraint, you who rejoice in victory: speak as your Sefa whets / urges you."

(All are my translations.)

I like the last quotation from *Beowulf*. Here, hospitable King Hrothgar is telling Beowulf how welcome he is; he doesn't need to guard himself among these strangers, but can let go of constraints and relax. Beowulf and his words and thoughts are welcome at this festive gathering. (It actually turns out that Hrothgar is wrong: during the feast Beowulf is challenged about his deeds and reputation by Unferhð (whose name means 'not-ferhð', not-wise). So Beowulf actually still needed to keep his guard up, but good old Hrothgar's heart was in the right place!)

We can see from these various quotations that Sefa feels not only positive emotions, but negative ones too, including worry, sorrow, sometimes even grimness and savagery. I think that all of these emotions can be tied to 'caring about something.' When something you love or care greatly about is threatened or lost, you may become worried, sorrowful, grim, even savage in reaction to what happened: these emotions grow out of the fundamental emotion of caring.

Here is a picture of the purest, fullest expression of Sefa that I can think of: Sefa is the soul within you who is filled to overflowing at the moment when you first hold your longed-for newborn child or grandchild in your arms. Relationship, kinship, tenderness, love, attentive care, protectiveness, whole-hearted commitment: these are the blessings of Sefa.

Sjöfn, Sif, and their Companions

Snorri Sturlason, in his *Gylfaginning* (35; p. 30, prose Edda) tells us that the Asynja or Æsir-goddess Sjöfn "is much concerned to direct people's minds to love, both women and men. It is from her name that affection is called *siafni*." Simek suggests that "Sjöfn is a goddess of marriage and love, or else one of relationships, and is one of several goddesses named by Snorri who are matron-like guardian goddesses" (p. 286). I like his last point: Sjöfn not only inclines one toward love, friendship, and loving attitudes toward one's kin, but also helps to ward the relationship and keep it strong. I see her as a 'daughter' or hypostasis of Frigg, whose name means 'Beloved' and who is focused on marriage and family ties, among many other things.

Sjöfn's sister-Goddess Lofn helps bring about marriages and relationships even when many obstacles stand in the way. (As a Heathen, I would give Lofn great credit for the progress that has been made in legalizing same-sex unions.) The Goddess Var hears the oaths and private agreements that men and women make to each other, and punishes those who break them. Vör is the Goddess of Awareness, which ties in with our Sefa's awareness, perceptiveness and concern for whatever it cares about.

The Goddess Sif's name itself means 'related, relative', connected to the plural ON word *sifjar* meaning one's relations, family, kindred. The German word *Sippe* is the same: kinship, consanguinity, family, relatives, kith and kin; also the word for a genus (one step higher than a species) in biological terminology.

There is a lovely term used of Queen Wealhtheow in *Beowulf*: she is called *frithu-sibb folca*, the frith-sib of the folk (l. 2017). Heathen frith is the outgrowth of strong relationships; it is woven from the mutual trust and support that healthy interrelationships foster among us. Sif is the mother of Ullr and Thruðr, the wife of Thor, the stepmother of Magni and Moði. I like to think of Sif as the frith-sib of all Heathen folk, related and relating to us all as a kinswoman and a leader in the kindly arts of weaving frith-relationships among us.

Queen Wealhtheow, frithu-sibb folca, offers Beowulf hospitality in her hall. (George T. Tobin.)

The Goddess Frigg, whose name means 'beloved', is a promoter of frith: the fabric of healthy relationships that support a peaceful family or community, where mutual obligations, responsibilities, commitments, and benefits are acknowledged and acted upon. Frigg's assistant or her emanation, Hlin, is a Goddess of protection and refuge, something that Sefa is sometimes in need of during turbulent interactions with the outside world. Sefa, in turn, longs to protect those it loves, and provide a home-like refuge for them: duties that Hlin can help with.

The whole matter of 'relationships' is both challenging and of utmost importance to humans, and it is no surprise that a whole team of Goddesses is needed to deal with the challenges and promote the rewards of relationship! I would say that it is our Sefa soul through which all these Goddesses work, and through which we relate to them, at least with respect to our relationships and the skills of perception that are needed for this. And I would say the same for our own Disir / Idesa / Matron-Goddesses, our ancestral spirits and the demi-goddesses who watch over our kin-lines. Promoting and defending the ties, obligations and rewards of any kind of kinship or relationship is a major focus of theirs.

Vulnerability of Sefa

It becomes clear, as we learn more about Sefa, that it is naturally a tender, affectionate inner self, the one within ourself that we would call warm-hearted and kindly, who feels that we are 'kindred spirits' with other people. It is from Sefa that we have our capacity for empathy, sympathy, understanding, and emotional commitment.

I think that when the old poems talk about a warrior's 'grim or savage Sefa', these warriors have had to harden and encapsulate their originally tender, childhood Sefa as a result of their brutal life experiences. Sefa is vulnerable because of its tenderness and warmth, its desire for loving and affectionate relationships. As we well know, the 'world out there' can be very cruel, threatening, and manipulative toward this innermost, tender part of ourselves, seeking to take advantage of it.

Our vulnerable Sefa needs a warder, and in fact it has two of them: our Hugr and our Mod souls, who interact with Sefa in subtly different ways. Here are some quotations showing Hugr's relationship with Sefa.

Havamal v. 94 (v. 95 in translation): Hugr alone knows that which lives near the heart; (Hugr) alone knows Sefa.

Havamal v. 161: I know a sixteenth (rune or spell-song): if I wish of a woman to have her *geð* (attention, awareness, consideration) and play, I turn (away) the Hugi of the white-armed woman, and shift / turn all her Sefa (toward me).

(For more discussion of these verses and of Hugr's involvement in love and relationship, see Chapter 10.)

These verses tell us that Hugr is very close to, and very aware of, our Sefa. Hugr also loves, and desires friendship and trust, and I believe that it is the close connection between our Hugr soul and our Sefa soul that causes these desires to arise within them.

Hugr, however, is not by nature tender and vulnerable, as Sefa is. Hugr is strong and wily, courageous and deep-thinking. One of its important soul-functions is that of the Warder, who can to an extent foresee or intuit what is coming toward us, and who has very good insight into the inner motives and intentions of others. Hugr can warn us, and bring to our attention that things may not be as they seem to be on the surface. Hugr counteracts naivete, and guides us into deep, hidden knowledge. In the second verse I quoted above, we see that the woman, warded by her Hugr, could not be unwillingly seduced unless the seducer used a spell to turn her Hugr away from its warding function, leaving her tender Sefa vulnerable to the wiles of the seducer.

Our Sefa can become hardened and grim, no longer warm and tender, due to the cruel pressures of life. I think that when this happens, it means that the Hugr is not well-connected with Sefa, and is not doing its job of warding Sefa's essential nature.

Hugr can itself be a grim, manipulative and cynical soul, and in fact it is the Hugr within an ill-meaning person who preys on other people's Sefas. When Hugr is like this, it likely doesn't appreciate or care about its own Sefa, and doesn't work to ward it. The appreciation and desire for love, friendship and kinship that should naturally flow between Sefa and Hugr is instead blocked and crushed, causing an overall hardening of the person's character and souls.

This woodcarving is entitled 'Holy Kinship', yet these figures offer examples of fully hardened Sefas. None are engaged with each other, all have grim or cynical expressions. There is no sense of joy, or kindred feeling. To me, this seems like an illustration of 'unholy kinship,' or unfrith, where selfishness, power over others, and cynical greed are the only unifying factors. (Silesia, Bode Museum, ca. 1500.)

People fall into this kind of situation because they fear for their tender emotions; they know these emotions can be disappointed, abused, mocked, threatened, exploited. But it is a mistake to try to deaden these emotions and desires as a way to protect oneself. A Heathen conception of soul lore can teach us that it is possible to have a thriving, warm-hearted, loving Sefa within us, in spite of all the threats from the outside world, as long as our Hugr does its job of warding Sefa.

Hugr has good judgement and clear sight. It can tell us when it is safe to reveal our Sefa and pursue its desire for relationship, versus Sefa needing to stay sequestered and protected inside ourselves while strong and wily Hugr takes care of any outer defense we might need. Awareness of both these souls will help us to live a life well-balanced between open-hearted, trusting relationships on the one hand, versus a well-protected inner self, aware of the many pitfalls within human society, on the other. This is not all up to Hugr to do, however: Sefa's ability to perceive and be aware of others should feed into Hugr's strategic decisions.

There is another way that Hugr and Sefa are connected: through ancestral ties. In my understanding, our ancestral spirits, the Alfar and Disir, are the Hugr-souls of our departed kin. The Hugr-soul within us is also likely to be a reincarnated soul, connecting us with past lives and relationships. Hugr and Sefa are both souls who desire and value kinship and close relationships. Their interaction and mutual support helps us pursue these desires across time and generations, as well as in the present and reaching out toward the future.

Modsefa / Modsebo

Modsefa in Anglo-Saxon is translated as "heart, mind, spirit, soul, thought, imagination, purpose, character." Old Saxon *modsebo* is very similar. As far as I know, this word-combination was not used in Old Norse or Gothic, languages where the word 'mod' was not developed into

Sefa

such soulful meanings as it was in the Saxon-root languages and Old High German.

The words *modsefa* and *modsebo* are widely used in Old Saxon and Anglo-Saxon texts, often as an indication of 'where', within oneself, emotions and thoughts are occurring, the way we would say 'in my heart, in my mind' about some thought or feeling. The Modsefa often seems to be the 'place' where the Mod-soul 'does things' within ourselves. In the *Heliand*, a person speaks of holding enmity against another "in his Modsebo." Elsewhere, it says that a priest "in his Modsebo never forgot God." In *Beowulf*, when describing the people's desperate prayer to the Gods to protect them from Grendel, the Christian poet mocks the Heathens' trust in their Gods by saying "that was their custom, their heathen hope: they were mindful of hell in their modsefas" (ll. 178-80).

Modsefa also seems to refer to character and reputation. Some examples from *Beowulf*: in speaking of a prince, "his Modsefa was known by many" (l. 349). Likewise, Beowulf says that "as soon as Hrothgar knew his Modsefa", Hrothgar offered him great hospitality (l. 2012).

The textual evidence we have seems to show little difference between the meanings of Mod itself (see Chapter 8) and Modsefa, but I must assume that originally these words did not have identical meanings. Certainly, in Old Norse where the combination-word does not exist, there is a very great difference in meaning between *móðr* and *sefi*. Actually, they are radical opposites in meaning. I have an interpretation of Modsefa, however, that fits into the theme of this exploration of Sefa.

I have not come across texts in Anglo-Saxon or Old Saxon that show any great connection between Hugr and

Sefa, in the way we see it in Old Norse; no special indication that Hugr is considered the warder of Sefa. In place of that understanding, I propose that in the Saxon-root languages *modsefa* originally meant the Mod-soul linked with Sefa, in a relationship with Sefa, that parallels the Norse relationship between Hugr and Sefa.

There are a great many parallels between the Norse understanding of Hugr, and the ways the southern and western Germanic peoples understood Mod. Mod and Hugr have much the same qualities of courage and strength, strategic intelligence, determination and will. Both of them can bring these qualities to bear, to protect our Sefa and give it room to grow and express itself safely. In turn, Sefa can pour out its drive toward relationships, trust, and kinship through both Hugr and Mod, so these drives can be put judiciously into action.

Hugr is well-known as a warder and advisor spirit in Scandinavian lore, so the understanding that it can ward our Sefa flows naturally from that. Mod is not known as a warder; it is more our 'inner self', in many ways, our persona or ego, at least as it was seen in Anglo-Saxon and the Continental Germanic languages. But, as I discussed in Chapter 8, Mod is thought to have originally been an independent nature-spirit or power, which expressed itself in the form of overbearing strength and rage, a state-of-being also called *mod*. These powerful spirits gradually became incorporated into the human soular-system (and that of other beings, too), bringing their powers with them. Those powers are primitive and amoral, originally; they are not shaped or controlled by human ethics, customs, emotions and values.

Sefa

I think that as Mod became incorporated with our other souls and our Sefa, our Mod-sefa developed as a bridge between the original Mod-daemon and our human, and humanizing, Sefa-self. This bridge is the Modsefa-space referred to in the old texts, the place where the blended emotions and thoughts of both Mod and Sefa reside.

I see Modsefa as a buffer zone between Sefa's warm-hearted caring, the world of the heart, and Mod's powerful will and drive to achieve in the world: the world of the hand, if you will, the world of action. Thanks to Mod's strong actions, directed by Modsefa, Sefa can express its caring into the world of actions and deeds. Thanks to Sefa's goodness and value for healthy relationships, Mod's actions can be shaped through Modsefa to promote, rather than damage, these goals of relatedness and caring. Without Sefa and Modsefa, Mod alone would pursue its own will and power without concern for the consequences to others.

There's a nice instance in *Beowulf* that shows the power of the blended Mod and Sefa. As Beowulf was battling the dragon, facing his death, his war-band was too frightened to join him, except for young Wiglaf. Even though Wiglaf was facing his first battle, 'his modsefa did not melt within him' (l. 2628) as he armed himself and approached the dragon.

The word 'melt' is very telling, to me, because I think that 'melting' is something that Sefa does. Under the power of overwhelming love and tenderness, Sefa melts and flows outwards, meeting the flow of Sefa coming forth from the other one toward whom one feels love, to blend together in frith and kinship and powerful bonding. Melting is good under the right circumstances, but not when one is facing a deadly dragon!

Heathen Soul Lore

Wiglaf loved his lord, Beowulf, and was also kin to him. He was furious that the other thanes stood back from the battle. It was Wiglaf's Sefa, his kinship and care for his lord, along with his stalwart Mod-character, that motivated him to face the dragon by Beowulf's side, and to deal with the consequences of Beowulf's mortal injury by the dragon.

Wiglaf faces the dragon, and his lord's death. His Modsefa does not melt.

Sefa

Wiglaf's Mod and his Sefa blended together: love and strength, character and courage, to act as an honorable thane when everyone else was holding back. His Mod and his Sefa were engaged together, and his Modsefa did not melt.

Another instance of Sefa modifying Mod can be seen in the tale of Modthryð that I discuss in Chapter 8. Modthryð was a cruel and selfish princess who engaged in horrid deeds until she was wed to the great king Offa. After that she mellowed, loved her spouse, and became a fine and generous queen. I would attribute this change to the transformation of her Sefa-soul as the result of a loving marriage. Sefa, in turn, softened her brutal Mod-soul, and her Modsefa became a benevolent meeting-ground for Sefa and Mod together, leading to her generous activities as queen. (*Beowulf* ll. 1931-66; Rodriguez p. 59.)

Both Hugr and Mod serve, in their subtly different ways, to buffer and protect our tender inner self, our Sefa, the root within us of the desire for good relationships and for a world where people care deeply about good things and work to bring them about. At the same time, Sefa encourages Hugr and Mod to value and pursue good relationships. Hugr is Sefa's warder, advising Sefa of potential dangers and standing forth to protect it when necessary. Mod is Sefa's strength-in-action. Our Modsefa is (or should be) a seat of inner wisdom, healthy emotion, and sound character. It is backed by Mod's strength and will, and by Sefa's gentle wisdom of the heart.

The Wunjo Rune

Wynn is of great use to those who want for little,
Who have few sorrows and cares, and have, themselves,
Well-being and bliss, and a sufficient 'burg' (protected place).
(Anglo-Saxon Rune Poem, my translation.)

In Anglo-Saxon, the word *wynn* meant: joy, rapture, pleasure, delight, gladness. It's the root of the word 'winsome': pleasant, delightful, joyful, merry, that includes also a sense of innocence within the joy, a joy which is untarnished, whole and hale. Many other words in Anglo-Saxon are based on this lovely word, *wynn*. Diana Paxson, in her analysis of Wunjo, speaks of the happiness it brings as something that comes from relationships and community, and from our celebration of these ties (*Taking up the Runes*, p. 90). The relationship-gifts of Sjöfn and Sif, and their sister-Goddesses, bring frith and security in all their forms, and the joy and contentment that arise from these things.

The 'protected space', the burg, spoken of in the Wynn Rune Poem points toward our Hugr as the warder of our Sefa, with Hugr as the burg, and Sefa as the joy within. It also points toward our Mod and Modsefa, who provide a safe and lovely space within which our Sefa can interact with others and pour its caring attention out into the world. When our Sefa is well warded and supported by our other powerful souls, it is enabled to share its loving care, its joy and delight, its goodwill and kinship, judiciously and to best effect.

In working with Sefa and its warders, consider making a bindrune of Wynn / Wunjo, along with the runes Mannaz and Uruz. Mannaz, as a mind-rune and a representative of human beings, can stand for the Hugr. The

Sefa

Mannaz rune-poem tells us that 'man is the joy of man' (humans derive joy from other humans), which ties in well with Wunjo. Uruz can stand for Mod, with its reference to the 'mody wight', the courageous aurochs who fights to defend its territory. Meditating and working with the three of them together is helpful to further understand and develop Sefa, Mod and Hugr, and their life-supporting interactions.

Summary

Sefa is essentially our inner Self, and engages closely in relationships with family and kin, spouse and other romantic relationships, with friends and community. It is aware, perceptive, understanding and caring, and uses those qualities to enhance its relationships. These qualities support relationships, but also make Sefa vulnerable to manipulation and exploitation, and vulnerable to developing hardness and cynicism if abused for too long.

Sefa is, or should be, warded by our Hugr soul, who cares about many of the same things that Sefa does, but has a tougher, wilier makeup and serves as our spirit-warder and spirit-advisor, involved in protecting our tender inner Self. Our Mod-soul and our Sefa are also closely connected, creating between them our Modsefa, which combines the qualities of both souls. Meditation on the Wunjo rune can open up insights into our Sefa.

(Note: The Sefa is further explored in Chapter 17: "The Arising of the Self.")

The Ash Yggdrasil, by Friedrich Wilhelm Heine

Chapter 13

13: Hel-Dweller

Saiwalo and Dwimor, Part 1

In the next several chapters I will discuss the soul that was called *Saiwalo* in primitive Germanic and has descended into modern English as our word 'soul.' Academic authors I have read concur that the Heathen concept of the *Seola / Sawol / Saiwala* was an afterlife soul, with little involvement in Midgard life except in keeping the body alive by its presence, and that it naturally heads to Hel after physical life, where it continues existing as an individual being often known as the 'shade'. This is based on studies about this soul in the early Continental Germanic and Anglo-Saxon writings; I examine this evidence in more detail in Chapters 14 and 15.

The Old Norse word *sál* did not exist during Heathen times, and was borrowed during early Christian times from Old English *sawl*. However, here I will argue that the rich and vivid imagery of 'the dead' in Old Norse tales includes beings which in other Germanic cultures would be called *Seolas, Sawols, Saiwalas* and so forth.

As with other life-souls (Ferah, Ahma / Ghost, Aldr), the presence of Saiwalo in the body is essential for physical life and its absence causes death. Yet, it is not as involved in our personality and Midgard activities as many of our other souls are, except in one important way: it is the source of our ability to create images in our 'mind', or actually in our Saiwalo soul, whence our mind can access them. This is a conclusion I've drawn about Saiwalo, and I shall provide my evidence and reasoning as this series of chapters about Saiwalo proceeds.

Each of our souls has characteristic ways of shaping our perceptions, experiences and actions, and through them, shaping the world around us, as I've discussed about the various souls in previous chapters. In the case of Saiwalo, its characteristic way of action is 'imaging' and populating our imagination with these images.

These images then shape our perceptions and reactions, for example: forming stereotypes, forming our own self-image, dreams and daydreams, aspirations and longings, setting goals for ourselves by imagining desired outcomes, developing fears based on our inner images of threatening people and circumstances, using images to degrade ourselves and others…the list could go on forever, covering both 'good' and 'bad', beautiful and ugly forms of imaging. PTSD, the uncontrolled eruption of terrible images into one's awareness, reflects a type of spiritual injury to the Saiwalo soul in addition to its physical dimensions.

So much of what we perceive, think, feel, and act upon is rooted in and motivated by these images in our minds. And yet, my sense of our Saiwalo is that it is the *generation* of images itself, and not the resulting thoughts, emotions, and actions, that forms Saiwalo's primary activity. Consistent with ancient understandings of this soul, Saiwalo does not play an active role in our Midgard life and our personal characteristics. Its role in Midgard is passive: generating, absorbing and transmuting images according to

Hel-Dweller

its own inner processes, which are rooted in Hel. Our other souls in Midgard, our mind and body, all actively pick up and respond to those images, and in turn generate material that our Saiwalo uses to modify its images and create new ones.

This leads to one other aspect of Saiwalo's nature that I want to mention briefly here; I will pursue it in more detail in Chapter 16. I think that Saiwalo itself is always rooted and present in Hel, even while we are alive in Midgard, and absorbs powerful cosmic energies filtering up from Ginnungagap, Hvergelmir, and Niflheim, the realm of proto-being. These are the energies which form and feed our Saiwalos. These energies rise into Hel and are picked up and used by all the Saiwalos there: those who are currently supporting living humans in Midgard and those who currently are not.

In Hel, all these energies and imageries mix together, decomposing and recombining, fermenting and fertilizing, and from this seething soup of potential, Saiwalo forms the images, the language of imagination, that rise back into Midgard through Saiwalo's *Dwimor*, its phantom projection into the Midgard plane, and shape the perceptions and experiences of Midgard beings. (This process will be explained in more detail farther on.) This resembles the activity of the Hagalaz rune in its form as a seed-crystal that thaws and freezes repeatedly (hail forming and melting), each time producing a new crystalline shape out of the formless, primal water.

In my perception, these activities are a fundamental aspect of Hel's function in the spiritual ecology of the Worlds. Among other things, Hel serves as a sort of wetland, processing spiritual 'waste' through metaphysical analogs of microbiological activities, mysterious roots and worms and wriggling things, soil and water chemistry and the like, and provides fertile soil and pure water for all the teeming spiritual life growing on the Tree of Worlds.

In this context, we can see the damaging nature of the Christian insistence that Hel is a terrible place of punishment and despair, from which our Saiwalo souls must be 'saved' and sent to 'heaven'. 'Heaven', the God-Homes or divine realms, are the proper domain of our Ahma / Ghost, our 'spirit', not of Saiwalo, which has its own important work to do in Hel. This misrepresentation of Hel and its resulting cultural impacts and imagery leads to severe disruption not only for our individual souls, but for the spiritual ecology of the Worlds as well, including the spiritual health and wellbeing of our own Midgard.

So, this is the nutshell version of where I'm going in this study of our Saiwalo soul over the course of this and the next three chapters. I'll start with a rather circular definition: I define Hel as the 'place' where Saiwalo souls dwell and do their work, and define Saiwalos as the beings who dwell in Hel. Hel and Saiwalos define each other, just as an ecosystem is defined by its characteristic components acting together, while the components function thanks to the interactions of the ecosystem. This seemingly pointless definition will make more sense, I think, as we proceed to examine old tales, not only of Hel and the dead, but also tales of 'Hel-like places' and people who are 'like dead' but not entirely. The main purpose of this chapter is to gain a broad, visceral sense of Heathen Hel and the beings who dwell there.

A final note before we begin: I conceive of Saiwalo as a soul-being settled and functioning in Hel, who sends up a projection of its being into Midgard, which I call the *Dwimor*, meaning a 'phantom' in Anglo-Saxon. The Dwimor, projected into Midgard, provides a matrix which attracts and holds together all of our other souls during our life in Midgard. It is not a stand-alone soul, but is formed from the essence of the Saiwalo, and bears the image of our physical being. This image is imprinted into our Hama-soul during gestation, which uses it as a blueprint for developing our physical characteristics, our Lich-Hama. After death, our Dwimor or phantom retains our physical image. It is this image, this Dwimor-phantom, which appears in many of the tales and anecdotes about afterlife figures that I discuss below. I cover the Dwimor in more detail in Chapters 14 and 16.

Hel as the Hidden Land

The imagery that we have of the afterlife is one of the areas where Saiwalo's image-generating activity is especially powerful, since it comes from Saiwalo's very roots: Hel itself. In fact, I suspect that Hel itself, or the human perception and experience of Hel / the afterworld of the dead, is the product of multiple Saiwalos imaging their surroundings together.

There are beautiful places in Hel, such as the feasting hall of Baldr and Nanna, and tales of Odainsakr, the Field of the Not-Dead (see Simek p. 239). And there are horrible places such as Nástrǫnd or Corpse-Strand (*Gylfaginning*, in Faulkes p. 56). Feasting halls of the dead, entered through cliffs and mountains, welcome newly-dead kinsfolk, as is told in *Eyrbyggja Saga* ch. 11. Even the implacable Sea-Goddess Ran provides pleasant accommodations to some of the dead: "In those days it was believed that drowned people had been well-received by Ran, if they came to their own funeral feast"(*Eyrbyggja Saga* p. 138).

These are just some of the Heathen images of Hel or the afterworld of the dead. In my perception, Saiwalos of folks from other beliefs shape their own regions of Hel based on what living people are taught and believe about the afterlife domains, including the Christians' idea of hell as a horrible place of punishment.

"In Germanic mythology, Hel is not a place of punishment, hell, it is simply the residence of the dead" (Simek p. 137). Grimm also says it is "not a place of torment or punishment." He continues with an interesting observation: "When Ulphilas (the Gothic translator of the Greek Bible) uses *halja* (Gothic Hel) it is always for Hades (the Greek realm of the dead, not a place of punishment)...whenever the (Greek) text has *geenna* (Gehenna, the Hebrew place of punishment) it remains *gaiainna* in Gothic—it was an idea for which Gothic had no word." (vol. II, p. 800.) Grimm is here saying that there was no word for, and thus no concept of, a place of punishment in the Gothic afterlife.

Hel comes from proto-Indo-European **kel*, meaning 'to cover, conceal, save.' It is related to many relevant words including *Heliand*: the 'one who saves', hall, helmet, hollow, hold, coverings. (Watkins p. 40.) A number of Germanic Goddess names may be related to this word, including Nehalennia, Huld, Hlodyn, Hludana, and Frau Holle (Simek p. 154). These Goddesses are protectors, guides and teachers, Earth-Goddesses; they are not presiders over lands of torment. Hel is a place of concealment, of refuge: it is the Hidden Land.

Faring to the Edge of Hel

Let's proceed by looking at some vivid images of afterlife scenes from Old Norse literature. One of my favorites comes from *Hervör's Saga*, a part of *Heidrek's Saga*. The relevant portion of it is included in Larrington's translation of the *Poetic Edda* as "The Waking of Angantyr", and is also discussed in Ellis (pp. 159-161, 174-5).

According to Christopher Tolkien, *Heidrek's Saga* is "one of the most ancient of all extant Germanic heroic lays" (p. xiv) and shares features with much of the West Germanic poetry and the earliest Edda poems (p. xii). It is likely that the oldest material goes back to the wars of the Goths north of the Black Sea in the late 4th to early 5th centuries, and the characters may overlap with those of the early Old English poem *Widsith* (p. xiii).

Given the great age of this saga and its connections with other early Germanic poetry / history, we can figure that its portrayal of afterlife beings and places is not too heavily influenced by Christian theology.

Hervör's Tale

(Quotations are from Peter Tunstall's translation, Chapter 5, except as otherwise noted.)

Hervör, the posthumous, headstrong daughter of the berserker Angantyr, and leader of a band of Vikings, decides to go claim the famous sword Tyrfing that was buried with her father and his eleven berserker brothers on the 'haunted island' of Samsey. Her Viking band refuse to set foot on the island after sunset, so she proceeds alone.

Hervör finds a shepherd, who is terrified when she asks the way to the burial mounds and tries to persuade her to turn back, telling her that "all out here is horrible to humans" (Larrington v. 4). "Fire is blazing, barrows open, field burns and fen"...after telling her this, the shepherd runs off. Undaunted, Hervör continues until she "sees where the grave-fire is burning" and is "not afraid though all the mounds were in her path and the dead standing outside. She waded through the flame as if through fog until she came to the barrow of the berserks."

Though the dead stand at the doors of their howes, shadows against the fire, they apparently are in a state resembling sleep, for Hervör calls out to them: "Awake,

Angantyr! Hervör wakes you! ....Under forest roots I rouse you all." As she receives no response at first, she resorts to threats and curses. Her father finally rebukes her for shouting and cursing at the dead: "Hervör, daughter, what drives you to call so? Brimful of bale-runes...mad have you gone, waking up dead men." Her father doesn't want her to take Tyrfing because it is cursed, and an argument ensues.

As the father and daughter argue, "then the mound opened and it was as though the whole barrow was fire and flame," leading Angantyr to say: "Helgrind (Hel-gate) gapes and graves open, all is fire on the island's rim." He urges her to hurry back to her ship, but she refuses: "your daughter's *muntun hugar* does not tremble though dead men there in the door she see." *Muntun* I take to mean a combination of *muna*, her mind (cp. Muninn) plus *tun*, a hedged enclosure, thus 'her mind enclosed within her Hugr' is not afraid.

Larrington, using a different version of this verse, translates: "Hervör's hard-forged spirit (Hugr) swelled in her breast" (v. 8). This is interesting phrasing considering what I have written in previous chapters about the Hugr-soul 'swelling in the breast' as it builds up power. Hervör's Hugr soul, swollen with power, enables her to deal with these terrifying scenes and the otherworldly fire.

Angantyr warns her that the sword will bring evil not only to her but to all her house and descendants. Hervör, in her frustration, responds by threatening to cast a very interesting curse (*vigi*): unless they give her the sword Tyrfing, Angantyr and his brothers shall "all lie there, undead with dead (*dauðir með draugum*) in the dank rotten". The translation in Ellis says: "I will ordain it that you dead shall all lie and rot with the corpses, lifeless in the grave" (p. 180).

I think that the *draugr* or animated corpse (animated, I believe, by its decomposing Hama soul) is different from the image of its living self, the 'shade' or Dwimor that Saiwalo creates, even though they have similar appearance. This passage, distinguishing between 'the draugr' and 'the dead', is a strong piece of evidence for this argument. There would be no point inflicting a curse that 'the dead will rot with the corpses / draugar' unless 'the dead' (apparently not rotting) and the 'corpses / draugar' (subject to rot) are not the same thing.

Another corroboration is that the draugr, guarding its treasures, is usually shown to be hostile and savage in the tales, not acknowledging even its closest kin or beloved friends: it tries to kill all comers. By contrast, the dead

Angantyr is calm and caring towards his daughter, trying to persuade her to abandon her dangerous intentions. He is not acting like a draugr.

Though Old Norse did not have the soul-word *sál* until they borrowed it from Old English *sawl* during early Christian times, I believe that the 'shade' or the 'image of the dead person which is not a corpse', that often appears in Old Norse tales, is the same as the being referred to as '*saiwala, sawol, sele, seola,* etc' in all the other Germanic languages. More precisely, I see this image of the dead person as the creation of the Saiwalo soul: a Dwimor or phantom image of the person.

Angantyr tells his daughter, "I say you aren't, girl, like other humans, to walk among howes." Hervör answers "I did think I was human, at home with the living, till down I came to your dead men's hall."

He finally gives in, telling her that the sword is "wrapped right round in flame; one girl only on earth up there I guess would dare to take that glaive in hand." These words, along with the otherworldly fire and the images of the dead, show that this scene takes place within the domain of Hel. "Down I came to your dead men's hall" and "one girl only on earth up there" indicate that they are in an underworld setting, even though there is no account of Hervör traveling downwards in the story.

As Hervör departs she bids the '*heilir in haugi*', the 'hale men in the howes', to rest. It's rather remarkable to call dead men 'hale', meaning healthy, whole, unharmed, especially since these twelve berserks were all killed in battle. This goes along with my argument that the beings Hervör encounters are not rotting corpse-draugar, but are natural beings, healthy in their own way, in the realm of the

Hel-Dweller

dead: beings which I believe would be called 'Sawol / Seola / Saiwala' etc. in other Germanic languages. Hervör may be congratulating her kinsmen for having escaped her threatened *vigi*, her harmful curse-magic, by giving her the sword. Instead of being cursed to rot with their corpses, these shades or phantoms remain whole and unharmed.

Hervör's final words are "I thought I trod between the worlds when all about me fires burned." I think it's very clear that this is exactly what Hervör did: as she passed through the fires she entered the otherworld of the dead, no longer, for that brief time, in Midgard at all. The fires formed a boundary between Midgard and the regions of Hel.

A final note about Hervör's ancestry; the relevance of this will appear when I discuss story-motifs relating to Hel and faring to Hel. Tunstall's Appendix A presents the prologue from one of the versions of *Hervör's Saga*, which explains that Hervör is descended from giants, and from Alfar as well. Chapter 6 of Tunstall's translation tells how Hervör, in her male guise as Hervard, visited Jotunheim and Ymisland, populated by a great blending of giants and humans, from whom she was descended. She stayed with the giant-King Godmund, who ruled Glasisvellir. Odainsakr, the Deathless Acre, was said to be within his domain as well. Gudmund, Glasisvellir, and Odainsakr appear in many ancient tales about journeys to otherworlds, the dead, and Hel, which I have no space to recount here (nor to sort through the mixed Heathen, Christian, and Classical Pagan strands), but want to note that Hervör / Hervard traveled there.

Her connections with giants, alfar, and afterworlds / otherworlds are hinted at in the Saga, when Angantyr tells his daughter he doesn't think she is like other humans, and she answers that 'I thought I was human...till down I came to your dead men's hall.' I will show with more examples that journeys to the land of the dead or the Hidden Lands often feature giants, and Alfar, too, are related to the dead.

Common Motifs Relating to Hel and the Dead

There are motifs or patterns in this wonderfully descriptive Saga that show up in many other encounters with the otherworlds and with the dead. (1) A difficult journey to the world of the dead or its borderlands. (2) An eerie fire which marks the place of the dead and the treasures of the dead, and forms a boundary which is difficult for the living to pass. (3) The dead are apparently 'sleeping' and need to be awakened before responding to those who call them. (4) Necromancy, the ability of the dead to foretell the future, as Angantyr does when he tells Hervör that the sword will bring ill to herself and her kin-line. There's another theme that shows up surprisingly often in these tales: (5) the presence or influence of giants. Two other common motifs which are not shown in Hervör's Saga are (6) the presence of a dog or dogs, and (7) the idea that living folk make a great deal of noise when they enter Hel, but the dead are very quiet. Let's look briefly at some other tales that feature these motifs.

Brynhild's Ride to Hel

The Valkyrie and wife of Gunnar, Brynhild, was placed within a funeral wagon after her suicide; then the wagon was burned. The poem "Brynhild's Ride to Hel" in the

Hel-Dweller

Poetic Edda describes her journey to Hel riding in this wagon. Note that Brynhild's corpse and the wagon were burned in Midgard, but their 'images' or Dwimors proceeded on the Hel-way as recounted in the poem.

The Oseberg funeral wagon.

This is not Brynhild's only encounter with otherworldly flames. She had previously been a Valkyrie, a chooser of the slain and thus someone on the border between life and afterlife. She chose death for the 'wrong' person, according to Odin's commands, and was punished by being cast into a magical 'sleep', surrounded by a high fire which only the bravest man and horse in the world (Sigurd and Grani) could pass through.

Brynhild's and the Valkyrie Sigrdrifa's tales are conflated in the various poems of the Poetic Edda, treated as being the same story. When Sigrdrifa, surrounded by otherworldly flames, is awakened from her magical sleep by Sigurd she tells him: "Long I slept, long I was sleeping" (*Sigrdrifa's Lay*), sounding much like the dead Völva being reluctantly awakened in *Baldr's Dreams*: "I've been dead a long time."

The magical sleep has much in common with the sleep of death, the sleep from which Hervör must awaken her father. As the dead Brynhild (her Dwimor or phantom image) travels on the Hel-way, she passes through the homestead of a giantess with whom she trades insults, and tells the giantess her tragic tale.

Baldr's Dreams

Here's another journey to Hel, as shown in the Edda poem *Baldr's Dreams* (Larrington's translation). After Baldr has a series of baleful dreams, the Gods and Goddesses gather in council, and it is decided that Odin will seek an explanation from the dead *Völva*, the Seeress. Odin fares to Niflhel, where he meets a fierce dog coming from Hel. Then, "on rode Odin, the earth-road resounded," and from there he approaches the east gate of Hel where he knows that the dead Völva lies. He awakens her from death using *valgaldr* or galdors of the slain, and demands that she 'tell me news from Hel.' Here is the motif of necromancy.

Interestingly, the Völva complains about having to travel 'this difficult road' in response to Odin's val-galdor, showing that the dead as well as the living may have to travel far in order to meet together. The other motif that shows clearly here is the 'sleep' of the dead soul, who is reluctant and resentful about being awoken. This is similar to Angantyr and his brothers' very slow awakening, where

Hervör has to shout curses at them to get them to wake up. Finally, Odin accuses the Völva of being 'the mother of three ogres', implying that she also is a giantess.

Odin rides to Hel.

(W.G. Collingwood)

Hermóðr's Journey

After Baldr was slain, his brother Hermóðr rode toward Hel for nine nights through valleys dark and deep, and came to the bridge Gjöllr at the boundary of Hel. Its giantess-warder Modguð told him that recently five battalions of dead men had ridden over this bridge, but had made no more noise than the living Hermóðr riding over it alone. When Hermóðr succeeds in reaching Baldr and Nanna in their feasting hall in Hel, he sees them and the hall adorned with wealth and beauty. Nanna gives him rich gifts to take back with him for Frigg and Fulla. (*Prose Edda*, p. 50.) Here we see the theme of wealth and beauty in Hel, as well as the theme of 'soul-mates', Baldr and Nanna reunited in death; themes I will return to later.

Thorstein Cod-Biter

Moving from the Eddas to the Sagas, we see a beautiful and eerie tale of welcoming the dead in *Eyrbyggja Saga* ch. 11. Unbeknownst to his kin, Thorstein Cod-Biter and his fishing crew had recently drowned. One autumn evening Thorstein's shepherd was out near Helga Fell, the holy mountain of Thorstein's kin, when he saw a sight both tragic and marvelous.

Thorstein Cod-Biter's doom, as Helga-Fell looms in the background.

"He saw the whole north side of the mountain opened up, with great fires burning inside it and the noise of feasting and clamor over the ale-horns." The shepherd saw that "Thorstein Cod-Biter and his crew were being welcomed into the mountain, and that Thorstein was being invited to sit in the place of honor opposite his (dead) father." This was how Thorstein's kin realized he had drowned. (p. 38.) I would call this holy mountain hall of the dead an antechamber or region of Hel. Hel, I think, includes all of the many locations where the Saiwalo-dead (not draugrs) may dwell.

These are just a few of the plentiful tales of encounters with the dead in Old Norse. Hilda Ellis's book *The Road to Hel* offers many examples of such tales, and discusses many of the themes or motifs I listed above. (It is easily available as an e-book, which may be under her married name, Hilda Ellis Davidson.)

Hel-Motifs in Tales of Hidden Lands

Now, it's interesting that there are a number of tales which show many of the motifs relating to Hel or the world of the dead that I identified above, but which involve living beings (Gods, giants, heroes) rather than dead ones. I find this very meaningful; I believe it shows that ancient Heathens had rich and varied imagery about the world of the dead, and the interactions that were possible between the living, the dead, and those in-between those states, as well as with the Gods, Goddesses, Giants, Alfar, and other beings. Let's look at two examples here.

Skirnir's Journey

(Translations are from Carolyne Larrington, Poetic Edda*)*
Skirnir, the friend and servant of Frey, is another traveler who journeys far, passes through eerie flames and encounters a giantess. Frey has conceived an overwhelming longing for the giantess Gerda, and Skirnir offers to go to her dwelling and gain her favor for Frey. Though there is no suggestion that the actors in *Skirnismal* are actually dead, this poem is intriguingly full of motifs relating to the otherworld of the dead, including its connection with Frey,

the lord of Alfheim and of dwellers in the mound: also the dead.

Skirnir asks Frey to give him "that horse which will carry me through the knowing, dark, flickering flame". This flame is clearly not a normal Midgard fire, which is neither 'knowing' nor 'dark'; it is an otherworldly flame like the ones Hervör and Sigurd encountered. The 'knowing' quality of this flame can 'decide' who is allowed to pass through it, as we see in the tale of Brynhild / Sigrdrifa, where only Sigurd and his horse Grani are able to pass through the flames around the Valkyrie. Likewise, Hervör was able to wade through the flames as though they were fog, and was 'the only girl up there' in Midgard who would dare lay hand on the flaming sword Tyrfing.

Skirnir begins his journey by noting that it is dark outside, just as Hermod rode to Hel through dark and deep valleys for nine nights (not days). He next reaches Gerda's steading, defended by dogs. We see the world of the dead defended by dogs in other Edda poems, including *Baldr's Dreams*. Dogs also show up in German folklore as companions of Goddesses associated with the dead, as I describe below.

Gerda's watchman sits on a mound, reminiscent of a burial howe, and asks Skirnir "are you doomed, or are you dead already?" Apparently, it would be no great surprise to him if Skirnir had approached him as a dead man. Gerda, inside her hall, asks what is the noise she hears outside? "The earth trembles, and all Gymir's (her father's) courts shudder before it." The realm of the dead trembles, resounds, makes a loud noise when the living approach it, as we see in Hermóðr's and Odin's journeys to Hel. This description is striking here, because normally one would not

Hel-Dweller

expect that a puny non-giant, Skirnir, would be able to make the earth tremble when approaching a giant's hall!

Gerda asks: "Why do you come alone over the wild fire to see our company?" just as the dead Angantyr asks Hervör the same question. One of the gifts Skirnir offers Gerda is Odin's ring Draupnir, which was "burnt with Odin's young son" Baldr, after his death, went with him to Hel, and was later returned. Skirnir also offers eleven gold apples, possibly apples from Idunn. If so, these apples would offer life to the one who eats them, another hint that this may be an afterlife setting. Gerda refuses, saying that "I lack no gold in Gymir's courts, my father's wealth is at my disposal."

Gerda at first resists Skirnir's threats. (Lorenz Frølich).

Skirnir follows with threats of many horrible curses, finishing with naming the giant "who'll possess you down below the corpse-gates", clearly a Hel-location, though there is no mention in the poem that Skirnir threatens to actually kill Gerda. Again, I am not suggesting that the players in this drama are 'dead', but rather that the drama takes place in an otherworld that shows many of the characteristics of the world of the dead, including the idea that giants live there and / or are encountered on the way there.

This poem, as a whole, is often considered to celebrate Frey's powers of fertility overcoming Gerda as a representative of frozen ground or barrenness. The Saiwalo / Hel-Dweller soul may also have connections with fertility, a topic I have not yet developed. In this light, Gerda can be seen as an underworld-being until brought into a different realm, to meet the fertile God and come to life.

Svipdag's Quest

Young Svipdag begins his quest in *Gróa's Chant*, and continues it in *The Sayings of Fiolsvin*. (Larrington, Poetic Edda). His stepmother is angry with him and forces him to go on an extremely difficult, complicated and dangerous quest to woo the maiden Menglöð.

Although the poem is of very late composition, the tale itself may reflect a fertility myth similar to the tale of Frey and Gerda. Svipdag reveals his father's name as sun-bright (Solbjartr, v. 47) and his mother's as Gróa, derived from 'grow'; both aspects (sun and growth) relating also to Frey and to fertility. (Simek p. 307.) One of the "girls who sit peaceably at Menglöð's knees" (vs. 37) is Aurboda, who is also named as the mother of Gerda (*Song of Hyndla*, v. 30; Larrington p. 319), and hence a giantess. As with the *Skirnismal* poem, in Svipdag's quest we see many of the same motifs relating to the Hel-world, though the protagonists are not dead.

Hel-Dweller

Svipdag goes first to the grave of his mother Gróa and calls her to awaken from her sleep, begging for her help on the quest by providing him with protective galdors or magical spells. Gróa asks why he calls on his mother "who has turned to dust," showing that she is not a corpse-draugr. Several of the galdors she gives him indicate that he will be faring through the land of the dead during his quest.

Verse 8 says that if mighty rivers threaten his life, they will diminish and turn back toward Hel. Verse 9 says "if your enemies lie in wait on the gallows-path (the road of the dead), may their Hugrs turn *(hverfi)* into your keeping, and turn *(snuisk)* until their Sefas are reconciled (to you)" (my translation here). Verse 13 says "lest night overtake you...on *niflvegi* (the misty path, or the Niflheim-way)," Svipdag will be protected from being harmed by "a dead Christian woman."

It sounds to me like Gróa anticipates that Svipdag will be faring through Niflheim / Hel and will encounter harmful spirits there. It's tempting to read this as Svipdag actually having to fare through the very worst, most run-down neighborhood down there, namely the Christian version of 'hell', for which he will certainly need protective spells!

Having received his mother's galdors, Svipdag presumably passes through a number of adventures, the 'long and difficult journey,' and then arrives at the gates of Menglöð's hall. We can assume, considering Svipdag's need for all the arcane galdor-protections en route, that this hall is in the Hidden Lands, the Underworld. Ellis has a long discussion of the idea that Menglöð's dwelling is indeed in the land of the dead (p. 177-8).

The keep or fortress Svipdag approaches is described as the 'seat of the Thurs-tribe' (Jonsson p. 174), showing again a connection between the underworld and the giants. It is guarded by a pair of savage dogs. The warder of this fortress is Fjölsvinn, meaning 'much-wise', which is a by-name of Odin, though it's unclear whether he is actually Odin. He "stands before the entrance and keeps watch on all sides of the threatening flames" (Ellis's translation of vs. 2, p. 178), showing the presence of otherworldly fires as we have seen in other tales.

The same fascination happens to Svipdag as happened to Frey: Frey, sitting on Odin's High Seat, saw Gerda with her white arms shining all the way from Giant-land to Asgard, and fell in love with her. Svipdag says from outside the great hall: "these courts glow, it seems to me, round the golden halls; I would love to make my home here." He asks about the ruler of these halls, and is told that she is Menglöð, who has power over the wealth-filled halls. (Vs. 5, 8). Gerda, too, lives in a hall filled with wealth, and hidden treasure is characteristic of the halls of the dead, as I shall return to.

Later (vs. 31-32) Svipdag asks a question of Fjölsvinn: "what that hall is called which is encompassed with knowing, flickering flame?" He's told it's called *Lyr*

Hel-Dweller

according to Larrington, but *Hyrr* according to Jonsson, which he interprets as meaning *tillokkende* or 'expanding, increasing, enlarging.' This ever-enlarging feature is characteristic of the land of the dead, which must continually expand to fit all the dead into it. "This treasure-store is one which, through all the ages, men will know only by repute."

It isn't clear which hall Svipdag is asking about, whether it's the hall standing in front of him or some question of lore. Since at the beginning of the poem the 'threatening flames' are mentioned, and since most of the questions and answers between Svipdag and Fjölsvinn relate to Menglöð's hall and the complicated activities that are demanded of Svipdag so he can enter it, I choose to think that the 'knowing flame' and the treasure-store do refer to Menglöð's hall, as they also relate to Gerda's hall, the halls of the wealthy dead, and Valkyries thrown into a magical, deathly sleep. In the end, it is revealed that Svipdag and Menglöð are soul-mates, destined for each other, and they join together in love and joy.

Fairy Tales

The late poem about Svipdag and Menglöð shows many similarities with more recent fairy tales from Germanic lands. In "Sleeping Beauty" and "Snow White" we see the deathly sleep of the heroine, that can only be overcome by a lover undertaking a difficult quest which has killed others who have tried it. Only one prince makes it through the wall of thorns, or the forest guarded by dwarves, to awaken his soul-lover with a kiss and bring her back to life. A review of

other classical fairy tales will show many of the same Hel-related motifs I listed above.

La Belle au Bois Dormant, by Gustave Doré.

Frau Holle and Walburga

The tale of Frau Holle's Well contains some of these themes as well. A girl falls into a well, which was a not-infrequent tragedy that killed young children in times when the family well was the necessary source of water. This girl, however, does not die but falls into Frau Holle's Underworld land through the well. 'Holle' is of the same derivation as 'Hel': that which is hidden, or that which hides, conceals and protects. Frau Holle is a great Being who rules not only a Hidden Land below Midgard, but also the airs above Midgard where she shakes snow down upon the earth.

This kind-hearted girl, landing in Holle's Land of green meadows below, helps beings who call out to her, including an overloaded apple tree about to break, and bread in an oven, at risk of burning. She then meets Frau Holle and works diligently as her servant for a period of time. Frau Holle then rewards her by literally showering her with gold and sends her through a gate, back to her home. (Told in Jacob and Wilhelm Grimm's *Children's and Household Tales*; in Goos pp. 66ff, and in various places on the internet.)

Hel-Dweller

Frau Holle's faithful helper.
(Relief from Mother Hulda / Frau Holle Fountain, Eschwege, Hessen.)

The resemblance between Frau Holle's realm and the underworld of souls is strengthened by the saying that "nurses fetch babies (I would say, babies' souls) out of Frau Hollen Teich," Holle's pond or pool. Another saying is reminiscent of Hervör wading through the flames around the burial mounds as if it were fog, and the glimpse of the feasting halls of the dead inside the holy mountain. "When fog rests on the mountain, 'Dame H(olle) has lit her fire in the hill.'" (Both quotations in Grimm v. 4 p. 1367).

As I mentioned earlier, one of the motifs that shows up in tales relating to Hel and the dead is the guardian dog or dogs, which also appear in other Indo-European mythologies such as the famous three-headed dog Kerberos guarding Hades' realm of the dead in Greek mythology. According to Rochholz (p. 20), writing about German folklore in 1870, "Grey hounds accompany the three Norns.

The fertility Goddesses Frau Harke, Frau Gode, and Frau Frick have always a hound beside them," as well as Frau Berchte. Walburga has power over dogs: speaking her name is a charm to tame fierce or even mad dogs. Nehalennia's altars usually show her accompanied by a dog. In German folklore there is a "Windhound" which apparently runs with the Wild Hunt but sometimes stays behind and must be placated with offerings during Spring to protect new crops from wild weather (p. 22).

All of the Deities mentioned: Norns, German Goddesses, and the Wild Hunt, have some association with death and the dead. Some of the German Goddesses as well as the Wild Hunt, in their own different ways, collect wandering souls of the dead from Hallows-tide through Yuletide, and we can envision the dogs playing their roles as hunters, herders, guides and guardians of the souls in these activities.

I see Wal-burga's name as meaning 'the burg or refuge of the slain', though Simek gives it as coming from 'Wald-burga' (p. 370). The latter could mean 'the burg or refuge in the woods', though *wald* also means 'power, the wielding of power'. Hence Wald-burga can mean 'the burg or fortress of she who wields power', a fitting name for a Goddess of the dead. The Woods are also a metaphor for the Otherworld, a dark place where one may well encounter death. All of these meanings shape Walburga, or Wælburga as I like to call her, in my mind as a Goddess who protects and guides the dead, and gives them a refuge (Hel). Urglaawe, a branch of modern Heathenism based on Deitsch lore, considers that Walburga is the same being as Frau Holle, who "guides the cycle of life, death, and rebirth in all areas of existence" (Schreiwer pp. 40, 66.)

Some Overarching Themes

So, these are a tiny fraction of the many fascinating, richly-imagined tales of the Hidden Lands, the dead, the Hel-Dwellers, as well as those who visit there and those who rule in those domains. There are several overarching themes in these tales that can help us in our quest to better understand Hel and its Dwellers.

One is the theme of Hidden Treasures and Arcane Knowledge. The dead are buried with riches, heirlooms, objects of power. The residence of these treasures in the company of the dead seems to add further power or main to them. Someone courageous (or foolhardy) enough might be able to retrieve such treasures for themselves, after being subjected to grueling tests of courage, endurance, or in fact tests of good-heartedness, as Frau Holle requires. Through the powers of necromancy, humans, Gods, and other beings may be able to obtain valuable hidden knowledge from the dead in Hel.

Another theme is the quest for the 'Soul Mate', as we saw in a number of these tales. This theme has several layers: the simple enjoyment of fairy tales, possible cultic purposes for fertility rites, as well as a more soul-oriented layer. This latter layer features heavily in Jungian psychology, which interprets the quest for the soul-mate as a quest to know and integrate with one's own soul. I agree with this interpretation and approach it from a Heathen standpoint, though it is more complex given that we have multiple souls. These tales of the underworld and Hel lead us more specifically on the quest to know our own Saiwalo souls.

The theme of 'hidden treasure' can be seen as 'Power': the powers of heirlooms, wealth, weapons, and other items imbued with the magical energies of the Hidden Lands. The theme of 'arcane knowledge' picks up the thread of 'Mysteries' which pique and draw our imaginations along a questing path. The theme of 'soul mate' is triggered by 'Beauty' which irresistibly calls to the soul, a great source of creative inspiration.

Menglöd and Svipdag, soul-mates.
("Day-Spring finds Menglöd", W.G. Collingwood.)

Hel-Dweller

These all lead to another theme, one I call the 'Fascination of the Imagination.' We saw examples of fascination in how Frey was struck by his view of Gerda, and how Svipdag was struck by his view of Menglöð's home.

Combining the search for hidden treasures / power, arcane knowledge / mystery, the soul mate / beauty, and all the challenges and eerie settings involved in questing for these, results in tales that are irresistible and fascinating. We always want more! Ancient tales going all the way back to Gilgamesh's quest for immortality, Odysseus's ventures into Hades, Orpheus's attempt to rescue his wife Eurydike from Hades, medieval wonder tales and heroic quests, fairy tales, ghost stories, modern fantasy tales in books and films: these all build on, and contribute to, the activity of imaging that our Saiwalos engage in.

These tales and images can lead our awareness toward our own Saiwalo and to the Hel-domain, the Hidden Land, in which it dwells. And in fact such tales, and new tales of our own, can help us shape, and re-shape, our own experience and perception of Hel, its Dwellers, and its Rulers, allowing our Saiwalos to create a domain of beauty, mystery and power around themselves, rather than one of torment and degradation, or of barren emptiness and despair.

"Odin am Brunnen der Weisheit" by Robert Engels.

"Odin at the Wellspring of Wisdom."

Odin savors the water of wisdom for which he pledged his eye, as the Warder of the Well, the Giant Mimir, looks on.

We, too, are called to walk the paths of wisdom, as well as we can discern them, and as far as we can follow them. The footprints of those who have gone before us are there to be seen, once we open our eyes, and the vista of new, untrodden ways stretches ahead of us into unseen distances. But always, as we travel, we need the waters of wisdom to nourish our souls.

Chapter 14

14. The Soul and the Sea

Saiwalo and Dwimor, Part 2

As souls (psyches) are born through the death of water, water is born through the death of earth. And as water comes into being from earth, so from water does the soul.
Heraclitus (ancient Greek philosopher) fragment DKB 36 (my translation).

The surging sea, by Dale Wood.

In this chapter I will explore the fascinating connections between the Saiwalo soul and water: water in the form of the sea, lakes, marshes, ponds and wells. I will also look at the connections between various Deities associated with water, and discuss their links with our Saiwalo soul.

Where does 'Saiwalo' come from?

The etymology of the word 'soul', from Proto-Germanic *Saiwalo, is not firmly established, but its most likely source is from the Proto-Germanic word for 'sea', *saiws, *saiwi-z, *saiwa-z, and this is what we'll be exploring here. It adds to the challenge, that the etymology of 'sea' is even more obscure!

I've read a number of different derivations of this word. Many philologists, but not all, conclude its root was borrowed from a non-Indo-European language. But the etymologist Anatoly. Liberman writes that: "According to some indications, the protoform from which *saiws* and its cognates were derived sounded approximately like *saikwi-*. Probably saikwi- and its Indo-European ancestor *soigwi–* designated a body of stagnant water..." (He is using 'stagnant' in the sense of 'still' here, a lake rather than the moving ocean.) I find in Watkins' Indo-European Roots dictionary that *seikw* meant "to flow out," which would make sense. So this is a possible Indo-European root, but as I said, many scholars think 'sea' may stem from a loan-word, which for us here, further confuses the source of the word 'soul' deriving from 'sea.'

Another layer of confusion arises, due to the changes in meaning of the word 'sea' and its Germanic relatives. There is another word-root for the meaning of 'sea', namely *mar-*. In Gothic it was *mari*, in modern German *Meer*, in English an old-fashioned word *mere*, in the Celtic languages *mor*, in Latin *mare*. In English, 'sea' means 'ocean' and 'mere' is a lake. In German, *Meer* means 'ocean', while *See* is a lake or inland sea; Gothic is the same with *mari* as the ocean, *saiws* probably as a lake or inland sea. Old Norse has *sær* and *sjór* meaning the sea, especially with respect to sea-related personal names and names of sea-related things, even though they also have *haf* meaning the ocean. So, assuming that we accept the general idea that **saiwalo* the soul comes from **saiws*, a body of water, there is still the question of 'what kind of water body', and what does this mean for our understanding of 'soul'?

This is very often what happens as we search for roots of words, in my case, Germanic soul-words: academic study takes us up to a point, and then leaves us hanging there. Academics are supposed to stop when the evidence runs out, but modern Heathen soul-practitioners are not limited thereby! I have found a very fine scholarly analysis by Josef Weisweiler, an older article but very linguistically detailed, that I find offers the most meaningful and satisfactory insight into 'soul and sea' that I've come across.

I have enough basic linguistic knowledge to understand Weisweiler's arguments, but not enough to know whether there are better ones that would refute him, though he details a number of counter-arguments himself. In any case, I find that Weisweiler's insights offer a very enriching perspective for understanding Germanic Saiwalo-soul, and I choose to follow his path into this knowledge. In the following section I summarize his findings, with additions from myself and other authors, as noted.

Weisweiler's Exploration of *Saiwalo

Weisweiler bases much of his argument on a Saami word for one of their soul-concepts: *saiva, saivo* (I've seen this spelled *sajva* online, and other spellings as well). (Note: Weisweiler, writing in 1940, used the word 'Lappish' to refer to this language, but the people who speak it prefer the term Sami or Saami, so I will use that here except in direct quotations.) Saami is a non-Indo-European language spoken by nomadic peoples whose range covers northern parts of Norway, Sweden, Finland and Russia.

According to many studies conducted over several centuries, the Saami adopted and modified a number of words, Deities, and other beliefs from their Germanic-speaking neighbors during the many centuries of contact they have shared. Among them is likely the word *saivo, saiva*. According to Weisweiler, this word has slightly different meanings among different branches of the Saami. In the northern Saami area, it means a freshwater lake, and is combined with other words to form names of certain freshwater fish and birds.

Among the western and southern Saami, the regions where they would have interacted the most with people of Norse culture, *saiva* or *saivo* means a 'holy or sacred lake'. These lakes are understood to be full of fat fish, but strangely, these holy lakes are divided into an upper layer of the lake, and a lower, separated by a lake-floor in between, which has a 'smoke-hole' or access hole in it. These 'two-bottomed lakes' are also known in Swedish folklore. At times the fish appear in the upper lake, at times they disappear to the lower.

Many practices from Saami lore and folk-religion focus on satisfying the Deities or spirits who control the access and behavior of the fish between the upper and lower layers, so as to have access to rich fishing. Offerings were made at significant locations near these lakes, generally large boulders or hills, and these were called 'saiva-stones, saiva-mountains, etc.'

There was a belief, especially in southern Saami territory, that many kinds of spirits lived in these sacred saiva-areas: Huldren / elves or land-wights, souls and spirits, underworld beings in the form of humans. Underworld was the territory of the Ancestors, who had the power to grant luck, prosperity, and fertile sources of food. These ancestral spirits were also called *saivo*, and Saami customs were heavily focused on interaction with their saivo-ancestors. Some saivo-spirits, both humans and sacred animals, become tutelary or warding spirits, much treasured by Saami shamans or *noaidi*. Saivo or sajvo are considered to be holy and well-meaning humans and certain animals, while the general world of the dead, *jabmi-aimo*, also includes ill-intentioned and dangerous spirits.

Pakassaivo: Saivo-lake, called the 'Hell of Lapland'.

Weisweiler follows this with about eight pages of linguistic discussion, drawing on many other scholars, showing that *saivo* is a loan-word from Proto-Germanic. In agreement with a number of other linguistic and folklore scholars, he points to the influence of Proto-Germanic language on Saami, going back to the Bronze Age before the separation of the Germanic languages into different branches. Significantly, they conclude that the Germanic root of *saivo* came from this very early period of influence, based on the morphology of both the Germanic **saiwalo* and related words, as well as Saami *saivo / saiva*. In particular, it is clear that *saivo* was borrowed from the Proto-Germanic word **saiwalo*, not from the later Norse word *sál*, which was itself borrowed from Anglo-Saxon during the conversion to Christianity.

(It is baffling why the word *saiwalo* and its expected descendants dropped out of proto-Norse at some point, while being retained in all the other Germanic languages from Proto-Germanic times up to the present day. If *saiwalo* was indeed a loan-word, that could be explained by saying that some branches of the Germanic tribes encountered the culture from whom they borrowed the word, but not other branches. Except that the word was borrowed into Proto-Germanic, before the Germanic languages split off from each other, so that explanation doesn't work. Weisweiler discusses these issues, without coming to any firm conclusions.)

Weisweiler considers the construction of *saiwalo* to be a diminutive form meaning 'belonging to the sea (lake),' *saiws*. This parallels the construction of other words such as *eichila*, 'little oak, or belonging to the oak', meaning an acorn, and *armilo* meaning 'sleeve', something that belongs to the

The Soul and the Sea

arm, and many other such words. Thus, *saiwalo* would mean 'belonging to the sea', or more poetically in German, 'sea-daughter', since saiwalo is a feminine noun. A good Germanic-type word I made up for the same idea is 'sea-ling', the little one from the sea.

Weisweiler links this back to the saivo-spirits, men, women, and children: the ancestral dead, the dwellers inside the holy mountain, the *huldre*-folk or elves, and spirit / power-animals. As he remarks, "These (beings), and everything else that belongs to the Lapp. *saiva*-concept of the 'holy lake', stand in the closest relationship to beliefs about the dead and the soul" (p. 43). He notes the commonality of these beliefs with those of their Scandinavian neighbors: two-bottomed lakes, huldre-folk, the dead (and other spirits) dwelling within mountains, rocks, and water-bodies, the ability of these spirits to provide luck and protection, and Scandinavian beliefs about lakes as the dwelling of souls.

Though Weisweiler does not discuss this, I would add the many Heathen connections with bogs and marshes here, as sites of offerings, sacrifices, and God-posts. The connection also shows in the name of Frigg's holy hall, Fensalir or 'fen-halls,' 'fen' meaning a marshy area, and Saga's hall Sökkvabekkr, meaning 'sunken benches.' The connection with Ran's hall where she takes the souls of the drowned is also obvious. Weisweiler does bring up the Norns in a footnote, briefly noting that they live near a lake or water body called *sæ* in Voluspa v. 20, though in the previous verse it is called a wellspring, *brunn*, and linking them with later beliefs about where children come from (p. 44n).

Weisweiler quotes Olrik and Ellekilde, explaining that the Scandinavian belief in an ancestral dwelling-place of the dead within a nearby mountain shows up only occasionally during the Viking period, and has no connection with Elf-beliefs. They conclude that the Saami belief, and their adopted word *saivo* that goes with it, dates back to Bronze Age practices and beliefs that they held in common with their Scandian neighbors, about an 'elf-world' or ancestor-world within mountains and other landscape features, where the newly dead return to their ancestors, and then become protecting spirits of the living.

All of these scholars conclude that the concepts relating to *saivo* were borrowed in very early times, before the Germanic languages split off from each other. This goes along with the linguistic evidence of saivo being borrowed from *saiwalo rather than from a later form of the word. In other words, both linguistic analysis and analysis of beliefs about the dead lead to the same conclusions. (p. 45-6.)

Weisweiler goes on to say that other Germanic lands outside of Scandi-navia have beliefs about lakes or pools as the dwellings of the dead, in the form of 'bottomless lakes' that lead down to hell. Even more widespread are the beliefs that unborn children are found in bodies of water, from which they are 'fished out.' This is where the folk-belief that storks bring

The Soul and the Sea

babies comes from (I would suggest, babies' souls rather than the physical baby). These long-legged wading birds fish the babies out of ponds or marshes, and deliver them to their parents.

Weisweiler mentions the *Hollen-Teich*, the Goddess Frau Holle's Pond, in this context, along with many other locations in Germany having their own *Kinder-wasser* or 'children-water' which hold (the souls of) unborn children. These 'waters' can be lakes, ponds, or well-springs. He quotes Kummer, who makes this very interesting observation: "Beliefs about where children come from do not stand under the sign of a Heathen God-figure, but rather under the sign of a Heathen conception about the origins of soul-life" (p. 49). Weisweiler sums up his conclusions in this way:

> Comparing these German folk-belief remnants with the northern images of lakes as homes of souls, and with the Lappish *saiva*-beliefs, results in this: the (proto) Germans who had not split up into individual peoples saw certain 'holy' water bodies as dwellings of souls. Within or underneath such lakes, the unborn awaited the moment of their birth, and thence returned the souls of the dead to the others (the other dead). In this way the proto-German…*saiwa-lo, 'the one from the sea / lake, the one belonging to the sea / lake', is constructed from *saiwa-z (holy) sea / lake (p. 49-50).

The *Online Etymology Dictionary* quotes the *Barnhart Dictionary of Etymology*, that the root of 'soul' means 'coming from or belonging to the sea' because that was supposed to be the stopping place of the soul before birth or after death, assuming that the word derives from *saiwalo*. It also draws from Klein's *A Comprehensive Etymological Dictionary of the English Language: *saiwaz* meaning 'from the lake' as a dwelling place for souls in ancient Europe. I suspect both these sources drew from Weisweiler. *Wikipedia* on soul-etymology offers the same information, along with English ideas about holy wells.

A graceful sculpture of Frau Holle, reflected in her pond, from which she draws out babies' souls as they prepare for birth into Midgard. She is holding her feather pillow, which she shakes to make snow fall on the Earth.

The Soul and the Sea

Other Folklore about Souls and Water

Here are some more images relating to souls, soul-powers, and water.

The Goddess (referring to Holda / Holle) "loves to haunt the lake and fountain; at the hour of noon she may be seen, a fair white lady, bathing in the flood and disappearing; a trait in which she resembles Nerthus. Mortals, to reach her dwelling, pass through the well" (Grimm p. 268).

Grimm's mention of the Earth-Goddess Nerthus is apt here, too: all those who laid eyes on her, save her priests, had to be drowned, that is, sent to her domain by means of drowning.

"Children falling into wells pass through green meadows to the house of friendly Holle" (Grimm p. 822). "Newborn babes are fetched by the nurse out of Dame Holle's pond" (Grimm, note p. 268).

According to folklore from the German lands, newborn children (or their souls) are brought from trees, cabbage-fields, wellsprings, ponds, water, also cliffs and boulders. (Compare this list with the Saami beliefs about saivo-locations.) They are brought from these places by various entities; the stork is the most widespread, but also the Water-man or Wassermann can bring the babes. (Erich & Beitl p. 409.)

In German language-speaking areas, Wassermann is one of the most widespread images, and also appears in children's games and songs (Erich & Beitl p. 858). "The water man (Wassermann), like Hel and Ran, keeps with him the souls of them that have perished in the water, in pots turned upside down...but a peasant visiting him tilts them up, and in a moment the souls all mount up through the water" (Grimm p. 496). "In some German lakes (*See* in German) the dead wait", and the Bretons, too, regard lakes and ponds as dwelling-places of the dead (Weisweiler p. 47).

("Der Wassermann", Hanus Schwaiger.)

I have a thought here: the Christian practice of baptism may perhaps have been relatively acceptable to Heathens because of their own beliefs about the soul and water. Heathen belief would have tied into the image of dipping the baby in the baptismal font: drawing the baby out of the water would have perfectly imitated their ideas about drawing babies / souls out of the water, with the priest in place of the stork, or of Frau Holle! As an aside here, the image of a stork drawing our soul from the water, perhaps from Holle's Pond or from Fensalir, and flying over the airs of Midgard can be fruitfully used for Heathen meditations on soul-cleansing and renewal.

In Norse lore, of course there is the sea-Goddess Ran, who keeps the souls of those who have drowned. Ship-symbols, and ships themselves, are common burial motifs in northern Germanic lands, and there are many tales throughout the Germanic lands about ships of the dead, and ships carrying souls, elves, and wights off into otherworlds. There is a very large body of material relating to ships, the dead, the Otherworlds, and Deities associated with them, especially the northern German Goddess Nehalennia. There is also the beautiful imagery toward the end of *Völuspá* (Poetic Edda), where the Earth sinks into the sea during Ragnarök, and after it is over, Earth rises again from the waves, eternally green and renewed. This is indeed an image of death and rebirth through water, as well.

All of these matters I've written about so far should be enough to establish a firm connection between water and the Saiwalo-soul. Now, let's add a dash of salt to the mix. I'm going to leave the research and lore domains now, and turn to my own thoughts about Saiwalo, linking it with the previous chapter, "Hel-Dweller". The image of the soul in that chapter seemingly bears no resemblance to the imagery in this one, so it's time to pursue that riddle, too.

A Dash of Salt

I am no more than an armchair alchemist, but I'll put on an alchemist's hat for a few minutes here. Salt is a primary substance in alchemy, both literally and symbolically. Salt represents condensation and crystallization that results in the body and physical matter. Mineral salts are what remain after alchemical processes of combustion and purification, after all else has been dissolved away. These salts hold within themselves the seeds and crystalline patterns of new earthly life, new physical shapes and functions. Hagalaz, a rune associated with Hel, represents this salty, crystalline seed-shape. Combined with Ingwaz rune, another crystalline shape, they hold all potential within themselves.

Heathen Soul Lore

All of the material I discussed above refers to the connection between the Saiwalo soul and sweet or fresh water-bodies, and there's lots of evidence for that. But anyone who has seen the sea has, I think, felt how that endless, restless, salty, mysterious expanse of water echoes something deep within all of us: the unknown, dimly-seen, protean, shape-shifting water-being that lies within our own depths, or within whose depths we ourselves lie. Have you ever listened to recordings of whale-songs? Sonorous, eerie, long drawn-out undersea echoes....these are the songs of the soul, of Saiwalo.

This image appears to reflect a double-bottomed lake and the mysterious, deep-dwelling beings within it.

I believe that Saiwalo partakes of the nature of salt water and of the sea. Salt water is heavier and denser than fresh water, and layers itself underneath lighter lenses of freshwater.

The Soul and the Sea

This reflects the double-bottomed lake of Scandinavian folklore. I envision the bottom layer of these holy lakes as denser salt water, the top layer as lighter fresh water, as often occurs in nature where aquifers are near the sea, and deeper salt water intrudes underneath the lens of freshwater.

I think that Saiwalo is a deep-dwelling being, rooted in its ecosystem, which is Hel. I think that the flitting shades or phantoms of the dead, which are referred to in the Germanic languages using words derived from Saiwalo, are actually image-projections sent out from these Hel-dwelling Saiwalo beings. I call these images *Dwimors*, from Anglo-Saxon *gedwimor*, meaning a phantom or apparition, to distinguish them from Saiwalo itself for purposes of discussion, though I see Saiwalo and Dwimor as one being in essence.

Here is my vision: when Saiwalo is ready to send forth a new Dwimor-phantom into Midgard to form the spindle around which the other souls will gather, it begins an alchemical process. It separates out the salt from itself, which condenses and crystallizes into the Dwimor, the phantom that Saiwalo projects into Midgard as our earthly soul, who bears our unique physical image. The beings whom I discuss in the previous chapter, "Hel-Dweller", are Dwimor-phantoms, either after-death phantoms, or phantom forms of still-living beings who are experiencing a temporary, altered state of awareness rooted in their own Saiwalo / Dwimor.

Returning to Saiwalo's alchemical creation of its Dwimor: Saiwalo sends up a fountain, which is salt at its lower level, then at the upper level separates into a salt-being, a crystallized soul-image, floating on an upwelling tide of sweet water. Though I didn't include details in my Weisweiler summary, there are a number of species of fish and water-birds whose names include the *saivo*-root. This mirrors the action of the Dwimor as it is condensed and sent forth from Saiwalo, rising through a fountain of sweet water as a saivo-fish rises through the sacred saivo-lake.

That sweet water of Saiwalo's upper extension wells up into Holle's Well or Pond, carrying with it the crystallized Dwimor, Saiwalo's projection into Midgard, for Frau Holle to draw out of her Well. She takes this Dwimor-spindle and twirls it, and the threads of our other souls wrap themselves around it, conforming to the Dwimor, the phantom image which Saiwalo projects into Midgard as a pattern for a new, unique being.

Here I'll bring in the fascinating Heraclitus fragment I quoted at the beginning:

As souls (psyches) are born through the death of water, water is born through the death of earth. And as water comes into being from earth, so from water does the soul.

Though he was a Greek philosopher, not a Germanic one, I think this enigmatic thinker has a lot to say to us here. Heraclitus is described as the first Greek to develop the idea of *psyche* as the complete, living human soul (Snell p. 17). *Psyche* is the Greek word that Wulfila, the translator of the Christian Bible into the Gothic language, rendered as *Saiwala* in Gothic.

I see this enigmatic saying of Heraclitus as a way of describing the process of the Saiwalo soul rising through Holle's Well. First there is elemental earth, and this serves as a metaphor for Hel, the Hidden Land that lies below the surface of the Earth. In its center, earth 'dies' and transforms into elemental water, thus becoming a water-well surrounded and contained by earth. This serves as a metaphor for Saiwalo, a watery being dwelling in earthy Hel, which reaches up toward Holle's Well. Then the water in the center of the well 'dies' and is transformed into a soul surrounded by water, a metaphor for our Dwimor: our earthly soul-image condensed from, and projected by, our watery Saiwalo in the form of a phantom.

The Greek philosopher leaves it at that: from earth, to water, to soul. The Germanic visionary brings in the lovely figure of the Goddess Frau Holle as the tender midwife of the soul, drawing it from the water into her sheltering arms. Holle places this soul-image, the Dwimor, which was born through the 'death' or transformation of elemental Saiwalo-water, into a mother's womb. There it gestates and condenses further, while surrounded again by the waters of the womb.

Thus Saiwalo's Dwimor becomes fully rooted in a solid body and is born into the earthly plane, together with its complement of the other souls. As I see it, Saiwalo itself remains in Hel, but is tied to, and in communication with, its earthly body through its projection, the Dwimor-phantom, which is also called by 'soul' words in the various Germanic languages.

Salt / Sweet, Grasping / Giving

Here's an interesting thing to think about. The death-Goddesses Hella and Ran (sea-Goddess) are both said to hold tightly to the souls in their domains and never let them go, though it's also said that if drowned men (their Dwimors) appear at their own funeral, it is a sign that Ran has received them well (see *Eyrbyggja Saga* ch. LIV).

Contrast this with Frau Holle, whose name stems from the same root as Hel's name. But unlike hard-grasping Hella and Ran, *Holle gives back*. It is through her own pond or well-spring, and her own blessed hands, that the souls of newborn children arise into Midgard. There is the implication here of an endless cycle of life and death and life again: souls flowing back and forth through Holle's hands and her Well of life and death.

(See discussion in Goos p. 364-5 about other roots of Holle's name, which all indicate benevolence, graciousness, mercy, kindness, and related words, also leading to the idea that Holle not only takes, but gives back, and that her giving is a higher priority than her taking.)

Let's look at this process of grasping versus giving from an alchemical perspective, as is appropriate for Saiwalo, an alchemical being in my understanding. Salt is a strong attractor of water: it absorbs water and holds onto it, as happens in our salt-shaker during humid weather. Only by the application of fire (heat and dryness) will salt release the water it has absorbed. Salt water is heavy, dense, and deep, and only beings who are fully adapted to it can live in a salt-water environment. Likewise Saiwalo, unlike our other souls, is adapted to function in Hel.

Sweet water, by contrast, is an essential requirement for all earthly life, except for the lives beneath the sea. Sweet water gives life to all of us on the surface of the Earth, hence the imagery of souls being drawn from sweet water as new babies. But even on Earth, traces of salt are needed for earthly bodies, while sea-creatures are adapted to excrete excess salt from seawater so as to use sweet water within their bodies. Sweet water and salt mingle in various

The Soul and the Sea

proportions within living beings, both of them necessary for life.

Saiwalo is an alchemically active being who can rise up from its foundation of saltwater, and condense and precipitate salt out of itself, separating itself into a salt-being, a Dwimor, arising out of sweet water. What triggers this process? Fire is the medium by which salt and water are separated, and fire is what happens when egg and sperm of earthly life meet in the womb and together ignite the Fire of Life, our Ferah soul. (See Chapters 2 and 3.)

As our Saiwalo soul is elemental water and earth, so our Ferah soul is elemental fire and earth. When the spark of Ferah ignites in the womb, Saiwalo senses the new Ferah and rises up to meet it. Working together, fiery Ferah and watery Saiwalo pull Saiwalo's salty crystals out of solution and condense them into a Dwimor, Saiwalo's gift and its foothold within the newly-conceived infant in Midgard. Thus are their powers earthed in Midgard life.

Salt grasps life; when salty Dwimor is united with Lich and the other souls, it grasps and holds life within our Lichama and soular-system; hence the life-soul nature of Saiwalo with its Dwimor-projection. Other life-souls: Ferah, Aldr, Ahma, Ghost, Hama, constantly draw ambient life-force in various different forms into our body-soul complex. Saiwalo-Dwimor does not generate life-force itself; rather, it provides the salty medium that absorbs and holds those life-forces within our soul-body matrix, ensuring that we remain alive in Midgard.

Within Saiwalo in Hel, its natural and ever-renewing saltiness causes it to grip hard onto its hidden potential for life, holding onto its treasure down in Hel and not letting go, giving Hel a reputation for grasping and holding....until

Ferah-fire once again sets the alchemy in motion. Then Saiwalo condenses its salt, changes its upper reaches to sweet water, and releases its Dwimor into Midgard. Thus: salt and sweet, grasping and giving, in an endless cycle flowing between Midgard and Hel.

Summary

The Proto-Germanic word *saiwalo* most likely comes from the word *saiws*, meaning a body of water, and may be a diminutive term for 'the little one from the lake / sea.' Many tales and beliefs from Germanic and Saami lands tell of how souls come from bodies of water, and head for the afterlife through bodies of water. The German Goddess Frau Holle is especially associated with babies, souls, and with wells, ponds, streams and other freshwater bodies. She is the midwife of Saiwalo-Dwimor as it enters Midgard.

Saiwalo souls have the nature of salt water (see further discussion in Chapter 16). When it is time to send a Dwimor up to Midgard to ensoul a newly-conceived infant, Saiwalo condenses the salt out of itself and forms the Dwimor, a salty, grasping soul-matrix who holds all our souls and body together during life in Midgard. After Saiwalo has condensed its salty Dwimor, its waters are sweet, and it reaches up through Frau Holle's well or pond to deliver Dwimor into her hands. There, she places it in a mother's womb, where, again surrounded by water, Dwimor begins its work of collecting the baby's souls and linking them with its body.

Hail the Holy Ones

So, here we have many connections between Saiwalo and waters of various kinds, and beings who live in these waters, ships which sail across these waters, life-giving treasures hidden deep below water and earth, and Deities and spirits who mediate passages between these realms.

I've written here of Frau Holle, and mentioned the Goddess Nehalennia as a matron of sea-faring. Personally, I believe that Nehalennia is a soul-mother as Frau Holle is, but her domain is the salt-water aspect of Saiwalo, rather than Holle's sweet-water aspect. The Norns, too, are associated with water, with birth and with our Aldr soul, as I discuss in Chapter 7, and I believe that Mother Frigg, with her marshy dwelling of Fensalir, ties into these watery Saiwalo matters as well. I also find Mimir's head, placed deep within his Well of memory and inspiration, to be a very potent, multi-layered symbol of Saiwalo's nature.

.... Njorð, by Andromeda Whitefeather.

Then there is the God of seafaring, wealth and prosperity, Njorð. Though there is no clear basis in the lore for doing so, I hail Njorð along with these other Deities as a patron of Saiwalo. Njorð adds his godly power to the activities of Saiwalo. His Seas represent the deep, mysterious, surging substance of Saiwalo. His ships represent the way we gather and transport and share out the treasures of Saiwalo, drawn from the depths of the Sea and from distant, unknown lands, borne across the Sea to the place where humans live. His gifts of wealth and harvest represent what we can gain by living a deeply Heathen spiritual life.

Njorð is famed for his beautiful feet, and his footprints can point us toward a rich path of soulful life, leading us toward misty shores where seabirds cry, calling us to explore the vast unknown. Njorð teaches us to respect the waves and winds, the currents and shoals, of the sea and of life itself: to meet them with courage, strength and clear sight ahead. While Holle presides over the entry and exit of our Saiwalo's Dwimor into Midgard, Njorð joins her in overseeing all the activity that happens in the middle, our active life in Midgard that enriches and fulfills our Dwimor, and at last sends it back to its Saiwalo-origin, fully laden with treasures from the Sea.

Chapter 15

15. What Happened to Heathen Saiwalo?

Saiwalo and Dwimor, Part 3

Primitive Germanic *saiwalo; Gothic saiwala; Old Saxon seola, siole; Anglo-Saxon sawol, sawl, sawel; Old High German seula, sele; Old Frisian sele; Old Frankish sela; Old Norse sál (a later word borrowed from Anglo-Saxon).

In Chapters 13 and 14, I primarily explored views of Saiwalo and its Dwimor before and after Midgard life, from the point of view of tales and folklore. Here, I use more 'educated' sources to pursue old Heathen views of Saiwalo's nature and role during life in Midgard, without distinction between Saiwalo and Dwimor. As we shall see, major changes occurred in views of what the Saiwalo is, as the transition to Christianity progressed. Please note that I use many different forms of the word 'Saiwalo / soul' here, depending on the language source I'm discussing.

Old Heathen Saiwalo is a mysterious, nebulous soul. During Midgard life it is not closely involved in our personality, emotions, thoughts, will, motivation, nor with the activities of the physical body, other than preserving its life. Thus it is different from the more Midgard-oriented souls we've explored: Ferah, Hama, Aldr, Mod, Hugr and Sefa.

Eggers relates that early Germanic Christian usage shows only an eschatological (afterlife) concept: the living soul must be prepared for its journey to God, and be protected from sin so as to ensure this destination after death. It doesn't play any direct role in earthly life. Where the Latin word for 'soul', *anima*, is used in relation to earthly life, in the southern and western Germanic languages it is translated using Mod or another soul-related word, not Seola, Sele, etc. Saiwalo is never part of the activity-realm of Hugi, Mod, Sebo / Sefa; it is very unlike them: never 'happy, sad, grim, cruel,' etc. (p. 19). In other words, it is not involved with the normal activities of Midgard life, nor with aspects of our personality.

Almost no compound words, adjectives or verbs are made in the Old Saxon *Heliand* out of *Seola* or modifying *Seola*, in sharp distinction to other soul-words such as Hugi and Mod, which are combined into a huge number of compound words and word-forms (Becker p. 30-1), such as the forty different adjectives used to modify Hugi (Becker p. 51). My thought is that Heathen Seola is far removed from everyday life, simply not involved with it, and so it isn't necessary to come up with compound words and phrases to describe its activities and nature.

Becker (p. 86 f.) notes that in the Old High German poems of Ottfrid, one cannot speak of the Sela with respect to emotion, thought, or volition (will), namely our normal Midgard life-functions. Sela is not the subject nor the actor of action-words, in contrast to other actor-souls, especially Muat (Mod). Even the activity of worship itself is not done

What Happened to Heathen Saiwalo?

by the Sela, but by Muat and other souls, as also are the activities of 'sinning'. The body and the Midgard-oriented souls do the sinning, while the Sela pays the price in the afterlife. (In contrast to this, I will note that the Saiwala in the Gothic Bible does sometimes take action in the context of worship, for example in the Magnificat of Mary (Luke 46): "my soul / Saiwala magnifies the lord.")

In spite of its lack of involvement in Midgard-life activities, Saiwalo is nevertheless essential for the maintenance of physical life in Midgard. Living persons are called *gesawelod* (be-souled) or *sawol-berend* (soul-bearing) in Anglo-Saxon, while lifeless persons are *sawol-leas* or soulless. The body is called the *sawolhus* or soul-house (compare also the body as the *ferh-hus*, home of the Ferah soul, and as the *ealdorgeard* or the yard / enclosure of the Aldr soul), while physical life is the *sawol-hord*, the sawol's treasure-hoard. *Sawlung* or 'souling' is a noun meaning 'the death-process'. It aptly refers to the process of changing from a physically living-being having a body and a number of Midgard-involved souls all wrapped together, into a shadowy, mysterious Sawol-being.

Here is something to keep in mind as we proceed: although our modern word 'soul' comes from the Primitive Germanic **saiwalo* and its Anglo-Saxon descendant *sawol* or *sawle*, our modern concept of 'the soul' is greatly changed from its Heathen antecedents. This is due to the heavy influence of Christianity and of Classical Greek, Hellenistic, and Neoplatonic philosophy which in turn influenced the early development of Christian thought on this subject.

The consensus of the modern academic scholars I've read is that in ancient Heathen belief, Saiwalo (Sawol, Siola, etc.) is what is left after we die: the 'shade' of a once-living person which sinks down into Hel. According to Eggers, based on the Old Saxon *Heliand*, "the Germanic Seola has no psychological function during life; it is only the afterlife being" (p. 19).

"The Seola fares to Hel, and many Seolas gather together there" (Eggers p. 21). The souls which are active in Midgard life, such as Ferah, Hugr, Mod, Sefa, are not spoken of in the plural in the *Heliand*; they remain within the living person and act within that person individually. But the Seola souls are seen as independent beings continuing their existence after death, as entities gathered together in Hel, and can be spoken of in plural form. In fact, Eggers notes that five of the seventeen uses of *seola* in the *Heliand* are plurals, even though the Latin word *anima* they are translating does not occur in the plural (p. 20). He considers this to be the ancient, pre-Christian understanding of Seola: a shade which naturally descends to Hel in the afterlife, and continues its independent existence there, in company with other Seola-souls.

Archaic Greek imagery of the *psyche* or afterlife shade of a person in the Homeric poems gives us the same picture. "The only meanings of *psyche* clearly attested in Homer are the 'shade' and the 'life destroyed at death'." This *psyche* is not an abstraction (such as 'life force'); it has an objective existence as an entity. (Claus, p. 61.)

Archaic Greek texts are valuable for supplementing an understanding of pre-Christian Heathen beliefs because they are the oldest European writings that deal with such subject matter, written hundreds of years before Christianity and well over a thousand years before the earliest Germanic writings. Yet the archaic (Homeric period) Greek and the Heathen Germanic cultures and traditions have a good deal

What Happened to Heathen Saiwalo?

in common in spite of this great span of time-difference. Thus, Greek concepts about the various souls can in some cases enhance an understanding of the Germanic ones, as I show, for example, in Chapter 7 with the Aldr and Aion souls.

The Gothic Bible, translated from Greek around 360 C.E., used Gothic *saiwala* to translate Greek *psyche*. It's notable that the meaning of Greek *psyche* changed radically under the influence of later Classical Greek and Hellenistic philosophy, in the same ways as the meaning of Germanic *sawol* etc. did under the influence of Christianity. Our modern understanding of what 'the soul' is reflects these changes: we generally think of 'the soul' as our inner self, our spirit, playing an important role, even the defining role, in the conduct of our life in Midgard. We don't much think of it as being a shadowy afterlife-being lurking at the fringes of Midgard life. Here, I'll explore how and why this concept of 'the soul' changed, and offer thoughts about its implications for Heathen spirituality.

The Sawol in *Beowulf*

I examine Scandinavian and German lore and folklore views of the Saiwalo soul in Chapters 13 and 14. Here I'll begin with a view of the Anglo-Saxon poem *Beowulf*. Though the author of the *Beowulf* poem writes as a Christian, there are some expressions he uses that hark back to Heathen usage, in my view. For example, the warriors fighting Grendel are "seeking his soul" (*sawol secan*, l. 801), and this isn't intended in a Christian sense at all. They want to kill him and remove his soul, not convert him or save his soul in a Christian sense. The same type of expression is used, in this and other writings, about other Heathen life-souls, for example killers are called 'Aldr-snatchers', Aldr-robbers', 'Ealdor-banes', and the Ferah life-soul is considered the debt that must be paid by criminals in verdicts of capital punishment (see Chapters 3 and 7). Seeking the sawol or any of the life-souls, in the ancient texts, meant 'the intent to kill'.

Beowulf in his old age must fight the dragon, and knows he will die in this struggle. There are beautiful lines in the poem describing the upcoming separation of his souls:

> His Sefa was troubled, restless and wael-fus *(eager for death, eager to go on the death-road). Wyrd was immeasurably close, greeting / challenging the old man, seeking his Sawol-hoard, dealing the blow to sunder life from lich (body). Not for much longer would the ætheling's Feorh be wrapped in flesh.* (Lines 219ff., my translation.)

Here we see Sawol as something which maintains life, a hoard that will be ravaged by the dragon under the impetus of Wyrd's power.

The death of Beowulf. (George T. Tobin.)

As Beowulf lay dying after killing the dragon, he spoke to his brave thane Wiglaf, the only one with the courage to

What Happened to Heathen Saiwalo?

follow him into the lair. Beowulf told his thane that Wiglaf was the last of Beowulf's own kin:

"*Wyrd has swept all my kinsmen toward* metod-sceaft *(the shaping of* metod, *similar to wyrd: their doom), those undaunted eorls. I shall go after them.*" That was the old man's last word from his breast-gehygd *(the Hyge or Hugr in his breast)* before he chose the high war-wylm *(whelming flames of the bale-fire) as, outgoing from his breast, his Sawol sought its soothfast doom.*" (Lines 2814-20, my translation.)

Soothfast (*soðfæst*) means 'true, trustworthy, honest, just, righteous.' ('Sooth' is an old-fashioned word for 'truth', as we see in the old word 'sooth-sayer'. 'Soothfast' is a very fine word, well-deserving of being brought back into the language, especially now when we need trusty truth-tellers more than ever!) The Christian poet probably had the idea of Christian 'righteousness' in mind here, yet he knew that Beowulf had not been Christian, and there are other indications of Heathen attitudes in these lines. The last thing Beowulf speaks of is his brave, undaunted kinsmen (also Heathen) gone before him, and he intends his Sawol to follow them. The kinsmen were trustworthy, faithful to their beliefs and their people, and have gone to a soothfast doom. The poet could not place Beowulf in a Christian heaven, and so portrayed his death in the Heathen way of going to join his famed and trusty kin.

I think the use of *sawol* in this context stands in between Heathen and Christian usage. The idea of the Sawol as the entity subject to the doom or judgement of a Deity is more Christian than Heathen, while the Sawol as an entity that leaves the body at death is indeed Heathen as well as Christian. All of the souls leave the body at death, of course, with various different fates when this happens.

My observation is that the tendency of different souls to head toward a specific location, fate, or condition after death, without the controlling influence of a judgmental Deity, is a characteristic of the ancient Heathen tribal beliefs as well as most other tribal beliefs I've studied through anthropological writings. The more we see moral judgments affecting the afterlife, in the old texts, the more I believe we are seeing Christian influence blended with Heathen thought. In Anglo-Saxon poetry, interestingly, we often see that it is Wyrd, a power that we can understand as a natural process, which brings about the fates of souls, rather than the judgment of a Deity. The two quotations from *Beowulf*, above, are examples.

This is not to say that 'moral worthiness' was not an issue for the ancient Heathens; of course it was. The dying words of Beowulf are that he will follow his worthy, 'undaunted' kin to his soothfast doom, his honorable place of trust. And the thing is, he is fully expecting this to happen naturally, for his Sawol to join his kin; he is not pleading with a Deity for a merciful judgment on his Sawol. He knows he has earned his honorable place in the afterlife by the worthy deeds of his lifetime, and he makes a confident statement to that effect. No Gods need apply here, to pass judgment on his soul!

In Chapter 7 I discuss the idea of the Gods' doom or judgement upon the worthiness of our Werold-hama, the weaving our Aldr soul makes out of all the deeds and experiences of our lifetime, which establishes the quality of our 'reputation' and lays it in the Well as a layer of ørlög. The Heathen Deities, in this view, pass judgment on the

What Happened to Heathen Saiwalo?

totality of what we've accomplished during life, in order to decide whether it is worthy to become a layer of orlay in the Well. This is a different thing from the Christian God's judgment of the soul as a being in itself, and sending that soul-entity to torment in Hell or bliss in Heaven. Beowulf fully expected that his deeds and reputation were enough to win him a 'soothfast doom' with his honorable kin, without going through a divine process of judging his Sawol.

This engraving depicts a Frisian king or duke, named Redbad or Radboud (d. 719 CE.) He fought against the Frankish efforts at Christianization, with wins and losses. At one point, he considered baptism as a political expedient, but backed out at the last minute, as shown here. The story goes that as he was about to be baptized, he asked the bishop whether he would see his departed kin when he went to the Christian heaven. Upon being told that no, his Heathen kin would not be in the Christian heaven, Redbad stated that he would rather be in Hel with his Heathen kin, than go to heaven by himself. A typically Heathen sentiment! To me, this indicates that Redbad was not concerned about facing terrible torments in Heathen Hel, but rather considered it a reasonable, and more homelike, alternative to Christian heaven as a place to spend his afterlife. His reaction also indicates a genuine and firm belief in the afterlife and in Heathen Hel.
(https://en.wikipedia.org/wiki/Redbad,_King_of_the_Frisians)

The Ferah-Saiwalo Dynamic

Let's move on now to another important aspect in our quest to understand the mysterious Saiwalo soul. Again and again in the Continental Germanic and Anglo-Saxon writings we see a sharp contrast between the Saiwalo soul and the Ferah soul (see Chapter 3 about the Ferah). Both of them are life-souls; when they depart the body then physical life is over. In a Heathen context this did not cause any ambiguity. Ferah is the life-force, a vital soul engaged in the flows and powers of life in Midgard; the word itself (*feorh, ferhð, fjör, verch, fair, etc.*) was used synonymously with 'life'. Saiwalo (*sawol, seole, sele, saiwala, etc.*) was most definitely not the life-force. Saiwalo was what was left after the Ferah, Hugr, Mod, Ahma, etc. departed the dying body: a shade or wraith who headed for the afterlife domain in Hel.

Saiwalo's natural domain is Hel, as I explored in the previous chapters. The key thing is that in Heathen thought, it is clearly implied that the state of Saiwalo in Hel is not 'life'. It is 'existence,' certainly, but 'life' is what happens in Midgard. 'Life', in Heathen thought, is not simply a physical state of being. 'Life' itself is substance, energy, flow, ensoulment, interaction with the powers of nature at all levels within Midgard space-time. I discuss in Chapter 16 my understanding that, rather than being composed of life-force / life-energy as the other life-souls are, Saiwalo's Dwimor is a spiritual-alchemical matrix which, during life in Midgard, attracts and holds together our other souls and the life-forces and energies that they draw into our 'soular-system.' Saiwalo itself is not directly involved with the flow of life-energy.

What Happened to Heathen Saiwalo?

I showed in earlier chapters that the Ferah and the Aldr souls were conceptualized in quite physical ways. Ferah is a substance that 'fills' the living body and drains away at death, as many expressions in the Old Saxon *Heliand* show. The life-soul Aldr was considered so close to the physical level that a spear shot at a sea-serpent 'stood in the Aldr' of the serpent (*Beowulf* ll. 1433-5). This is an image of the flesh or body, the Ealdor-yard, permeated by the Aldr soul-substance, and the Aldr being endangered by the spear piercing the flesh.

Ahma and Ghost souls provide Athom / Ǫnd, the breath of life, which Saiwalo does not possess on its own. Humans and other Midgard beings are alive, not simply because we are physically functioning, as modern materialism would have it, but because we possess souls which generate, gather and contain active powers, energies, and spiritual substances of life.

When Christianized Germanic-speakers began to translate and write Christian texts in Old Saxon and other Germanic languages, they had a great many linguistic and conceptual difficulties to deal with. For one thing, the Latin words for various soul-functions and soul-entities did not map neatly onto the richer and broader vocabulary of the Germanic soul-related words; they could not use a one-to-one translation of specific words, but had to vary the words according to the context.

Even more difficult for them, however, was the whole Christian concept of 'everlasting life' of the soul in the Christian heaven or hell. Germanic-speaking peoples already knew about the Saiwala / Seola / Sawol which dwells in Hel, so the Christian idea of souls surviving death must have come as no surprise. When Latin Christian texts mentioned the *anima* soul in the context of afterlife survival, Germanic-speakers knew they were referring to the Seola: so far, so good. The idea of the Seola having 'life', however, simply didn't work for them. 'Life' is what all our souls, gathered together in Midgard, give to us. When Saiwalo separates from the other souls and leaves Midgard, 'life' does not go with it.

In fact, I have noticed in the *Heliand* and other southern and western Germanic writings, the phrase that writers often used to describe Christian afterlife and heaven was not 'everlasting life' but 'everlasting light' (*langsam lioht*, literally 'long-lasting light'). Here is one example from the *Heliand*, describing Jesus' death: "Christ's Seola was sent along the soothfast way, to the long-lasting light; his limbs cooled, the Ferah was gone from the flesh." (*Heliand* 5710-3.)

Referring to the 'long-lasting light' (though they did sometimes use 'long-lasting life' as well), as the place where Seola dwells, seems to have been one of their solutions to the problem of Seola being the recognized afterlife soul but not having 'life' as Heathens understood it, so that the Christian promise of 'everlasting life' could be described and accepted by converted Heathens. The idea of a world of 'everlasting light' was not difficult to imagine and accept. They already knew that the Saiwalo has an ongoing existence after life. Imagining Saiwalo in a 'land of everlasting light' was attractive and posed no philosophical conundrums about what 'life' is and whether Saiwalo could be described as having it.

Here is an important passage from the *Heliand* (4057-60) showing the Ferah-Saiwalo dynamic, and also the challenges of translation. To make my point here, I need to provide, first, my translation of the original Latin passage from which the *Heliand* material was drawn, and then show how it was changed when rendered into Old Saxon. (The original text passages are from Becker p. 40. I provide the original Latin and Old Saxon texts at the end of this chapter, page 418, for those who wish to cross-check my translations.)

These were Jesus' words to the women who came to attend his body after his crucifixion, and arrived to find him resurrected. He told them that whoever believed in him would not die, and continued as follows. Latin version:

Though he dies out of time because of the death of the flesh, he is not dead in eternity because of the life of the spirit, and is resurrected into immortality.

Old Saxon version:

Though the Eldibarn (children of Aldr) bury him...he is nevertheless not dead. The flesh is buried, the Ferah is retained / held onto, the Seola is in good health / is sound.

Overall, one can see here that there is a considerable difference in concepts, between the Latin-Christian version, and the Saxon version which makes use of Heathen-rooted words and concepts to try to explain Christian concepts. (The poet's use of 'Eldibarn' is relevant, since the Aldr soul is associated with life in Time, so there is that link with the Latin text.)

All modern translators I have read translate 'Ferah' as 'spirit' in this passage, and say that it is 'saved' rather than 'held onto.' Presumably they might be influenced by the original Latin text, which does say *spiritus*. However, the Latin text is referring to *vitam spiritus*: 'the life of the spirit'. In my understanding, 'Ferah' is not translating *spiritus* itself, but rather the *vitam* part of this phrase, meaning 'life, the life belonging to the spirit'.

The Ferah is 'held' (*gihaldan*) in this text, which I read as 'it is held onto, it is not let go.' The life-soul Ferah is retained, even after death, and according to this Christian interpretation, its presence gives health / life to the Seola-soul.

It's interesting to compare this phrasing with Hervör's farewell to her father's and uncles' Saiwalo-Dwimors in their graves, bidding the 'hale men in the howes' to rest, as I described in Chapter 13, p. 346. 'Hale' means 'healthy, sound, unharmed'. In the passage above from the *Heliand*, the Seola is described as 'sound, in good health,' because of Jesus' actions and the preservation of the Ferah. But in *Hervör's Saga*, there is no need for a Deity's intervention nor for the 'preservation of the Ferah'. The Saiwalo-Dwimors are 'hale' on their own. Certainly, Beowulf's soothfast Sawol is likely to be 'hale' after death, as well, as described in the passage above about his death. The important take-home here is that Heathen Saiwalo can be 'sound' and 'hale' after death, in its dwelling-place in Hel, without any godly intervention.

But, in the Heathen conception, though Saiwalo can remain sound and in good shape after death, it is not 'alive,' and this was the conundrum for the early Christian missionaries. In Heathen thought, without Ferah, it would be impossible for Saiwalo to have 'eternal life,' even though it does have 'ongoing existence.' This existence is not 'life'; 'life' is bestowed by the presence of Ferah. Old Heathen concepts could not envision 'life' without Ferah's presence, not even life for the soul / Seola.

What Happened to Heathen Saiwalo?

This is not the only example of how early Germanic Christians struggled to conceptualize and explain Christian ideas in Germanic Heathen languages and contexts. In spite of the superlative poetic skill of the authors of the Old Saxon *Heliand* and other early Christian texts in poetic form, there are awkward, ill-fitting passages describing death scenes, trying to express Christian concepts in Heathen vocabulary. Here is another example.

The beggar Lazarus died of hunger outside a rich man's house. Then:

"God's angels received his Ferh and led him forth from there, so they could set the poor man's Siole in Abraham's bosom." (*Heliand* 3349-3353).

This is indeed awkward: the angels received the Ferh soul, then led either the Ferh soul (a neuter noun in Old Saxon) or the 'man himself' ('him', a masculine pronoun) away from there. When they arrived at Abraham's location, presumably heaven, they set Lazarus's Siole (a feminine noun) in Abraham's bosom. So here, grammatically, we have three different entities: neuter Ferh, feminine Siole, masculine 'him / Lazarus,' along with a lot of confusion.

Where did the Siole come from? Did the Ferh turn into the Siole en route to heaven? Did the Ferh disappear somewhere and the Siole magically appear in the angels' hands upon reaching Abraham? Was only the man's Siole set in Abraham's bosom, and not the man 'himself'? If so, what happened to the 'him' which the angels led forth, after they received his Ferh? And what happened to the Ferh received by the angels, after the Siole was deposited? To me, this illustrates the difficulty and confusion of trying to translate Christian ideas into a language and culture that have very different ideas of what 'souls' and 'life' really are.

Heathen Soul Lore

Here is another example, showing Grendel's death in the *Beowulf* poem. As he received his death-wound, Grendel "knew that his Aldr had come to an end" (l. 822), and then he "laid aside his Feorh, heathen Sawle, there Hel received him" (ll. 851-2). First, the Feorh must be laid aside, before anything else can happen. Then the Sawle takes center stage, and then Hel receives 'him'. Sawle is a feminine noun, so the 'him' which Hel receives must be Grendel 'himself'. Again, the Sawle is somehow involved here, yet the entity received by Hel is 'him'—apparently Grendel 'himself.' My impression is that this passage illustrates, again, the awkwardness of translating Christian ideas about the afterlife using Heathen terms and concepts.

From a Heathen perspective, the Sawle / Saiwalo is the afterlife representative of who the living person was, but this representative is missing other souls who provide the actual substances and powers of 'life', including the breath of life provided by Ahma / Ghost, and the full life-force and substance of Ferah. This afterlife being, the Saiwalo, is an image of who the person was, but does not possess the powers, essences and energies of 'life'. I want to note here the very clear contrast between Ferah and Saiwalo souls. A dying person can't simply give up their Saiwalo forthwith; their Ferah has to go first. Only when Ferah / life is definitely gone can the Saiwalo take up its natural afterlife existence.

Here is an example of this point. The *Heliand* says that "Christ gave Ferah to the fey, those who were ready to go forth, heroes on the Hel-way; the savior himself quickened them (brought them to life) after death" (ll. 4704-9). The word 'fey' is used in its Germanic sense: 'ready to die, knowing death is near, doomed to die soon.' This passage says that Christ gave Ferah-souls / Ferah life-substance to those who were dying and even to those who were already dead, the 'heroes on the Hel-way', and thus returned them to a state of life. The souls on the Hel-way presumably turned around and went back to join their living persons, after Jesus gave Ferah soul back to their Lich-Hamas in Midgard.

Ghost versus Soul

It's interesting to note that throughout the whole Grendel episode in *Beowulf*, Grendel, while living in a physical body, is referred to as a *gast* or ghost, often an *ellorgast*, an alien spirit or ghost from elsewhere, and once even a *helle-gast* (l. 1274), a spirit from Hel (though he is still alive). The folk of Heorot, plagued by the Grendel-gast, pray to the *gast-bona*, the ghost-bane or ghost-slayer (presumably Woden) to rescue them (l. 177). The physical dragon that Beowulf killed is also called a *gast* while alive.

A gast or ghost in this context is an otherworldly being roaming in Midgard, often a fully physical being, while a Sawol is a non-physical being attached to a physical being living in Midgard, which goes to an otherworld after death. There's a very clear difference between 'ghost / spirit' versus 'Saiwalo soul' here that's important to keep in mind when studying Heathen souls.

This is in contrast to modern English, where it's often difficult to pinpoint the difference between 'spirit' and 'soul'. This fuels my annoyance that all *Beowulf*-translators I've read (and the Anglo-Saxon Dictionary, too) inaccurately translate *gast-bona*, used to describe a Heathen God, as 'soul-slayer' rather than as 'ghost-slayer / ghost-bane / ghost-buster'. The desperate folk of Heorot are not praying to a soul-slaying God; they are begging their powerful God to get rid of Grendel, a bloodthirsty ghost-monster, which the God does by sending Beowulf as his response to their prayers. A 'soul-slayer' and a 'ghost-bane / ghost-buster / monster-slayer' really are not the same thing!

This picture of the energy and strength of otherworldly gasts roaming Midgard can carry over to our understanding of human Ghosts. Our own Ghost / Gast, during life and after death, is more active and powerful in a personal way, while Saiwalo is more passive in this respect; its activities are more in the nature of alchemical / ecological phenomena, rather than personally-oriented activities.

The activity and personal power of our Ghost is strengthened by what I believe is a partnership formed between our Ghost and our Mod-soul during Midgard life, which continues after death (see Chapter 8). Picture the difference in these traditional afterlife views, between Ghost as an Einherjar warrior in Valhalla, daily fighting and feasting, versus Hel-dwelling Saiwalo's need to be awoken from 'sleep' by a living person who wishes to speak with it, as is told in the ancient tales. Saiwalo's 'sleep' is a productive state of ongoing alchemical transformation (see Chapter 16), but it is a different kind of activity than our afterlife Ghost engages in: less personally-oriented, more cosmic in nature.

One of my favorite Heathen-flavored views of the Ghost and Athom, the sacred breath, comes in the *Heliand*, after Jesus has been crucified and is lying dead in the sepulcher: "then did the Gast / Ghost come, by God's power, holy Athom under the hard stone, into his Lich-Hama." (ll. 5770-2). Here is a picture of the holy Athom, the breath of Spirit, literally creeping under the stone that was rolled in front of the sepulcher and entering Jesus's body to bring him back to life. This is very literal, and definitely ghostly! It is not something the Saiwalo could do, returning from Hel and restoring life. Saiwalo has no breath of life to give; if it miraculously returns from Hel, this is because Ferah has first been restored to the Lich, as I described earlier. Only then, could Saiwalo return to life.

The life-giving abilities of the Ghost are shown again in the description of how Mary conceived Jesus. The Holy Ghost didn't just *cause* the conception to occur; "the Helago Gest *became* the child in her womb" (*Heliand* 291-2). Again, this would not be said about the Seola. In fact, none of the Germanic languages, past or present, have ever named the Christian Holy Spirit as "Holy Soul" or the equivalent. It is always "Holy Ghost / And / Ahma / Athom / Spirit." Soul and ghost / spirit are not the same thing.

The understanding that 'Ghost / spirit' and 'soul / Saiwalo' are different entities is strengthened by looking at what happened in the Old Norse language during the Christian conversion process. I mentioned in previous chapters that, while the 'soul' word (*saiwalo, sawol, sele, siola, etc.*) existed in all the other branches of the Germanic languages, and in Proto-Germanic, it dropped out of Old Norse, though I argue in Chapter 13 that I believe their afterlife concepts included beings that the other Germanic languages call 'soul, sawol, sele,' etc. This loss of 'Saiwalo' is a mystery, and another one is layered on top of it: the question of why the Old Norse language found it necessary to borrow (from Anglo-Saxon) the soul-word *sál* back into their language during the process of Christianization.

The Norse already had the word *and*, that referred to ghosts, spirits, wights, dwarves, monsters, as well as referring to the living human spirit and the breath of life (see

Chapter 4). They used this word to name the Christian 'Holy Spirit / Holy Ghost', as *Heilagur Andi* in Icelandic and Faroese, *Helige Ande* in Swedish, *Hellige Ånd* in Norwegian. Their usage of *and* clearly paralleled Anglo-Saxon and Saxon usage of *gast*.

As Heathens, the Norse already had the idea that disembodied people go to Hel after death. They apparently didn't need a 'soul-word' to express this concept; instead, they referred to the person after death simply by name, as the ongoing 'personhood', so to speak. In other words, they didn't say a person's 'soul' went to Hel; instead they said the person himself or herself went there. In other words, the Scandinavian languages seem to have had the concept of the afterlife-entity already covered, either as *'and'* or as the person by name.

Once Christian spiritual ideas started taking root, it was necessary to have accurate terms to express them. Why was the already existing word *and*, meaning 'spirit' not adequate for describing human afterlife-beings? Apparently, to express Christian ideas about the afterlife, they needed to borrow another word: Sál / soul. Latin and Greek languages, from which the Germanic language Bibles were translated, also had two different soul-terms: *spiritus / anima*, and *pneuma / psyche*. These words in turn translated Hebrew *ruach, neshama*, and *nefesh*. All these languages had, and have, more than one word for souls. Why?

One answer is clear to me: because we all have more than one soul. But there are some other subtleties here. As I described earlier, *Ande* and Ghosts were considered to be supernatural but physical beings in Midgard, beings possessing the breath of life and other life-characteristics. They are 'alive' in Midgard, even though they have supernatural traits, and they are potentially subject to death. Essentially, though these entities might die, they are not really 'afterlife beings', from the old Heathen viewpoint. A Germanic afterlife-being is something else, something which is not involved with, nor characterized by, Midgard life and breath. Instead, it comes into its own full nature and existence only after the body has died and the breath of life has departed.

My thought about the reason that the Old Norse language needed to borrow the soul-word *sál* during Christianization, is that they needed a word for the specific afterlife-soul, the soul which comes into its own after death. They certainly had this *concept*, as I discuss at length in Chapter 13, but they didn't have a *word* for it that fit into the context of Christian afterlife beliefs, so they needed to borrow one.

Looking at these two concepts, 'spirit / ghost / ǫnd / *and*' versus 'soul / Saiwalo', the difference between them is that 'spirit / ǫnd' is the breath of life, and Midgard-embodied wights possess this breath. Saiwalo soul, on its own, has no breath; its existence does not depend on breath, though its tie to a living human body does depend upon the breath. Saiwalo in Hel does not breathe, yet it continues its existence. Saiwalo, in itself, does not possess 'life' as it is understood in Midgard, though it does exist as a spiritual phenomenon with powers of its own.

What's the Big Deal?

We might wonder what's the big deal about whether we consider Saiwalo's afterlife situation to be 'life' or simply 'existence'. This issue, and the relationship between Saiwalo and the other souls that is defined by this issue, *was* a big deal for elder Heathens, so big a deal that it was a major underlying cause for all of the transformations and losses of the old soul-related words as Christianity permeated Germanic cultures. And as the soul-words transformed or fell out of use, so too did the old understandings of what souls are.

It boiled down to a Heathen understanding that 'to be alive' meant 'to be in possession of life-souls, and especially of the Ferah soul.' Once Ferah, Ghost with Athom, and the other life-souls departed, one simply could not be considered 'alive.' The powers, the energetic flows and substances, of 'aliveness' were gone. So when Ferah was gone from the corpse and from the 'shade', the afterlife remnant, one could not speak of this shade or Saiwalo possessing 'everlasting life.' Yet, this was the Christian promise: that if one believed (and 'behaved'), one's soul would be 'saved' and given everlasting life. If the Christian missionaries couldn't back up the promise of everlasting life in heaven or torment in the Christian hell, then they would lose much of their power to tempt and coerce people into Christian belief and practice.

In order for the Christian 'hell' to be perceived as a terrible place that people wanted to avoid at all costs, Heathens had to be persuaded that their Saiwalos could suffer, could react to this place of torment and despair the way a living person would. Likewise, to enjoy Heaven's everlasting bliss, a soul would need to have the capacities to appreciate and participate in it. This meant that the abilities and natures of the other souls: life-souls and Midgard personality-souls, had to be grafted onto Saiwalo, so that it could 'live forever' with full capacity after death, either suffering in hell or rejoicing in heaven.

What Happened to Heathen Saiwalo?

A telling example of this process is how King Ælfred the Great (848-899 CE) in his translation of some of the biblical Psalms into Anglo-Saxon, translated the *two* Latin-Christian soul-words 'spiritus / spirit' and 'anima / soul' into *three* Anglo-Saxon soul-words, namely Gast (Ghost, spirit), Sawle (Saiwalo, soul), and Mod. When the poet of the Psalms cried out to his God to save his 'soul / anima' from the power of death in Psalm 15:10, Ælfred translated this as a plea to save "my Sawle and my Mod" together (O'Neilll). It was not enough for him to plead salvation for his Sawle; his Mod, representing his sense of himself, his Midgard-life faculties, needed to be included, as well.

Mod, in late Heathen and early Christian times in the Southern and Western Germanic branches, was seen as a soul which contains the Inner Self, the Personhood of a person, along with their character, their volition, and other components that make up a person (see Chapter 8). The afterlife souls, Ghost and Saiwalo, were not considered to possess the full complement of these aspects of personality and Selfhood. Ælfred took the Christian promise of salvation of his full 'self' seriously, and thought very carefully about how to translate Christian texts so as to convey this belief to his people.

Heathens already had beliefs about survival of Saiwalo after death. What was new, was the idea that the full, living Selfhood of a person could be 'saved' or 'damned', and consequently rejoice or suffer as a living person would. Therefore, Ælfred cried out for salvation for his Ghost / Spirit, his Sawl / Soul, and his Mod-soul, and in fact, he references Mod at least as often as Sawle, and far more often than Gast, in his translation of the Psalms. Without all three of them, his experience of the afterlife could not be complete, so it was vital that his Mod be included.

This makes it clear that Ælfred, a very thoughtful, spiritual and philosophical person, did not consider that his full personhood resided in his Sawl or his Gast. To receive the promise of everlasting life, he needed a soul associated with life and personhood, not just shadowy afterlife-souls.

I do not see Alfred's attitude as coming from Christianity. Christianity teaches that by 'saving the soul', everything that matters is saved. I think that Ælfred's understanding of these matters was still influenced by Heathen thought, even though he was a dedicated Christian. The very words he used were rooted in Heathen thought from centuries of use; he could not fail to have his own thoughts shaped by the soul-words and their original, Heathen meanings.

I'm going to make a fundamental point, that requires more discussion than there is room for here: the native words for 'soul, spirit' and all their complex associations differed significantly among the Hebrew, Greek, Latin, and Germanic languages. In addition, there were several quite different philosophical and belief systems through which the terms in the various languages were understood and further developed. These included various forms of Jewish religion, Classical and older Greek philosophy, Hellenistic and Jewish-Hellenistic philosophy and Neoplatonism, Pagan Roman beliefs and culture, various hotly-disputed versions of early Christianity, and various Heathen beliefs of the Germanic peoples.

The Christianized soul-words reached Heathen lands carrying an immense amount of complex baggage, and met a whole different, and much larger, set of soul-related words with baggage of their own. The result of pushing Heathen terms and concepts, during the conversion process, through this philosophical and linguistic meat-grinder is what usually comes out of meat-grinders: sausage! The various distinct ingredients become mashed together and have quite a different flavor as they come out the other side. My efforts at forensic Heathen soul lore are focused on sorting out the sausage, to the best of my ability, and approaching some idea of what the original ingredients were. (For an interesting perspective on the conversion process, refer to Russell's *The Germanization of Early Medieval Christianity*.)

Impacts of Changing Ideas about the Soul

The new ideas about 'the soul' came with some highly significant corollaries, big changes from Heathen ways of thinking. The Christian establishment deliberately wanted to keep people's eyes off of 'worldly matters' and fixed on the rewards and punishments of the Christian afterlife. Afterlife was 'what it's all about' in Christianity, as it was taught during that period of time. There was a radical change from focusing on all the domains and activities of the non-Saiwalo souls, acting in Midgard in both embodied and disembodied states, to focusing solely on the Saiwalo's future existence in heaven or hell.

As people were encouraged to shift from a Heathen focus on human life in Midgard, to a Christian focus on 'being saved from hell and going to heaven', Saiwalo went from being an obscure, shadowy, remote soul-being, to being 'The One-and-Only Soul' which must constantly be protected from the 'sins' that all the other Midgard-oriented souls, now demoted to soul-parts, supposedly commit every day during their time in Midgard.

Ælfric of Eynsham, an influential cleric and a prolific writer and speaker, flourished about a century later than Ælfred, and a good deal changed during that century. Rather than expanding the number of afterlife-souls to three, as Ælfred did, he shrank it down to only one soul, and threw everything else into that one 'soul-basket'. Here is how Ælfric described the soul:

> Soul is called many names in books, according to its functions. Its name is *anima*, this is *sawul*, and this name is fitting to its life. And *spiritus, gast*, appertains to its contemplation. It is *sensus*, that is *andgit* or *felnyss*, when it perceives. It is *animus*, that is *mod*, when it knows. It is *mens*, that is *mod*, when it understands. It is *memoria*, that is *gemynd*, when it remembers. It is *ratio*, that is *gescead*, when it reasons. It is *voluntas*, that is *wylla*, when it wills something. But nevertheless, all these names are for *sawul*. (Inciuraite, p. 38; she is quoting Harbus p. 35.)

Inciuraite describes this as the Sawul becoming superordinate (the one on top of everything), and all the other soul-related words becoming hyponyms ('under-names') of Sawul (p. 37). In this passage, Ælfric followed the example of earlier Christian church fathers, themselves much influenced by Greek and Hellenistic philosophy. He took all of a human's souls / soul-like attributes, and put them under the single umbrella of the Sawul, amazingly, even the Spirit / Gast.

Ælfric's view of the soul now falls squarely within the 'psychological theory of the soul' that I discuss in Chapter 1, and moves away from the 'existential theory of souls' on which I base my own analysis, and where I think King Ælfred was coming from.

If one takes the psychological approach, as is common in our culture today, then Ælfric's system is helpful for understanding Old English terms relating to the functions of 'the soul'. From my own perspective, though, this version of the Saiwalo is entirely unrecognizable when compared to the earlier understandings that I have discussed here and in the previous chapters.

The new 'soul' gradually absorbed many of the older soul-words, and they dropped out of the Germanic languages entirely. Other soul-words remained, but altered their meanings and became less important, less influential within the human 'soular system.' Gradually, the ancient Heathen meanings of the soul-words disappeared, and with them went the old Heathen understanding of what souls really are.

Summary

During life, Saiwalo / Dwimor is shadowy and detached, not heavily involved in our Midgard activities. Dwimor is busy absorbing images from Midgard, and transmitting images from Saiwalo into Midgard. It is gathering its 'sawol-hoard': a word used for 'life' in Anglo-Saxon, and a word I like to use to describe what Dwimor is doing during our life in Midgard: gathering its soul-hoard of image-treasures.

I discussed the polar differences between our Ferah-soul which confers life, versus our Saiwalo-soul which comes into its own only after death, and the Heathen understanding that you cannot mix these two together. 'Life' is not simply a 'condition'; it is a *substance* that we possess while we are in Midgard, with all our souls together.

Life consists of flows of energies and powers, the presence of life-souls. Saiwalo doesn't have access to these things after death; they are part of the Midgard-environment.

I think that the Christians chose to elect the Heathen Saiwalo, out of all the possible soul choices, as the supposed 'one and only soul' of human beings because Saiwalo was already known to go to Hel after death, and also known to be little involved in Midgard life. This suited the Christian focus on the afterworlds, on 'heaven' and 'hell', as opposed to the Heathen focus on Midgard life, the domain of all the souls working together.

'Ghost / Spirit' and 'Soul' are not the same entity in old Heathen thought. Ghosts were considered to be wights or other beings with physical characteristics, residing in Midgard or able to travel back and forth between Midgard and whichever otherworlds they stemmed from. They possess the breath of life, and are capable of being killed. The Grendel-monster in *Beowulf* is an example of a gast or ghost.

The Soul / Saiwalo / Seola, on the other hand, has no breath of life. Saiwalo-Dwimor does not exist in Midgard on its own, as a gast can do. Saiwalo must be connected with a living body in Midgard, but is itself a shadowy entity on the fringes of Midgard life. It comes into its own nature only after the death of the body, the separation of all the souls, and its Dwimor's descent to its natural dwelling-place, Heathen Hel.

Old Heathen Ghosts were seen as powerful entities, difficult to overcome when their desires conflicted with those of living humans. Saiwalos, on the other hand, if they appeared on their own in Midgard at all, appeared only as fleeting phantoms, 'poor souls', whose only real power in Midgard, if any, lay in their ability to cause fear in the living.

The Christian 'Holy Ghost' has never been called the 'Holy Soul', showing a clear difference between the two. The Holy Ghost is an entity with great spiritual power, is able to travel between Midgard and 'Heaven', and confers the breath of life. A Saiwalo / Soul entity would not have these powers.

Saiwalo is vague and otherworldly, in many ways a *tabula rasa*, a clean slate, upon which Christians could draw their own picture of 'what a soul is', as opposed to the stubborn and well-known characteristics of the more Midgard-oriented Heathen souls, such as Mod and Hugr, which would be difficult to re-interpret. However, this re-interpretation did gradually occur over longer periods of time. Saiwalo absorbed Ferah, a primary life-giving soul. It absorbed Mod, Hugr and Sefa, with all their qualities and abilities that enable us to thrive in Midgard. Aldr and Hama dropped out of consideration as souls, at least in formal religious contexts, though Hama (and Hugr) continued to show up in folklore contexts. Ahma / Ghost / Athom / Ǫnd still retain their nature as 'spirit and divine breath.'

Now our Saiwalo-based 'soul' is considered our comprehensive Inner Self, including thought, emotions, will, memory, reason, and all the rest. The psychological approach to understanding what a soul is, comes to the fore, and the existential theory of multiple souls as individual beings taking part in a 'soular system' or soul-household, becomes lost in the mists of time. My work, and my hope, is to bring it back into the foreground of Heathen thought and awareness, to support a rich, vigorous, dynamic

Heathen Soul Lore

spiritual and philosophical life for Heathens, in Midgard and in the other Worlds as well.

Translation reference:
Here are the Latin and the corresponding Old Saxon verses that I referred to on page 401 of this chapter:

Si morietur ad tempus.........thoh ina eldibarn erthu bithekkian
Propter mortem carnis.........that flesk is bifolhen
Non morietur in aeternum.......nis he dod thiu mer
Propter vitam spiritus......that ferah is gihaldan
Et immortalitam resurrectionis........is thiu seola gisund.

(Becker p. 40; *Heliand* lines 4057-4060. The Latin comes from Tatian's *Diatesseron*, a conflation of the four canonical gospels that was much used by early Germanic Christians.)

A general note on sources: Although there is a great deal of learned writing in Anglo-Saxon / Old English that goes into much detail about 'what the soul is,' most of this is, in my view, so heavily influenced by both Christian and Classical philosophical thought, that I don't find it of much use in trying to understand ancient Heathen concepts. One of many indications of this is the very tidy, rational and systematic categorization of soul-like faculties offered by early Christian writers such as Ælfric in his Catholic Homilies. One might as well be reading Aristotle or St. Augustine of Hippo, translated into Anglo-Saxon!

Far more useful, I find, are the passionate and beautiful poems, such as the Old Saxon *Heliand*, that are addressed to and intended for laypeople, often still Heathen or only recently converted. King Ælfred's translation of the

What Happened to Heathen Saiwalo?

Psalms, *Beowulf,* and many other poetic works are more helpful than the old scholarly works, in my opinion.

In these poems, terms relating to the souls are used as the common people would understand them. They are not intricate philosophical concepts, stacked into castles of towering logic. They are ancient words rooted in Heathen consciousness and understanding, used as they would be used in everyday life. The same can be said for folklore sources. I find that this more poetic approach guides us on a less tidy and logical, but more genuine and deep-rooted pathway into Heathen thought about the souls.

My silver 'Eormen-soul' necklace, made and given by a Heathen friend.

Interlude: A Short Essay on the Eormen-Soul

The **Irminsul** was a great wooden pillar or tree with religious and ethnic meaning to the Heathen Saxons; effectively it was the axis mundi, the World-Pillar. The Christian Frankish emperor Charlemagne conquered the Heathen Saxons and commanded the Irminsul to be cut down in 772.

The word 'Irmin' in Saxon, 'Eormen' in Anglo-Saxon, meant 'great, powerful, wondrous, immense.' The Anglo-Saxon word eormen-cynn meant 'human-kind', the great-kin, while eormen-grund meant the 'great ground': the wide world. Eormen-laf meant a great legacy: what is left for us by those gone before. I am here using a play on words to imply that, like the Irminsul, the **Eormen-soul** or 'great and wondrous soul-concept of the Heathens' was 'felled' by the imposition of Christian ideas. (Heinrich Leutemann, artist.)

Heathen Soul Lore

An engraving from the mid-1800s entitled "Wesley's Tree." (The British Museum.) Here, the people are gathered around a great tree, in time-honored custom. But their focus is on the Christian preaching of John Wesley, rather than on the World-Pillar and the World-Tree, and all that these concepts imply. The focus has shifted from Heathen attention to the sacred <u>connections</u> between Midgard and other Worlds and Beings, to a focus on the <u>separations</u> between 'Heaven, Earth and Hell' and the dire implications these separations have for the Christian concept of the human soul.

The Eormen-Soul

This may be a depiction of the fallen Irminsul, a detail from a relief-carving of the crucifixion (the Externsteine), of uncertain date, but probably around 1160CE. Here we see an image of the Heathen 'Irmin-soul' bent to the ground, but not broken. Our work as modern Heathens can raise our 'Eormen-Soul', our full and complete Heathen soular-system, to its upright, natural position again.

This is an artist's rendition of what the fallen Irminsul, shown in the stone carving above, might have looked like when it was upright and whole, though we do not know for sure what the historical Irminsul looked like. The shape pictured in the stone carving, and above, was commonly used during the Heathen period to depict trees in general, and may, or may not, have been specifically intended as the Irminsul in the Externsteine stone-carving. (See discussion in Waggoner 2021, pp. 162-3).

Though the Irminsul has been used as a symbol by many modern groups, some with hostile attitudes, it existed long before such groups and philosophies did. The medieval chronicler Rudolf of Fulda (9th century) called the Irminsul "the column of the *universe upholding all things" (Waggoner 2021, p. 144). Although the word 'Irmin (eormen, jörmunn, *ermanaz)' means 'great, huge', it was also the name of a legendary divine or semi-divine founder of the Germanic tribe called the Herminones, as recounted by the 1st-century Roman historian Tacitus (p. 64). Most modern scholars and Heathens associate the Irminsul, and possibly the shadowy figure of Irmin or Hermin, with the Heathen God Tyr / Tiw / Tiwaz.*

Let's connect this with the Anglo-Saxon Rune Poem for the rune Tiwaz / Tir, which calls Tir a 'tacna' ('token'), *meaning a "sign / symbol / wonder / banner / standard": something to be seen and followed with hope and reverence, like the great Irminsul. Though the rune Tiwaz / Tiw / Tyr is the God's name, the 'token' it refers to is thought to be the North Star. (For more in-depth discussion of this rune-poem, see Waggoner 2021, pp. 145-7.) Here is my rendition of the poem. I include more word-variants than most translations, because I use the poem as inspirational material.*

> Tir is a *'tacna / token, sign'*, holding troth well
> With æthelings (nobles); always shows the true path
> Over the mists of night; never fails, deceives nor betrays.

I put all of this together: the Irminsul, the Rune Poem, the God Tiw / Tyr / Irmin, the North Star, and the 'Irmin-soul' play on words, and relate it all to the pursuit of Heathen soul lore. Our own Eormen-soul, the great-soul or over-soul comprised of our full soular-system, is our own North Star, our own true path, that shines through the fogs and confusions of the world. It is a path of nobility, faithfulness, and perseverance: a path unique to each one of us, that calls us onward toward great wonders of the souls.

Chapter 16

16. The Alchemy of Hel

Saiwalo and Dwimor Continued

In this chapter I present my own thoughts about the nature and dynamics of the Saiwalo soul, its Dwimor or phantom-image, and about Saiwalo's ecosystem: Hel, the Hidden Land of mystery and power. This chapter is less a scholarly analysis, and more a series of esoteric and mythic symbols and tales, presented from several different angles, with the purpose of homing in on a visceral understanding of what Hel, Saiwalo and Dwimor are.

    I want first to make a clarification, and distinguish between understandings I've derived from the lore, versus on my own. I described traditional beliefs about the afterlife-being called by variations of the word *Saiwalo / Seola / Sawl*, etc., in the previous three chapters. Both the *Saiwalo* (soul) and the *Dwimor* (phantom) are old, native Germanic words and concepts, but the specific relationship between them that I present is based on my own ideas, and so is the idea that Saiwalo stays in Hel while sending up a Dwimor-projection into Midgard to support a living person. The more traditional idea is that a Saiwalo-soul enters a living person at birth, perhaps first drawn from a body of water (physical or spiritual) by a Goddess or Norn, and that the Saiwalo-soul heads back to Hel / the Hidden Land after death, perhaps also by diving through a body of water, or entering a cave or other landscape feature.

My own soul-explorations through the years have led me to the ideas that I present in these chapters about the Saiwalo, Dwimor, and Hel. These beliefs of mine include:

~ that Hel is a metaphysical ecosystem whose primary components are the Saiwalo souls, and that Hel and the Saiwalos are interdependent;

~ that this ecosystem and its alchemical processes play a vitally important role in the health and vitality of all the life-bearing Worlds, especially Midgard;

~ that Saiwalos remain in Hel and continue their work there, while also sending up Dwimor-projections to ensoul living beings in Midgard, which remain connected to the Saiwalos in Hel during life;

~ that the Dwimors return to Hel and their Saiwalos after death in Midgard, and that this Dwimor-traffic to and fro constitutes a major part of the important interactions and exchanges between Midgard and Hel, the Hidden Land.

I hope this helps to distinguish between traditional beliefs and the new ideas that I am presenting through my soul lore work, for those who are concerned about such distinctions. This chapter explores and expands on the understandings I listed above.

Part 1. Alchemy, Ginnungagap, & the Coalescence of Hel

Alchemy in this Context

Approaches to alchemy range across a wide area, from the precursor to modern physical chemistry, to various forms of material transformations (including the production of medicines), to the rarefied reaches of psychospiritual development. Alchemy is "a form of chemistry and speculative philosophy….any seemingly magical process of transforming or combining elements into something new." (*Dictionary.com*) "Alchemists attempted to purify, mature and perfect certain materials…the perfection of the human body and soul was thought to permit or result from the alchemical *magnum opus* (great work), and, in the Hellenistic and Western mystery tradition, the achievement of gnosis." (*Wikipedia*.)

I like Greer's explanation of alchemy as more than simply a field of study. He sees it as a universal method, in the same way that science is a universal method, with its own procedures which can be applied to explore many fields of knowledge and transformational processes. The basic approach of alchemy is called *solve et coagula* (dissolve and coagulate or bring together): find the primal material, separate the subtle from the gross (material) components, purify and transform them, then recombine them into something similar to, but more powerful and pure than the original (Greer p.145-60). I am here applying a basic alchemical approach to a subject of metaphysical study, namely the origins, nature and functioning of Hel-world.

One of the theories about physical alchemy in older times was the idea that minerals *evolve*, as long as they are underground and subject to heat and moisture, transforming from lead through various other metals and finally into silver and gold.
(https://www.sciencehistory.org/distillations/magazine/gold-secrecy-and-prestige.)

The understanding was that while minerals do 'evolve' while they are buried underground and are subject to various chthonic influences, once they are brought up under the light of the Sun and Moon, they cease evolving. Alchemists who sought to bring about further evolution of metals into gold tried to duplicate these chthonic processes in order to bring about metallic evolution, and as a result, invented many of the processes and equipment used in modern chemistry.

The concept of underground evolution of substances still applies in certain contexts, such as the transformation of igneous rocks and sediments into metamorphic rocks due to chthonic forces of heat and pressure. Overall, though, the alchemical idea of the evolution of metals no longer fits into the modern scientific processes of material transformation, but it still holds meaning for some forms of spiritual alchemy, as we shall explore further.

Among the many applications of alchemy, the one of interest to us here is using it to understand something about cosmogony: how the Worlds and some of the beings of the Worlds come into existence through processes of transformation, including the type of transformation that is mythically expressed as 'sacrifice.'

I began the discussion of Hel's ecosystem in Chapter 13, and I began discussion of Saiwalo's alchemy in Chapter

14. In this chapter I will lay out a broader picture, as I presently understand it, of how Saiwalo and its ecosystem of Hel function. What I present here can be understood as a perspective on mythic-alchemy and mythic-ecology, under the umbrella of Heathen metaphysics.

Why Alchemy?

Before we proceed to the main topics, I want to explain my reason for using alchemy and ecology as a way of describing and understanding Hel, Saiwalo and Dwimor. I think that there are various different conceptual contexts that allow us to explore and understand each of our various souls, and by using these contexts, we can deepen our understanding in ways that would not be available without those contexts.

The best context for Ahma and Ghost is 'spiritual' and 'spirit-mind'. For Ferah, Aldr and Mod, the context is 'metaphysical energies and patterns relating to Nature / Spirits / Deities / Wyrd'. For Hama, it is the 'etheric body'. For Hugr, Mod, Hama, Ferah, Sefa, we have the 'personal' context: personality, character, will, physical and social abilities, ego, emotions, relationships, etc. And for Aldr we have the context of Time and our life in time.

Saiwalo and Dwimor are very different, and don't fit well into any of these contexts. They are 'spiritual' sort of by default, in the sense that they are not physical, but they don't have the connotations, activities and meanings that we, in the modern Western world, usually associate with 'spirituality.' The 'metaphysical energies and patterns of Nature, etc.' are associated with Midgard and with the other realms of action of the upper-worlds Deities and Spirits, and these are not Saiwalo's domain or concern. Nor are Saiwalo and Dwimor associated with the day to day activities, connections and concerns of the body, ego, personality, and so forth. 'Time' as it is experienced in Midgard has little relevance for Saiwalo. These other souls (except for Ahma as primal, unchanging Spirit) have motives, will, desires, interests and connections that orient and direct them in Midgard space-time during life.

Saiwalo exists in a different kind of conceptual space, not closely associated with any of the above. It has no personality in and of itself, at least as we understand it in Midgard, though its Dwimor will carry the image or reflection of the person's personality and physical appearance after death. This Dwimor-image is not true personality and personhood; it lies only at the level of surface appearance, and lacks depth and substance.

However, Saiwalo definitely has functions and processes associated with it, which I perceive as being more like metaphysical analogs of ecological systems and alchemical processes, rather than like being 'persons' in any sense that we understand it in Midgard. Alchemy is a good conceptual context for Saiwalo and Hel, because it allows room for metaphysical and speculative exploration, as well as providing a foundation for viewing Hel and its dwellers in ecological terms, as we shall explore further.

The Mighty Gap of Potential

Early it was, in ancient times, when Ymir settled into being. Neither sand nor sea, nor cool waves were there. Earth was not, nor high heaven; only the yawning gap of mystery, nowhere green.
(Völuspá vs. 3, Poetic Edda, my rendition.)

Starting from the beginning, we are told in the prose Edda (pp. 9-11) of how the first powers and beings came about,

The Alchemy of Hel

within the space called Ginnungagap, the Void containing all potential. Even here, in an organized tale narrated by one person, there are contradictions in the story, and it is likely that Snorri's account was somewhat garbled, distorted, and misinterpreted, as all oral records are. Nevertheless, we will work with this!

The 12th-century author, Snorri Sturlason, tells us that Hvergelmir, the Roaring Cauldron, formed in the center of Niflheim, the world of mist and cold, and out of it flowed the Elivagar, a river(s) of cosmic power. According to Snorri, the name means 'eleven rivers', which he names in the text. In other places in the lore, Elivagar is treated as a single river-ocean that surrounds Midgard and separates it from Jotunnheim. In this understanding, *Elivagar* may mean 'stormy sea', an interpretation that fits better with other Indo-European myths about the world-circling ocean. (Simek p. 73.) My own view is that Elivagar is an outflow of cosmic power from Hvergelmir, the wellspring of the cosmos, which branches off in braided patterns to surround, support and nourish each of the Worlds of our mythology.

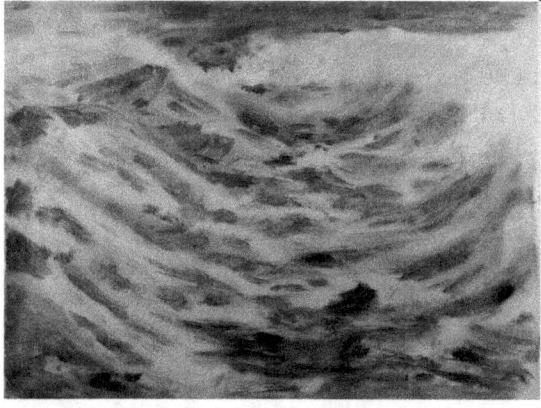

Ginnungagap fills with the freezing waters of Hvergelmir. By Dale Wood.

Elivagar contained something that is referred to as venom or poison, as well as salt. As the water of Hvergelmir flowed out, it began to freeze, filling the northern end of Ginnungagap. The venom separated out on top, and as the cold winds blew ice and rime across the Gap, the heat from the world of fire, Muspelheim, at the southern end began to melt the rime. This melted rime formed into Ymir, the hermaphroditic proto-Giant. The implication is that Ymir, and all the giants after him-her, are composed of venom / poison, condensed and coagulated from frozen Elivagar.

Then, Snorri describes how Ymir was fed. The second being who coalesced out of the rime was Auðumla the Cow, whom I call the Ur-Mother. Auðumla fed Ymir with her milk. She fed herself by licking the ice and frost still filling Ginnungagap, which, having had all the venom drawn out of it to form Ymir, was now salty rather than venomous. As Auðumla licked the ice, she gradually uncovered or freed the sleeping body of Buri, who would become grandfather of Odin, Vili and Ve, and fed him with her salty milk, as well.

I want to note here that when the old Germanic languages translated the Christian terms 'create, creation', with reference to their view of cosmogony, the native words that were used involved not 'creation out of nothing', but rather 'shaping': *skapa* in Old Norse, *gesceap* in Anglo-Saxon, etc. 'Shaping' is also what the Norns do with wyrd or 'fate'. In this scene, Auðumla is 'shaping' Buri out of ice with her tongue, bringing him into being in the living world. Thus, she takes her place among the primal shapers of the worlds.

We can see parallels between Auðumla freeing Buri from the ice, Sigurd freeing the 'frozen-in-sleep' Valkyrie Sigrdrifa / Brynhild from the enspelled fire that surrounded

The Alchemy of Hel

her, and the fairy-tale motif of the enspelled, sleeping young woman being freed by the rescuing prince in tales such as Sleeping Beauty and Snow White. Such parallel symbolism is rife in some forms of alchemy. Awakening from the enspelled sleep is the balanced opposite of transformational sacrifice.

In the reverse of Auðumla freeing Buri from the ice and thus awakening him, here Wotan has put the Valkyrie Brunhilda to sleep, and surrounded her with a magical, binding fire, where she must remain until she is awoken. Such reverse-parallels are among the mysteries of Hel, the Hidden Land. (Arthur Rackham, artist.)

So, here we have the first alchemical processes: the fire and ice providing transformative energies, and the outflow from Hvergelmir condensing into ice which contains venom and salt. It's said in the story that Ymir's body coagulated from the 'clinkers' or fragments of frozen venom as Elivagar froze into ice and rime. This equates to a process of purifying the ice from the venom, which was all drawn out of the ice in order to form Ymir, much like the process by which alcoholic drinks like applejack are distilled by freezing. Once Ymir is formed, venom no longer remains in the ice, but salt does. Both Auðumla and Buri are formed through coagulation or freeze-distillation from this salty ice. They are salt-beings, but do not contain venom.

Though we are told by Snorri that Buri fathered Borr, the father of Odin-Vili-Ve, it is a mystery who the mother of

Borr was. My own view is that she was Auðumla herself, whom I consider the Ur-Mother, able to shift her shape. Other Indo-European myths link ancient Mother-Goddesses with cows, as well. I believe that Auðumla mothered Borr (thus becoming the grandmother of Odin-Vili-Ve) before going on to the next phase of her existence.

The Coalescence of Hel

And what is that next phase? We hear no more about Auðumla (nor about Buri) in the lore: she's done her job of feeding Ymir, shaping and freeing Buri from the ice and feeding him, and perhaps mothering Borr. Then she apparently wanders off into the mists, never to be seen again, though perhaps the Milky Way is a clue to her path! I have another idea about her: that she actually becomes the world of Hel.

Let me talk about some other examples of sacrificial transformation of primal beings, before I turn to these thoughts about Auðumla. (1) Ymir was sacrificed by Odin, Vili, and Ve so that they could shape the Earth out of his body: the physical world with its sky and its encircling waters, where humans and other beings live. (2) I believe that Mimir's baffling execution, while he was hostage to the Vanir, was also a cosmogonic sacrifice. ("Ynglingasaga" p. 3, in *Heimskringla*.) Wise Mimir, admired by all, was beheaded by the Vanir, supposedly because they were angry with his fellow-hostage, Hœnir, who was handsome and charismatic, but lacked the qualities of wisdom needed by a chieftain. Hœnir, however, suffered no consequences for his apparent vapidity; it was Mimir who was executed. The Vanir returned Mimir's head to Odin, who preserved it using rune-power and placed it within Mimir's own Well.

"Mimir's Head" stone carving by my husband Rosten Dean Rose. It is placed above a small pond on our homestead that we call Mimir's Well, overshadowed by a huge Yew, reminiscent of Yggdrasil.

There is no sense or logic to this story of Mimir's execution, which leads me to look for a more mythic, symbolic underpinning. As I perceive it, these events led to the coming-into-being of World-Mind, represented by Mimir's Well of Memory and Inspiration. World-Mind is my concept of the intangible space, the energetic matrix, where Thought occurs: both individual thoughts and the thoughts of multiple beings which influence and build upon each other.

As Ymir's body became physical Midgard, Mimir's head / brain / mind became the metaphysical space where Thought occurs. The skull of Ymir became the sky of Midgard, and his brains became the clouds. I see Mimir's head / World-Mind superimposed over Ymir's skull and brains as the sky of Midgard, with the movements of clouds and winds in the physical world mirroring the movement of thoughts through World-Mind (also called the Noösphere, after Greek *nous* = mind.)

I think that Mimir and his sister Bestla, the uncle and mother of Odin-Vili-Ve, were the two beings who grew under the arm of Ymir (*Gylfaginning* p. 11, in the prose Edda), the first generation of cosmic offspring along with Borr son of Buri. As I see it, both Ymir and his-her son Mimir were cosmogonic sacrifices, sacrificed by the Æsir and the

Vanir. They were sacrificed at different times: Ymir at the beginning, the foundation of the physical world, and Mimir much later, after beings capable of Thought had multiplied in Midgard and the other Worlds.

A cloud-face seen in profile on the right reflects the idea of Ymir's brains as the clouds, and Mimir's head as the space of World-Mind.

In this story so far, we have a group of the earliest progenitor-beings, and most of them are involved, either as sacrificers or as victims, in sacrifices for cosmogonic purposes, in my understanding. I think that Auðumla follows the same path, except, in contrast to the usual fate of cows, she is not sacrificed by others, but gives herself over to a self-directed process of living transformation.

The Alchemy of Hel

I see the coming-into-being of the world of Hel as two overlapping processes, or rather, as an alchemical process that can also be represented by mythological beings, which is frequently how alchemy is presented in traditional lore.

Alchemically, here is my vision. The primal polarities of Fire and Ice generate the Roaring Cauldron of cosmic energy, Hvergelmir, within the center of Ginnungagap, which sends up clouds of mist and steam over the Gap. (The account by Snorri places Hvergelmir at the Ice-polarity, Niflheim, but my own understanding is that it lies in the center of Ginnungagap. It is the cosmic-energy wellspring balanced and energized between the polarities of Ice and Fire.) This mist that rises from Ginnungagap is Ahma or Ond, primal Spirit, out of which all that is, is formed. As Ahma-mist rises over Ginnungagap and attains some distance from the roaring cosmogonic energy-fountain, it 'cools' or steps down its energy and condenses into the first of the worlds where human souls are able to exist as individual beings: Hel, the place I call the Womb of Souls, among other names.

Here is a mythical picture of this process. Auðumla can be seen as the Cosmic Mother, but she is not the mother of individual beings, except perhaps of Borr. The womb of the Mother, and the womb of any mother, is a hidden place, a place of shelter, shaping, and magical growth, a place that is different from the living-spaces of physical Midgard, and within the womb lie beings which are both like and not-like already-born humans in Midgard.

There are a number of Germanic Goddess-names that derive from Proto-Indo-European *kel* = to cover, hide, conceal, through Proto-Germanic *haljo*. Their names include Hel, Holle, Nehalennia, Hludana, Hlodyn. This covering and concealment refers, presumably, to the grave and to the world of Hel, but it also refers very clearly to the state of the child in the womb, who is covered, concealed, nourished, shaped and protected by its mother's body. After-life and before-life have many similarities and connections. The mother who holds before-life within her has many similarities to the one who holds after-life within her, the Mother of Souls. In many beliefs around the world, she is one and the same being, a Goddess through whom life and death pass as they come and go through her doorway.

My view is that Auðumla, as the Ur-Mother, transformed herself into Hel-world, the Womb of Souls, and that Germanic Goddesses connected with Hel-world are transformations or 'daughters' of her essence, as well. She offers her transformed body as a place of concealment, sheltering, nourishment, a place where beings in the afterlife can go through their own transformational processes.

Auðumla's name means "The Hornless Cow of Plenty / Wealth", and that ties into the idea of Hel as a place of hidden treasure and wealth (see Chapter 13). This shows up not only in Germanic folklore but in other mythologies as well, such as Greek and later Roman Plouton / Pluto, one of the names of the God of the Underworld, whose name means 'wealth, riches'.

As for Auðumla's 'hornlessness': cow's horns are often considered to be a symbol of the moon in the feminine mysteries. In Hel, I perceive that there is no visible moon. Hel is the interior of Auðumla, the nourishing, hidden land, permeated by its own mysterious, unearthly light. Auðumla has no horns; Hel has no moon. And, having no moon or sun, Hel is a place well-suited for the chthonic processes of alchemical evolution and transformation, as we shall explore further, later on.

Auðumla Ur-Mother begins her sacrificial transformation into the world of Hel, the Womb of Souls. By Dale Wood.

We saw, earlier, that Auðumla was formed out of salty ice, and fed by licking salty ice: she is a salt-being. Salt is a preservative, keeping things from spoiling, and is thus symbolic of the preservative qualities of Hel where Saiwalo souls continue their existence and empower living souls in Midgard. Through Auðumla we can see Hel as containing alchemical salt and water, as well as elemental earth in the form of her body. This leads us to the next development: the arising of the salt-water Saiwalo souls in their earthy underworld of Hel.

Summary of Part 1

In my perception, Hel-world, and the later Hel-Goddesses, arose from the great Ur-Mother in form of a cow, called Auðumla. She herself embodies the primal powers of Fire and Ice, Ginnungagap, Hvergelmir and its outflow called Elivagar. Her elemental nature is formed of salty ice. As the sacrifice of Ymir provided the matrix for the creation of Midgard and other life-worlds, Auðumla's self-sacrifice of transformation provided the matrix for Hel-world to come into being. Her sacrifice sets the pattern of 'transformation' which is the ecological function of Hel, as I discuss below.

Part 2. Generation, Coagulation, Dwimor and Dwimoring

Spontaneous Generation

In the foregoing section, I discussed my understanding of the substrate / matrix / womb of Hel, which is Auðumla: a salt-being who offers herself, her being and nature, as the ground for a new World, the world of Hel. (Note that 'matrix' comes from the Latin word for 'womb'.) Now we're ready to look more deeply into the beings that populate Hel: the Saiwalo souls, and how they arise. Let's look at a another parallel development for a moment. Ymir was sacrificed to form Midgard, and Worlds that lie close to it. We are told that the Dwarves came into being as 'maggots' consuming the flesh of Ymir after his-her sacrifice, and were later transformed into humanoid beings, the Dwarves, by the Deities (*Gylfaginning*, in the Edda, p. 16).

In ancient times, maggots were thought to arise through spontaneous generation from decomposing flesh.

The Alchemy of Hel

Apparently, ancient Norse considered this to be a logical explanation for the origins of the Dwarves, who burrow through the earth / Ymir's body as maggots burrow through decaying flesh. This is somewhat distasteful and insulting imagery, perhaps not surprising since ancient Heathens had a rather negative view of Dwarves, with their tendency to consume or suck energy from other beings (such as humans and domestic animals) on occasion.

I have a different way of looking at this mythic tale. I view Dwarves as master mod-power transformers, who began their existence as energy-larvae absorbing mod, might and main from mighty Ymir's flesh, and condensing it within themselves. (See Chapter 8 for more about mod-power.)

A dwarf ponders his next great work.

In fact, I like to think that it was the Dwarves, not the Deities, who initiated their own transformation once they had accumulated and refined enough mod, might and main from Ymir to achieve this great work.

Simek notes that the Dwarves were known for their wisdom and skill, and, in addition to their smithcraft, were also known as miners and as custodians of treasures (p. 68). They are strongly associated with Earth and its elements, minerals and metals. If we accept the alchemical ideas I've laid out, then we must conclude that the Dwarves, feeding from Ymir, also partake of the 'venom' from which Ymir is formed.

In alchemical terms, the venom can represent strong acids and bases that have the power to dissolve various substances, and are also used in the dangerous processes for refining pure metals out of mixed ores. It's wise to keep this 'venomous' or dangerous aspect of Dwarves in mind, when dealing with them: though they are wise and skilled, they must be dealt with cautiously. They are generally not 'warm and fuzzy' beings.

The World of the Dwarves is considered to be 'underground', beneath the level of Midgard, as Hel is, also. I think there are a number of parallel processes in these two Underworlds, including a process of spontaneous generation of the native beings or dwellers in these worlds, arising out of a primal matrix as the Dwarves did out of Ymir's flesh. I might note also that Dwarves are sometimes associated with the dead, as shown by some of their names, such as Nar (corpse), Nainn (ditto), Dain (died), Blainn (blue-black). The World of the Dwarves, full of riches and infused with danger, death and power, and the World of Hel, the Hidden Land of Saiwalo souls, filled with hidden wealth, power and mystery, have some significant overlaps that are worthy of exploration.

Coalescence and Coagulation

Now let's take a look at this parallel process: the Saiwalo-souls arising spontaneously within the substance of Auðumla / Hel. Here, instead of the 'decomposition' of Ymir's flesh and the extraction and condensation of his-her mod-power by the Dwarves, we have coalescence and coagulation of individual Saiwalo-souls out of the foundational matrix of Hel. 'Coalescence' means a process of gathering together around a center, and 'coagulation' refers to thickening and sticking together more firmly.

This process is driven by the alchemical properties of salt and water. Auðumla's body, as all bodies, is earthy, but it was generated from salty ice, that is, from salt and water. In Chapter 14, I quoted a fragment from the Greek philosopher Heraclitus, and reiterate that quotation here:

> *As souls (psyches) are born through the death of water, water is born through the death of earth. And as water comes into being from earth, so from water does the soul.*
> (Heraclitus fragment DKB 36, my translation.)

I see this enigmatic saying of Heraclitus as a way of describing the process of the Saiwalo soul arising. First there is elemental earth, and this serves as a metaphor for Hel, the Hidden Land that metaphysically lies below the surface of our physical Earth. In a certain locus, earth 'dies' and transforms into elemental water, thus becoming like a water-well surrounded and contained by earth. The water in this well is permeated by elemental Earth in the form of salt. This describes my perception of the Saiwalo soul, a salt-water being nestled within its earthy-watery ecosystem of Hel. Please note that these 'elements'—earth, water, salt (and venom) — are not the literal substances we're familiar with in Midgard, but are metaphors that carry clues to their subtle alchemical and elemental natures.

Next, the water in the center of the well 'dies' and is transformed into a soul surrounded by water. This is a metaphor for our Dwimor: a salt-being condensed from, and projected by, our watery Saiwalo-soul in the form of a phantom, which is our earthly soul-image. This water-well, surrounded by earth and condensing salt out of itself, is an image of a Saiwalo-soul condensing its Dwimor-projection in preparation for a new life in Midgard.

An image of a Saiwalo soul in the form of water surrounded by earth. The Dwimor condenses from the salty water, and is drawn up into Midgard. By Dale Wood.

These 'deaths' or transformations come about through solution and coagulation, alchemical *solve et coagule*. The coagulation and condensation of the Dwimor is necessary because Saiwalos are diffuse, non-material entities, very different from the environment of Midgard. Even though the Dwimor is a phantom or a wraith, only vaguely materialized, it is still considerably denser than its Saiwalo, which is necessary so that Dwimor can carry a body-image with it and cohere with the Hama and Lich in Midgard.

The energy for Dwimor's condensation and projection comes from our Ferah-soul, a soul aligned with elemental Fire and Earth. In my understanding, the Ferah-soul comes into being in Midgard when egg and sperm unite in the womb, during the process of conception, and Ferah's coming-into-being is accompanied by an intense flash of lightning.

The alchemical fire of Ferah's conception provides the heat necessary for the condensation of a new, salty Dwimor-phantom to form from the salt-water Saiwalo-soul grounded in Hel. The Dwimor rises up, a projection from its Saiwalo in Hel, and is drawn to join with the newly-conceived Ferah-soul, the Fire of Life, to form the foundation of a new living person in Midgard.

While in the womb, the Dwimor is again surrounded by 'salty water' as the child gestates within the amniotic fluid: a physical-metaphysical mirroring, of which there are many examples in Heathen soul lore. (See Chapters 2, 3, and 14 for more details about conception and development of these souls.)

The Roots of Dwimor

Dwimor comes from Anglo-Saxon *gedwimor*, and has two sets of meanings. One is 'phantom, ghost, apparition,' and the other is 'illusion, delusion, error,' a meaning which was heavily used by those in the Christian religious establishment to castigate Heathen ideas and beliefs. Dwimor's root goes back to Proto-Germanic as **dwemra* =

'vapor, smoke, apparition', and is related to *dox* = twilight, dusk.

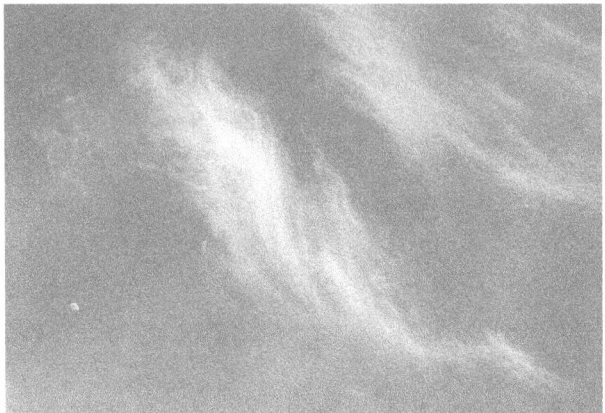

Dwemra in turn comes from Proto-Indo-European *dheu*, meaning 'to rise in a cloud' as dust, vapor or smoke. It is also related to words indicating breath, and 'defective perception or wits'. The Proto-Indo-European root and its Germanic descendants go off in several directions, including 'to rise as a cloud', 'to die', 'to dwindle, diminish' (*dwinan*), 'to lead or go astray' (*gedwelian*), 'beclouded in one's senses and perceptions,' dizzy, drowsy, doze, hence the meanings of 'illusion, delusion.' *Gedwolcraft* means 'occult art, magic,' perhaps dealing especially with illusions.

There is also a connection with 'breath, breathing creature', leading to Proto-Germanic *dheuzam* = 'animal'. Its descendants include *deor* = wild animal in Anglo-Saxon, *Tier* = animal in German, and modern English *deer*. It is also the root of *thymos*, an ancient Greek soul very similar to Hugr and Mod, which was said to exit like smoke from a dying person. Our thymus gland, located in our chest where our breath dwells, is named from this source. The herb thyme was burned as incense, rising up in smoke. (Linguistic roots from Watkins p. 19-20, Hall p. 91.) I show more information about the word-roots relating to breath in Chapter 4, Table 1, and in Chapter 5 where I note the connection between these words and shamanic practices.

The Dwimor in Midgard

Here is my understanding of the soul-processes that occur during human conception. The heat from the lightning-flash of Ferah-soul's conception condenses the salty Dwimor out of its watery matrix in Saiwalo, and draws it up into Midgard to join with Ferah. Dwimor bears with it the image that Saiwalo has generated for this new, living person.

The flare of power that is released when Dwimor and Ferah merge gives rise to the Hama-soul, which is then imprinted with the spiritual image borne by the Dwimor. The Hama, a soul intimately involved with the physical dimension, connects with the genetic inheritance of the newly conceived being. Hama then takes over the process of shaping the infant into a physical human with its many characteristics and abilities, based on Saiwalo's image that has been imprinted in the Hama by the Dwimor.

The other life-souls—Ferah, Ahma, Ghost, Hama, Aldr—each have their own specific ways of keeping a person physically alive and embedded within living systems. Ferah is the vital life-force and life-substance that circulates throughout the world of Nature, and links Midgard Nature (including living humans) with the Deities and other spirits of Nature. Ahma and Ghost provide the breath of life and inflowing inspiration, energizing physical, mental and spiritual life. Hama shapes and maintains the living physical body with its many skills and abilities. Aldr fills, nourishes and heals the living person with a dense, close-to-physical energy, and governs their lifespan and the timing of important life-events.

Saiwalo is also traditionally considered a life-soul, whose departure from the body coincides with death, yet unlike the other life-souls, it is not clear from the oldest lore in what way Saiwalo contributes to life. (See Chapter 15.) Here, I use alchemical metaphor to describe my own view of how Saiwalo maintains life within us during our time in Midgard.

Here is the basic principle: salt is a grasping substance; it attracts and holds 'moisture', which we can view as a metaphor for 'life-energy and life-substance.' Hvergelmir, the cosmic wellspring, exudes a salty flow from itself, which shaped and fed Auðumla. Auðumla transformed herself into the World of Hel, and from her salty substance Saiwalo-beings emerged through spontaneous generation. When the Ferah-soul arises in a flash of lightning during conception, the heat from this life-fire reaches into Hel and condenses a core of salt from a Saiwalo-being, drawing it up into Midgard. This core is the Dwimor, a phantom-being projected out from Saiwalo to join with a new life in Midgard.

Dwimor's salty nature forms a core of alchemical attraction at the center of our being, around which our other souls gather as gestation proceeds in Midgard. Our other life-souls: Ferah, Aldr, Ahma, Ghost, Hama, constantly draw ambient life-force in various different forms into our body-soul complex. In my understanding, Saiwalo does not participate directly in this process of drawing in and metabolizing life-forces. Instead, it is Saiwalo, through its Dwimor, who provides the salty medium that absorbs and

The Alchemy of Hel

holds those life-forces within our soul-body matrix, ensuring that we remain alive in Midgard.

Saiwalo uses its alchemical nature to create the ionic bonds which hold our soul-body complex together, allowing the formation, circulation and preservation of all the patterns of energy and matter that coalesce to form our Midgard life, body, personhood and functionality. When the body dies and Dwimor returns to its Saiwalo in Hel, the removal of its coagulating force leads to separation among all the souls and the Lich; our soul-body complex is dissolved and death occurs.

The rune Hagalaz, associated with Hel and considered to be a primal seed-crystal in modern runic thought, can be seen as the underlying pattern for this activity. Hagol in Anglo-Saxon means 'hail, hailstorm', which is associated with thunder and lightning, phenomena which are, in turn, associated with the Ferah soul (see Chapter 3).

Here is the Anglo-Saxon Rune Poem for Hagalaz or Hagol:
Hagol (hail) is the whitest of grains,
Tossed about by the airs of heaven,
Billowing in showers of wind,
It soon returns to water.
(my translation)

Looking at the process runically, we have a thunderstorm (Ferah soul) generating hail-stones (Saiwalo producing Dwimor in response to Ferah-fire). The hail-stone forms a crystal, mimicking the formation of our souls and body around our Dwimor-core. After a (life-)time tossed about in the turmoil of life in Midgard, the hail melts, releasing our accumulated souls from Saiwalo-Dwimor's crystalline bond, which leads us to our next topic.

Dwimoring

I've offered my thoughts about the alchemical involvement of Saiwalo and Dwimor at conception and during Midgard life. Now we'll look at the end of Midgard life, when our Dwimor is 'Dwimoring' (a word-form I made up). As it is leaving Midgard, the Dwimor undergoes another alchemical process, mirroring its condensation into salt at the beginning of its journey: that of sublimation. Sublimation occurs when matter changes directly from the solid to the gaseous state, without going through a liquid phase first. You can sometimes see that happening over a field of snow under the sun, when the air is too cold to melt the snow, but the solar energy draws up a haze of vapor from the surface of the snow.

I believe that our Ferah-soul emits a flash of light and heat as it separates from our Lich and other souls at death, just as it does when it forms at conception. I see this flash as a metaphysical form of atomic energy, which is mythically expressed as the power of the Thunder-God's Hammer and the lightning it causes. At conception, we have the fire of fusion between egg and sperm. At death, we have the fire of fission: the explosive separation of that which had been fused together. I think that this fire of fission causes the sublimation of the Dwimor, transforming it from a metaphysically 'solid' core which holds us together, into a waft of vapor that can be perceived as a phantom spirit set loose from the body at death.

Let's review the meanings of *dwimor* and related words, that I discussed earlier: *phantom, ghost, apparition,*

The Alchemy of Hel

illusion, delusion, dizzy, dozing, vapor, rising as smoke or dust, twilight, dwindle, diminish, beclouded in wits and senses, to wander astray, etc.

I'm going to suggest here that if we imaginatively put ourselves in the place of our own Dwimor as it is released from our body and heads back to Hel, we would experience all of the meanings I just described. We would be sublimated out of the physical body, no longer in the form of crystallized salt around which a living person coagulates, but now rising as a cloud, as sublimated vapor. Others who perceived us would see us as a phantom or apparition, and imagine we are an illusion.

The dim and twilight world of the disembodied Dwimor.

As we head back toward our Saiwalo in Hel, we would perceive a dim and twilight world around us. Separated from the other souls and body we shared life with in Midgard, and not yet joined with our Saiwalo in Hel, we would feel diminished, dwindled away from what we were in Midgard. Norse tales tell of the dead having no weight or sound to their steps, as they cross the bridge to Hel: they have dwindled from what they were as living beings.

Our Dwimor's senses and perceptions, no longer fortified by the Lichama, Ferah, and the other souls, would feel dizzy, dim, confused, beclouded, dozy, during the dying process and after leaving the body. This is the Dwimor during the temporary state between its life in the physical body in Midgard, and its return to its Saiwalo in Hel.

Dwimor is not a stand-alone soul, it is a phantom-form, a projection of the Saiwalo, and it cannot function well in its dwindled state when it is detached from the other souls and the Lich. Many accounts of afterlife experiences and observations are, I believe, told from the perspective of this Dwimor-experience, and show Hel and the afterlife as Dwimor sees it at this stage of its existence.

This stage of sublimation of the Dwimor, though unsettling, is a temporary one, part of a natural process of transformation that it undergoes. The Dwimor itself, bewildered and diminished, is only vaguely aware that it bears a rich cargo of treasure from its life in Midgard, as it heads back to its Saiwalo in Hel. This is the subject of the next section: the involvement of Saiwalos, Dwimors and the ecosystem of Hel in generating and transforming the 'treasure-house of images' that flow constantly into and out of our awareness, and influence our thoughts, actions and reactions as we pursue our lives in Midgard.

Part 3: Images; Polarity of Saiwalo and Ahma; Precipitation

Dwimor-images

In my previous chapters about the Saiwalo, I've made reference to its ability to generate images, foremost among them being the Dwimor, the phantom-projection of Saiwalo. I showed at length in Chapter 13 how images of the dead, as opposed to dead bodies themselves, play a great role in the lore and folklore of Scandinavian lands.

The continental Germanic-language speaking countries have many, many tales about souls of the dead who appear in phantom form, images of who they were in life. Lore from many other lands and cultures speak of the same thing: encounters with beings who were humans, and look like who they once were, but they are not dead bodies. These encounters sometimes appear to occur in Midgard, other times they seem to happen in afterlife domains or otherworldly settings.

This ability of the Saiwalo to create a Dwimor, a phantom image, is, I believe, an indicator of its facility for generating images overall, including the images that come to us in visions, dreams and daydreams.

One of the influences on my ideas about Saiwalo, Dwimor and images comes from ancient Greek usage of the words *psyche* and *eidolon*. *Psyche* is the Greek word that the Gothic bishop Wulfila translated as *saiwala*, as he rendered parts of the Bible from Greek into Gothic. *Eidolon* in ancient Greek meant, among other things, the spirit-image of a person, living or dead. This is also the root of our word 'idol', the image of a Deity or other object of veneration. To give an example of ancient Greek usage of these two words, here is part of the story about the Greek hero Achilles, mourning for his slain friend and lover, Patroklos. (*Iliad* 23, 65-109.)

In grief and exhaustion after battle, Achilles fell asleep on the shore. The *psyche* of Patroklos came to him then, 'in all things like himself.' He told Achilles that the *psyche-eidolons* of the dead prevented him from faring over the river of death to join them, leaving him alone and restless, with no place to go. The reason he was not accepted into the blessed lands was because of the lack of funeral rites, which had not yet been performed due to the battle.

When Achilles tried to embrace his friend, Patroklos' psyche dissipated like smoke, yet later, 'psyche and eidolon' returned, and continued to appear to Achilles all night long, "like Patroklos' very self", giving Achilles instructions about the funeral as well as wailing and weeping about its lot.

Here we see the juxtaposition of 'soul / *psyche*' with 'image or phantom / *eidolon*'. In our terms, these are Saiwalo with Dwimor. When living Achilles tried to embrace the psyche, it vanished like smoke, which is one of the meanings of Dwimor's word-root, 'rising like smoke'. Yet later it / they returned, the soul along with its shape or phantom.

There's another intriguing mention of the eidolon in the *Odyssey* (ll. 690 ff). The hero Odysseus has entered Hades to seek knowledge from the dead, and encounters many 'shades' there, both familiar and unknown. He meets the eidolon of Herakles, but strangely it is only his eidolon, his image. The poem states that Herakles 'himself' dwells on Mt. Olympos with the other Deities, wed to a daughter of Zeus.

The Alchemy of Hel

This is a perplexing 'image' for us to contemplate! In the context of our usual cultural understanding, it's hard to envision a situation where the image of the person is in Hades / Hel, while the person 'himself' is basically in 'heaven'. These kinds of metaphysical riddles, like the Zen *koans*, can spark some intriguing insights when we work with them meditatively over time. In the context of Heathen soul lore, I interpret Herakles' situation as a description of his Ghost-soul, including his Ghost's spiritual body, living in the God-Homes on Olympos, while his Dwimor-image is situated in Hel / Hades.

The Poles of Saiwalo and Ahma

Though there is no requirement for me to adhere to the ancient Greek concepts, I find them intriguing for two reasons. One is that there is a good deal of similarity between some of the archaic (Homeric period) concepts of souls, and the Germanic concepts as I understand them. The Homeric poems were written centuries before the existence of Christianity and the changes it brought, making them a good source for understanding ancient Pagan thought. The second reason is that my own soul-explorations over the years have steadily led me to the perception that Saiwalo is 'more' and 'other' than the shade, the fleeting image of the dead, the eidolon or Dwimor, that sometimes appears to the living.

In my perception, Saiwalo is greater and stronger than a flitting shade; it surges and thrums with the fundamental, upwelling cosmic forces that arise from Hvergelmir and the Elivagar. Saiwalos are powerful: deep, slow, world-transforming souls, and they are very unlike any image or being we are familiar with in Midgard.

Meditating on the odd pairing of psyche with eidolon as a composite afterlife-being in Greek lore is one of the many metaphysical puzzle-pathways or spiritual labyrinths that led me toward my understanding of Heathen Saiwalo and Dwimor. Dwimor is the fleeting image, the shade; Saiwalo is the strange and powerful being who generates that shade.

Saiwalo is a very deep-level being, not directly associated with Midgard itself, but only through its Dwimor or image. It is deeply rooted and settled in Hel, in my perception of it. I see it as the opposite pole to Ahma, our 'high', transcendent Spirit-soul. Our entire being is anchored between these two non-earthly poles: Ahma in 'high' transcendence, Saiwalo in 'deep' transcendence. (The use of these directions, high and deep, is metaphorical, based on how these things feel or seem to us.) We are beings wrapped around the spindle formed by the connection between these two souls and their domains.

Each of these souls has a mediator who serves as a transformer of their natures and powers, buffering between the otherworldly domains of Ahma and Saiwalo on each end, and Midgard / living humans in the middle. Ghost and Dwimor can each be seen as shapes, hamas, or vehicles of their respective root-souls. Ghost is formed of a membrane or pod which encloses and shapes our portion of Ahma within it, while Dwimor is a condensation and projection of a portion of Saiwalo's essence into Midgard. Both Ghost and Dwimor can sometimes be seen as phantoms in Midgard, or during otherworldly experiences by living humans, yet neither of them fully expresses the nature of their transcendent originators.

Inspiration / wode, formed of Air and Fire, comes from Ahma / Ǫnd, through our Ghost and into our Ghost-mind (*gastgemynd* plus *gastgehygd*). Images, formed of Water, come from Saiwalo through our Dwimor and into our deep-mind, our unconscious and subconscious levels. As they blend within living humans and interact with our other souls in Midgard, the results of their earthing can be all over the map of human experience and endeavor. Great art, new inventions, new ways of doing and perceiving can result from this blending of inspiration and imagery. So can great suffering and destruction, brought about by negative images fired by inspiration that is more of a wode-conflagration than a vitalizing, holy Fire of purified wode.

On a personal level it is the same: the inspiration-imagery blend within us, resulting from all the experiences, attitudes and strivings of our life, can result in anything: from the suffering of PTSD, to the misfires of relationships based on misunderstandings and stereotypes run amok, to the quiet satisfactions of a well-balanced life, to the high reaches of spirit-infused creativity and spiritual activity.

The Alchemy of Images

I'll summarize these points by repeating a paragraph from Chapter 13. So much of what we perceive, think, feel, and act upon is rooted in and motivated by images in our minds. And yet, my sense of our Saiwalo is that it is the *generation* of images itself, and not the resulting thoughts, emotions, and actions, that forms Saiwalo's primary activity. Consistent with ancient understandings of this soul, Saiwalo does not play a direct, active role in our Midgard life and our personality. Its role in Midgard is passive: generating and absorbing images according to its own inner processes, which are rooted in Hel. Our other souls in Midgard, our mind and body, all actively pick up and respond to those images, and in turn generate material that our Saiwalo uses to modify its images and create new ones.

Now let's look at this process alchemically. I described previously how Dwimor is formed from Saiwalo through a process of coagulation and condensation of elemental salt, in preparation for its projection into the Midgard-plane. It enters Midgard as a salt-being, and there forms the alchemical matrix that holds together our souls and body, and the various energies that they draw into our soul-body complex. But these are not the only things embedded in Dwimor's matrix: Dwimor also collects the images that constantly swirl within us and around us, the images that shape our own perceptions and experiences of the world around us, and shape our reactions to the same.

Here is an important point: Dwimor, and Saiwalo, do not have the abilities of evaluation and judgement. Saiwalo generates images, Dwimor absorbs and transmits images, but neither of them *chooses* the images for these activities. Images float up from Hel like bubbles, entering into our Midgard minds through our Dwimor. Everyone's Saiwalos are filtering these images up into Midgard through their Dwimors, and everyone's soular-systems are processing and using these images, passing them around and picking them up from one another, and as all of this happens, the images coalesce, transmute, combine, evolve and multiply.

We exist in a sea of images, far more so than in earlier times due to phenomena like photography, cinema, the internet, advertising, the media, the world-wide spread of telecommunications, news, songs, books, art, speeches, messages, education, etc. The images we derive and share from these sources have a great impact on us, and through our actions, they impact our physical and non-physical worlds.

We exist in a sea of images. (George T. Tobin, artist.)

All of the imagery that we are exposed to coheres in our Dwimor, with its function of providing a grasping, salty matrix to hold all the aspects of our living-being together. Dwimor can't sort out healthy from unhealthy images, productive versus damaging or worthless images, inspiring versus time-and-energy wasting images. Such sorting and choosing is not within its abilities; it just holds onto everything it encounters. We have to rely on our other souls with the capacity for judgement and choice, if we want to keep some inventory-control of images going on within us: our Hugr, Mod, Ferah, Sefa and Ghost.

Our own health and well-being in Midgard are maximized when our souls capable of judgement take on the responsibility of sorting through and winnowing the images that our Dwimor collects throughout every day and night. The use of critical thinking, and many types of spiritual and mental-health practices are designed to do this, as well as treatments for more severe situations of imagery-run-amok, such as schizophrenia, PTSD, hallucinations and paranoia. (If you'd like some further reading about the process of maintaining a healthy and clear 'imaginarium', one approach for doing this is discussed by John Michael Greer on his *Ecosophia* website in this article: https://www.ecosophia.net/the-care-of-the-mind/)

Precipitation

However well or poorly our other souls perform these processes of image-monitoring, winnowing, cultivating and combining, the time comes when our Midgard life is over and our souls go their various ways. Dwimor heads off to its Saiwalo in Hel, bearing the hoard of imagery that it has collected over a lifetime.

I wrote previously about how Dwimor leaves the body through the process of sublimation, transforming from a metaphysically 'solid' state as a salt-being, into a vaporous state as a disembodied phantom, as it begins its journey from Midgard back to Hel. As it proceeds on its journey, approaching its salt-water Saiwalo origin, Dwimor gradually becomes more liquid in nature. We can see an analogy of this, when envisioning the properties of physical earth: air / vapor can penetrate a certain distance into the ground, but not very far. Water / liquid is able to penetrate earth much more deeply. As Dwimor sinks into metaphysical / elemental Earth, heading toward the underworld of Hel, it coalesces from an airy into a watery state.

When Dwimor returns to its Saiwalo, it undergoes another alchemical process: that of precipitation. Precipitation occurs when some kind of stimulus causes a dissolved substance to coalesce into larger particles and separate out into a sediment, sinking down as a solid at the bottom of the liquid. Dwimor bears its particles of imagery 'in solution', dissolved within its salty-watery self, as it heads toward Saiwalo. When it reaches Hel, its hoard of image-particles is precipitated out into Saiwalo.

There are many things that can stimulate or catalyze precipitation, including various chemicals, heating or cooling, or vibration. I perceive that Saiwalo catalyzes precipitation from its Dwimor by means of singing, that is, by vibration. I mentioned in Chapter 14 that I perceive Saiwalos' singing as being similar to whale-song: long, deep, sonorous echoes under the sea, heavy on vibration. Saiwalo sings the images from Dwimor into itself, by means of precipitation out of Dwimor. There is also a cooling effect as Dwimor sinks from the hotter, active plane of Midgard life, into the cooler, quieter plane of Hel, which promotes precipitation as well.

What does Saiwalo do with these precipitated images? Here we begin to move into the ecology of Hel, the subject of Part 4.

Part 4. Hel: An Ecological Perspective

So far, I've discussed my thoughts about how Hel and the Saiwalo souls arise, how Saiwalo condenses a Dwimor-phantom out of itself and projects it into Midgard to ensoul a new life, how that Midgard-Dwimor alchemically attracts and holds together all our souls, body, and energy flows during life, and how, at death, Dwimor sublimates out of the body as a wraith and returns to its Saiwalo in Hel, bearing a lifetime's worth of images as its treasure-hoard. Saiwalo draws its returning Dwimor toward itself through its long, echoing, sonorous song, and once Dwimor has arrived, the vibrations of the song and the cool environment of Hel cause Dwimor's hoard of images to precipitate into Saiwalo.

During its journey between Midgard and Hel, which may be swift or may be drawn-out and lingering, Dwimor's perceptions and experiences are shaped by the images it bears from its years of life in Midgard. Unlike many of our other souls, Dwimor has no ability to evaluate, to judge, to think critically. *Dwimor's images are its reality.* This is important for us to understand, as living, fully ensouled humans who can make choices about what we accept into our personal thought-spaces, our perceptions and interpretations of reality, our Hugr's framework of thought.

If Dwimor has a lifetime's worth of threatening, debased, ugly, frightful, painful, corrupt, meaningless or worthless images of what reality is like, as it heads back to Hel it will populate its surroundings with these perceptions, and experience them as real, both during its journey and after it reaches Hel. If living persons—relatives, loved ones—happen to be in contact with this Dwimor after death through dreams or visions, they also will perceive and be influenced by the Dwimor's perceptions, and will assume that 'this is what death and Hel are like.' Thus, Hel develops a reputation as a negative, fearful place, or a place empty of meaning and of hope.

The most widespread world religions deliberately paint horrific pictures of what their versions of hell are like, in order to draw their believers toward a God, or a spiritual path, that can save their soul from this terrible fate. This picture of hell then becomes a lasting part of the cultures influenced by these religions. During times and places in Midgard (including much of Heathen history) where people

The Alchemy of Hel

suffer from war and conflict, slavery, oppression, famine, epidemics, disasters and other terrible experiences, whole populations become imbued with the awful imagery that these experiences leave in their minds. This, too, is carried by their Dwimors into Hel.

So Hel ends up, over time, carrying a heavy load of negative imagery, absorbed through the negative experiences and beliefs of people during their lifetimes in Midgard. This imagery is not passive or static: it continues to bubble back up into Midgard through the Saiwalos and Dwimors of living people, perpetuating not only negative imagery in Midgard, but all the harmful beliefs, behavior and deeds that people engage in, in reaction to this imagery. All of this establishes a vicious circle, in the most literal sense.

But...all is not gloom and doom! There is a great deal of activity going on under the surface of Hel, activity which is not really perceptible to the Dwimors who have recently returned from Midgard. I perceive Hel and its Saiwalos as something like a wetland ecosystem, similar to both freshwater and estuarine (brackish, shallow seawater) ecosystems, which are among the most biologically active and productive types of ecosystems in the world.

Not only are they productive of great biodiversity, they are also great detoxification organs of our planet. Wetlands receive, and also produce, a lot of 'yucky stuff': rotten, stinky, toxic stuff, including human waste and pollution. They have an amazing facility for purifying material that is toxic and corrupted, to the point where humans can deliberately use natural or artificial wetlands to process waste and pollution and produce clean water.

This is what I envision as the major role of Hel and its Saiwalos in the spiritual ecology of the Worlds: it is a great, metaphysical 'wetland' which accepts the harmful spiritual waste-products draining down from all the Worlds, and

very slowly but steadily transmutes this waste into pure, life-giving spiritual water which fertilizes the Worlds.

A beautiful, healthy wetland in the ecosystem of Hel. By Dale Wood.

The Impact of Christianity on Hel

When we understand the function of Hel as I have described it here, it becomes clear how damaging it was when Christian ideas came in and transformed Heathen beliefs about the nature of Hel-world (seen as simply the place where souls go after death) and the destination and role of Saiwalo / 'soul'. I don't believe for a moment that Christian beliefs were really able to change the natural functions of Hel and the Saiwalos. But one of the great powers of our Saiwalo soul is the ability to create images that affect how it and others around it perceive and experience their surrounding environment.

So when Christians convinced living humans, including their Saiwalo souls, that 'hell' is a terrible place of burning flames, punishment and despair, and convinced them that 'bad' / Heathen souls would go there while 'good' / Christian souls would go to a remote 'heaven' detached

The Alchemy of Hel

from all Earthly concerns, connections and energies, it was—and still is—possible for people's Saiwalo souls to create images of these beliefs and experience them as though they were real.

Christians said that 'good' Saiwalo souls would go to 'heaven', to dwell in serene bliss with Deity. In fact, dwelling with Deities is the natural destination of our Ghost soul, while our Ahma soul is at home within the undifferentiated primal power/substance of Ginnungagap and Hvergelmir, experienced in all religions as oneness with the primal source of all.

Saiwalo, however, has different work to do, a different role to play. Sending Saiwalo to these 'heavenly' places would be an unnatural displacement, made worse by the idea that if Saiwalo's Dwimor does go to its natural place, Hel, this is considered a horrific punishment and failure, rather than its proper destination.

All of this disrupts Saiwalo and Hel-world from pursuing their proper functions within the cosmic ecosystem of the World Tree, and causes suffering and distress among Saiwalo souls and their Dwimors in Midgard and in Hel. This spiritual suffering is reflected into Midgard through the roiling and spoiling of Saiwalo's imagery.

Compare the flames of torment in the Christian concept of hell with the magical flames of the Hidden Land, as I discussed in Chapter 13. In the painting on the next page, Sigurd has passed through the flames around Brunhild, and comes to awaken her. She had been punished by Odin, sequestered behind a wall of flames, which only the bravest man in the world could pass through. But here is the important point: the flames themselves are not a

torment to Brunhild. She is sleeping peacefully, if unwillingly, and awakens unharmed. The fires here, and in other tales of the Hidden Lands, are magical, 'knowing' flames: gateways to the otherworlds, wardens of the lands of the dead and the fairytale lands, emanations from treasures, powers and places of the otherworlds. These fires are Mysteries, not agonies.

Hel-world's true role, in my perception, is to serve as a metaphysical analog of a healthy wetland, involved in composting, refining, purifying, fertilizing, recycling, regenerating, and gestating energies, evolving new spiritual forms, and shaping the 'roots' of events and entities in Midgard. Under Christian influence, Hel was supposedly transformed from this perhaps messy and uncomfortable, but necessary and healthy, set of functions into a horridly polluted, dead-end spiritual cesspit called 'hell'. The result is an apparent—an experiential—disruption of cosmic forces and processes affecting both spiritual and physical worlds.

In my view, this has created a severe spiritual and cultural PTSD, except that it is not *post*-traumatic stress disorder, it is *ongoing* traumatic stress disorder, rooted deeply in the spiritual disruption of Saiwalo and Hel-world, and the disrespect, fear, and denial of the Deities and powers associated with them.

The Alchemy of Hel

Humans, and Midgard as a whole, really need the functions of a healthy Hel as I described above: a place and a means to clear out psychic and spiritual gunk, poisons, pollutions, to purify and recycle them. Physical Midgard pollution is a reflection of the spiritual 'landfills' and 'superfund sites' and 'ocean dead-zones' that accumulate in Hel without proper processing, breaking down, and reuse of the components for fresh spiritual energy. We need Hel's natural, spiritual processes of cleaning up what is decaying, 'dead and done with', what doesn't serve life and well-being, and forming fertilizer from that to feed what is fresh and new, nourishing and revitalizing.

I think it's interesting to look at the evolution of our culture's understanding of 'hell' in light of these ideas. The Christian notion of 'hell' that I described above reached its heyday during medieval times and the following several centuries, and had many social repercussions, such as the Inquisition and the burning of heretics, witches and others. (The theological rationale for burning people alive was that the fire would purify their heretical souls and thus save them from hell and eternal fire. Burning people was really 'saving' their souls, but strangely enough, the victims failed to be suitably grateful.)

Though there are still many Christians who take these older beliefs about 'hell' literally, there are many others whose concepts have evolved in a different way. A belief among many modern Christians is that 'hell' means 'separation from their God', eternal loneliness: a form of psychological / spiritual suffering, rather than the 'physical' torment, degradation and depravity of the medieval hellscapes. And of course, many modern Westerners don't believe in 'hell' at all. I think that an important influence on this gradually changing concept of 'hell' is due to the work of the Saiwalos over centuries of Midgard time, slowly breaking down the horrific hellscape imagery that seeped into Hel from Midgard and creating space and energy for new imagery to arise.

Our Responsibility during Midgard Life

Each of our Saiwalo-souls is a part of this great task of ongoing spiritual regeneration, though we likely have no awareness of this during our Midgard life. This work is powerful and transformative, but it is also slow, in terms of Midgard time. Transformation takes time, and is not accomplished in one go-around.

Dwimors returning to Hel, and Saiwalos sending up images into Midgard, stir the churning soup of imagery and keep it active. Negative, positive and neutral images and energies mix together, mutating and recombining. A lot of good stuff arises from this, but negativity is also churned up and passed around. Eventually it all gets processed and purified by the 'wetland', but in the meantime, new imagery is produced, passed around, and amplified: some of it good, some not so good.

This is where our Midgard life and its responsibilities enters in. As I mentioned before, Saiwalos and Dwimors have no judgement, no analytical abilities, whereas most of our other souls do. Our lifetime in Midgard is our great opportunity, the time when all our souls can interact with each other, each with its own strengths, counterbalancing one another and creating within us a spiritual environment where our souls can grow together into greatness.

We have the option, during our Midgard life, to take on the responsibility of 'image-management', creating our

The Alchemy of Hel

own images of beauty, spiritual health, life-enhancing power, richness of experience: gifts we can give not only to the Midgard-world, but to Hel and the Saiwalos as well.

Every time we communicate, we pass images back and forth with each other. Every story that is told through whatever medium, every item of news reported, every interpretation of events, every dream or nightmare, every creative work, every fear and hope: all of these, and more, generate images that stick in our minds and in our Dwimors. It's a lifetime's work to learn to filter these, to take control of the images that we take in and accept, and images that we give out to others, so that we shape our Dwimor's treasure-hoard, over the course of our life, into richness, power, beauty, meaningfulness and goodness. Thus, we shape a true treasure for Dwimor to bear back to Hel and share with our Saiwalo.

Here is an eerie but beautiful verse from Shakespeare's *The Tempest* (I, ii) that poetically illustrates this process, using the image of a drowned man lying on the floor of the ocean:

> *Full fathom five thy father lies,*
> *Of his bones are corals made,*
> *Those are pearls, that were his eyes.*
> *Nothing of him that doth fade,*
> *But doth suffer a sea-change*
> *Into something rich and strange.*

This passage takes an image of death and decay, and transforms it into an image of enduring treasure and mysterious beauty. Strange and unsettling, yes, but meaningful, significant, transformative. Hel is an unsettling place from the perspective of the living, no question. But Hel and the Saiwalos have an essential, life-supporting role to play in the cosmic processes that maintain the Worlds. We can choose to play a conscious and supportive role in this process during our life in Midgard, by mustering the powers of all our souls to create, within and around ourselves, an environment of spiritual health, beauty, power, knowledge, and goodness, and spread it as far as we can. In this way, we consciously and willingly participate in our Saiwalo's vital role of purification, transformation and fertilization of the spiritual energies of the Worlds.

When I talk about managing, transforming, recreating the imagery that we take in and that we give out to others, I am not suggesting that we pretend things are other than they are, that we choose denial over hard-edged truth. Think about the many, many instances, in all times and places in the world, where people have undergone terrible experiences but have turned them to good.

Great poetry, art, music, social change, personal transformation, are often born of suffering. Adversity can turn good people into great people: generous, loving, heroic inspirations to others. A person living a quiet, boring sort of life can turn to pointless or even harmful pastimes and habits to liven things up, or can choose instead to find creative and worthwhile ways to give their life meaning and share that meaningfulness with others.

We can choose the sources, the media, the amount of time we spend taking in information and images every day, and use some of the time we save by limiting this, to engage in creative and positive endeavors. We can cultivate healthy habits of thought, spiritual practices, deep and genuine relationships, self-awareness, gentle humor, honesty and generosity. We can choose to transform adversity and the challenges of life into wisdom, compassion, and the motivation to bring about change where it is needed.

Through all of these activities, we transform potentially negative, destructive images into images which inspire us, strengthen our determination and resilience, and encourage us and those who associate with us. In doing all of this, we help our Dwimor gather its hoard of the true treasures of life, to carry back to Saiwalo and Hel, and enhance the great transformations that they perpetually carry out.

This is my view of the ecology of Hel. In Part 5 we'll explore an alchemical perspective on these phenomena.

Part 5. Stages of Alchemical Transformation

In Part 4 I used the analogy of a wetland ecosystem to describe the spiritual-ecological functions that Hel serves, the role it plays in the spiritual health and well-being of all the Worlds upon the Tree. Here I will return to alchemical symbolism and processes in order to cast light on these functions from a different direction.

Alchemy is about transformation, both material / physical, and metaphysical transformation. This transformation is seen as a series of operations or processes, summed up in the Latin phrase *solve et coagula*: dissolve and coagulate or bring together. There are various schools of thought in alchemy that present the steps of this process in different ways, such as different numbers of steps, and differences in the order and methods by which they are

Heathen Soul Lore

carried out. The seven steps or stages I use here are the basic, traditional ones.

An interesting aspect of alchemy that makes it well-suited for our purpose is the very rich library of symbolic images that esoteric alchemy makes use of to communicate its mysteries: kings, queens, lions, mythical beasts—all portrayed in different colors; Sun, Moon, gardens, gems, metals, weapons, walls, gates, castles, and many more. The conceptual world of traditional alchemy is a fully-populated fairy-tale realm, among many other things, and all the beings and images in this realm are laden with mythical and symbolic significance.

After studying all the foregoing chapters and material about Saiwalo, it should be very clear now, how well the richly symbolic imagery of alchemy fits as a way to perceive and describe the nature and processes of Hel-world and its dwellers. Transformation, and the arising of images, are primary activities of Hel and the Saiwalos, in my understanding.

I'm going to return to something I mentioned in Part 1, because now the time is ripe to pursue that in more depth. The older view of alchemy held the belief that *metals evolve*, but only as long as they are underground, sequestered from the light of Sun and Moon, but exposed to chthonic (underground, underworld) forces. Thus, in this belief, lead goes through a series of transformations into various metals, and finally into the pinnacle of metallic evolution: gold.

These transformational processes were also applied by alchemists to achieve other 'states of perfection' such as spagyric medicinals and states of health, as well as states of spiritual development and enlightenment. All of these various 'states of perfection' or ultimate development were

The Alchemy of Hel

considered equivalent to the 'gold of the alchemists,' and the 'philosopher's stone.'

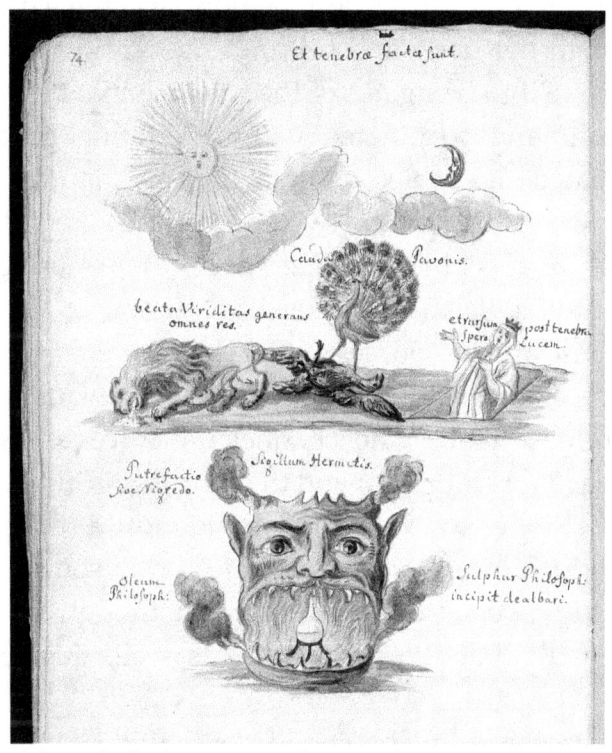

A sample of symbolic images used in traditional alchemy. Note that there are clouds that block the light of Sun and Moon from these processes. At the top of the page, the Latin words mean 'and darkness fell', which is a quotation from the Gospels referring to the time of Jesus' death, when he 'bent his head and gave up the ghost.' In Latin, the words used are 'he emitted his spirit' (emisit spiritum). *This phrase, the emission of spirits, refers to the process of distillation. The ghostly figure of the Queen arising from the grave may illustrate this concept as well. The images on this page, and the choice of words, are packed with esoteric nuance and symbolism pertaining to alchemy.*

The Chthonic Forces

Now, let's take a look at Hel and its Saiwalos from this perspective. I wrote, in Part 1, about my idea that Auðumla, the mythical cow of earliest beginnings, the Ur-Mother, transformed her body and self into the world of Hel. She herself came into being out of the salty ice that flowed from Hvergelmir and coagulated within Ginnungagap: blown about, heated and cooled by the winds emanating from the poles of Fire and Ice at the two ends of the Gap. The giant Ymir was formed in the same space, then sacrificed and shaped into the Earth of Midgard.

These are the sources of the 'chthonic energies' which power the alchemical transformations of the Underworlds: Auðumla and Ymir, who channel the forces of Fire, Ice, Ginnungagap, Hvergelmir and the Elivagar. (Buri also came from the same sources, but he is not a chthonic or underworld power. Rather, he is the source of the overworld powers, the Gods of Asgard, though they are all blended with underworld powers as well, due to Jotun-ancestry.)

I discussed in Chapter 13 how often Giants / Jotnar seem to be associated with the world of the dead and the underworld. Ymir was sacrificed and his-her body shaped into the Earth of Midgard. So Ymir and the Giants are associated both with physical earth / underground, and with the underworld of the dead.

Another race of beings, the Dwarves, are also involved here. The Dwarves arose as energy-larvae ('maggots') feeding from Ymir's body, then were transformed or transformed themselves into the tribe of Dwarves, as I wrote in Part 2. Their domain is underground / underworld, they also are associated with the dead, and are

The Alchemy of Hel

even more strongly associated with gems, metals, magical treasures, and the skills and craft involved in obtaining and creating these things.

Thus, the Dwarves join Ymir, Auðumla and the Giants as chthonic powers. Ymir is 'primal substance', and the Giants descended from him-her are considered, like the Titans of Greek myth, to embody primal substance and primal powers of the Earth, including weather and the oceans. Dwarves are 'consumers and shapers' of primal substance, consuming Earth-energies and shaping Earth-substance into treasures.

Auðumla is both the 'primal substance' of Hel, in my understanding, but also a primal shaper in her role as shaper of Buri, as well as her self-transformation into the world of Hel. Her shaping and transforming power is further shown through the spontaneous generation of Saiwalo souls out of her primal substance, and Hel / Saiwalos' roles in transformation of images and spiritual waste-forms of the Worlds. Her transformative influence on Hel and its dwellers is primary, but Ymir / Giants and Dwarves have their roles to play, as well.

In taking an alchemical perspective, we can think of all these beings and the primal cosmic phenomena as emanators or representatives of energies which act upon the Hidden Land of Hel and its dwellers, the Saiwalos and their Dwimors. These energies have different effects, which we'll examine here, step by step as they are carried out in a series of alchemical processes that result in transformation and evolution of the materials they are working upon: that is, images and the energies associated with them, and the Dwimors themselves.

I should mention here that living humans who spiritually perceive events and beings in Hel, through dreams, visions, spirit-journeys, may perceive any of these stages of alchemical processes, and may interpret them in very individual ways. Our perceptions may pick up chaotic or un-interpretable scenes: images of stillness / darkness / emptiness where everything is happening imperceptibly beneath the surface; scenes of mystery and beauty; familiar scenes and persons; scenes that seem frightening, upsetting or unsettling. Though I describe the alchemical processes of Hel as a sequence of events in time, Hel does not experience time as we do in Midgard. These events can 'be happening', 'have happened', 'will happen', all at once, which makes it difficult for us to interpret what we perceive of Hel and its dwellers.

Differences between Hugrs and Saiwalo-Dwimors

A quick digression, before we proceed with the alchemical stages, because the question may come up: "I've been in contact with some of my departed ancestors, and they are not much like you're describing here. What's going on?"

When living people contact departed ancestors and others they knew during life, or want to get to know after life, my sense is that it is usually the Hugr-souls who are the ones contacted, especially if the spirits one encounters seem very human-like, with personalities, emotions, thoughts, similar to those of living humans. Many Heathens enjoy having cozy, low-key ceremonies with ancestral spirits during holy days or any other time. I like to have what I call 'a tea-party with my Disir', laying out cups of tea for myself and for them, sitting with my Daybook, and writing down

The Alchemy of Hel

what comes to me as conversation and advice from these ancestresses.

Spirits who engage in these kinds of human-like, Midgard-like relationships and behaviors are, as I said, likely to be Hugrs of the departed. Saiwalos, Dwimors, and their environment of Hel have a different feel to them: they are imbued with mythic or fairy-tale overtones, archetypal, otherworldly characteristics, subtle and strange differences in light, color, sound, movement, etc., compared to what we are familiar with in Midgard.

It's harder to relate deeply to these beings on a personal level. Though they have great depth, their depths are not those of character, personality, experience, thought, emotion, as we experience them in Midgard. In the ways I just listed, they may seem superficial or detached from our Midgard concerns, perhaps taking a mild interest, or engaging with us for a short time, but we get a sense that they are not deeply engaged.

This is very different from the Hugr-souls, who are fully engaged with the concerns of human Midgard life, whether they are embodied or disembodied. In a nutshell: the more human-like and Midgard-like a contacted spirit and situation is, the more likely that it is a Hugr soul. The more archetypal and fairy-tale-like overtones a contact or scene has, the more likely one is perceiving scenes and beings of Hel.

There are some similarities and overlaps between Saiwalo and Hugr as well. Contact between either of them and our conscious mind can result in hidden, arcane, or mystical knowledge coming into our awareness through images, intuitions and insights. Our imagination, working through our conscious mind, may 'dress' these contact-experiences as familiar scenes and images, or as eerie and unfamiliar.

The other overlap between Saiwalo and Hugr is that much of our Hugr's framework of thought is formed from images provided by Saiwalo-Dwimor. Hugr's job is to evaluate these images and decide whether they are worthwhile and beneficial components of its framework of thought, or whether they need to be modified, or culled and removed.

The Alchemical Processes

Now let's proceed with the step-by-step alchemical processes of Hel.

Calcination
Calcination is symbolized by Fire; it breaks down something into ashes or residue. The fission-fire of our Ferah-soul at the time of death separates our souls from our body, and the body is then burned to ash or decays in the ground. In mythical imagery, Ymir's energy is that of 'venom' or corrosive force; this corrosion is fiery and breaks things down into their component parts, ashes, or residue. This step corresponds to the death process of our soul-body complex, the sublimation of the Dwimor, and its departure from Midgard.

Dissolution
Dissolution is symbolized by Water, and involves dissolving the ashes of calcination in water or other liquid. In my view it comprises the actions of the Dwimor after death. Dwimor is released from the Lich and the other souls by Fire, and separates from them as an airy wraith, a phantom.

The Alchemy of Hel

As Dwimor sinks into the underworld and returns to Hel, it cools and condenses. It becomes watery, and bears the treasure-hoard of images it has collected during life as suspended particles within its watery matrix. Thus, after the fiery separation and sublimation of death, Dwimor cools, sinks, and becomes a watery matrix containing the ashes or particles of its image-hoard.

The rib-cage, face and hand of Ymir can be seen here, as he-she dissolves in a flood, prior to coagulating into Midgard surrounded by ocean.

This step in the process reflects the Elivagar, the braided, twining rivers of power which flow endlessly out of Hvergelmir, the cosmic wellspring. The Elivagar, back in the beginning of things, carried dissolved salt and venom within its flow, as I discussed in Part 1, just as the Dwimor bears the dissolved particles of its image-hoard within its watery matrix. This stage is also an image of Ymir dissolving into component parts, on the way to formation of Midgard.

Separation
This stage is associated with Air. Saiwalo is very much a shape-shifter, fluid of form, and takes on the likenesses of many different images as it pleases. At this point in our discussion we can envision the Saiwalo, awaiting the return of its Dwimor, as something like a landscape, a parcel of land that is formed of Saiwalo-stuff.

Saiwalo sends out its song that echoes and reverberates across the Saiwalo-landscape like horns blowing among mountain crags, as its Dwimor slowly descends to a landing, there within the Saiwalo-landscape. During the descent, the vibrations of Saiwalo's song cause the image-particles in the Dwimor to condense into larger, heavier complexes of images, to separate from the Dwimor, and to precipitate into the Saiwalo-land like rain or snow, watering and fertilizing it with image-energy. Whatever these imageries consist of, Saiwalo absorbs them and is 'flavored' with their energies.

Dwimor's load of images condenses into fog and precipitates down over the Saiwalo-landscape.

This parallels the events in Ginnungagap, when the venom which was dissolved in the Elivagar precipitated out and formed Ymir, who took on the nature of venom. This process of separation is also one of the skills of the Dwarves, who must separate and refine precious metals from the ore in which they are bound, before they can make them into treasures. In the same way, our Hugr souls must sort, separate and clarify the images that it incorporates into our framework of thought.

The Alchemy of Hel

Conjunction

This is a phase of recombination. The images that Dwimor has brought back and precipitated into Saiwalo mix and recombine with other imagery and energies already present in Saiwalo and in Hel. During this phase, Dwimor itself is reincorporated within its Saiwalo.

Traditionally, this phase is considered to involve the union of opposites: male and female, light and dark, etc. In my perception, things are a great deal more complex in Hel, and in the world of images. Unions of opposites certainly occur at this stage, but many other mixtures are possible, too.

My own image of what is happening at here is that of adding culture to milk, to make cheese or yogurt, or yeast to bread dough or to fruit juice to make wine. 'Things' are mixed in with the image-hoard that bring about transformation. These are the seeds of change.

The parallel cosmic action is Auðumla licking the salty ice within Ginnungagap, turning it into milk within herself, and feeding Ymir and Buri, thus combining elements of all the primal forces and beings. The salt from Auðumla's milk, which bears the seeds of transformation, becomes the salt in Ymir's blood, which, after he is sacrificed, becomes the salty seas of Midgard. The salty sea is a powerful image of the Saiwalo soul, as I discuss in Chapter 14.

Fermentation

Auðumla is a cow, a ruminant animal. Ruminants possess four hard-working stomachs, each involving different digestive processes, to turn tough, indigestible grasses into the fatty acids that provide them with energy and nourishment. Microbial fermentation plays the major role in this: in effect, a ruminant is an enclosed, walking wetland! Auðumla's giant, bio-active stomachs power the wetland ecosystem functions of Hel that I discussed in Part 4. I realize that this imagery is not very 'spiritual'...what can I say? Heathen mythology tends to be very literal at times, and this imagery works, at least for me. This phase is associated with Earth, and the imagery here is definitely 'earthy'!

So, in the previous step, 'seeds of change' or 'microbial cultures' were mixed in with the images and energies, and now the fermentation and wetland processes occur: breaking down, mutating, recombining, evolving: all the processes of transformation. Hel's / Auðumla's ecosystem is doing its work.

Distillation
Now the energies and imageries have gone through a process of fermentation and change. The next step is to distill and purify the resulting fermented mass. This is also the stage during which Saiwalo may begin the formation of a new Dwimor for its next association with Midgard life.

This is a phase of Fire and Air, as the fermented mass is subjected to high energies that cause it to 'boil' and rise as steam, then condense into a purified form. The images that arise during this stage have been mutated and transformed from their previous forms.

Dwimors and images begin to distill into shapes, out of the mist arising from the wetlands of Hel.

During this phase, the essence of the previous Dwimor, which was earlier reincorporated with its Saiwalo, begins to re-form as a shade, a phantom image, within the landscape of its Saiwalo. Image-essences are also distilled, which will become new treasures, powers, and arcane knowledge to enrich the Hel-domain.

The cosmic analog of this phase is the Ahma-mist rising from Hvergelmir-fountain and distilling into the Ahma / Ǫnd souls of humans and other beings. This stage also brings in the skills and powers of the Dwarves as they finish refining metals, gems, and arcane energies in preparation for the final formation of their beautiful and magical treasures.

Coagulation
This is the final step of the alchemical process, the gathering-together or crystallization of what has been burned, dissolved, separated, recombined, fermented, and distilled. It results in pure gold, in a crystalline jewel or stone, in a precious medicine or elixir, in a human spirit that has gone through great trials and been purified and integrated into a new form. In our study of Saiwalo, this stage results in transformed images capable of sparking new, original, beneficial ideas and behaviors among humans in Midgard.

Salt crystals photographed in Death Valley, USA. Soul lore translation: Dwimors coagulated from salt-water Saiwalos in Hel.

This is when a new, salty Dwimor becomes fully crystallized out of the salt-water matrix of Saiwalo, and heads up to Midgard to join the Ferah-soul of a newly-conceived human, to begin the process of gathering all the other souls and their energies together around its crystalline, salty matrix.

The Dwimor from the previous Midgard life is now fully re-formed, still very much a part of its Saiwalo, but possessing the appearance and surface characteristics of the

The Alchemy of Hel

person it was once a part of. If living humans—loved ones, descendants, etc.—manage to contact this Dwimor spiritually, they will perceive the form of the human being they knew and expect to see. The Dwimor may seem 'wiser' or 'better' than the original human in some ways, due to its evolution through these alchemical processes. Or it may seem little changed from what it was before, depending on its willingness and ability to be transformed.

Dwimors will go through multiple repetitions of these processes, as each new Dwimor the Saiwalo sends into Midgard returns and triggers a new round of transformations for the whole Saiwalo-landscape and all its indwelling Dwimors from previous lives. Thus, the Saiwalo-landscape becomes ever more populated by Dwimors from all previous lifetimes.

At this time, the re-formed Dwimor obtains its 'adornments' and 'treasures': treasure-images that have been distilled through these transformational processes and have grown in power and beauty. Thus, living humans who spiritually perceive the Dwimors within their Saiwalo-landscape may envision decorated feasting-halls or beautiful palaces, stores of treasure, and human shades adorned with precious garments, jewelry, weapons, and so forth. Of course, these images may not conform to medieval ideas of beauty and richness, when we perceive them, but instead match more modern ideas and conceptions.

Adorned Dwimors may possess great beauty and take on the powerful attraction of a mystical 'soul-mate', which may in turn be projected onto a living human through our own Saiwalo. Distilled and coagulated treasures of arcane knowledge are also produced during this phase, and may be imbedded into objects of magical power.

Cosmically, with this step of the process we come full circle, back to Auðumla and her living transformation into the world of Hel, crystallizing Hel-world and its souls out of all the elements that went into her making, and providing the foundation for the ever-recycling processes of alchemical transformation undertaken by Hel and its Dwellers.

Necromancy and Arcane Knowledge

As this cycle completes itself, this is also the time when the arcane, necromantic knowledge rooted in Hel is shaped into something that living humans have some hope of understanding. (Necromancy is here used in its literal sense of 'prophecy or arcane knowledge from the dead.') It is necessary to provide a seed-crystal around which this knowledge can coagulate, so it can take on a humanly comprehensible form.

The seed-crystal is often a question, asked by a living person, through an intermediary who may be a living spaewife or spaeman, or a Deity or helping Hugr-spirit. The question, and the powers and energies of the underworld, catalyze and coagulate relevant images drawn from the Saiwalos and crystallize them into an image-answer to the question. The image-answers may take visual form, or auditory form as a galdor or song, or other sensory forms.

Here is something to note, that links us back to the old tales about living people contacting Dwimors in Hel, as I described in Chapter 13. The Norse tales frequently envision that the dead are 'asleep' or out of touch in some way, and need to be called or even coerced through runes and magical spells into paying attention to what the living want.

The Alchemy of Hel

My interpretation of this observation is that Saiwalo-Dwimors in Hel are generally busy with their alchemical, 'wetland' processes; this is where their focus lies. If living people call or coerce them, Dwimors need to go through a process of shifting their attention, their energy, their appearance and ways of expression, and their plane of existence, in order to respond in a way that the living can perceive. It can take awhile, in terms of Midgard time-perception, for Saiwalo-Dwimor to make this happen. This creates the perception that the dead are asleep, and / or far away, and must be called and awoken in order to interact with the living.

The process of crystallizing knowledge can occur in another way, as well, in my experience. We can open our spiritual perception to *our own Saiwalo* (it is inadvisable to walk into the widely populated, strange domain of Hel itself) and walk into our Saiwalo's 'hall' or 'landscape', bearing with us a symbol or image of something that is deeply mysterious to us, and about which we wish to learn more.

Words and verbal questions are not useful, here within our own Saiwalo. Visionary images (using any or all of our senses, including 'feeling') are the medium of communication. We present this question-image within the hall or landscape of our Saiwalo, and prepare to 'absorb' the response. To do this, we can imaginatively take on the form of something that gathers and absorbs, like the soil of a landscape, a living sponge beneath the sea, a mountain meadow under a fall of snow, or a pool of water in the rain. We absorb the knowledge-essence that precipitates into us from our Saiwalo, and crystallize it within ourselves into an image that expresses this knowledge.

This is our knowledge-seed, our treasure, our philosopher's stone, but though we bear it back with us into Midgard, it will not be immediately available to us. It's wise to take our time and put this seed or image through the alchemical processes I've outlined here, perhaps repeatedly, in order to unpack its rich nuances, its treasures of knowledge and beauty. This is a process I've followed for years, to try to learn more of Hel and its mysteries. It is a strange and unusual undertaking, but very rewarding.

Part 6. The Permeability of Hel

In this final part about the nature of Hel and its beings, we'll consider two other subjects that result in connections between Hel and other Worlds. One is the source of the Hugr-souls; the other concerns 'back doors' between Hel and other beings and Worlds.

Where do Hugrs come from?

In the previous parts of this chapter, I discuss my own ideas about the origins of Hel-world, and of the Saiwalo-souls and the Dwimor-phantoms that they produce. I also write of my idea that Hel-world is like a giant wetland, which receives spiritual waste from Midgard and other Worlds, and gradually transforms it through ecological-alchemical processes into nutrient-rich elemental Water that fertilizes the Worlds.

There is another phenomenon that I perceive happening during these processes: the arising of proto-Hugr souls, the first stirrings of what will eventually become full-blown human Hugrs. I wrote in Chapters 9 and 10 about the Hugr as an ancestral soul, one that survives physical death, continues its connection with Midgard through its living kin

The Alchemy of Hel

and others it was close to, and often reincarnates. But where did Hugr come from originally, and how do more Hugrs arise as new souls for increasing populations? Here are my current thoughts on this question.

Let's picture the great wetland of Hel, here: a watery, marshy land busy fermenting and transforming the mass of spiritual material it contains. In terms of the alchemical processes I described in Part 5, we are looking at the fermentation stage. Marshes in Midgard sometimes produce the phenomenon called the 'will-o'-the-wisp', luminous wisps of mist that hover and waft over swamps and marshes at night. Scientifically, these are formed from chemoluminescent phosphorus and methane gases arising from decaying matter. In folklore around the world, they are considered to be spooks and spirits of the marshes, which are said to lead people dangerously astray if they follow these wisps across the nighttime landscape.

"Will-o'-the wisp and snake," by Hermann Hendrich.

Let's look now at the next alchemical step, after fermentation: distillation, where the fermented mass is raised to a higher energy level by heating until it steams or boils, and purified vapors arise from this mass. In our Hel-landscape imagery here, the fermentation process itself raises energy and results in distilled vapor-wisps dancing over the surface of the Hel-marsh. The marsh is itself fermenting, distilling and coagulating image-energies collected from Midgard and other Worlds.

These rising wisps are the proto-Hugrs, formed of image-energies that arise from the great transformational wetlands of Hel. As they dance over the surface of the wetland they gather more images, wrapped around themselves like yarn on a spindle. This is the alchemical stage of coagulation, and the result of images coagulating together is the arising of some form of desire, relating to the images.

The desire may be a longing to reach toward these images, motivating the urge to achieve or realize them in some way. In some cases, negative images will instead spark a desire to get away from them or overcome them. These images of the Hugr's formation lay the groundwork for the Hugr's motivating forces: longing, yearning, desire, shaped by the originating images, which crystallize into this Hugr-ling's core essence. Thus, images crystallize into desires, forming the wispy proto-Hugr whose roots lie in desiring, yearning, longing, wishing.

At this stage, the Hugr-ling has no power or knowledge of how to attain its desires; it is simply a wisp of longing. But the energy of its longing is enough to draw it up toward the Midgard-plane, the source of the imageries that the Hugr-ling is formed from, and the place where its longings and desires will be played out.

When it reaches the spiritual-energy planes of Midgard, it encounters other, more developed Hugr-spirits, who have already lived human lives, once or many times. Through association with these disembodied but experienced Hugr-souls, the Hugr-ling is 'apprenticed', so to speak, and begins to develop its powers. Ancestral, experienced Hugrs guide the new ones into association with parents-to-be, spurring their desire and, hopefully, love for each other and their desire for a child. Thus, a new home is created for the Hugr-ling: a child with its full household of souls, and the young Hugr can begin its long journey toward experience, wisdom and power.

Back-Door Connections

In my understanding of Hel, the Saiwalo-Dwimors and proto-Hugr souls, I catch a glimpse of some fascinating back-door connections between Hel, Hugrs, Midgard, some of the God-Homes, and their associated Deities. The reason I call these 'back door connections' is that Hel is traditionally considered to be a place from which dead souls can never escape, nor can the living or the Deities go there except under extraordinary circumstances. The 'front door' between Hel and the living worlds of humans, Deities and others is considered to be firmly closed. Yet if we look at folklore and beliefs stretching across many Germanic peoples and many centuries, there are clues that hint at all sorts of 'back door' connections, some of which I briefly outline here.

I've sensed for years a strong connection between afterlife Hugrs and Hel, yet I don't believe that Hugrs actually populate Hel itself, as Saiwalo-Dwimors do. Rather, I think there are 'back doors' between Hugr's afterlife hangouts and Hel, not to mention my belief that proto-Hugrs arise from Hel, as I wrote above. Hugrs can readily pick up the images that Saiwalos are generating, absorbing and processing. Afterlife Hugrs can use those images to 'clothe' themselves and their surroundings when interacting with living humans in dreams, visions, and oracular work.

Thus, when working with afterlife Hugrs, we may see similar kinds of imagery of feasting halls, ancestral gatherings, and strange environments, that we might expect to see in Hel, as well as the more homely memories of known people and environments left over from Hugr's life in Midgard. Hugr's active involvement with before- and afterlife as well as Midgard life creates a bridge of understanding and familiarity between itself and the Saiwalo souls.

Now, let's look at the Goddesses Frigg and Saga, and their homes. Mother-Goddess Frigg's hall is called Fensalir, meaning 'fen-halls'. A fen is a marsh or wetland. In Chapter 14 I wrote about various Germanic beliefs that associate souls with water: babies' souls being drawn out of water by a Goddess or Norn, and the souls of the dead sometimes appearing from and disappearing into lakes or other water bodies.

A depiction of Frigg. Note the presence of the stork, a bird that wades in the marshes and delivers babies, and two babies hidden under Frigg's robes, whose souls are drawn up from the waters by the stork.

In ancient Heathen times, bogs were frequently the recipients of rich offerings and sacrifices to the Deities. Here, we have combined images of birth, death, souls and treasures being placed into, and drawn out of, water bodies, with the strong association of Deities' involvement in various ways. I draw the conclusion

The Alchemy of Hel

that Frigg's hall Fensalir is a 'back door' or hidden life-death-life passage into and out of Hel's treasure-troves of souls, offerings, spiritual wetlands, and the phenomena that arise from there.

The Goddess Saga's hall is called Søkkvabekkr, meaning 'sunken bench/es'. This seems to indicate an underwater hall, similar to Fen-Halls. Some modern Heathens think that Saga is another name for Frigg, or a hypostasis of her, because of the similarity of their hall-names and the fact that Odin, Frigg's husband, joins Saga in her hall every day, where they drink together from golden cups (*Grimnismal* v. 7 in the Poetic Edda). This makes sense to me!

Saga's great skill is that of telling tales, sagas, history. In order to weave these tales, she makes full use of dramatic images, which then link us with Saiwalo-souls and their ability to generate and transform images. So here is another back-door between a watery God-Home and the output of Hel: images shaped into stirring tales, arising from the 'hall of sunken benches'.

The Earth-Goddess Nerthus, who in the past lived on an island, was bathed annually, and whose sanctity was protected by drowning anyone who glimpsed her other than her priests, is another Deity who, I would say, has a back-door to watery Hel-world. I suggest that the purified elemental Water from Hel's wetlands rises up to Nerthus' lands, and under the power and direction of her Earth-Goddess nature, it fertilizes the earth of Midgard.

Odin's hall Valhalla with its name and decorations reminiscent of slaughter, its Einherjar warriors who are slain in battle and revived every day, and Odin's association with the dead, also sounds to me like it has some serious back door connections with Hel, even though it is considered an overworld abode.

Frau Holle, a German Goddess whose name stems from the same root as 'Hel', roams freely between underworld, overworld and Midgard; her doors are wide. People enter her realm by falling down a well or entering a mountain cave, descending into the underworld. She is also a sky-Goddess, shaking her feather-bed so that feathery snow falls down on Midgard, and laying out her clothes to dry, seen in the long, low lines of clouds lying on the horizon, and in the dense mists draped across the sides of mountains. She is heavily involved in everyday life in Midgard as well, including birth and death processes. Frau Holle experiences no barriers between the Worlds; all doors, back or front, are open to her.

Frau Holle is so good at communicating between the Worlds, that this mailbox has been set up for her in Hastrungsfeld, Germany!

There are also the many versions of 'lost souls, poor souls' (*arme Seelen* in German folklore), 'wandering souls', processions of gathered souls led by Goddess-figures, the Wild Hunt, Halloween flights and lurking of spirits from the afterlife and so forth, common especially among the Continental Germanic branches up until recent times. Much of the imagery associated with these phenomena indicates that these wandering souls either escape from and return to Hel at designated times, or have failed to reach Hel after death and need to be gathered up and guided there. There are many landscape features such as caves and water bodies that are considered to be the gateways through which such wandering souls exit and return, as I wrote about in Chapters 13 and 14.

Walpurga or Walburga, as the Lady of the Dead, at times allows wandering souls into Midgard; at other times she gathers them up to return to Hel. Some modern Heathens consider Walburga and Frau Holle to be the same being. ("Klassische Walpurgisnacht" by Edmund Friedrich Kanoldt.)

Putting together clues such as these, and the evidence of 'Hel-like places' populated with living beings that I discussed in Chapter 13, I draw the conclusion that Hel is a much more permeable and nuanced place than we are told to believe by some of the Norse lore and the lore of other religions such as Christianity. Though I believe that our Ghost-souls head for the God-Homes while our Saiwalos are rooted in Hel and our Hugrs remain connected to Midgard,

Heathen Soul Lore

the existence of these back doors indicates that there may be less distance and estrangement between these Worlds and souls than one might assume.

A ray of light through the trees reflects in the water, illustrating the meeting of the worlds of air and water, light and earth.

Worlds reflect off each other, and we perceive those reflections through the images that capture our awareness.

Chapter 17

17. The Arising of the Self

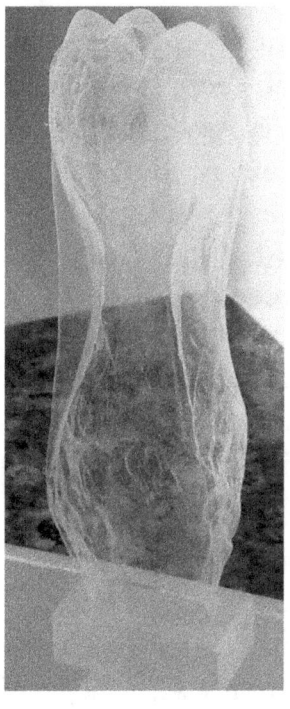

The Self arises from interacting energies of our souls, as a hologram like this one arises from interacting wavelengths of light.

We've gone through a long, complicated list of multiple souls here, which leaves us with some fundamental questions. Where, in this sea of souls, does our sense of unitary Selfhood reside? How do our souls functionally coordinate during life in Midgard? What happens to our sense of Self after we die and our souls each move on to their own afterlife fates?

To address these questions, I will examine a new perspective on the Sefa soul. I wrote in Chapter 12 about my thought that *sefa* is related to 'sib' and that they both stem from the same Proto-Indo-European (PIE) root **s(w)e-*. The word 'self' also comes from this root. **S(w)e-* is the third-person pronoun, and also in various forms refers to the social group as an entity: 'we ourselves'. The suffixed form **s(w)e-bho* leads to 'sib' (and, I believe, to the Old Saxon soul-word *sebo*: the 'b' is crossed, and indicates the 'bh' sound), while the suffixed extended form **sel-bho* leads to 'self'. (Watkins p. 90.)

Proto-Germanic **selbaz* leads to the words for 'self' in the various Germanic languages: *self / seolf / selbo / silba / selb*, etc. (*Online Etymology Dictionary.*) Essentially, the only difference between some of the Germanic-language words for 'self' and 'sefa-soul' is the addition of an 'l': Anglo-Saxon *self / seolf* and *sefa / seofa;* Old Saxon *sebo / selbo*. My own thought is that Old Saxon represents the eldest and clearest linguistic connection between *self / selbo, Sefa / Sebo*, and *sib / sibbia*.

So, here we have a strong connection between 'self', 'that which belongs to myself', and 'that to which I belong': relatives, social ties and bonds. Both 'self' and 'sib' are linked to the Sefa soul. This leads me toward a new vision of the Sefa, expanded from the meanings I've been able to draw from the old literature, that I discussed in Chapter 12.

I have not found evidence in the old lore that would make Sefa fit my definition of 'a soul-being': it is not a life-soul, nor a daemon-soul, and I've seen no indication of an independent afterlife. Yet I don't see Sefa as a 'soul-part' either: it is too extensive and too oriented toward the larger world outside the self, to be limited like that.

Then, we have another issue: our full household of multiple soul-beings, our 'soular-system'. What links them all together in a functional, daily-life sense? Where does our sense of Selfhood lie, in this vision of multiple souls that I present? I approach these questions using two analogies drawn from modern science and philosophy: the systems-theory phenomenon of 'emergent properties', and 'holograms'.

The Emergent Self

The question "what is the Self?" is a perennial favorite of philosophers, scientists, and religious thinkers, with many explorations in interesting directions. Within our domain of Heathen soul lore study, an answer to this question gradually unfolds as we pursue this knowledge in depth. This 'answer' is not a dogmatic or credal statement, imposed by any authority or belief system. It is an inner knowing, a recognition of what is there, that grows slowly out of personal experience of our souls and our self.

From our Self's perspective, and that of our everyday, conscious mind, the souls seem like 'parts' of itself, or 'soul-parts', and the Self has the idea that 'I have a soul, it belongs to me'. *From the perspective of the souls, however, the Self is something they create and maintain together, an outgrowth of their synergy during life in Midgard.*

I see the Self as an 'emergent property' of the souls. An emergent property arises out of a coordinated system of various entities, for example the cells that comprise the various structures and systems of our brain. None of these cells 'think', yet when they work together in a coordinated fashion, 'thinking' arises from that activity. An emergent property is not contained in any of the parts of the system, but arises or emerges out of the integrated activity of the system as a whole. There are large fields of study in the sciences and philosophy that examine this fascinating phenomenon of emergent properties as they appear in physical, biological, ecological, and social systems. In Heathen soul lore study, we examine it in a spiritual context, that of our own 'soular-system.'

Here is what I offer in response to the question "what is the Self?" from the perspective of Heathen soul lore. *Our Self is a song, and the singers are our souls.* Our Self-Song is sung by all our souls harmonizing their 'voices' or vibrations together during our lifetime in Midgard. Each Self-Song is unique, and fluctuates its tones from minute to minute, day to day, as our souls act and react in various ways to their activities and surroundings. This song of the Self, I believe, is how our Sefa-soul arises. It is an emergent property of our full soular-system.

Sometimes our Self-Song is harmonious, sometimes it is dissonant and jarring; sometimes it is muted and blurred, sometimes strong and clear. At different times, different souls have louder or softer voices, depending on the nature of each of our souls and our life circumstances. Tonal balances shift and change. Our song evolves through time, as we grow and move through different stages of life. Yet always, there is a core that holds it all together: the expression of our own unique Self by our souls singing it into being, here in Midgard.

The Arising of the Self

Beethoven's souls are singing his Self and his music into being.

The Midgard Self

Thus, Sefa, our soul focused on relationships, is the soul who arises from the relationship among all our souls together. While the life-soul Saiwalo-Dwimor holds our soular-system together in an alchemical / metaphysical sense, Sefa is the bond of relationship which coordinates our soul-household as a functioning system within the domain of Midgard life, with all its demands and complexities. Sefa is not a soul which *gives* life; it is a soul which *is given* life, by the interactions of all the other souls. We our Self do not 'have a soul'; rather, our souls create and sustain our Self during life in Midgard.

Though I argue that our everyday sense of 'being a Self' is centered in Sefa, it is vital to keep in mind that each and all of our souls are truly our Self, as well. Sefa-self would not exist if the other souls, our deep-selves, were not singing it into being during every moment of our life.

Sefa focuses on relationships, on knitting-together, on sensing, perceiving, understanding, and working with what matters most to us in life. It focuses equally powerfully on the inner relationships among our soul-household; on our outer relationships with family and kindred, friends, lovers, colleagues, neighbors, others; and on our relationships with the Deities and other spirits.

Sefa's perceptiveness, insight, understanding and caring also enable us to see the relationships among intangibles like ideas, images, situations, creative elements, problems, solutions—all the different ways we strive to understand and address the complexities and the opportunities of our lives as thinking, feeling, responding beings here in Midgard.

Making connections among the multitude of tangibles and intangibles that comprise our Midgard life is Sefa's strength and purpose. This is also Sefa's vulnerability: the strong focus on, and need for, relationship and caring can result in exploitation and manipulation of Sefa by unscrupulous or selfishly needy people (and possibly by spirits, too), and in becoming overwhelmed by the sheer volume and intensity of all the interrelating and caring going on. Even though Sefa is perceptive and insightful, these abilities can be overridden by its need for relating, whether wise or unwise in any specific situation. Here is where the warding function of our Hugr-soul comes in. Other souls as well, especially Mod, can strengthen Sefa's resistance to exploitation and to being overwhelmed.

The Sefa is created by our other souls during Midgard life, and its purpose is to act and have its being in Midgard.

The Arising of the Self

The question now arises: what becomes of this Self, after death and separation of the souls?

The Holographic Self

Our sense of being a unitary Self resides in Sefa, but each of our other souls is just as much our true self, our own, our essential being, an individual participating within a holism. This situation is a paradox or a quandary that takes a long time to for us to perceive and settle into; it's kind of like trying to understand what living in five or six dimensions, instead of three or four, would feel like. How can we shape this insight into something that is understandable for us? The image of a hologram might help.

A hologram is a three-dimensional image created through the use of laser technology.

This charming hologram re-creates the Hama of an archaeopteryx named Yghol.

A unique trait of a hologram is that if you divide it, each piece of the divided hologram contains the image shown in the entire hologram, though small pieces will contain somewhat less detail than the original.

As Sefa weaves together our soul-household with all its experiences and activities in Midgard, it creates a hologram of our life-experience, which is its hama, its soul-skin or soul-shape. Each soul's essence and experiences are shared and woven into the Sefa-hologram during life; the hologram of our Selfhood contains the meaningfulness of all the souls' full Midgard lives, woven together.

After death, the soul-household or Hiwship of souls breaks up, but each soul still carries the hologram of the Self that the whole soul-household created during life in Midgard, though some of the smaller details may be lacking. These holograms enrich each of the souls with all that the person experienced in Midgard. Here is what the hologram means to each of our souls, after death and separation from the others.

For the Aldr soul, that holographic image is its Werold, the tapestry it has woven of our deeds, ørlög, achievements, that it presents at the Doom-stead of the Holy Ones and lays in the Well of Wyrd. For the Ferah soul, the energies of the hologram are woven back into the webs of life: the patterns and rhythms of the life-force, and the natural 'laws' or patterns that interconnect throughout and between Midgard, the Deities, and the other life-worlds. This weaving may be done deliberately by the Ferah as a transformed spirit-being, such as a Landwight or other nature-spirit, or may happen as a natural process of dispersion of Ferah-energies.

Ahma has contributed its beauty and power to the hologram during life, but has no need of the holographic Self after death. Ahma is pure, unchanging Spirit, that lies beyond matters of individual selfhood. Ghost, however, carries the full hologram of selfhood with it, into the God-Homes or divine realms, where it may choose to continue as an individual, personal being, interacting with the Deities in personal form. The Ghost embodies the hologram very strongly, including bearing the shape and many of the

The Arising of the Self

abilities of its original physical body, thus creating a Ghost-hama, a spirit-form, for itself.

Earthly Hama-soul slowly disperses, along with the decay of the physical body, its Lich. In folklore, sometimes the dead body is reanimated as a draugr, a zombie-like being, by the reattachment of the Hama with the Lich. As the Lich decays, however, the hologram that shapes the lingering selfhood of the Hama also decays. Draugrs do not last forever, and as they 'age', they become less and less like their original, living human, as their self-pattern, their hologram, naturally breaks down and disperses.

Mod, I believe, sends out buds or seeds of itself during life, which bear aspects of the living Selfhood. These floating 'Mod-seeds' attach to infants at the beginning of their life and bring their Mod-qualities with them. In my understanding, Mod itself generally partners with Ghost after life is over, and brings with it its strong hologram of life, its willpower, strength and experience.

Hugr strongly holds to the holographic-self after death, and keeps up with its Midgard connections and involvement as an ancestral or guiding spirit, or as an afflicting wight. The natural connection between Hugr and Sefa continues after death through the hologram, their life-long experiences of relationships and all they have learned therefrom. Hugr is likely to reincarnate at some point; the degree to which it retains traces of its previous selfhood-hologram varies a great deal from person to person. Hugr, Mod and Ghost are the ones who inherit or incorporate the Sefa-hologram most strongly after death.

Saiwalo-Dwimor's holographic inheritance consists of its treasure-hoard of images, which it collects during Midgard life.

Summary

Our whole soul-household sings our Sefa-soul into being, which holds our sense of Self, and creates a hologram of the shared life of all our souls as we live our lifetime in Midgard. Sefa is focused on relationships both within our soul-household, and in the greater world outside ourselves. It connects tangible and intangible beings and things together, and has powers of perceptiveness, insight and understanding that give it the skills necessary for these tasks. After death, our Sefa-self's holographic being is shared among all of our surviving souls.

© *Tomas Castelazo, www.tomascastelazo.com / Wikimedia Commons / CC BY-SA 4.0*

The souls cast reflections across the Worlds, which coalesce into the image of the Self.

Chapter 18

18. Closing Thoughts and Topical Summaries

Evaluating and changing our concepts and understanding about something as fundamental as 'soul' and 'self' is a long and challenging process. The rewards come as we gradually feel a more coherent and steady sense of who we are, how we want to live our lives, how we can relate to others (physical and spiritual beings) in better ways, and perhaps most fundamentally, how we can express who we really are into Midgard life, and fulfill the full promise of our wyrd, of all the sacred strands that go into our making.

This book offers the knowledge-foundations to point us in these directions. Book II in this series, *Heathen Soul Lore: A Personal Approach,* provides further discussion and insights on each of the souls, and offers exercises and guidelines for those who wish to begin applying personalized Heathen soul lore to any or all aspects of their daily life.

As we bring this book to a close, I want to return to the idea with which I began this study: that we have multiple souls, with different sources, natures, footholds and connections with our body, and afterlife fates.

Another Look at Multiple Souls

In Chapter 1, I offer a definition for what I call the existential theory of souls. The criteria for defining a soul using this approach are: (1) the soul confers life by its presence, and its absence means death. These are the life-souls. Or, conversely, (2) the soul can exit the living body temporarily and take action on its own, without causing death; these are the daemon-souls. And / or (3) the soul has an independent, stand-alone afterlife. One of the souls I have discussed here, the Sefa / Sebo, does not fit into these criteria. Instead, I believe it is a soul sung into being by all our other souls together, and functions as the coordinator of our souls and the residence of our 'sense of Self' during life.

Having laid out my research and thoughts about the nature of the souls, I want to offer another argument in favor of the idea that we have a number of different souls, rather than having several dependent soul-parts fitting into a single soul, as is more commonly assumed. My argument here is based on cosmology: on the perception that our multiple souls are connected to multiple worlds, cosmological processes and beings. They come into being in different ways, are connected by various flows of energies to different worlds and beings, and have different fates in the afterlife. To me, these are indications of individual soul-beings, rather than soul-parts. Here is a review of these souls, focused on cosmological details, to support this argument.

Closing Thoughts and Topical Summaries

Origins, Nature, and Destinations of the Souls

Our life-soul Ferah comes into being as a flash of lightning during physical conception; I might call it a flash of 'lifening'! Ferah's powerful life-energy and life-substance are most closely aligned with Deities of Earth, Thunder and Lightning: those whose own powers flow through the living world of Midgard and support the life processes therein. Ferah-souls comprise an interconnected network of vital energies, linking together humans, other living beings, flows of natural energies, Deities and spirits into an ordered system governed by natural laws in Midgard.

After death, Ferah may become a spirit associated with Midgard nature in some way, or may join the ambient surges of Midgard life-energy and life-substance. Powerful Ferahs may become the kind of guardian spirits reflected in the Matronae of Roman times: place-based spirits or *genii loci* of rivers, cities, regions, clan and tribal domains rooted in a specific area.

I think that one possibility, among others, for the Ferah soul after death is to accompany its partner Hugr soul, and perhaps one or more landwights as well, to form together a powerful ancestral or semi-divine land-warder spirit. Alternatively, we can make our own Ferah a deliberate gift to the Gods: growing our Ferah's strength, beauty and connections throughout our lives, and at the time our death comes to us, offering it to the Holy Ones with love and dedication.

Ahma / Ǫnd is eternal, unchanging spiritual essence, rising from the primal energies of Fire and Ice, from the great Ginnungagap of all potential which opens up between these

Heathen Soul Lore

polarities, and from Hvergelmir, the Roaring Cauldron, the Source of proto-being which flows forth from the Gap. Ahma brings our breath of life with it, and bears it away when it leaves. Birth and death of the body have no direct effect on Ahma.

Ghost is formed from and filled by Ahma, wrapped in a pod or soul-skin, generally by one or more Deities. The unshaped spiritual essence of Ahma is shaped by the soul-skin of the Ghost into a personal being with its own characteristics and nature. Ahma flows into Ghost as divine breath and inspiration, and enters Midgard through our breath and our Ghost-Mind, with their connections to our other souls and body. The human Ghost mirrors the personal Deities, who are shaped, by their own power, from Ahma, the essence of impersonal Godhead or Source, into personal beings with their own distinct natures.

Ghost is formed for us at the time of our birth, and rides in upon our first breath of life to take root within us. It departs upon our last breath, as we 'give up the Ghost.' The usual afterlife of Ghost is residence with whichever Deities it was closest to during life, to participate in the God-Homes with the activities and purposes of those Deities. In some cases, Ghost may choose to disembody itself and return to the primal Ahma, impersonal Spirit, from which it was formed, rather than heading to the God-Homes. A severely unhealthy or damaged Ghost, or the Ghost of a person who is extremely tightly connected to living persons or Midgard affairs, may end up as a haunt drifting in the spiritual plane of Midgard, until the situation or condition that caused this is resolved.

The Hama is closely linked to the body both during life and after death, in the form of our Lich-Hama, our ensouled physical body. It comes into being in the womb, imprinted and energized by Ferah, Saiwalo-Dwimor, and one or more Deities, and bears the spiritual blueprint for our body and physical life: our appearance, physical and social abilities, and living energies, in the form of La, Læti and Litr. The structures of the womb itself (caul, placenta, afterbirth) are considered to contain a spirit of luck, the *hamingja*, which accompanies the person throughout life.

After death, if the body is cremated, then the Hama dissolves and its energy returns to the ambient pool of natural energies. If the body goes through the process of decomposition, then the Hama's energy gradually decomposes along with the flesh, but some of the energy will remain as the 'soul of the bones.' Some necromantic and shamanic practices make use of this soul-energy lingering in the bones of people, and of animals.

Aldr is given to us by the Norns at birth, and with it comes the ørlög or orlay they have spun for us. As our life proceeds, Aldr continues its connection with the Norns, feeding strands of new orlay back and forth between them and our Midgard life. Orlay builds up this way in the Norns' Well, and in our Werold-hama, the cloak that Aldr weaves, containing all the experiences and deeds of our life: our personal world. Aldr continually feeds nourishing and healing spiritual energies into our Lich-Hama, seeking always to extend our life-span, our vigor and vitality. Thereby, it fills our Ealdoryard, the spiritual container of Aldr which coincides with the outline of our physical body.

Aldr governs the timing of events in our life, and our relationship with Time itself. It can be considered our body-in-time, as our Lich-Hama is our body-in-space. When our life is over, Aldr, dressed in its Werold-hama, proceeds to the Doom-stead of the Gods and Norns. There, our lifetime's experience and deeds, our Werold-hama or cloak, is observed and acknowledged by the Holy Ones, and—if deserved—is blessed and fastened into the Well of Wyrd. There, it waters the sacred roots, thereby becoming one more layer of All-That-Is upon the Tree of Worlds.

Mod souls develop, over evolutionary time, from elementals, nature-based spirits or daemons, associated with microbes and other natural beings. Through association with humans and their other souls over generations, especially with Sefa and Hugr, Mod-daemons become humanized, strongly influencing our temperament and character, our mind and motivations, but keep their basic characteristics as powerful daemon-souls.

Mod is characterized by its Will, strength, power, determination, might and main: physical, mental and spiritual, and uses its access to natural flows of Midgard energy to maintain its might. It is especially connected with Thor and his family, and their flows of might and main. Highly developed human Mod-souls have *modcraft:* strategic intelligence and wisdom, characteristic of leaders, counselors, elders, wise queens and kings. Frigg embodies this modcraft, and can guide its development among humans. After death, Mod is likely to accompany our Ghost-soul, either in its afterlife in the God-Homes, or as a haunt. In some cases, it may return to being an elemental or nature-spirit, or migrate to become the Mod-soul of a different kind of being.

Hugr arises as a wisp of longing from the wetlands of Hel, and filters up into Midgard. There, it encounters afterlife Hugr-spirits who have previously incarnated within human soul-households. After further development, the new Hugr incarnates and begins its long cycle of learning through successive reincarnations. During this process it develops many aspects of character, thought, emotion, temperament, willpower, and the need for and interest in human attachments and human life. Through the experience of lifetimes, Hugr becomes wise, subtle, and powerful.

After death, the experienced Hugr may become an ancestral spirit, a guide and warder for a time, a Dis, Alf, or Fylgja, until reincarnating again. Ill-intentioned afterlife Hugrs may become afflicting spirits, given many names in folklore, who cause illness, nightmares, bad luck, loss of fertility and other problems for living humans. Odin is the exemplar of Hugr's nature and its powers, a patron of this soul among humans.

Saiwalo is the Hel-dweller, who remains rooted in Hel and sends an image or phantom, a Dwimor, into Midgard to ensoul a person. The Dwimor serves as an alchemical matrix, attracting and holding all a person's souls and body together during life. Saiwalo-Dwimor is not closely involved with our Midgard personality and activities, but it generates, gathers, and mutates mental-emotional images which influence us and those around us. After death, the Dwimor-phantom returns to its Saiwalo in Hel, bearing with it a hoard of images that it collected during life, which then shape our Saiwalo soul's perceptions of its habitat and existence in Hel.

Sefa arises from within a person, the expression of all their souls singing or vibrating together. Sefa holds our sense of Self, of how all our souls interrelate and interact together during Midgard life. Sefa focuses on 'self and other': the relationships among our own souls, among humans (living and after life), and between humans, Deities, and other spirits. It is perceptive, understanding, insightful: qualities that it uses to strengthen its relationships. The Goddesses Sif, Sjöfn, Frigg, Vör, and the other companions of Frigg are matrons of Sefa. During life, Sefa creates a hologram of all the souls' experiences, which is retained by the other souls when they separate after Midgard life is over.

My argument is that these souls are different enough, in their origins, nature, connections, and afterlife fates, to reasonably be regarded as individual soul-beings, rather than as dependent parts of one soul.

Soul-Footholds

In my understanding, our souls have what I call footholds in our physical body and its life-processes: places where that soul interfaces most powerfully with our physical life. Here is a review of each soul's foothold in the body. These different footholds give further illustration of the nature and functions of each of the souls.

Ferah fills our entire body with its etheric life-substance. I think the channels of energy that are identified in Eastern systems as Qi and Prana run through this Ferah-substance, as do our sensations and many of our instinctual reactions. Our perceptions, both physical-sensory and metaphysical, are also linked with our Ferah.

Ahma and Ghost have their foothold in our breath, lungs and diaphragm, while Ghost-Mind hovers over our brain and interpenetrates it.

Hama is integrally connected with its creation, our Lich-Hama or living body, and especially with the blood, hair, skin and outer appearance. It shows itself in the activities, skills and abilities of our body, including our voice, body language, expressions, behavior and personal characteristics.

Aldr's foothold lies in our bone marrow and in the many fluids of our body, whose subtle energies are held within the body by our Ealdoryard, the Aldr's boundary that coincides with our physical exterior. Many of our body fluids are regulated by cycles of time: the rise and fall in levels of hormones, neurotransmitters, digestive / reproductive / immune-related fluids, the fluids that bathe and nourish our brain, spinal column and bone marrow, and many others, influenced by diurnal, lunar and seasonal cycles and by our age and stage of life. These are among the means by which Aldr influences our physical body and our body-in-time; they are Aldr's foothold in our body. The fluids ruled by Aldr symbolically mirror Aldr's source in the waters of the Norns' Well.

Aldr is also a soul which feeds nourishment to our body, especially the spiritual and energetic nourishment contained in food that is close to its natural state. Emotional nourishment is gained through all the work that humans do together to grow, obtain, prepare, celebrate, and share the food. These aspects of nourishment work together to optimize our life-span, vitality and wellbeing.

Mod is seated in our solar plexus and abdomen, meshed with our microbiome and with the powerful energy centers in this region. Mod gives us strength and vigor at all levels: physical, mental, emotional, spiritual. The interactive processes of digestion, metabolism, energy production, muscles and tendons, reproductive system, and immune system all influence and are influenced by the state of our Mod. Mod can express its power through the gaze of the eyes, as we see in Thor's intense, fiery gaze, the fierce gaze of wild beasts, and the deep wells of wisdom seen in Frigg's eyes.

Sefa resides in the heart, and Hugr in the breast, around and in the heart. They are also associated with our organs of perception, our brain, and the many biochemical processes that generate and are generated by our emotions. With their focus on relationship and kinship, and Hugr's root in desire, these souls are heavily invested in the body's involvement with sexuality, mating and reproduction.

Saiwalo-Dwimor, in my perception, has no actual physical connection with the body, except in the sense that in phantom form it is the image of our body. Dwimor is the metaphysical (non-physical) matrix which attracts and holds together the other souls and their energies during Midgard life.

Different Religions, Different Perspectives

Here is another question that comes up, as we consider the perspective on Heathen souls that I present here. What should we make of the fact that different religions, philosophies, and schools of psychology all have different ideas about what 'the soul' is, where it comes from, where it goes to, and 'who is in charge of it' during, before, and after our physical life? Wars are fought, people are ostracized, impoverished, enslaved, tortured and killed over these questions, not to mention defined as being 'insane' or 'evil' based on 'wrong beliefs.' What is 'the soul', and how many of them do we have?

As I make clear in this book, I perceive us as having multiple souls. I also perceive that souls are not like physical entities with clear, firm boundaries, where we can say with certainty where one ends and another begins. I see them as

Closing Thoughts and Topical Summaries

being more like Venn diagrams of overlapping circles, or 'fuzzy sets' where the properties of one category blur into the properties of another. I perceive them as being multidimensional, extending into dimensions beyond our familiar space and time, which makes putting them into any definitional boxes more difficult.

I think that religions, philosophies, and sciences each define souls in ways that fit with their overall worldview and understanding of theology, cosmology, psychology, biology, neurology, and the like. And this works for each of them in context, because the souls are amorphous, elastic, fractal, holographic, multidimensional beings. Souls can adapt to the 'containers' of belief in which they are placed. Or, more accurately, our understanding and experience of our souls can so adapt. Souls can be sorted in different ways, placed into different containers of belief. My own approach to Heathen soul lore is one such container.

This gives rise to another question: are some 'containers' of belief more desirable than others? More healthy, more expansive, more compassionate, more 'soulful', more insightful, or whatever? I think this is so, and I am biased in favor of the Heathen ideas about the souls that I pursue in my soul lore studies. This is based on my values, interests, beliefs and aspirations. I fully acknowledge that a follower of a different belief system would see the landscape of soul lore quite differently, and I would not try to argue them out of it.

It's like looking at light. Is light all one color, white? Or is it a spectrum of rainbow colors? The answer to both questions is 'yes'; it depends on what kind of lens one is looking through. Don't forget: our human eyeball is a lens, and so are the eyes of insects, fish, animals, who all see light somewhat differently or very differently. There is no way we can perceive light without looking through some kind of lens.

My soul-lens is a Heathen one, colored by Heathen understandings of multiple Deities, multiple Worlds, multiple Beings across the worlds, multiple states-of-being for souls before, during and after physical life, multiple strands of time and wyrd, history, genetics, kinship, and many other influences interwoven to make us who we are, day by day, life by life. It is no surprise, then, that I see the rainbow spectrum when I look at soul-light. I see our souls as being the players, the actors, in this great game of Being, and I think that one soul, and one color of light, would not be enough to capture, experience, enact and express everything that is really going on.

"It takes a village to raise a child," and it takes a soular-system of interactive beings to create a fully responsive, aware, active, multidimensional Self for each person, during each lifetime, while at the same time interacting with other worlds and beings, outside of the space and time of our everyday lives. There's a lot going on out there, in our World and in all the others, and we benefit by approaching it as a team of soul-beings, each with its own strengths and abilities, perceptions, origins and destinations.

The Meaningfulness of Soul Lore Study

It seems to me that the study of ancient words, and their etymologies or histories, taken in context within ancient writings, can be a key to waking up and recognizing our own souls. The word-complexes are like lures or songs, or runes, that awaken the relevant souls, calling to them through the mists of time and worlds. Even the confusions and contradictions that arise from these studies are alluring, like the pieces of a jigsaw puzzle or an intriguing riddle that we want to keep working on until we've solved it to our own satisfaction. The solutions that we find might be unique to us, or might be relevant to others, too. They might, or might not, be something that can be firmly supported by scholarly references. But that is not the point, nor the end-goal, of this endeavor.

The end-goal is to know our own souls, and to understand their relationships with each other, with the Holy Ones, ancestors, powers and spirits of nature, with living people and all the other beings of this and other worlds. There are many ways such goals may be accomplished, of course. But the study of ancient soul-words offers a unique gateway to forgotten knowledge, a place from which to begin our journey toward understanding. It starts us off in the direction we want to go, and helps us make sense of all the knowledge and experience we gather along the way as we live our life.

Pursuing soul lore through ancient languages also offers a direct and vital link to ancestral pools of knowledge, and to one's ancestors themselves, an important consideration for many Heathens. I suggest that the methods I use for soul lore study can be extended into other historically-based Pagan religions and their ancient languages, for the same purpose.

I also envision that modern Heathens from all different ancestral backgrounds can enrich their own practice by pursuing language roots that connect them with their own kin and the ancient cultures of their kin. For so many people, in so many times and places of the world, ancestral connection is deeply meaningful. Learning even a few relevant words from the ancient languages of our kin-lines, whatever they may be, is one way of awakening our souls, who stretch their roots through Time, Wyrd and Worlds.

There is another very good reason for pursuing soul lore. In today's world, overwhelmed with waste-products of both material substances and energy emanations, we need to focus more on meaningful activities that do not require much material and energy input, and that do not generate much waste. Inner exploration, and shared exploration of these realms with others close to us, offers each of us endless opportunities for worthwhile activity that generates little in the way of harmful waste and by-products. Quite the contrary, it encourages us to value non-material activities more, and to rely less upon material and energy-consuming things and activities.

Pursuing soul lore is life-changing, life-enhancing and enriching. It gives us the power of knowing who and what we are, and the ability to express this out into the world in a multitude of ways. It gives us the ability to understand others more deeply and interact with them in better ways: not only other humans, but other beings of this and other Worlds as well.

I wish you Gods'-speed on this great, ever-expanding journey of exploration!

Acknowledgements

True acknowledgement and appreciation are due to generations of people, known and unknown, over thousands of years of human spiritual exploration, and their efforts to express these explorations through language. But to bring it down to the personal and the present time, I want first to thank Dale Wood for his inspiring artwork and his proofreading. His art provides a whole new dimension to what I am trying to communicate with this book. I'm also grateful to Andromeda Whitefeather for the lovely sculpture of Njorð in Chapter 14.

Diana L. Paxson deserves great appreciation for her work, and her encouragement of writers, as long-time editor of *Idunna: A Journal of Northern Tradition*, where many of my original soul lore articles were first published. (This journal has recently been retitled *Idunna: A Journal of Inclusive Heathenry*.) Her many books relating to spiritual exploration and to Heathenry are an essential resource for Heathen spiritual work. The outstanding spaeworking / seiðr workshop that she and Laurel Olson Mendez offered in 1995 provided me with a solid foundation for Heathen spiritual exploration as a spaewife, for which I am forever grateful.

My warmest thanks and appreciation to John Michael Greer for reading and recommending this book, and for the great riches he offers with his own many books and blogs on wide-ranging topics of esoteric, philosophical, and cultural significance.

Cat Heath provided detailed proofreading and valuable pointers for correction, as well as inspiration from her own, truly outstanding book, *Elves, Witches and Gods:*

Spinning Old Heathen Magic in the Modern Day. I'm grateful for her kind words on the cover.

I offer further thanks for proofreading and feedback to James Martin and to WolfDraco.

To my dear husband Rosten Dean Rose, I'm grateful for all your support, help and love that nourish my life and souls. Thank you for many technical rescues during the writing process! I also want to say how fortunate I am, unlike many modern Pagans, in the friendly interest and support I've always received from my entire extended family, especially from my daughter and my mother, for my Heathen path and work, even from those whose religious or philosophical beliefs differ significantly from my own. For us, kinship trumps dogma as the higher value, a belief that is close to my own heart.

I feel the need to inject a note of humor here, as friends, family and I come up with ever-more ornate titles for the work I do. I mentioned in Chapter 15 that pushing Heathen soul-concepts through the meat-grinder of the Christian conversion process resulted in, effectively, soul-sausage, and referred to myself as a forensic soul-specialist trying to sort out the sausage. Diana Paxson's kind words of recommendation on the cover of this book have suggested another title for my work, while my husband has dashed off a haiku poem to tie it all together. Hence, the text for my next set of business cards:

"Forensic Soul Lore Specialist and Philological Adventurer for Hire: No words too long or too short; no soul-sausage left unsorted!"

Acknowledgements

Reverse linguistics:
Delectable morsels to
Unpack the sausage.

I owe a great deal to many modern Heathens: other authors, friends, acquaintances, colleagues, teachers, partners, fellow explorers of Heathen paths. I have learned from them all. Though each of us walks our own path, there are broad ways where many of us meet, as we wander back and forth across each others' paths, learning and sharing along the way.

Last, and greatest, comes my appreciation toward our Heathen Holy Ones, and all I have learned from and experienced through them, and with them. No words can express this, but they know of the trust and commitment that lie at the root of my souls.

I'll close with a verse about appreciating friendship (my own rendition of verse 119 of the *Havamál* in the Poetic Edda). I like to apply this aphorism not only to human friends and kin, but to the Holy Ones, and indeed, toward my growing knowledge of my own souls, the most intimate friends of all.

If you have faith in a friend of yours,
Fare you to find them again and again.
Brushwood and grass will soon grow high,
Covering the path no wayfarer walks.

Heathen Soul Lore

Let us keep the paths of wisdom, friendship, trust and faithfulness clear and well-trodden: the paths which weave together our own souls, our friends and kin in this World and the others, and the Holy Ones who bless us all.

Winifred Hodge Rose
Midsummer Day, 2021

Word-Hoard / Glossary

Æweweard, Éwart: Anglo-Saxon and Old High German terms, respectively, for a Heathen priest. The meaning is 'warder of the troth / covenant / law'.

Æsir: A tribe of Heathen Gods. Prominent members are Odin, Thor, Frigg, Tyr.

Ahma: The Gothic term for 'spirit', including the breath of life. I also use this word to indicate the cosmic field of spiritual proto-being that I envision arises from the meeting of Fire and Ice within Ginnungagap.

Aldr: One of the Heathen souls, which governs our lifespan and the timing of events in our life, and channels spiritual nourishment for us. Its meaning is closely related to 'old' and 'age, age of time.'

Alf (sing.), Alfar (pl.): This term can refer to a divine tribe of beings closely associated with the Æsir Gods, and is also used to designate the spirits of deceased male ancestors.

Asgard: The divine realm of the Æsir Gods, which includes many individual God-Halls within it.

Ask & Embla: The mythical first human couple, formed from trees or logs by Odin, Hœnir and Loðurr, or by Odin and his brothers Vili and Ve.

Athom: An Old Saxon word for the spirit and the breath of life.

Auðumla: In Norse mythology, a primal being in the form of a cow, whose name means 'the hornless cow of wealth / prosperity.' She appeared in Ginnungagap at the beginning of things, licked the shape of Buri, the first God, out of the enclosing ice, and fed Buri and Ymir with her milk. In my thought, she is a shape-shifting Mother-Goddess, and transformed herself into the realm of Hel. I believe she was the mother of Borr, the progenitor of the Æsir.

Bestla: The mother of Odin, Vili and Ve, and the sister of Mimir. I believe Bestla and Mimir were the unnamed pair who were generated under the arm of the primal Giant, Ymir. Thus, she, her brother Mimir, and her consort Borr were the first generation of offspring from the primal powers.

Borr: The son of Buri and consort of Bestla. As the father of Odin, Vili and Ve, he is the progenitor of the Æsir Gods.

Buri: In Norse lore, a primal being, progenitor of the Gods, who formed within the ice of Ginnungagap. He was licked free of the ice and fed by the Ur-Mother in the form of a cow, Auðumla.

Daemon, Daimon: A Greek word with complex meanings; here it is used to designate a soul or spirit which can exist and take action independently of its living physical body.

Dis (sing.), Disir (pl.): Literal meaning is a lady or a noblewoman; sometimes a demi-goddess. Most commonly used to indicate the spirits of one's deceased female ancestors.

Doppelgänger: The double or etheric twin of a person, a term used in reference to occult phenomena.

Draugr: A reanimated corpse; can also refer to a ghost. In my thought, the corpse is reanimated by the Hama soul.

Dwarves: Otherworldly beings who appear in many forms and roles in all the branches of Germanic folklore. Considered to be very wise and full of craft, but can be deceptive and are famed for bearing grudges. In Norse lore, Dwarves formed within the sacrificed body of the primal Giant Ymir; according to one account, they began as 'maggots' within Ymir's flesh, absorbing his-her energy and substance. In my view, Dwarves are masters of mod-energy, which they 'suck' or absorb from the natural and otherworldly environments, and sometimes from other beings as well, causing fatigue and illness. Dwarves absorb mod-energy, transform it, and use it to power their craft.

Dwimor: A phantom or apparition. I use this term specifically to designate the phantom of a living person which is created by the Saiwalo soul, and which serves as a matrix for holding together the energies of all the person's souls during life in Midgard.

Elivagar: A sea, encircling river, or multiple rivers that flow out of the great wellspring Hvergelmir in Norse mythology.

In my thought, Elivagar is a braided system of 'rivers' of energy which arise from the cosmic wellspring Hvergelmir, and surround, separate and nourish the various Worlds upon the World-Tree.

Ferah: One of the Heathen souls, which confers life, life-force, sensation, thought, feeling, behavior, piety, wisdom.

Frigg: The great Goddess of Asgard: mother, wisewoman, wife of Odin, mother of Baldr, leader of a group of helping-Goddesses, diplomat and frith-weaver / peace-weaver. Her name means 'beloved.'

Fjǫrgyn, Fjǫrgynn: An ancient Goddess and God, about whom little is known, except that Fjǫrgyn is one of the names of Thor's Mother, the Earth Goddess, and Fjǫrgynn is the father of Frigg. Presumably they are brother and sister, and perhaps spouses as well. Their names are cognate with the Proto-Indo-European Thunder-God, *Perkwunos.

Ghost: As I use this term, Ghost is one of our human souls, our 'spirit'. It is formed from primal, unshaped, transcendent Ahma-Spirit by being enwrapped in a soul-skin which gives it shape, coherence, personal characteristics, and personal consciousness.

Ginnungagap: In Old Norse lore, Ginnungagap is a place of primal chaos or nothingness. At either end are the primal powers of Fire and Ice, and in the temperate center is where the World Tree takes root. The ancient Giant Ymir was formed from the frozen rime at the icier end of Ginnungagap. The ancient divine Cow, Auðumla (whom I regard as the Ur-Mother) also arose from Ginnungagap, as did the progenitor of the Gods, Buri.

Hama, hama: The literal meaning is 'a covering'. In Norse folklore, the Hama manifests as a magical being, an occult shape with paranormal powers, which can fare forth from a person in spirit form, and is also associated with the womb, the caul, and the processes of gestation. In my soul lore theory, Hama shapes and ensouls our physical body, the Lich, and provides it with many abilities such as speech, behavior and action.

Hamingja: In Norse folklore, Hamingja is both a form of luck, and a spirit who bears and gives that luck to the person with whom it is associated. As with Hama, Hamingja is considered to reside in the womb / caul / afterbirth. It accompanies the child it was born with throughout life, as long as nothing dire occurs to destroy its luck or its connection to the person.

Hel: Hel, with its linguistic variations, is the term in all the Germanic languages for the place where souls go after death. It was not considered a place of punishment, but simply the residence of the dead. In Norse lore, Hel is also the name of a daughter of Loki, a Goddess of the dead and ruler of Hel. The word Hel is derived from Proto-Indo-European *kel-, meaning 'to cover, conceal.' Hel is the Hidden Land. The German Goddess Frau Holle derives her name from the same root, and is considered to be a guide and protector both during life and after death.

Heathen Soul Lore

Hiwscip, Hiwship: An Anglo-Saxon word referring to a household or group of people living together. I use it to refer to the household of soul-beings which makes up our personal 'soular-system.'

Hlin: A Goddess and companion of Frigg, whose name means 'protectress'. Quite possibly she is an aspect or emanation of Frigg's own protective powers. Germanic Goddesses were considered protectors of warriors in battle, as well as of all men, women, and children.

Holle, Frau Holle: A German Goddess much involved in all matters of daily Midgard life, especially those traditionally relating to women and children, and to food, agriculture and home. Her care for all humans extends before and after Midgard life, as well as during it. Her name is cognate with 'Hel', and Holle's domains of action include not only Midgard and Midgard's sky, but Underworld as well. Other roots of her name include words for 'benevolent, kind, gracious'. Holle is especially revered by the modern Heathen sect called Urglaawe.

Hugr: A powerful soul focused on Midgard activities, using faculties of thought and emotion to navigate the complexities of human social life. In my thought, Hugr is the soul which periodically reincarnates, and which continues its involvement with Midgard life even after death by becoming an ancestral spirit, an Alf or a Dis, or a guiding spirit, or if ill-natured, becoming an afflicting wight.

Hvergelmir: In Norse mythology, a well or wellspring located in the cold, Niflheim side of Ginnungagap, under a root of the World-Tree, from which the Elivagar river(s) flows. In my thought, Hvergelmir is centered in Ginnungagap and is the source of the energy flows that form the cosmos.

Jotnar, Giants: Considered to be descended from the hermaphroditic proto-Giant, Ymir. Norse Giants are grouped into several tribes, including Thursar, Jotnar, Rises, Frost-Giants, Berg- or Mountain Giants, Trolls, etc. Giants such as the Anglo-Saxon Eoten and German Riesen play a role in the folklore of other Germanic lands as well. In the Norse pantheon, many of the Æsir Gods are of Jotun descent through their mothers, including Odin, Thor, Vidar, Magni and Modi.

La, Lö: Life-force that expresses itself through blood and the warmth it gives to the body, and through the health and beauty of hair and skin. Given to Ask and Embla by Loðurr, or by one of Odin's brothers, Vili or Ve (Vili, in my view).

Læti: Another gift given to Ask and Embla by Loðurr, consisting of speech, the ability to move and take action, and of the characteristic behaviors of human beings.

Landwights: Land-spirits, beings who inhabit spiritual planes of Earth / Midgard, and involve themselves with the features and processes of landscapes and ecosystems. They range in size / power from smaller beings inhabiting trees, rocks, small spaces, up to mighty warders of large areas and phenomena such as mountains, lakes and storms. At the latter end, they merge into the domains of the Jotnar and Deities.

Heathen Soul Lore

Lich-Hama, Lich: Lich is the physical body; Lich-Hama or Lichama is the living body ensouled by its Hama.

Litr, Wlite: A gift of Loðurr / Odin's brother, consisting of our physical shape and appearance, enlivened by the energies of our souls shining through that appearance. *Litr* is the Norse term, *Wlite* is Anglo-Saxon.

Magni: A son of Thor and the giantess Jarnsaxa, embodiment of might and main. He survives Ragnarök and is one of the leading Deities of the new world that comes after.

Matronae: A multitude of Goddesses, demi-Goddesses, ancestral warding spirits of tribes and clans, and land- and river-warding spirits, who flourished during the time of the Roman empire. Both Germanic and Celtic Matronae are recognized, as well as some whose provenance is not clear. Many stone altars and thanks-offerings to them have been found, especially in the region of what is now Germany, but extending all over Europe and Britain in the wake of the Roman Empire and their troops. These matronly beings are honored by modern Heathens, as well.

Mægen, megin, main: Power, force, energy that is inherent in living beings, magical objects, and otherworldly beings.

Midgard: The World of Earth and all it encompasses. It means 'middle yard, enclosure', a word and meaning that existed in all the Germanic languages, often in the form of 'middle earth' meanings. This term implies an assumption that there are 'upper' and 'lower' worlds as well. According to Norse lore, Midgard was formed from Ymir's sacrificed body by Odin, Vili and Ve.

Mimir and his Well: Mimir is an ancient, wise Giant, the uncle and teacher of Odin. He was beheaded while a hostage with the Vanir, but Odin preserved his head and continues to receive wise rede from it. Mimir's Well is considered a place of great wisdom and mystery. Odin pledged his eye to this well in exchange for runic knowledge, and the well also is said to contain Heimdal's horn and his hearing or his ear. My idea is that Mimir's Head / Well is 'World-Mind' or the Noösphere, the realm where Thought occurs.

Mod: One of the Heathen souls, which has a powerful influence on our character and actions in Midgard. Mod's strengths include our Will, energy, determination, and courage, and reflects in our moods.

Mod-power: I envision this as a form of energy similar to mægen / megin, except that it is shaped by the mood and character of the being who is accessing and expressing it.

Moði: A son of Thor and the giantess Jarnsaxa, embodiment and channel of mod-power. He survives Ragnarök and is one of the leading Deities of the new world that comes after.

Niflheim: In Norse lore, the cold, icy end of the primal space called Ginnungagap. The word means 'mist-world'. In my thought, the term Niflheim describes the mist of spiritual proto-being, the field of Ahma, that continually arises from Ginnungagap, generated by the primal polarities of Ice and Fire. This mist is the basis for all subsequent shapings of worlds and beings.

Norns: Three womanly beings, possibly Giants though their origins are unclear. In Norse lore they are named Urðr, Verðandi, and Skuld, representing 'What-Is', 'What Is Becoming', and 'Debt, or What Should Be.' They live beside the Well of Wyrd / destiny, called Urðarbrunnr, and nourish the World-Tree with mud and water from the Well. They speak ørlög or fate for humans, and the council or doom-stead of the Gods takes place near their Well; presumably they participate in these councils. There are also lesser norns, who appear as fairy godmothers and similar beings involved with people's fates. In Anglo-Saxon, these beings are called the Wyrdæ.

Odin, Oðinn, Woden: One of the chief Gods of the Aesir, son of Borr, brother of Vili and Ve, husband of Frigg, father of Thor and Baldr. He involves himself heavily in Midgard affairs.

Ǫnd: Old Norse word meaning both 'spirit' and 'breath'.

Ørlög, Orlay: This word means the 'ur-layers, primal layers', and is related to the words for 'law.' These layers are laid by the Norns, shaped from the deeds and events of humankind and Midgard, as well as the other Worlds and beings. In turn, ørlög influences the lives and life-spans of living humans. Ørlög is the Old Norse term, Orlæg or Orlay is Anglo-Saxon.

Proto-Germanic: A language which has been reconstructed by modern scholars; the prehistoric ancestor of Germanic languages such as Anglo-Saxon, Old Saxon, Old Norse, Frisian, Old High German, Frankish, etc. Gothic is the closest historical language to Proto-Germanic.

Proto-Indo-European, PIE: The prehistoric, reconstructed root of all Indo-European languages, ancient and modern.

Ragnarök: 'The destiny or fate of the Gods,' a great battle between the Gods and the Jotnar or Giants, with the dead from different realms participating on different sides. Some modern Heathens regard Ragnarök as having already happened, in the form of the forcible conversions from Heathenism / Paganism to Christianity during the early Middle Ages. Others regard it as an event yet to come, and some see Ragnarok as a cyclical, recurrent event, having already happened in the past, and still to come again in the future.

Saiwalo, Sawl, Seola, etc: The root of our word 'soul'. In Heathen belief, this is the afterlife soul, which naturally goes to Hel as the realm of the dead.

Sefa, Sebo: In old Germanic texts, a soul or soul-part especially attuned to emotions and relationships. The word probably relates to other words for 'sib' and 'relative', and to words for 'self.' In my thought, Sefa is a soul which arises from the interactions of all our other souls. It contains our perception of 'self' and 'self in relation to others.'

Seiðr, Seidh: In Nordic cultures, a practice similar to witchcraft, with a strong focus on oracular work and faring in spirit-forms. In modern Heathen use, it often refers to oracular trance practices.

Sif, Sibbe, Sippe: A Goddess, in Norse mythology the wife of Thor and mother of Ullr and Thruðr. Her name is related to the words for 'kinship, relationship' in all the Germanic languages, and she supports and protects this important domain of life. Some also consider her to be the Goddess of grain, with a belief that thunder and lightning are necessary to cause the grain to ripen, reflecting the relations between Sif and Thor. I envision her as the 'frith-sib of the folk', a peace-weaver who graciously shares her home and blessings with living folk and with the many human spirits who reside with her, Thor and their family in the afterlife.

Sjöfn: A Goddess and companion of Frigg; a promoter and protector of love, marriage and relationships generally.

Soular-system: An expression I invented to designate the group of soul-entities who collectively create a living person here in Midgard.

Spaecraft, spaework: As used here, and in modern Heathen terminology, these words refer to a practice of oracular trance work, often performed in a group setting, other times performed individually, to explore questions and issues of interest to the querents.

Syn: The Goddess Syn wards the doors of the hall, and closes them against those who must not enter. She is called on at the Thingsteads (assemblies) when one wishes to refute an accusation, and is considered the Goddess of Denial. (*Gylfaginning* p. 30, Edda). I view her as the "Just Say No" Goddess, the one who helps us protect our healthy and necessary boundaries against intrusion.

Thor, Thunor, Donar, Donner: A well-loved and much-trusted God among ancient and modern Heathens, wielding the power of thunder and lightning. His great Hammer is used to defend the Deities and Midgard against destructive forces, and is also used for hallowing and blessing. Thor is Sif's husband, and is the father of Magni, Modi and Thruðr. His hall Bilskirnir ('ray of light lightning-strike') lies within his domain, Thruðheim ('strength-home, strength-world'), and is the afterlife residence of many human spirits whose patron he was during life.

Thorlings: A term I invented, based on the Germanic suffix "*ling, lingas*" that implies 'belonging to or descended from' the name the suffix is attached to. Thus, Thorlings are those who are descended from Thor: Magni, Moði and Thruðr.

Thruðr: Daughter of Thor and the Goddess Sif. Her name means 'Strength'. Presumably she, like her brothers Magni and Modi, survives Ragnarök and becomes one of the leaders of the new world. Her father's godly domain bears her name: Thruðheim or 'strength-home, strength-world.'

Valhöl, Valhalla: 'Hall of the slain', Odin's hall where spirits of slain heroes—Einherjar—reside.

Heathen Soul Lore

Werold: A word meaning 'man-age', used in Anglo-Saxon, Old Saxon and Old High German, and referring to the totality of a person's life-span and life-experience. In Old Norse, the word is Veraldr.

Wode: One of the gifts given by Hœnir / Odin's brother when two trees or logs were transformed into the humans Ask and Embla. Wode refers to an ecstatic state of heightened spiritual—and sometimes physical—energy, which can take forms ranging from inspired eloquence and prophecy, artistic and intellectual genius, warrior focus and strength, to berserker rage, or outright madness. I see the gift of wode as a divine spark or a bridge, that enables humans to reach divine consciousness and communication with the Deities. If the person is not fit nor prepared for this, if their motives are skewed, or if they approach the Deities in inappropriate, offensive ways, the resulting flow of wode may backfire into negative forms.

World-Tree, Yggdrasil: The cosmic Tree, the structure of Space and all that exists within space. It is rooted in the three great Wells of power in Norse myth: Hvergelmir, Mimir's Well, and Urðr's Well, and the Nine Worlds are supported by its branches and roots.

Worlds, Nine Worlds: Norse mythology envisions nine worlds as the home-bases for different kinds of beings: Asgard for the Æsir, Vanaheim for the Vanir, Alfheim for the Alfar or elves, Midgard for humans, Svartalfheim for the Dwarves, Hel for the dead, Jotunheim for the Giants, and the Worlds of the primal energies: the World of ice and cold, Niflheim, and the World of Fire, Muspelheim.

Word-Hoard

Wyrd, and Well of: An Anglo-Saxon word derived from 'to become, to happen, to come to pass'; basically, 'to come into being.' This is the name of a being or a power that brings about destiny and fate in Anglo-Saxon lore, in particular, the circumstances of one's death. Wyrd is cognate with Norse Norn-name Urðr, and Wyrd's Well is the same as Urðarbrunnr: the Well of Fate (approximately). 'Fate, Destiny' and 'Wyrd' are not exactly the same, but overlap a good deal in meaning.

Ymir: A Giant, said to be hermaphroditic, who came into being within Ginnungagap at the beginning of the cosmos. Jotnar / Giants are descended from him-her, and I believe that the unnamed pair who were generated from beneath Ymir's arm were Mimir and Bestla, the uncle and mother of Odin, Vili and Ve. Ymir was sacrificed by Odin, Vili and Ve, and his-her body formed the foundations of Midgard and some of the other Worlds.

Yggdrasil: The 'steed of Ygg'. 'Ygg' means the 'terrible one', and is a byname of Odin. His 'steed' here is the World-Tree upon which he hung for nine days and nights to win the Runes.

"Yggdrasil, the Mundane Tree", by Oluf Olufsen Bagge.

Photograph and Artist Credits

Dale Wood's licensed artwork appears on the following pages: Cover; following the Dedication; 67; 91; 103; 113; 227; 249; 291; 367; 431; 439; 444; 464.

Other credits:

Page 28:
    Senja Norway: Ximonic (Simo Räsänen), CC BY-SA 4.0 <https://creativecommons.org/licenses/by-sa/4.0>, via Wikimedia Commons

Page 29:
    "Milky Way" ESO/S. Brunier, CC BY 4.0 <https://creativecommons.org/licenses/by/4.0>, via Wikimedia Commons

Page 30:
    "Turbulent gust front." NOAA Photo Library, NOAA Central Library OAR/ERL/National Severe Storms Laboratory (NSSL), Public domain, via Wikimedia Commons

Page 39:
    "Lightning ground storm." Brandon Morgan littleppl85, CC0, via Wikimedia Commons

Page 40:
    "Forest ray of sunshine." www.Pixel.la Free Stock Photos, CC0, via Wikimedia Commons

Page 44:
    Huge tree at Oakfield Demense by louise price, CC BY-SA 2.0 <https://creativecommons.org/licenses/by-sa/2.0>, via Wikimedia Commons

Page 46:
    Purple lightning. Jeremy Thomas jeremythomasphoto, CC0, via Wikimedia Commons.

Page 48:
    Lightning and tree. https://unsplash.com/photos/fiJolJjKoC8

Heathen Soul Lore

Page 50:
    Relief 07 of Mother Hulda Fountain, Eschwege. Photo by Oliver Cossalter, CC BY-SA 3.0 <https://creativecommons.org/licenses/by-sa/3.0>

Page 65:
    "Schnitzerei 'Weinende Frau Holle' am Ostufer des Oderteich. Kassandro, CC BY-SA 4.0 <https://creativecommons.org/licenses/by-sa/4.0>, via Wikimedia Commons

Page 69:
    "Waldimnebel." Reinhard Hurt, CC BY-SA 3.0 <https://creativecommons.org/licenses/by-sa/3.0>, via Wikimedia Commons

Page 70:
    "The sun hides in the clouds above Kathmandu." Abpaudel, CC BY-SA 4.0 <https://creativecommons.org/licenses/bysa/4.0>, via Wikimedia Commons

Page 72:
    "Blowing snow over Langstrandtindan mountains, Norway." Ximonic (Simo Räsänen), CC BY-SA 3.0 <https://creativecommons.org/licenses/by-sa/3.0>, via Wikimedia Commons

Page 82:
    Two raven fledglings. Brian Campbell, CC BY-SA 4.0 <https://creativecommons.org/licenses/by-sa/4.0>, via Wikimedia Commons

Page 90:
    "Ghostly eclipse from southern Africa." Bruno Sanchez-Andrade Nuño from Washington, DC, USA, CC BY 2.0 <https://creativecommons.org/licenses/by/2.0>, via Wikimedia Commons

Page 108:
    "Velleda: Effet de Lune." Eugène Lenepveu, CC BY-SA 4.0 <https://creativecommons.org/licenses/by-sa/4.0>, via Wikimedia Commons

Page 126:
    Relief 05 of Mother Hulda Fountain, Eschwege. Photo by Oliver Cossalter, CC BY-SA 3.0

Photograph and Artist Credits

<https://creativecommons.org/licenses/by-sa/3.0>, via Wikimedia Commons

Page 126:

<a href="https://www.freepik.com/photos/woman">Woman photo created by wirestock - www.freepik.com</a>

Page 131:

Burg Freudenberg Hexe: FHgitarre from Germany, CC BY 2.0 <https://creativecommons.org/licenses/by/2.0>, via Wikimedia Commons

Page 147:

"Foetus in placenta in utero."
https://wellcomeimages.org/indexplus/obf_images/ef/8b/490909253d240a35ebe235f5434b.jpg

Page 149:

Marble plaque showing parturition scene, Ostia, Italy.
https://wellcomeimages.org/indexplus/obf_images/45/53/1ca4947ef01a66b8b71e7cc0d498.jpg

Page 151:

Gold belt. Treasure case 04.2, Middle Bronze Age hoard from Burton, Wrexham. The Portable Antiquities Scheme/ The Trustees of the British Museum, CC BY-SA 4.0 <https://creativecommons.org/licenses/by-sa/4.0>, via Wikimedia Commons

Page 167:

"Tree of Hippocrates" Ad Meskens, CC BY-SA 3.0 <https://creativecommons.org/licenses/by-sa/3.0>, via Wikimedia Commons

Page 174:

Ask och Embla: Bengt Oberger, CC BY-SA 3.0 <https://creativecommons.org/licenses/by-sa/3.0>, via Wikimedia Commons

Page 179:

Three Norns and baby, photo by Taliesin, Pixabay.

Page 187:

"Ribe Vikinge Center, The Three Norns." Västgöten, CC BY-SA 3.0 <https://creativecommons.org/licenses/by-sa/3.0>, via Wikimedia Commons

Heathen Soul Lore

Page 191:
Flying bird. Matthew T Rader, https://matthewtrader.com, CC BY-SA 4.0 <https://creativecommons.org/licenses/by-sa/4.0>, via Wikimedia Commons

Page 192:
"Raddusch Aurochs." Pudelek (Marcin Szala), CC BY-SA 3.0 <https://creativecommons.org/licenses/by-sa/3.0>, via Wikimedia Commons

Page 199:
"Giant ocean wave," unknown author, Wikimedia Commons.

Page 214:
"Boom van Hippocrates." Ceescamel, CC BY-SA 4.0 <https://creativecommons.org/licenses/by-sa/4.0>, via Wikimedia Commons

Page 215:
"Pech Merle cave leopard spotting" (I must note that these are horses, not leopards, whatever the photograph-poster thought). HTO, User:Kersti Nebelsiek, Public domain, via Wikimedia Commons.

Page 226:
"Ritt zum Kufenstechen." Michael Gäbler, CC BY 3.0 <https://creativecommons.org/licenses/by/3.0>, via Wikimedia Commons

Page 231:
"Barn owl in flight." Worm That Turned, CC BY-SA 3.0 <https://creativecommons.org/licenses/by-sa/3.0>, via Wikimedia Commons

Page 232:
Borre Mound Cemetery. Bochum1805, CC BY-SA 2.0 <https://creativecommons.org/licenses/by-sa/2.0>, via Wikimedia Commons

Page 240:
"Awarded 1st Place The Owl by Col Richard Pugh." U.S. Army, CC BY 2.0 https://creativecommons.org/licenses/by/2.0>, via Wikimedia Commons

Page 244:
Short-eared owl on Seedskadee NWR.

Photograph and Artist Credits

Page 252:
"James Blalock: Harbinger." Elisabet Stacy-Hurley, CC BY-SA 4.0 <https://creativecommons.org/licenses/by-sa/4.0>, via Wikimedia Commons

Page 275:
"Grabstein von Niederdollendorf, Rückseite." Heiko Fischer, CC BY-SA 4.0 <https://creativecommons.org/licenses/by-sa/4.0>, via Wikimedia Commons

Page 277:
"De Makrallen Bever (Standbeeld van heks Marie Catier)." Erfgoedcel Pajottenland Zennevallei Parent institutionQ96098280 LocationDilbeek, BelgiumCoordinates50° 52' 04.836" N, 4° 12' 32.324" E Established2011 Authority control: Q94753063institution QS:P195,Q94753063, CC BY-SA 3.0 <https://creativecommons.org/licenses/by-sa/3.0>, via Wikimedia Commons

Page 311:
"Evolution of a tornado." JasonWeingart, CC BY-SA 4.0 <https://creativecommons.org/licenses/by-sa/4.0>, via Wikimedia Commons

Page 316:
Flying swan. EsterAce, CC BY-SA 4.0 <https://creativecommons.org/licenses/by-sa/4.0>, via Wikimedia Commons

Page 327:
"Holy Kinship, Silesia ca. 1500, Bode Museum." Daderot, Public domain, via Wikimedia Commons

Page 332:
Hans Thoma "Der Krieg", Städel Museum.

Page 344:
"Christian Gottlieb Kratzenstein-Stub: Hervör henter sværdet hos angartyr." (The original is spelled "angartyr" rather than "angantyr.")

Page 349:
"Fra Osebergfunnet." National Library of Norway, Public domain, via Wikimedia Commons.

Heathen Soul Lore

Page 352:
    Winslow Homer "Fog Warning". Boston Museum of Fine Arts.

Page 361:
    Relief 05 of Mother Hulda Fountain, Eschwege. Photo by Oliver Cossalter, CC BY-SA 3.0 <https://creativecommons.org/licenses/by-sa/3.0>, via Wikimedia Commons

Page 371:
    "Pakassaivo, 'Hell of Lapland'". Heikki Immonen, CC BY 3.0 <https://creativecommons.org/licenses/by/3.0>, via Wikimedia Commons

Page 374:
    White heron wading: Image by <a href="https://pixabay.com/users/kimdaejeung-7703165.

Page 376:
    "Hoher Meissner Frau Holle." User: Celsius at wikivoyage shared, CC BY-SA 3.0 <https://creativecommons.org/licenses/by-sa/3.0>, via Wikimedia Commons

Page 380:
    "Whales can fly (inverted)". Christopher Michel, CC BY 2.0 <https://creativecommons.org/licenses/by/2.0>, via Wikimedia Commons

Page 387:
    "Njordh" sculpture by Andromeda Whitefeather. https://www.etsy.com/shop/andromedaaltarcraft

Page 388:
    "Footprints in the sand." Rosendahl, Public domain, via Wikimedia Commons

Page 421:
    Externsteine relief Irminsul detail: Gunnar Ries, CC BY-SA 3.0 <https://creativecommons.org/licenses/by-sa/3.0>, via Wikimedia Commons

Page 423:
    Irminsul. Gunnar Ries, CC BY-SA 3.0 <https://creativecommons.org/licenses/by-sa/3.0>, via Wikimedia Commons

Photograph and Artist Credits

Page 441:
"Kowal (smithie) Wroclaw dwarf." Beata Zwolańska-HołodPnapora, CC BY-SA 3.0 <https://creativecommons.org/licenses/by-sa/3.0>, via Wikimedia Commons.

Page 446:
"Blue sky with wispy clouds." ProjectManhattan, CC BY-SA 3.0 <https://creativecommons.org/licenses/by-sa/3.0>, via Wikimedia Commons

Page 451:
"Foggy coastline." Alanthebox, CC0, via Wikimedia Commons.

Page 466:
Sigurd and Brunhild, by Harry George Theaker, 1920.

Page 473:
"Symbolic alchemical watercolour drawings Wellcome." https://wellcomeimages.org/indexplus/obf_images/59/32/8f4aae1a96ac4063e7518539ccdc.jpg

Page 479:
"Imir." Sokol_92, CC BY-SA 3.0 <https://creativecommons.org/licenses/by-sa/3.0>, via Wikimedia Commons

Page 480:
"Rain on the Mountain." Chris Light, CC BY-SA 4.0 <https://creativecommons.org/licenses/by-sa/4.0>, via Wikimedia Commons

Page 482:
"Highland cow." Elbert Alias, CC BY-SA 3.0 <https://creativecommons.org/licenses/by-sa/3.0>, via Wikimedia Commons

Page 484:
Salt crystals in Death Valley: Brocken Inaglory, CC BY-SA 4.0 <https://creativecommons.org/licenses/by-sa/4.0>, via Wikimedia Commons

Page 494:
"WAK Hastrungsfeld." (Frau Holle's mailbox.) Metilsteiner, CC BY-SA 3.0 <https://creativecommons.org/licenses/by-sa/3.0>, via Wikimedia Commons

Page 496:
"Crepuscular rays with reflection." Brocken Inaglory, CC BY-SA 3.0 <https://creativecommons.org/licenses/by-sa/3.0>, via Wikimedia Commons

Page 497:
"Pythagoras Award hologram." Zeptosecond, CC BY-SA 4.0 <https://creativecommons.org/licenses/by-sa/4.0>, via Wikimedia Commons

Page 503:
Archaeopteryx hologram, Wyoming Dinosaur Center. Greg Goebel from Loveland CO, USA, CC BY-SA 2.0 <https://creativecommons.org/licenses/by-sa/2.0>, via Wikimedia Commons

Page 506:
"Walking reflection." © Tomas Castelazo, www.tomascastelazo.com / Wikimedia Commons / CC BY-SA 4.0

Page 524:
"Walking between woodlands on the chalk" by Marathon, CC BY-SA 2.0 <https://creativecommons.org/licenses/by-sa/2.0>, via Wikimedia Commons

Page 558:
Fresco showing a woman so-called Sappho holding writing implements, from Pompeii, Naples National Archaeological Museum (14842101892) restored.jpg. Naples National Archaeological Museum, CC BY-SA 2.0 <https://creativecommons.org/licenses/by-sa/2.0>, via Wikimedia Commons.

Book-Hoard / Bibliography

Note: *Many of the older texts listed here can be found online for easy reference.*

Ælfric's Catholic Homilies, ed. Malcolm Godden. The Second Series, Text. Oxford UK: Oxford University Press, 1969.

Bang, Anton C. *Norske Hexeformularer og Magkiske Opskrifte*. Norway: Kristiania I Commission hos Jacob Dybwad, A. W. Broggers Bogtrykkeri, 1900-01.

Barber, Charles Clyde. *An Old High German Reader*. Oxford UK: Basil Blackwell, 1964.

Bauschatz, Paul. *The Well and the Tree: World and Time in Early Germanic Culture*. Amherst MA: University of Massachusetts Press, 1982.

Becker, Gertraud. *Geist und Seele im Altsächsischen und im Althochdeutschen: Der Sinnbereich des Seelischen und die Wörter gest-geist und seola-sela in den Denkmälern bis zum 11.Jahrhundert*. Heidelberg, Germany: Carl Winter Universitätsverlag, 1964.

Berr, Samuel. *An Etymological Glossary to the Old Saxon Heliand*. Berne, Switzerland:Herbert Lang & Co., 1971.

Bosworth, Joseph and George Waring. *The Gospels: Gothic, Anglo-Saxon, Wycliffe, and Tyndale Versions, fourth edition*. London, UK: Gibbings & Company, 1907.

Cathey, James E. *Heliand Text and Commentary*, Medieval European Studies II. Morgantown: West Virginia University Press, 2002.

Chesnutt, Michael. "Nordic Variants of the Guntram Legend." In *Arv: Scandinavian Yearbook of Folklore*, Vol. 47, 1991. Uppsala: The Royal Gustavus Adolphus Academy. Distributed by Almqvist & Wiksell International, Stockholm.

Heathen Soul Lore

Chickering, Howell D. Jr., transl. *Beowulf*. New York, NY: Doubleday,1977. (Dual language.)

Claus, David B. *Toward the Soul: An Inquiry into the Meaning of ψυχη before Plato*. New London CT: Yale University Press, 1981.

Cleasby, Richard, and Gudbrand Vigfusson. *An Icelandic-English Dictionary*. Oxford UK: Oxford University Press, 1894.

Colunaga, R.P. Roberto, and Laurentio Turrado. *Biblia Sacra iuxta Vulgatem Clementinam, nova Editio*. Madrid, Spain: La Editorial Catolica, S.A., 1953.

DeVries, Jan. *Altgermanische Religionsgeschichte. Band I*. Berlin, Germany: Walter de Gruyter & Co., 1956.

---. *Altnordisches Etymologisches Wörterbuch*. Leiden, Holland: E.J. Brill, 1961.

Diatessaron (Tatian's Harmony, four Gospels merged into one.) http://www.earlychristianwritings.com/text/diatessaron.html.

Eggers, Hans. "Altgermanische Seelenvorstellungen in Lichte des Heliand." *Jahrbuch des Vereins für Niederdeutsche Sprachforschung*. 1957 / 80. Neumünster, Germany: Karl Wachholtz Verlag.

Egil's Saga, transl. Hermann Palsson and Paul Edwards. Penguin Books, London. 1976.

Ellis, Hilda Roderick. *The Road to Hel: A Study of the Conception of the Dead in Old Norse Literature*. Cambridge University Press, London, 1943. (Some editions of this book have the author under her married name: Hilda Ellis Davidson.)

Erich, Oswald A. and Richard Beitl. *Wörterbuch der Deutschen Volkskunde*. Stuttgart, Germany: Alfred Kröner Verlag, 1955.

Book-Hoard

Eyrbyggja Saga, transl. Hermann Palsson and Paul Edwards. London, England: Penguin Books, 1989.

Goos, Gunivortus. *Goddess Holle*, 3rd revised and supplemented edition. Norderstedt, Germany: Books on Demand GMBH, 2019.

Greer, John Michael. *A Magical Education: Talks on Magic and Occultism.* London UK: AEON Books, 2019.

Grimm, Jacob. *Teutonic Mythology*, transl. James Steven Stalleybrass. London, UK: George Bell and Sons, 1882.

Gundarsson, Kveldúlf Hagan, compiler. *Our Troth, 2nd Edition, Volume I: History and Lore.* North Charleston, SC: BookSurge, 2006.

Hall, J.R. Clark, with supplement by Herbert D. Merritt. *A Concise Anglo-Saxon Dictionary, 4th Edition.* Toronto, Canada: University of Toronto Press, 1960.

Harbus, A. *The Life of the Mind in Old English Poetry*. Amsterdam and New York: Rodopi, 2002.

Heath, Cat. *Elves, Witches & Gods: Spinning Old Heathen Magic in the Modern Day*. Woodbury, MN: Llewellyn, 2021.

Heliand:
http://www.hieronymus.us.com/latinweb/Mediaevum/*Heliand*.htm.
(The line numbers I use for *Heliand* references in this book are taken from the numbering on this website, as being the most accessible for readers. Line numbering systems differ, in different references / versions.)

Heraclitus fragments: www.heraclitusfragments.com

Hervör's Saga: Peter Tunstall, transl. "The Saga of Hervör & King Heidrek the Wise", www.germanicmythology.com/FORNALDARSAGAS/HevararSagaTunstall.html. 2005. (Dual language version.)

Herrera, César E. Giraldo. *Microbes and Other Shamanic Beings*. Cham, Switzerland: Palgrave McMillan / Springer Nature, 2018.

Ibn Fadlan, Ahmad. *The Rus, c. 922*.
https://content.ucpress.edu/chapters/12938.ch01.pdf

Iliad, Book 23:
https://www.perseus.tufts.edu/hopper/text?doc=Perseus%3Atext%3A1999.01.0133%3Abook%3D23%3Acard%3D54

Inčiuraitė, Lina. "The Meaning of Soul in Ælfric's 'Catholic Homilies'." Vilnius University Institute of Foreign Languages. Verbum. Vilnius : Vilniaus universiteto leidykla. 2010, t. 1, p. 37-45. ISSN 2029-6223

Jonsson, Finnur. *De Gamle Eddadigte*. Köbenhaven, Denmark: G.E.C. Gads Forlag, 1932.

---. *Edda Snorra Sturlusonar*. Udgivnet efter Handskrifterne af Kommissionen for det Arnamagnaeanske Legat. København, Denmark: Gyldendalske Boghandel – Nordisk Forlag, 1931.

Kroonen, Guus. *Etymological Dictionary of Proto-Germanic*. Leiden Holland / Boston MA: Brill, 2013.

Laxdæla Saga, transl. by Magnus Magnusson and Hermann Palsson. Bungay, Suffolk, UK: Penguin Books Ltd., 1969.

Larrington, Carolyne, transl. *The Poetic Edda*. New York, NY: Oxford University Press, 2014.

Lecouteux, Claude. *Witches, Werewolves and Fairies: Shapeshifters and Astral Doubles in the Middle Ages*, transl. Clare Frock. Rochester, VT: Inner Traditions International, 2003.

Liberman, Anatoly. *Oxford Etymologist*.
https://blog.oup.com/2009/10/watered-down-etymologies

Kellogg, Robert. *A Concordance to Eddic Poetry*. East Lansing MI: Colleagues Press, 1988.

Koene, J.R., transl. *Heliand, oder das Lied vom Leben Jesu*. Münster, Germany: Druck und Verlag der Theissing'schen Buchhandlung, 1855. (Dual language, Old Saxon and German).

Mahlendorf, Ursula R. "OS Gest, OHG Geist." *Journal of English and Germanic Philology*, Vol. LIX, No.3, July 1960. Urbana, IL: University of Illinois Press.

Mallory, J.P. and D.Q. Adams, editors. *Encyclopedia of Indo-European Culture*. Chicago, IL: Fitzroy Dearborn Publishers, 1997. See especially entries under "Oak" and "Thunder."

Meyer, Elisabeth Marie. *Die Bedeutungsentwicklung von Germanischen *moda-*. Halle, Germany: Buchdruckerei des Waisenhauses, 1926

Mitchell, Stephen A. *Witchcraft and Magic in the Nordic Middle Ages*. Philadelphia PA: University of Pennsylvania Press, 2011.

Moalem, Sharon. *Survival of the Sickest: the surprising connections between disease and longevity*. New York NY: HarperCollins, 2007.

Motz, Lotte. "Of Elves and Dwarfs" in *Arv: Tidscrift for Nordisk Folkminnesforskning* (Journal of Scandinavian Folklore) Vol. 29-30, 1973-4. Published by The Royal Gustavus Adolphus Academy, Uppsala; distributed by The Almqvist & Wiksell Periodical Company, Stockholm, Sweden.

Murphy, G. Ronald. *The Saxon Savior*. Oxford, UK: Oxford University Press, 1989.

Odyssey, Book 11: http://www.perseus.tufts.edu/hopper/text?doc=Perseus%3Atext%3A19 99.01.0135%3Abook%3D11%3Acard%3D601

Heathen Soul Lore

O'Neill, Patrick, ed. *King Alfred's Old English Prose Translation of the first 50 Psalms*. Cambridge, MA: The Medieval Academy of America, 2001.

Onians, Richard Broxton. *The Origins of European Thought about the Body, the Mind, the Soul, the World, Time, and Fate*. Cambridge, UK: Cambridge University Press, 1954.

Online Etymology Dictionary, www.etymonline.com

Paxson, Diana L. *Odin: Ecstasy, Runes & Norse Magic*. Newburyport, MA: Weiser Books, 2017.

---. *Taking Up the Runes: A Complete Guide to Using Runes in Spells, Rituals, Divination, and Magic*. York Beach, ME: Weiser Books, 2005.

Phillips, J.B. *The New Testament in Modern English, revised edition*. New York: Macmillan Publishing Co., Inc. 1972.

Polomè, Edgar C. "Some Comments on Voluspà, Stanzas 17-18." *Journal of Indo-European Studies, Monograph 6*. Washington, D.C.: Institute for the Study of Man, 1989. (My thanks to Dr. Ben Waggoner for this reference.)

Poo, Mu-chou, ed. *Rethinking Ghosts in World Religions*. Boston MA: Brill, 2009.

Ramakrishna Rao, K.B. *Advaita Vedanta: Problems and Perspectives*. Special Lectures Series, University of Mysore 78. Parasanga, India: University of Mysore, 1980.

Rijckaert, Arseen. *Hippocrene Standard Dictionary Dutch-English / English-Dutch*. New York, NY: Hippocrene Books, 1997.

Rodriguez, Louis J. *Anglo-Saxon Verse Charms, Maxims and Heroic Legends*. Chippenham, Wiltshire, England: Anglo-Saxon Books, 1993.

Rose, Winifred Hodge. https://heathensoullore.net/
~ "An Anglo-Saxon Charm Against a Dwarf: Shapeshifting, Soul Theft, and Shamanic Healing"

Book-Hoard

~ "Disir, Hama and Hugr as Healing Partners"
~ "Images of Orlay"
~ "The Kindly Gods Go Wandering"

Rune Poems: https://en.wikisource.org/wiki/Rune_poems

Russell, James C. *The Germanization of Early Medieval Christianity: A Sociohistorical Approach to Religious Transformation.* New York: Oxford University Press, 1994.

Rydberg, Viktor, transl. by Rasmus B. Anderson. *Teutonic Mythology: Gods and Goddesses of the Northland.* New York, NY: Norroena Society, 1906.

Scavenius, H. and B. Berulfsen, *McKay's Modern Norwegian-English / English-Norwegian Dictionary (Gyldendal's).* New York, NY: David McKay Co. Inc., no date.

Schreiwer, Robert, and Ammerili Eckhart. *A Dictionary of Urglaawe Terminology.* www.urglaawe.org. 2012.

Simek, Rudolf. *Dictionary of Northern Mythology,* transl. Angela Hall. Stuttgart, Germany: Alfred Kroener Verlag, 1993.

Simpson, Jaqueline. *Icelandic Folktales and Legends.* Berkeley and Los Angeles: University of California Press, 1972. (Includes notes relating the "witch bridle" theme to those of other countries as well.)

Simrock, Karl. *Die Edda: Die ältere und jüngere Edda und die mythischen Erzählungen der Skalda.* Essen, Germany: Phaidon Verlag, 1987.

Skeat, W.W. *A Mœso-Gothic Glossary.* London, UK: Asher & Co., 1868.

Snell, Bruno. *The Discovery of the Mind: The Greek Origins of European Thought.* New York, NY: Harper & Bros. 1960.

Storms, Gustav. *Anglo-Saxon Magic.* New York, NY: Gordon Press, 1974. *Sið Gealdor,* p.216-223.

Heathen Soul Lore

Strömbäck, Dag. *Sejd: Textstudier i nordisk religionshistoria.* Stockholm: H Geber; Köpenhamn, Levin & Munksgaard, 1935.

Strömbäck, Dag. "The Concept of the Soul in Nordic Tradition" in *ARV: Journal of Scandinavian Folklore,* Vol. 31, 1975. The Almqvist & Wiksell Periodical Company, Stockholm, Sweden.

Sturlason, Snorre. *Heimskringla, or the Lives of the Norse Kings.* Ed. & transl. Erling Monsen. New York, NY: Dover Publications, 1990.

Sturluson, Snorri. *Edda.* Transl. & Ed. Anthony Faulkes. Rutland, VT: Everyman, Charles E. Tuttle Co. 1987

Tacitus, Cornelius. *Agricola and Germania.* Transl. Herbert Benario. Norman, OK: University of Oklahoma Press, 1991.

Taylor, Arnold R. *Icelandic-English / English-Icelandic Dictionary.* New York, NY: Hippocrene Books, 1990.

Tolkien, Christopher, "Introduction" in G. Turville-Petrie, general editor, *Hervarar Saga ok Heiðreks.* London UK: Viking Society for Northern Research, University College,1956.

Waggoner, Ben. *A Pocket Guide to Runes.* Philadelphia: The Troth, 2019.

---. *Hávamál: A New Translation.* Philadelphia: Troth Publications, 2017.

---. *Our Troth, 3rd Edition, Volume 1: Heathen History.* Philadelphia: The Troth, 2020.

---. *Our Troth, 3rd Edition, Volume 2: Heathen Gods.* Philadelphia: The Troth, 2021.

Walker, Benjamin. *The Hindu World: An Encyclopedic Summary of Hinduism.* New York, NY: Frederick A. Praeger, Publishers, 1968.

Watkins, Calvert. *The American Heritage Dictionary of Indo-European Roots.* Boston, MA: Houghton Mifflin Harcourt, 2011.

Book-Hoard

Weisweiler, Josef. "Seele und See: Ein etymologischer Versuch", in *Indogermanische Forschungen: Zeitschrift fur Indogermanistik und allgemeine Sprachwissenschaft.* Vol. 57. Berlin, Germany:Verlag von Walter De Gruyter & Co. 1940.

Young, G.V.C, and Cynthia R. Clewer. *Faroese-English Dictionary.* Peel, Isle of Man: Mansk-Svenska Publishing Co. Ltd., 1985.

Zimmer, Heinrich, ed. by Joseph Campbell. *Philosophies of India.* Bollingen Series XXVI. Princeton, NJ: Princeton University Press, 1951.

(Note: the title of the journal *Arv* changed slightly over time; in each reference above I give the title as it appeared in that issue of the journal.)

*Let's see….have I remembered everything?
Ah, just a little bit more….*

About the Author and Artist

About the Author

Winifred Hodge Rose is an Elder of the Troth, an inclusive, international Heathen organization, and has followed a Heathen path for the past thirty years, serving as a scholar, writer, leader, teacher, priestess, and oracular spaewife in many Heathen venues. She is retired from her career as a research scientist working on methods for watershed and natural resources management on military installations in the US and Germany. She grew up as the daughter of a US diplomat stationed in various countries during the 1950s and 1960s, attended a German high school for three years, and later lived for years in Greece and Germany.

These experiences enabled her to learn foreign languages through immersion, and to develop the ability to observe and adapt to different cultures and world-views. This has helped her efforts to understand, as well as possible, ancient Heathen world-views and adapt them for modern Heathen use.

Her life in retirement is focused on Heathen practice, research and writing, as well as enjoyment of extended family (especially grandchildren), pets, and nature. She lives in the Illinois countryside with her husband, and enjoys the presence of many animals both wild and tame that share their wooded homestead and ponds. Her website, with many articles, poems, ceremonies, meditations and more, can be found at *HeathenSoulLore.net*.

About the Artist

Dale Wood is a fine-artist, who enjoys delving into various forms of media, with a focus on watercolor, painting, and music. A practicing Heathen since 2005, his goal is to create art that stirs both the mind and the soul, while infusing his beliefs, and passion, into everything he creates. Based out of southeastern Massachusetts and the Pacific Northwest, Dale seeks to capture the raw energy sourced from the soul and everyday life through his art.

Dale Wood

A Word about Wordfruma Press

Fruma means 'origin, beginning' in Anglo-Saxon, and *ordfruma* means the fount or the source. The Anglo-Saxon word *Os* refers to a God of the Esa or Æsir tribe, and the Rune Poem for the rune Os / Ansuz goes as follows:

Os is 'ordfruma' of every speech,
The support of wisdom and the benefit of the wise,
And for every earl, prosperity and hope.
(my translation)

The Esa-God referred to here is Woden or Odin, the fount and origin of speech, eloquence and wisdom. Since my work relies in large part on understanding the roots and sources of words, I have made a play on words here, changing *ordfruma* to *wordfruma:* "the fount or origin of words". The origin or wellspring of meaningful words flows from godly inspiration: a divine gift that underlies the formation and emergence of our entire species, *homo sapiens*. Wordfruma Press thus honors the gift of speech, and the origins of the gift: all of the Holy Ones.

The trademark logo pictured here, conceptualized by myself and created by Forest Hawkins, shows the rune Ansuz, an analog of Os, rising up from a wellspring. Ansuz takes shape as a fountain that represents the power of speech and wisdom. The shape of the logo also represents the Well and the Tree, with dew from the Tree dropping into the Well. Wordfruma Press publishes scholarly and inspirational Heathen works.

www.ingramcontent.com/pod-product-compliance
Lightning Source LLC
Chambersburg PA
CBHW052008290426
44112CB00014B/2166